PENGUIN BOOKS

FROM PURITANISM TO POSTMODERNISM

Richard Ruland is a professor of English and American literature at Washington University in St. Louis. He has lived and lectured abroad as a Guggenheim fellow, and taught at the University of Leeds and, as a Fulbright fellow, at the universities of Groningen and East Anglia. His books include *The Rediscovery of American Literature: Premises of Critical Taste, 1900–1940, America in Modern European Literature: From Image to Metaphor*, and a two-volume collection with commentary of theories of American literature from the seventeenth to the twentieth centuries, *The Native Muse* and *A Storied Land*.

Malcolm Bradbury is a novelist, critic, television dramatist, and professor of American Studies at the University of East Anglia. His novels include *Eating People Is Wrong* (1959); *The History Man* (1975), which was made into a major TV series; and *Rates of Exchange* (1982), which was shortlisted for the Booker Prize. Critical works include *The Modern American Novel* (revised edition, 1992), *No, Not Bloomsbury* (1987), and *The Modern World: Ten Great Writers* (1989). He has edited *Modernism* (1976), *An Introduction to American Studies* (1981), *The Novel Today* (revised edition, 1990), and *The Penguin Book of Modern Short Stories* (1987). Among his television successes is an adaptation of Tom Sharpe's *Porterhouse Blue*, which won an International Emmy Award.

FROM PURITANISM TO POSTMODERNISM

A HISTORY OF AMERICAN LITERATURE

Richard Ruland and Malcolm Bradbury

PENGUIN BOOKS

PENGUIN BOOKS
Published by the Penguin Group
Viking Penguin, a division of Penguin Books USA Inc.,
375 Hudson Street, New York, New York 10014, U.S.A.
Penguin Books Ltd, 27 Wrights Lane, London W8 5TZ, England
Penguin Books Australia Ltd, Ringwood, Victoria, Australia
Penguin Books Canada Ltd, 10 Alcorn Avenue, Suite 300,
Toronto, Ontario, Canada M4V 3B2
Penguin Books (N.Z.) Ltd, 182–190 Wairau Road,
Auckland 10, New Zealand

Penguin Books Ltd, Registered Offices:
Harmondsworth, Middlesex, England

First published in the United States by Viking Penguin,
a division of Penguin Books USA Inc., 1991
Published in Penguin Books 1992

1 3 5 7 9 10 8 6 4 2

THE LIBRARY OF CONGRESS HAS CATALOGUED THE HARDCOVER AS FOLLOWS:
Ruland, Richard, 1932–
From Puritanism to postmodernism: a history of American
literature / Richard Ruland and Malcolm Bradbury.
p. cm.
ISBN 0-670-83592-7 (hc.)
ISBN 0 14 01.4435 8 (pbk.)
1. American literature—History and criticism. I. Bradbury,
Malcolm, 1932– . II. Title.
PS88.B68 1991
810.9–dc20 91-20944

Printed in the United States of America
Set in Simoncini Garamond
Designed by Victoria Hartman

These are the Gardens of the Desert, these
The unshorn fields, boundless and beautiful,
For which the speech of England has no name . . .
                    —WILLIAM CULLEN BRYANT

Why should not we also enjoy an original
   relation to the universe?

. . . America is a poem in our cyes. . . .
                    —RALPH WALDO EMERSON

And things are as I think they are
And say they are on the blue guitar.
                    —WALLACE STEVENS

CONTENTS

PREFACE

At the start of his book *A Homemade World: The American Modernist Writers* (1975), the American critic Hugh Kenner performs a characteristic and flamboyant act of critical magic. He links two elements in the history of the modern world that are independently celebrated, but not usually seen to be connected. One is the flight of the Wright brothers at Kitty Hawk in 1903, the first real powered flight and yet another demonstration of the way American technological know-how was rapidly changing the twentieth-century universe. The other is a work of fiction started the next year, in which the artist is portrayed as a modern flier, Stephen Dedalus. The book is, of course, James Joyce's *Portrait of the Artist as a Young Man*, about a Modernist artist who soars on imaginary wings into the unknown arts, breaking with home, family, Catholic religion and his Irish nation in the process. We usually consider Joyce one of the great rootless, expatriate artists of an art of modern rootlessness, which we call Modernism. In fact one of the marks of modern writing, George Steiner has said, is that it is a writing unplaced and "unhoused." But Kenner has a different point, and suggests that Modernism did actually find a happy home. Linking American technological modernity and international Modernism, he sees a new kind of kinship being constructed. He says of the Wright brothers: "Their Dedalian deed on the North Carolina shore may be accounted the first American input into the great imaginative enterprise on which artists were to collaborate for half a century." The Wrights set the new century's modern imagination soaring; when it landed again, it landed in America.

As Kenner admits, the Modern movement did not at first shake the American soul. But a collaboration between European Modernists and American Moderns did eventually develop—first in expatriate London and Paris during the years before the First World War, then when American soldiers and fliers came to Europe to fight it, then again in the expatriate Paris of the 1920s. As European avant-garde experiments and America's Modern expectations joined, the point came when it was no longer necessary for Americans to go to or depend on Europe. Gertrude Stein said that Modernism really began in America but went to Paris to happen. Extending this bold act of appropriation, Kenner argues that, as an American renaissance flowered at home, a distinctive American Modernism grew up. Modernism's "doctrine of perception . . . seems peculiarly adapted to the American weather," he says, adding, "which fact explains why, from Pound's early days until now, modern poetry in whatever country has so unmistakably American an impress." The idea that all Modern literature is American, whether it is or not, extends through Kenner's fascinating book. On European soil, he is saying, the Modern movement was born, but it appeared unrooted. In the United States it found what it needed, a "homemade world," where it could grow in what William Carlos Williams called "the American grain." Then it could be reexported to its origins as an approved twentieth-century product. Later history reinforced this exchange, as Modernist writers, painters and musicians fled to the United States from Nazism in the 1930s. So Bauhaus became Our House, or at least our Seagram Building, Pablo Picasso somehow translated into Paloma Picasso, and when something called Postmodernism came along everyone thought it was American —even though its writers had names like Borges, Nabokov, Calvino and Eco.

This appropriation of the new and innovative in art into an idea of American literature is not new. When the eighteenth-century Bishop Berkeley wished to celebrate the potential of colonial America, he told it that the arts naturally traveled westward: "Westward the course of Empire takes its way." A similar assumption dominated the thought of American thinkers in the years after the American Revolution. In *Pierre* (1852), Herman Melville saw Americans as history's own avant-garde, advancing into the world of untried things. When a hundred years ago Walt Whitman introduced later editions of *Leaves of Grass* with his essay "A Backward Glance O'er Travel'd Roads" (1889), he emphasized that since the United States was the great force of material and democratic change in the world, it therefore must create a great modern literature: "For all these new and evolutionary facts, meanings, purposes," he explained, "new poetic messages, new forms and expressions, are inevitable." Gertrude Stein similarly declared the United States—with its historyless history, its novelty and innovation, its spacetime continuum, its plenitude and its emptiness—the natural home of "the new composition." This was not simply an American idea: Europeans held it too. Philosophers from Berkeley to Hegel to Sartre to Baudrillard, poets from Goldsmith to Coleridge to Mayakovsky to Auden, novelists from Chateaubriand to Kafka and Nabokov, painters from Tiepolo to Picasso felt it. As D. H. Lawrence insisted in *Studies in Classic American Literature*, published in 1923 when not just Americans but Europeans were rethinking the American tradition,

> Two bodies of modern literature seem to me to come to the real verge: the Russian and the American. . . . The furtherest frenzies of French modernism or futurism have not yet reached the pitch of extreme consciousness that Poe, Melville, Hawthorne, Whitman reached. The Europeans were all *trying* to be extreme. The great Americans I mention just were it.

The idea that American literature was destined to become not only an expression of American identity but the great modern literature—and therefore more than simply an American literature—has long had great power.

The matters were never so easy. Just two hundred years ago, when Americans had just completed their Revolution and were proudly feeling their identity as the First New Nation, when the Romantic revolution was developing across the West, and when with the French Revolution the calendar itself seemed to begin again, there was American writing, but there was no American literature. What existed, in those fervent years when Americans began to contemplate a great historical and transcontinental destiny, was a *desire* for one—a novel literature that would express the spirit of independence, democracy and nationhood. "America must be as independent in *literature* as she is in *politics*—as famous for *arts* as for *arms*," announced Noah Webster, the great American dictionary-maker and patriot, expressing a powerful popular sentiment. But other voices sounded caution—not the least of them Philip Freneau, a poet-patriot who had fought in the Revolution and celebrated the "Rising Glory of America." He warned that political independence from Europe was not the same thing as artistic independence: "the first was accomplished in about seven years, the latter will not be completely effected, perhaps, in as many centuries."

A hundred years ago, a hundred years after Noah Webster's hopeful appeal to the coming of American literature was another revolutionary time; the ends of centuries, including our own, often are. The modern Industrial Revolution that had begun in the wake of the other revolutions a hundred years earlier was transforming all values, religious, scientific and political. A sense of modernizing change swept the Western world; in fact, this is the moment from which we can best date the modern revolution in arts and ideas, from the emergence of scientific principles of relativity, technological developments that generated new power systems like electricity and new communications systems like the streetcar and the automobile, new intellectual systems like psychology. Ibsen and Nietzsche, Schopenhauer and Zola, Freud and Bergson were transforming fundamental Western ideas. Now the great transcontinental and industrialized United States was in an imperial mood, outstripping the production of Germany and Great Britain combined and looking confidently forward to the role of world power and technological superforce in the coming twentieth century, which many were already naming "the American Century." Like Webster before him, Walt Whitman declared that in this new world "new poetic messages, new forms and expressions, are inevitable." But where were they?

Between 1888 and 1890, Edmund Clarence Stedman and E. M. Hutchinson compiled their eleven-volume *Library of American Literature*, from colonial times to the present. It appeared comprehensive, and the contents made it clear what its editors considered American literature to be. It was nothing like the view we have of it today; indeed it was, as Longfellow had called it, a branch of English literature. Its major authors were Washington Irving, James Fenimore Cooper, William Cullen Bryant, Longfellow, Lowell, Whittier, Oliver Wendell Holmes, a largely New England pantheon. Melville—he died in 1891—was all but forgotten. Whitman—he died in 1892—was granted small recognition. Poe was a morbid castoff of German Romanticism, Hawthorne wrote rills from the town pump, Thoreau was a misanthrope. The realist and local-color movements which had dominated American writing since the Civil War were hardly acknowledged. What was seen as American literature was effectively what came to be called "the Genteel Tradition." What, then, lay beyond the Genteel Tradition? In 1890 William Dean Howells, the "Dean" of American letters, having just moved to New York from Boston where he had edited the magisterial *Atlantic Monthly,* published his novel *A Hazard of New Fortunes*—a very '90s title. Henry James published *The Tragic Muse*, and his brother, William, the Harvard philosopher and pragmatist, produced *The Principles of Psychology*, exploring many of the ideas about the importance of consciousness that would preoccupy modern minds. Thought, consciousness, James explained, did not function in a logical chain and therefore needed to be described in a new language: "A 'river' or a 'stream' are the metaphors by which it [consciousness] is most naturally described," he wrote, and so gave us a notion, a "stream-of-consciousness," which would help unlock our understanding of the modern fiction that was to come. William James wrote exultantly to William Howells: "The year which shall have witnessed the apparition of your *Hazard of New Fortunes*, of Harry'o *Tragic Muse*, and of my *Psychology* will indeed be a memorable one in American literature." His words seem prophetic now, for the 1890s saw, in America as in Europe, a fundamental change of mood. But still there was no certainty about the direction of that eagerly awaited literature.

So we must look later yet for the coming of that imperial confidence about American literature that informs Hugh Kenner's book. By the First World War there was still searching doubt about the value of the American past or indeed of the American literary present. "The present is a void and the American writer floats in that void because the past that survives in the common mind is a past without living value," complained the critic Van Wyck Brooks in 1918; "But is this the only possible past? If we need another past so badly, is it inconceivable that we might discover one, that we might even invent one?" This invention of the American literary past was a significant enterprise of the 1920s, when American writing went through a remarkable modern flowering and made its international impact. Not only D. H. Lawrence but many American writers and critics undertook the task of devising a viable American literary tradition. The past that they constructed was a very different one—not a "Genteel Tradition" any longer (that was the enemy), but a literature that indeed went to the "real verge." Once-major writers became minor, and once-minor writers like Melville, Hawthorne and "our cousin Mr. Poe" became major. Writers seeking a new tradition, a fresh ABC of reading, as Pound called it, looked everywhere, at the American, the European, the Chinese and Japanese past and present. As the very American T. S. Eliot explained in "Tradition and the Individual Talent" (1919), tradition cannot be inherited; "if you want it you must obtain it by great labour."

Constructing a usable literary past for contemporary writers became one of the great projects of American fiction-making—and America's fiction included American criticism. During the 1930s, for obvious reasons in a time of political activism, it was chiefly the socioeconomic past of American literature that critics reconstructed. In the 1940s, as war came and American ideals had to be reenergized, books like F. O. Matthiessen's *American Renaissance* (1941) and Alfred Kazin's *On Native Grounds* (1942) began to insist increasingly that there was an encompassing American tradition made on American soil which had passed beyond inherited forms to construct a novel American imagination. In the 1950s, in the age of rising American confidence as its role as world power increased, works like Henry Nash Smith's *Virgin Land* (1950), Charles Feidelson's *Symbolism and American Literature* (1953), R. W. B. Lewis's *The American Adam* (1955), Richard Chase's *The American Novel and Its Tradition* (1957) and Leslie Fiedler's *Love and Death in the American Novel* (1960) sought for distinctive American themes, myths, languages and psychic motifs with the means of modern criticism and the conviction that there was a major tradition to be recovered and explored. As American writers grew famous across a world that sought to understand American values, a very American literature rose from the interpretation of American beliefs and American dreams, American theologies and American democratic ideologies, American landscapes and American institutions, American ideas of mission and destiny, the achievements of what was now seen as unmistakably a "homemade world."

These, of course, were versions, critical myths. Leslie Fiedler described his *Love and Death in the American Novel* as itself an American novel, and so it was—a fine one. All literary histories are critical fictions. But, because the needs of the American present have so often dictated the interpretations of the American literary past, to make it "usable," American literary history is more fictional than most—one reason, perhaps, why the Modernist spirit with its own sense of being history-less in history found America such a natural home. As the critic Percy Boynton observed in 1927: "Criticism in America is implicitly an attempt by each critic to make of America the kind of country he [now we would add "she"] would like, which in every case is a better country than it is today." At present there is something closely resembling chaos again—creative chaos, we may hope. We live or have lately lived in an age of Postmodern deconstructions, in which more energy has been put into demythologizing interpretive myths than constructing them. Earlier canonizations have led to a rage for decanonization as the desire to challenge the usable past of the moderns has become dominant. Some of this energy comes from writers who are seeking, as they should and must, to construct a new history, often a multiethnic or a more fully gendered one. Some comes from critics enjoying the lush fruits of an age of critical hyperactivity. The current flurry of theoretical debate suggests a Reformation revisited, not unrelated to the Great Awakening of the 1960s. Today there is no doubt that the map of the Postmodern world is itself changing fast. And so, of course, will its critical fictions.

As Hugh Kenner's book suggests, anxieties of influence, appropriations of tradition, have always abounded in American writing. Writers always seek to construct the history they would most like to have. Trying to do untried things, Herman Melville conferred Shakespearean powers on his recent friend Nathaniel Hawthorne ("Some may start to read of Shakespeare and Hawthorne on the same page"). A dedication to Hawthorne then graced Melville's own *Moby-Dick*—and so Melville appropriated the new Shakespearean heritage back to himself. Melville was soon to be forgotten but was recovered in the 1920s; he suddenly became a heritage again, for Hart Crane and so on to Charles Olson and many, many more. The transcendentalist Ralph Waldo Emerson, seeking the new American Poet, found Walt Whitman and hailed him "at the beginning of a great career." Whitman sought to be the grand encompassing poet of the new America that Emerson saw in prospect but found his reputation highest in Europe; he also died in relative neglect. It was not until the Modern movement that his "new messages" began to be fully read, and poets like Ezra Pound undertook their pacts with him ("I have detested you long enough"). Henry James made an antecedent of Hawthorne, though also of the great European realists like Balzac and Flaubert. Then Gertrude Stein, Pound and Eliot made an antecedent of James, just as later poets made antecedents of Pound and Eliot. Sherwood Anderson made an antecedent of Stein and led Hemingway, Fitzgerald and Faulkner to her. In the 1940s these three went through their own period of obscurity, until in the 1950s they too became antecedents, two of them with Nobel Prizes, fit to enter the boxing ring with Norman Mailer.

This constantly renewing search, this constructing and defacing of literary monuments, this borrowing and assimilating and intertextualizing, shows us one way in which literary traditions are constructed—from the inside, by writers themselves. The process resembles what Ezra Pound loved to call the *paideuma,* the cultural distillation the artist needs to create his work. Pound tried to write the *paideuma* into his modern epic poem *The Cantos,* his "portable substitute for the British Museum" (later American poets have usually used the Library of Congress and the Smithsonian). T. S. Eliot described this constructive process in a different way when he said:

> The existing order is complete before the new work arrives; in order to persist after the supervention of novelty, the *whole* existing order must be, if ever so slightly, altered . . . and this in conformity between the old and the new.

These were the Modernist versions of what we have come to call (in Harold Bloom's phrase) "the anxiety of influence," the process by which writers both construct and deconstruct traditions for themselves, though of course in doing that they also change the views and values of contemporary critics.

American literature is indeed preeminently a modern literature, one reason why the many anthologies devoted to it are frequently divided into two volumes on different chronological scales—one dealing with the vast period since settlement in 1620, the second with the last powerful hundred years. This helps explain why, perhaps more than most literatures, American literary history is frequently dominated by the interpretations modern writers make of their predecessors. No wonder we can find so many variants of the history of American writing. A look back at older versions shows how elaborate the construct, and how massive the reversals, can be. In *The Rediscovery of American Literature* (1967) one of the present authors has illustrated how any discussion of American literature draws on long-standing speculation as old as the settlement of America from Europe itself, shaped by large questions about the nature of American experience, the American land and landscape, American national identity and the nature of language and expression in the presumed "New World." The heterogenous elaboration of literary theories collected in his *The Native Muse* (1972) and *A Storied Land* (1976) makes clear that literary discussion is never a continuous, steady flow, but an eddy of currents which shift us from one concern to another and back again in new weather with relit landscape. They also show how obsessive the idea of the "American-ness" of American literature has been; indeed few major literatures have been as preoccupied with the idea of nationality. Yet just as the question "What then is the American, this new man?" was troubling when Crèvecoeur posed it in 1782, so it remains ambiguous and above all arguable to this day.

If we are today in a period of high argument about American origins and directions, we contend as well about the whole philosophy of literary interpretation. What we have best learned to do is multiply our questions. Is American literature writing about Americans, or by them, or even, as in Kenner's book, literature whose very spirit makes it neo-American? Where are the limits of that literature, the edges of writing, the suitable frames in which we can set it, the aesthetic values by which we judge it? What is a canon, what is a tradition, what is an intertextual sequence, and how subversive might these be of the idea of literary continuity? Is a reading of a literature simply the sum total of the readings that various selected texts (dubiously selected, many would say) have generated? What do we mean by American, by literature, by history? Literary history must always present a more tangled web than social, political or economic history, because in the end it is always bound up with complex subjective artistic judgments and with strong human and creative emotions. A political historian may know who was President of the United States in 1810 with far more certainty than a literary historian can "know" whether Ahab is mad or Whitman a great poet. Historians can analyze Lincoln's presidency to establish his impact on the nation with far more confidence than we can present the writings of Melville or Twain as culturally central, demonstrative of their time or of lasting value to the imagination. The fact remains that we must go with some vision of literature and history or we will simply not go at all.

We are also in a time when contemporary American writers are especially conscious of the need to reconstruct traditions for themselves: when the different ethnic groups must recover their own origins, when women writers deconstruct male fictions in the quest for a female literary past, when Modernism is over and Postmodernism is slipping behind us as we move toward a turn of the millennium and an artistic phase for which we have as yet no name. We live too in an age of rapid communications and vast, indeed parodic, cultural assimilation, where the boundaries of nations are no longer the boundaries of taste, perception or ideas. The world map of influence is changing all the time. New technologies transform the conditions of writing, the nature and transmission of the sign; new historical aspirations shape our sense of an impending era, and scientific possibilities energize us to new types of thought and new models for artistic form. As American culture has grown ever more fluid and various, its historical singularity has diminished in a world which has ever-increasing access to many things once considered part of a purely American dream. The twenty-first century offers its own prospects and its own fears, and writers are already beginning to find language for them. The modernity of Kitty Hawk and Stephen Dedalus is now a long way in the past, and our imaginative fictions will have to define themselves afresh while at the same time making or holding to a guiding tradition.

Our own book is no less a fiction than any other. We have thought of it as a story in two senses—our own tale of a nation's literature, and the fable a country told itself as it tried to understand its own becoming in writing. The nation called itself America, and the rest of the world has called it America too, even though its land mass is only part of the northern section of the world's Western Hemisphere. For the authors, this book is one way to impose an order on 350 years of writing in what is now the United States, an order that enables a vast range of written material to stand on a single narrative continuum. It is also one version of the story that material tells, the America summoned into being by the numberless imaginations that have striven to find words and forms for new experiences or familiar experiences encountered during new times in a new landscape. Ours is an introductory version, but we have aimed to inform it with the view that art is to be defined broadly, with a complex existence in its social, ideological and historical situation. Equally important has been the value of maintaining an international perspective; American literature, despite all its endeavor for a native distinctiveness, has remained part of a broad Western tradition, from which it has drawn at least some of its usable past, to whose present it has always contributed. Now, by virtue not only of its quality but its modern resonance, and indeed America's own power of influence and distribution as well as its possession of a world language, American literature more than ever exists for more people than simply the Americans. It is part of, and does much to shape, the writing of literature through much of the contemporary world. That is part of its power and an essential part of its interest.

One of the advantages of a collaborated book is a width of perspective, a breadth of methods and interpretations, a mix of critical attitudes and a dialogic way of writing. The authors come from the two sides of the Atlantic, and offer, as it were, both an internal and an international view. Malcolm Bradbury is a novelist and professor of American Studies at the University of East Anglia in Norwich,

England, who has written widely on American literature; he initiated the project and in the first instance contributed much of the discussion of the Modern period and of the novel. Richard Ruland, professor of English and American literature at Washington University, St. Louis, Missouri, lectures and writes about American poetry, literary history and literary criticism; he initially contributed most of the discussion of the colonial period, nineteenth-century poetry, modern poetry and drama, and criticism. Dialogue, interchange and travel over the years created the final text, as did changing theories and events over the period of the writing. Both of us have borne it in mind that the end of the twentieth century has been marked by a vast change in the ideological map, as many of the theories and attitudes fixed by the era of the cold war have begun to collapse and many modern critical assumptions have been, indeed still are, in process of transformation and dissolution. As we have said, there can be little doubt that the last decade of the twentieth century will be as transformative and revolutionary as the close of earlier centuries, in which patterns of thought and art changed radically. Writers' views of the world will change, as will reigning critical fictions. But, if our Post-Postmodern situation has served to remind us that there are never final answers, we will nonetheless continue to wonder what American literature is and try to construct some useful story of it.

The vision is ours. Of course it is also the sum of the experience won from the writers we have read and admired, the works that have stimulated and guided our sense of creative discovery, the accumulated readers who have used and so remade and rewritten those books, the teachers who taught us, the colleagues we have talked with, the students we have taught and learned from. We have both drawn as well, from time to time, on some of our previous discussions of American literature in various books and periodicals. Besides those who have worked with us in the general and ever-extending debate about the history and nature of American writing, we should acknowledge some very particular debts: to the Fulbright and Guggenheim fellowship programs that brought the American author to Britain for extended stays and to those who made him welcome and thus made this collaboration possible; to Janice Price (who first proposed this project), to Helen McNeil (who played a valuable part in the planning), Norman Holmes

Pearson, Marcus Cunliffe, Alan Trachtenberg, Chris Bigsby, Daniel B. Shea, Ihab Hassan, C. Carroll Hollis, Howard Temperley, Eric Homberger, Dominic Belasario, Kay Norton, Richard M. Cook and Birgit Noll Ruland.

RICHARD RULAND
St. Louis, Missouri

MALCOLM BRADBURY
Norwich, England

· PART I ·

THE
LITERATURE
OF BRITISH
AMERICA

———

CHAPTER

· 1 ·

THE PURITAN LEGACY

· I ·

A fundamental difference exists between American literature and nearly all the other major literary traditions of the world: it is essentially a modern, recent and international literature. We cannot trace its roots directly back into the mists of American antiquity. We need not hunt its origins in the remote springs of its language and culture, or follow it through from oral to written, then from manuscript to book. The American continent possessed major pre-Columbian civilizations, with a deep heritage of culture, mythology, ritual, chant and poetry. Many American writers, especially recently, have looked to these sources as something essential to American culture, and the extraordinary variety and vision to be found there contribute much to the complexity and increasing multiethnicity of contemporary American experience. But this is not the originating tradition of what we now call American literature. That came from the meeting between the land with its elusive and usually despised "Indians" and the discoverers and settlers who left the developed, literate cultures of Renaissance Europe, first to explore and conquer, then to populate, what they generally considered a virgin continent—a "New World" already promised them in their own mythology, now discovered by their own talent and curiosity.

The New World was not new, nor virgin, nor unsettled. But, arriving in historical daylight, sometimes with aims of conquest, sometimes with a sentimental vision of the "noble savages" or other wonders they might find, these settlers brought with them many of the things that formed the literature we now read. They brought their ideas of history and the world's purpose; they brought their languages and, above all, the book. The book was both a sacred text, the Bible (to be reinvigorated in the King James Authorized Version of 1611), and a general instrument of expression, record, argument and cultural dissemination. In time, the book became American literature, and other things they shipped with it—from European values and expectations to post-Gutenberg printing technology—shaped the lineage of American writing. So did the early records kept of the encounter and what they made of it. Of course a past was being destroyed as well as a new present gained when these travelers/settlers imposed on the North American continent and its cultures their forms of interpretation and narrative, their Christian history and iconography, their science and technology, their entrepreneurship, settlement practices and modes of commerce. We may deplore this hegemony and seek to reverse it by recovering all we can of the pre-Columbian heritage to find the broader meaning of America. The fact remains that the main direction of the recorded American literary imagination thereafter was formed from the intersection between the European Renaissance mind and the new and wondrous land in the West the settlers found—between the myths they brought and those they learned or constructed after they came.

This America first came into existence out of writing—European writing—and then went on to demand a new writing which fitted the continent's novelty and strangeness: the problems of its settlement, the harshness and grandeur of its landscape, the mysterious potential of its seemingly boundless open space. But "America" existed in Europe long before it was discovered, in the speculative writings of the classical, the medieval and then the Renaissance mind. American literature began, and the American dream existed, before the actual continent was known. "He invented America; a very great man," Mademoiselle Nioche says about Columbus in Henry James's *The American* (1877). And so, in a sense, he did—except that Columbus was himself following a prototype devised long before, the idea of a western land which was *terra incognita,* outside and beyond history, pregnant with new meanings for mankind. This place that was not Europe but rather its opposite existed first as a glimmering, an image and an interpretative prospect born from the faith and fantasy of European minds. Out of the stock of classical and religious tradition, out of vague historical memories and fantastic tales, an identity had already been given to the great land mass on the world's edge which waited to be summoned into history and made part of the divine plan. So, millenarian and Utopian expectations were already attached to this new land. Here might be found Atlantis or Avalon, the Garden of Hesperides, the Seven Cities of Antillia, Canaan or Paradise Renewed, great cities made of gold, fountains of eternal youth. Its wonders would be extraordinary, its people strange and novel. The idea of America as an exceptional place somehow different from all others endures to this day, but it is not a myth of modern American nationalism or recent political rhetoric. It is an invention of Europe, as old as Western history itself.

The America—to give it one of several possible names—that was opened up by exploration and discovery from the fifteenth century on was therefore a testing place for the imaginings Europeans long had of it. Columbus expected to find the East in the West and carried a complex vision to interpret what he found. It, in turn, confirmed some of his expectations and disproved others, in a process to be endlessly repeated as European exploration continued. There were wonders, cities of gold, pristine nature, strange civilizations, unusual savages, the stuff of Eden. There was also danger, death, disease, cruelty and starvation. Myth mixed with actuality, promise with disappointment, and that process has continued too. In effect, America became the space exploration program of an expansive, intensely curious, entrepreneurial and often genocidal era of European adventuring. It stimulated and shaped the direction and expectation of the Western mind, and also filled its treasure chests. It provoked Utopian social hopes, millenarian visions of history, new scientific inquiries, new dreams of mercantilism, profit and greed, new funds for the artistic imagination. "I saw the things which have been brought to the King from the new golden land," wrote the painter Albrecht Dürer in 1520, after inspecting the tributes from Cortés and Montezuma that Charles V displayed in Brussels before his enthronement as Holy Roman Emperor; "All the days of my life I have seen nothing that gladdened my heart so much as these things." Such wonders, such promises from the new golden land, entrenched it firmly in the European imagination, where it was to remain; very few travelers from Europe who afterward crossed the Atlantic were without some sense of expectation or wonder as they encountered the strange New World.

Because of this imaginary history, which preceded the real one and all but obliterated the history of those who had lived American lives before the Europeans came, we will never really find a single demarcation point to show us where American writing exactly starts, and certainly not when it became distinctive or broke finally loose from European writing. The invaders came from many different European societies to lands that had indigenous and often highly complex native cultures and a continent spread between the two poles with every conceivable variety of climate, landscape, wildlife, vegetation, natural resource and local evolution. These were complex frontiers, but on them the power of force *and* of language generally proved to lie with the settlers. Records of these early encounters thus exist, in prodigious variety, in most European languages: narratives of travel and exploration, of religious mission and entrepreneurial activity, letters home, reports to emperors and bishops, telling of wonders seen, dangers risked, coasts charted, hopes justified or dashed, souls saved or lost, tributes taken or evaded, treasures found or missed. From the European point of view, these are the first American books. Often these are practical reports or exhortations to colonization, but at the same time the imaginary myths began to extend; there was, for example, Sir Thomas More's famed *Utopia* (1516), which drew on Amerigo Vespucci's recorded voyages to picture an ideal future world. In a Britain anxious about maintaining and developing its sea power and its outposts abroad, the stories of the English navigators, told by the Elizabethan diplomat and promoter of colonization Richard Hakluyt in his *Voyages and Discoveries* (1589–1600), created intense excitement. They were expanded by Samuel Purchas in *Hakluytus Posthumus, or Purchas His Pilgrims* (1625); and such books, all over Europe, fed contemporary mythologizing and shaped literature. They passed their influence on to Tasso and Montaigne, Spenser and Shakespeare, John Donne, Michael Drayton and Andrew Marvell, all of whom wrote of the wonders of the "brave new world," or the "Newfounde land." American images have constantly been refracted in European art and writing, and so have the images traded in reverse, of Europe in America. That is another reason why even to this day it is hard to identify a separate space for American literature which makes it distinct from the arts of Europe.

Even when there was an actual America, with firm settlement, the process continued. Naturally, the imaginary story now began to change, taking on specificity, definition, geographical actuality, a stronger sense of real experience. Early explorers' accounts of navigation, exploration, privation and wonder began yielding to annals, geographical records, social, scientific and naturalist observations. When the first permanent English settlement was founded under difficult and dangerous circumstances at Jamestown in Virginia in 1607, it had its recorder, Captain John Smith. Both a practical sea captain and a romantic adventurer, a promoter of colonization forced to become savior of the colony, Smith told the tale in his brief *A True Relation of . . . Virginia* (London, 1608), which dispels some of the golden myths but develops others, not least some to do with himself. Smith emphasizes chivalry, adventure, missionary intention and the potentials of the rich American plenty; he also emphasizes practicality, privation and dangerous conflict with the Indians. Still, the story of his rescue from danger by the virtuous Indian princess Pocahontas—he made it yet more exotic in his *Generall Historie of Virginia, New-England, and the Summer Isles* (London, 1624)—gave Virginia and North America its first great romantic tale in English, creating a version of the Noble and Remediable Savage that prospered freely in the European mind. Smith's mapping, both actual and written, of American possibilities continued. Sent by the Virginia Company to explore the coast farther north, he gave it the name "New England," attached British names to many of its unsettled areas and recorded it all in his influential *A Description of New England* (London, 1616)—a reasonably accurate annals about the practical problems of travel, settlement and husbandry, detailing coasts, terrain, climate, crops and prospects for cultivation. But Smith's book was also full of American promise, defining a heroic and even divine mission for those who would undertake plantation's great task: "What so truely suits with honour and honesty as the discovering things unknown: erecting towns, peopling countries, informing the ignorant, reforming things unjust, teaching virtue; and gain to our native mother country a kingdom to attend her."

As author of the first English book written in America, Smith influenced much to come. He shows us both the need to narrate the new and the problems involved in such narration. Introducing the word into new space, he tries to give plot and purpose to travel and the landscape. Like all early records, his is shaped by Renaissance theories of history, Christian faith in mission, patriotic ideas of settlement, moral notions of the value of plantation, cultivation and honest toil. The excitement comes in his sense of crossing the strange frontier between the Old World and the New. Smith himself could not be sure whether his story marked a genuine new beginning, but his successors were more certain, for the English colonies he speculated about soon multiplied: Plymouth Plantation in 1620 and Massachusetts Bay in 1630, following Smith's own maps of settlement; Maryland in 1634, Rhode Island in 1636, New York in 1664, Pennsylvania in 1681. Among these settlers were some who truly believed this was the new beginning, a fresh start for history and religion, a millenarian enterprise. They were the Puritans, who, determined to maintain the purity of their separatist Protestant faith, did aim to begin anew and find in that process of erecting towns, peopling countries, teaching virtue and reforming things unjust a truly fresh start. The "Pilgrim Fathers" who—though hunting for Virginia—made landfall at Cape Cod in 1620 to settle Plymouth Plantation were following Smith, but with an urgent sense of independence. Like Smith, they chronicled all they did; indeed the larger colony soon to develop at Massachusetts Bay brought the technology of printing and soon produced an American book on American soil, the *Bay Psalme Book* of 1640. And, though they wrote first for themselves and their colonial successors, they also, like Smith, had in mind readers in Europe; they were still writing for English eyes, seeking to convert English minds.

What they wrote, prolifically, was another kind of beginning to the American story, another kind of narration that gave shape and significance to the process of plantation, settlement, social development. But now the voyager was not the explorer or the planter but the Pilgrim, entering new space and new history. The plot was providential; God guides these encounters between the traveler and the not yet written New World. The myth remains shaped by European sources, but now one source above all, the Bible, and especially its opening chapters, Genesis and Exodus, the tale of the Chosen People and the Promised Land. For the Puritans (different traditions shaped the narratives of the other non-Puritan colonies) the essential tale was a religious one of travail and wandering, with the Lord's guidance, in quest of a high purpose and a millennial history. When Puritans wrote of the New World and the allegory of the Puritan diaspora, they were, by following out the biblical types, telling nothing less than the tale of God's will revealing itself in history.

The Puritan imagination, it was acknowledged, was central to the nature of American writing. One reason for this was that it brought to the New World not only a Judaic sense of wonder and millenarian promise—the "American dream" that is still recalled in so much modern literature, not least in the famous ending of F. Scott Fitzgerald's *The Great Gatsby* in 1925—but a vision of the task and nature of writing itself. Puritan narratives defined a shape for the writing of America, but they also questioned how and whether language could reveal the extraordinary experience. As a result, from the very beginnings America became a testing place of language and narrative, a place of search for providential meanings and hidden revelations, part of a lasting endeavor to discover the intended nature and purpose of the New World. The Puritan millennium never did reveal itself directly, and so the task continued—long after early plantations evolved into permanent settlements, Puritanism turned into hard-working enterprise, relations with Europe and England became increasingly distant and estranged and the thirteen American colonies finally declared their independence and became the First New Nation. That New Nation then turned westward, to contemplate afresh the wide continent that continued to provide a sense of wonder and the promise of providential possibility. As it did so, the power and capabilities of language and narrative remained a central matter. Slowly, these historical turns created the modern, discovering writing that we now call American literature.

· II ·

"I must begin at the very root and rise," wrote William Bradford to begin *Of Plimouth Plantation* in 1630. A personal journal, much used by his contemporaries, it was completed by 1650 but not printed until 1856. Bradford was a leader of the Mayflower Separatists and governor of Plymouth for thirty years after its settlement; his account reveals his determination to set on durable record the entire pilgrim story— of departure, voyage, arrival, settlement, development and lasting dedication to God's purpose in history. Of these events and intentions, it offers the most vivid and vital description we have, in part because both its factuality and faith are driven by a fundamental conviction about the nature of style and language. Bradford is, he says, determined to render his account "in the plaine style, with singular regard unto the simple truth in all things." What the simple truth *was* was as plain to Bradford as to any other Puritan, whether one straining within the confines of the Established Church in Britain or forced abroad as a hounded Separatist for insisting on radical purification of religious belief and practice. That truth had special application, however, to those who had fled from the persecutions of British magistrates to the security of Dutch tolerance, only to realize they must flee once more if they were to preserve their religious and national identity. For them the voyage to New England was an act of faith, derived from the reading of providential signs in contingent events, and the "simple truth" was therefore nothing less than an account of the significant actions of God's Chosen People, sent on a divine errand into the wilderness. Their story sets them in a new land where history can be redeemed. The goal is the Christian millennium, and all events are signs.

Bradford's is a detailed, evocative annals, but behind it lay as type and meaning one of the greatest of biblical narratives, the story of the Promised Land found through the reading and following of providential intent. This was the essential Puritan vision of Bradford's book, and it shaped as well the account by John Winthrop, governor of the larger Massachusetts Bay Colony to the north founded ten years after Plymouth. Winthrop, too, kept his journal record, published eventually as *The History of New England from 1630 to 1649* in 1825–26. It was Winthrop who had declared in his famous shipboard sermon on the *Arbella* that "the eyes of all people are upon us" and that the Puritans were called to erect "a citty upon an Hill"—a city that would stand as lesson and beacon to the entire world. Both Bradford and Winthrop see the migrants as none other than new Israelites; both place their small bands firmly on the stage of cosmic history. Winthrop carefully reads every natural sign for meaning and like Bradford projects a drama rooted in time's beginnings, where God charges His people to confound the ever-vigilant machinations of Satan by building villages and lives that would embody and enact the divine will. For both, the arrival in the New World marks a specific point on a historical continuum which had begun with Creation and will cease only with the apocalyptic fullness of God's final judgment. In both books the facts are many and fully detailed, but beyond the facts are clear allegorical and transcendental meanings, evidence of God's participation in the successive stages of human history.

Nonetheless, as the millenarian process interweaves with daily events—the problems of harvest, troubles with the Indians, the hardships of founding a community—Bradford's diary-record must constantly amend and adjust. It eventually takes the shape of a "jeremiad," a primary type of Puritan writing. The writing that is more than a tale of woe or failure; it is an interpretative account of hardships and troubles and an anguished call for return to the lost purity of earlier times. Always the movement of history, the detail of daily event, demands scrupulous attention because these things partake of an allegorical mystery. The material of journals like Winthrop's and Bradford's is the stuff of millenarian epic, but it is epic without known outcome. Signs and meanings are always uncertain and satanic deception is always a possibility.

This is why the scrupulous simplicity and implied veracity of "the plaine style" that Bradford explicitly adopts seem to Puritan writers necessary to represent the essence of their experience. But it is also why Bradford's and Winthrop's accounts show a falling arc, from admirable yet impossible millennial hopes to the growing sadness of undeniable failure. In the understated eloquence of "the plaine style," Bradford, as the years pass, must record that his people, though desiring a community of saints, remain men who have found no clear pathway to sanctity. Indeed in the end Bradford comes to see a dream gone wrong, a second generation not like the first, beginning to forget or reject the piety of the first settlers and their dreams of a perfect community. Ironically, the snare of Satan that Bradford perceives drawing men from their appointed path is exactly their success—in meeting the challenges of a dangerous nature and a hostile environment, in dealing with the Indians, in developing an economy. Daily and symbolic history divide; the Separatist aim, to be in the world but not of it, slowly erodes, as the settlers develop adequate shelter, sufficient stores and finally, with the settlement of Massachusetts Bay, a profitable and rapidly expanding market for their surplus.

If Bradford's part-journal, part-history has a climax, this is it, as his tone turns toward irony and scorn:

> Corn and cattle rose to a great price, by which many were much enriched and commodities grew plentiful. And yet in other regards this benefit turned to their hurt, and this accesion of strength to their weakness. For now as their stocks increased and the increase vendible, there was no longer any holding them together, but now they must of necessity go to their great lots. They could not otherwise keep their cattle, and having oxen grown they must have land for ploughing and tillage. And no man now thought he could live except he had cattle and a great deal of ground to keep them, all striving to increase their stocks.

The settlers scatter, "the town in which they lived compactly till now was left very thin and in a short time almost desolate," and the prospect of building a Heavenly City in the wilderness has to be amended. Bradford expresses the same poignancy in a comment he adds to an early letter he had written to describe the way the settlers are "knit together as a body in a most strict and sacred bond and covenant of the Lord." His later note observes the decaying of this faithful bond, for the

> subtle serpent hath slyly wound himself under fair pretences of necessity and the like, to untwist these sacred bonds and ties. . . . It is now part of my misery in old age, to find and feel the

decay and want therefore (in a great measure) and with grief and sorrow of heart to lament and bewail the same.

Some two hundred years later, when that new acquisitiveness had come to seem the essential spirit of America, Ralph Waldo Emerson would observe that "The power of Love, as the basis of a State, has never been tried" and wonder whether a "nation of friends" might devise better ways to govern social and economic relations. The question is a natural one when the dream is of perfect community in a world where time dissolves the best that men can do. For here was a nation of friends indeed, united in a love for each other that they saw as a necessary emanation from the divine love that sheltered them all. But after a lengthy trial of communal ownership and labor, they reluctantly concluded that such were not the ways of the Lord.

> The experience that was had in this common course and condition, tried sundry years and that amongst godly and sober men, may well evince the vanity of that conceit of Plato's and other ancients applauded by some of later times; that the taking away of property and bringing in community into a commonwealth would make them happy and flourishing; as if they were wiser than God. For this community (so far as it was) was found to breed much confusion and discontent and retard much employment that would have been to their benefit and comfort. . . . Let none object that this is men's corruption, and nothing to the course itself. I answer, seeing all men have this corruption in them, God in His wisdom saw another course fitter for them.

William Bradford's *Of Plimouth Plantation* testifies repeatedly to the shortcomings of the sons when measured by the dreams of their fathers. As it sounds its call for a return to the primal vision and turns toward jeremiad, its lament for the gap between divine intentions and human fulfillment becomes a fresh assertion of divine selection. Despite their failings, the Puritans persist in writing for themselves a central role in the sacred drama God had designed for man to enact on the American stage, the stage of true history. In that recurrent conflict between the ideal and the real, the Utopian and the actual, the intentional and the accidental, the mythic and the diurnal, can be read—

as George Santayana was much later to observe—an essential legacy
of the Puritan imagination to the American mind.

From Edward Johnson's *A History of New England* (London,
1653), better known as *The Wonder-Working Providence of Sion's
Saviour in New England,* to Cotton Mather's vast *Magnalia Christi
Americana* (1702), the formal histories of American settlement, like
the personal diaries of the time, are presented as works of religious
interpretation, tales of election, wonder-working intervention and divine meaning. Johnson's elaborate history gives positive shape and
design to the daily events of New England by seeing everywhere God's
careful attention. The Puritans were, after all, attempting to found a
new order of society based on a new covenant of men and a new
relation of religion and law. Everything was thereby made ripe for
interpretation. For those charged with the quest, it seemed that the
whole world watched as God and Satan contested the meaning of
human time on the American shore. The writer's urgent task was to
displace the traditional center of historical significance in Europe and
direct it onto the small band of spiritual pioneers who, for the world's
sake, had accepted God's injunction to establish His Kingdom in the
wilderness.

As time went on, the process of typological interpretation grew
ever more complex as the extending facts of American history became
a long record of trials and proofs. Mather's *Magnalia Christi* marks
the culmination of this process. Cotton was third in line of the Mather
dynasty, which has come to seem the embodiment of American Puritanism, much as John, John Quincy and Henry Adams were later to
manifest the New England legacy of Brahmin virtue and civic responsibility. He felt himself destined for leadership of both church and
state; a man of great learning, with a major library that displayed the
density of the culture New England had developed and its access to
European thought and science, Mather wrote close to five hundred
books, essays, sermons, verses and theological treatises. At the close
of the seventeenth century, the *Magnalia Christi* looks back on the
now distant story of New England settlement and celebrates its endurance and cultural richness, displayed in such things as the early
founding of Harvard College. In its portraits of Governors Bradford
and Winthrop and its biographies of sixty famous divines, it moves

into hagiography, becoming a Foxe's *Book of Martyrs* for the Church of New England. But above all, it seeks to assert the presence of God's spirit in the colonies. "I write the *Wonders* of the Christian religion," his account begins, "flying from the Depravations of *Europe,* to the *American Strand.*" Eighty years after settlement the story is now less jeremiad than epic; indeed, it draws not only on the Bible but the Vergilian tale of trials overcome in Rome's founding, the making of the great city. Once again the aim is to underscore the essential Puritan version of history which placed the experience of a few transplanted Englishmen at the center of God's plan for the redemption of His creation.

· III ·

"The plaine style," the millenarian expectation, the ceaseless search for the relationship between God's and man's history, between providential intentions and the individual conscience: these were the essential elements the Separatists brought with them when they left Britain to found their Bible commonwealth. Running through their concerned recording was a metaphysic of writing which endlessly sought meaning by separating the word from ornate and ceremonial usage to attach it again to good conscience and to revelation. The plain style, said Thomas Hooker, came from "out of the wilderness, where curiosity is not studied"—from the life of ministers, land-tillers and artisans. Only apparently was it naive or unshaped; rather it was a subtle rhetorical medium devised to win acceptance for what Bradford called "the simple truth." It was often studded with elements of high art—elaborate imagery, prose rhythm, complex metaphor and scriptural analogy—but with the end held firmly in view. In Puritan experience, writer and audience alike distrusted "tainted sermons," talk or writing striving for decoration or ceremonial. Unlike the devotional elegance of Catholic or Anglican writing, this was language resacralized by its own congregation, shaped by specific theological, social and political assumptions: "Writings that come abroad," Hooker cautioned, "are not to dazzle but direct the apprehension of the meanest."

This was the lesson carried to America by Hooker's fellow minister

John Cotton, the eminent English preacher who in converting to Puritanism sacrificed his famous eloquence to the spare utility of the plain style. When without preliminary indication he addressed his Anglican congregation in the plain words of his new faith, some were said to pull their caps over their ears, so great was the difference in utterance. Migrating in 1633 to the Bay Colony, he was soon one of its most important spiritual leaders, "indeed a most universal scholar, and a living system of the liberal arts, and a walking library," wrote his grandson Cotton Mather. He had much to do with the beginnings of the American book, being the supposed author of the famous preface to the *Bay Psalme Book* of 1640. In his journal of March 1, 1639, Governor Winthrop noted that there was a new press at Cambridge, and "The first thing printed was the freeman's oath; the next was an almanack made for New England . . . ; the next was the Psalms newly turned into metre." All were evident American necessities, but the remaking of the Psalms for ready comprehension and easy singing required some justification. In his preface Cotton speaks of the "common style" of most Old Testament books and notes that "If therefore the verses are not always so smooth and elegant as some may desire or expect; let them consider that God's Altar needs not our polishings"—perhaps the most famous dictum on language and art to emerge from colonial America. Yet the famous phrase itself displays the fact that the plain style did not eschew metaphor. Metaphor and typology are the shaping elements of Puritan writing.

Just as the new colony acquired its own printing press, it sought to establish its own literary style, and there was no shortage of opportunity for expression. The hundreds of journals, sermons, devotional works, histories, accounts of church and social polity and volumes of religious controversy indicate a remarkable vitality. The sermon was the essential native form, as well as a central event of Puritan life in a congregation where the minister was a key figure in the sustaining of the social and religious covenant. It was a form of providential communication and communion and a testing place of the word itself in its capacity to expound and interpret God's meanings. Leading preachers like John Cotton, Thomas Hooker and Increase Mather testify to the way in which the community saw itself locked in a single great struggle for salvation; the sermon was affective discourse, purposeful and inspirational speaking and writing designed to generate emotion and faith. It was to become the main instrument of that Great Awakening that, one hundred years after settlement, brought a renewed burst of religious fervor when the old spirit seemed in decline. Its central voice was Jonathan Edwards; his "Sinners in the Hands of an Angry God" (1741) remains the most famous of Puritan sermons. In some ways this is a pity; it does not suggest the range of Puritan experience, and it does not fully represent Edwards himself, giving far too narrow a view of this extraordinary intellect, as we shall see. But it does demonstrate how the millenarian spirit was sustained through the ministry and how Puritan belief persisted in America.

Central to the Puritan's life was the question of individual election and damnation, the pursuit by each man of God's works, the relation of private destiny to predestined purpose. Besides the history and the sermon, there was the journal, the recording of the individual life. For each pious settler, personal life was a theater for an inner drama comparable to the history of the community as a whole. Each day's experiences could be scrutinized for indications of God's will and evidence of predestination, and so the story of individual lives grew in the pages of diaries and journals in much the way historians shaped their accounts of historical crises and public events. What the aspirant to holiness sought as he read his life was a pattern of salvation—some indication, however minute, that he belonged to the predestined regenerate. This commitment to self-scrutiny and conscience gives us, in the many journals, a remarkable access to the Puritans' inward life, their balance of self and society. In journals like Bradford's and Winthrop's, the public account, the history, of America begins; but their record is not only of public but private and inward events, not only congregational concerns but domestic experience. History and theology merge with autobiography in the Calvinist way, and autobiography—especially spiritual autobiography—became an accepted Puritan form, often intended for public circulation, from the personal accountings of the Reverend Thomas Shepard to the *Spiritual Travels* of Nathan Cole. From such works we begin to sense the destiny of the Puritan self, and as time went on and colonial life took on greater secular complexity we begin to know its domestic world too. As we shall see, it is in some of the later diaries that we find this early

American identity at its most various and complex: in the seven volumes by Cotton Mather; the detailed and much more secular record of Samuel Sewall, the most engaging account we have of Puritan domestic, social and commercial life; and the *Personal Narrative* of the great divine Jonathan Edwards. Such works created a legacy of self-scrutiny that was to shape later secular statements of individualism and conscience, like that famous gospel of the American Self, the *Autobiography* of the eighteenth century's best-known American, Benjamin Franklin.

· IV ·

As all this suggests, the main part of the abundant literary expression we have from the Puritan period is not what we would now call imaginative literature. History, annal, travel record, scientific observation, the diary, the sermon, the meditation or the elegy—these were the central expressions of the American Puritan mind. Theater was condemned, and prose fiction, in the age when the novel was finding itself abroad, was deeply distrusted. Poetry, though important, had a rigorously defined place. But the fact remains that there was a complex Puritan imagination that, drawing on the encompassing sense of allegory and typology, the Bible, and high notions of the transcendental and providential, opened up America and its new settlements to discovery through the word. No doubt the commitment of the Puritans to spiritual meditation and the "plaine style" cut their colonies off from the imaginative excitements of what in seventeenth-century Britain was a rich age of writing. The erotic and linguistic play of metaphysical poetry, the dark complexities of Jacobean tragedy, even the vast epicality of Puritan writers like John Bunyan and John Milton, whose *Paradise Lost* appeared in 1667, were not replicated in Puritan New England. Yet this intense British Protestant spirit had its own metaphysical and allegorical resources that marked early Puritan writing and later American literature. The Puritan view of the word as a potential revelation saw allegory and metaphor essentially as connective tissue linking humankind to divine truth and limited the larger play of the imagination but never totally denied it. Puritans considered many of the literary questions we still ask today; they answered them differently. Just as for the Renaissance Platonist the world's matter came to life as a reflection of pure idea, so for the Puritan, word and world alike were a shadowing forth of divine things, coherent systems of transcendent meaning.

In this, Puritan thought anticipated many aspects of Romanticism, especially that brand of it we call transcendentalism and find notably American; much of this was born out of the Puritan heritage. But where Romanticism celebrated the imagination as a path to spiritual understandings, the Puritan mind required piety. Believing that they would find either salvation or damnation at life's end, the Puritans demanded of all the arts they cultivated—pulpit oratory, psalmody, tombstone carving, epitaph, prose or poetry in general—that they help them define and live a holy life. That logically led to suspicion of pictorial, musical and verbal creations which served only for pleasure or distraction, but allowed for much metaphorical play, much witty observation, much gothic imagining constrained by the endeavor to comprehend spiritual life or their own destiny in the American world. As visible saints with the press of history on their shoulders, the New England settlers felt they had a special mission of interpretation. So they cherished moral and spiritual advice, valued the didactic and the pious, and set limits on other things. This reinforced their commitment to the familiar American doctrine of utility, the need to do or enjoy only what leaves us better for the experience.

So, to this day, the Puritan approach to the arts is typified by one of the most widely used books ever published, *The New England Primer* (1683?). Frequently reissued, selling some five million copies, it led generations of children through the alphabet with a dogmatic set of mnemonic rhymes, from "In Adam's fall/We sinned all" to "Zaccheus he/Did climb a tree/His Lord to see." Its purposefulness and instructive intent is typical of the Puritan approach to verse and rhyme. When Cotton Mather gave advice to those preparing for the ministry in his *Manuductio ad Ministarium* (1726), he both commended poetry and warned of its dangers. A "devil's library" exists, he says, whose "muses . . . are no better than harlots," and he warns that the powers of darkness have a library among us, whereof the poets have been the most numerous as well as the most venomous authors. Most of the modern plays, as well as the romances, and novels and fictions, which are a sort of poem, do belong to the catalogue of this cursed library.

A Mr. Bedford, he noted, had collected "near 7,000 instances" of pestilential impiety from the plays of the previous five years, a sign at least that such things circulated, as indeed Puritan libraries prove. But despite his strictures, Mather could say that

Though some have had a soul so unmusical, that they have decried all verse as being but a meer playing and fiddling upon words; all versifying, as it were more unnatural than if we should chuse dancing instead of walking; and rhyme, as if it were but a sort of moriscedancing with bells; yet I cannot wish you a soul that shall be wholly unpoetical. An old Horace has left us an art of poetry, which you may do well to bestow a perusal on. And besides your lyric hours, I wish you may so far understand an epic poem, that the beauties of an Homer and a Virgil be discovered with you.

Mather may have distrusted the "sickly appetite for the reading of poems which now the rickety nation swarms withal," but his own appetite for reading was substantial. He amassed a capacious colonial library of some two thousand volumes, drew on classical, contemporary and vernacular styles for the texture of his own prose, devoted himself to science, classics and the learning of seven languages and was elected to the British Royal Society in 1714. He was, as is evident from his observations, living in a society that welcomed crates of English books with every boat. And poetry was, in fact, an essential form of Puritan discourse. Much of it inclined toward useful doggerel, but verse anagrams, acrostics, riddles, epitaphs and elegies, often complex and playful, were popular forms and fill the writings of many of the major figures, from the early John Winthrop to Cotton Mather himself. Most are occasional, but there is one poem that did dominate New England—selling, it is said, one copy for every twenty persons there —Michael Wigglesworth's *The Day of Doom* (1662). It was not, admittedly, a joyous read: 224 eight-line stanzas of singsong doctrinal verse, it displayed the threat of the Day of Judgment and the Calvinistic doctrines of damnation and reprieve with three apparently contending aims—to instruct, to delight and to terrify. Wigglesworth, born in England and brought to America at the age of seven, became minister of Malden, Massachusetts. His intentions were always pious, but he wrote his famous poem with such dramatic intensity that a friend told him it would be read until the coming of the day it describes. Typically, he justified it according to the Puritan principle of utility:

> How sweetly doth eloquence even inforce trueth upon the under-standing, and subtly convay knowledge into the minde be it never so dulle of conceiving, and sluggish in yeelding its assente. So that let a good Oratour put forth the utmost of his skill . . . he will make a very block understand his discourse.

Wigglesworth did put all his poetic as well as his persuasive skill to the cause of making the "very block" understand. As the friend who wrote the prefatory verse to this most famous New England poem had it: "No Toys, nor Fables (Poet's wonted crimes),/Here be, but things of worth, with wit prepar'd."

Today we can still recognize the vigor of *The Day of Doom* and find it a useful mirror of seventeenth-century dogma. Nonetheless Wigglesworth has been superseded as the exemplary Puritan poet by two other writers whose vastly greater complexity displays far more richly the texture of doubt and struggle the Puritan poetic imagination was able to express. One of these was Anne Bradstreet, perhaps the first major woman poet in the English language. Also born in England, she sailed in 1630 on the *Arbella*. Both her father and her husband (by whom she had eight children) were governors of Massachusetts Bay, but it is partly because the poetry she produced between domestic duties and recurring bouts of illness is *not* about great political, historical or theological matters that she interests us. For today's women writers she represents a crucial antecedent, but other modern writers have also seen the continuing value of her sensibility and high metaphysical wit, not least John Berryman, who devoted his fine poem sequence *Homage to Mistress Bradstreet* to her in 1956. She acquired a contemporary reputation as the first author of a volume of American poems; her brother-in-law published her work in London in 1650, apparently without her knowledge, as *The Tenth Muse, Lately Sprung Up in America,* "compiled," added the title, "with great variety of Wit, and Learning, full of delight." These high claims were doubtless not her own, for her own note is essentially more restrained—as in the opening poem that addresses the want of themes in America and also the problems of being a woman poet:

> I am obnoxious to each carping tongue,
> Who sayes my hand a needle better fits,
> A Poet's Pen, all scorne, I should thus wrong;
> For such despight they cast on female wits:
> If what I doe prove well, it won't advance,
> They'l say it's stolne, or else, it was by chance.

The complaint is both personal and very compelling, and so is her best poetry.

Bradstreet ambitiously drew for models on the writing of Renaissance England, on Sidney and Spenser, and also on the French Guillaume Du Bartas, "great Bartas," for the large classical themes she first attempted. But it is the tug between such intentions and her own provincial and displaced world, between public issues and the stuff of domestic life, that creates the tension in her verse, as, indeed, does her typical Calvinist concern about the relation between this world and the next. A late poem, "The Author to Her Book" (1678), directly acknowledges the "home-spun cloth" from which she makes her poetry. But, though her strongest subjects are drawn from the stuff of daily life—many are poems of love and grief, some celebrating marriage in surprisingly intimate fashion ("If ever two were one, then surely we./If ever man were loved by wife, then thee") and others mourning the death of loved ones or the burning of the family house—they have a metaphysical wit and texture that anticipate the work of a New Englander of two hundred years later, Emily Dickinson. This comes in part from the struggle between dissent and acceptance in the life of a strong-willed woman living in a commonwealth which required double submission, to domestic and divine duty, but also in part from the sense of felt experience she inherited from British poetry, mixing an alert vivacity with an apparent simplicity. Her love is marital, her landscape plain but brightly seen, her meditations troubled but ultimately pious, her awareness of nature acute but also respectful of the Maker of it.

Bradstreet's poems were recognized in England old and new; the poetry of Edward Taylor was private and remained unknown until a bulky manuscript was discovered in the Yale University library in 1937. Slowly he has been recognized as the major Puritan poet, the best and most productive America would produce till the mid-nineteenth century. He too was born in Britain, in Leicestershire, and received his education there before emigrating in 1668. Besides those poets who influenced Bradstreet, he had also assimilated Donne, Herbert, Crashaw and Vaughan, the major metaphysical-religious poets of the age preceding his. A minister in Westfield, Massachusetts, he was a Puritan first and a poet second; his poetry never deviates from dedication to the glory and goodness of God. Yet there is something occult and Platonist about his thought, a baroque intensity in his writing, that still makes it seem a surprising product of Puritanism. With its elaborate conceits and complex rhythms, it could well have struck his contemporaries as popish—a possible reason why he made no effort to publish and indeed, according to legend, asked his relatives to destroy his verse at his death. If it had been, we would have been poorer by far more than some remarkable poetry, for the recovery of his manuscripts opened a window on the American seventeenth century that would have stayed closed forever. His poems portray a Puritan sensibility fruitfully nourished by the rich literary culture of Renaissance England—a belated, provincial poetry in some ways, for a contemporary of Swift—but thoroughly Puritan in its devotional piety. They also reveal what a gifted imagination could make of a world seen as only an American Puritan could see it, with a power of expression that less poetically skilled writers like Bradford or even Mather could only suggest.

Taylor's poetry shows that there is an extraordinary compatibility between the Puritan worldview and the wrought sensibility of metaphysical verse—that violent yoking of unlike things that so distressed

Samuel Johnson. For Taylor, soul and body, grace and sin, the will of God and the intransigence of His fallen creature, all require violence of conception and expression to resolve their contradiction:

> Alas! my soul, product of breath divine
> For to illuminate a lump of slime.
> Sad providence! Must thou below thus tent
> In such a cote as strangles with ill scent? . . .
>
> Woe's me! my mouldering heart! What must I do?
> When is my moulting time to shed my woe?
> Oh! Woeful fall! what, fall from heavenly bliss
> To th' bottom of the bottomless abyss?
> Above, an angry God! Below, black-blue
> Brimstony flames of hell where sinners rue!
> Behind, a trail of sins! Before appear
> An host of mercies that abused were!
> Without, a raging devil! and within,
> A wracking conscience galling home for sin!

These lines from "The Soule Bemoaning . . ." are part of a long sequence that Taylor called "God's Determinations Touching His Elect," an apocalyptic rendering of Puritan belief written about 1682. Taylor admired *The Day of Doom*, and once praised his wife because "The Doomsday Verses much perfumed her breath." Like Wigglesworth's poem a meditation on judgment, Taylor's sequence is essentially different in that it captures the passional aspects of faith, as Wigglesworth does not, by embodying the struggle between language and understanding. "God's Determinations" should be read whole. It starts brilliantly in its account of the summoning of Creation from infinity ("Who Spread its Canopy? Or Curtains spun? Who in this Bowling Alley bowld the Sun?"); it moves from the Fall, which caused the poet's exiled state, through to the joyous transit of Christ's coach toward the Heavenly City. If it lacks the epic grandeur and the intense dramatic sense that makes Milton's *Paradise Lost* the greatest of Puritan long poems, it nevertheless powerfully realizes the plight of the individual soul seeking both regeneration and a grasp of the compatibility between infinite justice and infinite mercy.

Taylor wrote many shorter poems as well—most notably two series of *Preparatory Meditations* that he used to explore scriptural texts and plumb his worthiness to approach the altar. These poems often have a charged erotic content and an appreciative physicality, along with the daring sense of language and willingness to extend analogies to near breaking point that make him a true metaphysical poet. His verse presents the drama of feeling as a struggle of strained discourse—"My tazzled Thoughts twirled into Snick-Snarls run"— where doubt and self-questioning have their proper, even startling, place—"I'm but a Flesh and Blood bag." His best-known poem, "Huswifery" (ca. 1685), illustrates a baroque sensibility that could transform homely domestic activity into symbolic exploration of the soul's dependence on God for the grace to deserve redemption:

> Make me, O Lord, thy Spinning Wheele compleate.
>   Thy Holy Worde my Distaff make for mee.
> Make mine Affections thy Swift Flyers neate
>   And make my Soule thy holy Spoole to bee.
>   My Conversation make to be thy Reele
>   And reele the yarn thereon spun of thy Wheele.
>
> Make me thy Loome then, knit therein this Twine:
>   And make thy Holy Spirit, Lord, winde quills:
> Then weave the Web thyselfe. The yarn is fine.
>   Thine ordinances make my Fulling Mills.
>   Then dye the same in Heavenly Colours Choice,
>   All pinkt with Varnisht Flowers of Paradise.
>
> Then cloathe therewith mine Understanding, Will,
>   Affections, Judgement, Conscience, Memory,
> My Words, and Actions, that their shine may fill
>   My wayes with glory and Thee glorify.
>   Then mine apparell shall display before Yee
>   That I am Cloathd in Holy robes for glory.

What is most remarkable is the way Taylor's verse employs the strained conceits of the metaphysical tradition to render the psychological and emotional pressures of New England Calvinism, thereby using the linguistic intensity of poetic creation as *itself* a means of reaching toward God and redemption.

Though discovered only lately, Taylor's large body of poetry now seems a convincing source for our sense of what Roy Harvey Pearce has called the continuity of American poetry. It has the spareness of Puritanism, a sense that the Bible and the troubled soul and conscience are sufficient locations for a struggle of the word toward revelation. But, unlike most Puritan verse, it is not doggerel, diagram or crude psalmody. Rather it displays triumphantly what Taylor's fellow Puritans might only suggest: that there is a relation between the way the world is seen and the aesthetic energy of the written vision. The Bunyanesque world of Holy War, where Grace abounds and the Pilgrim progresses toward the Holy City or the New Jerusalem, is presented as a powerful inward drama for which poetry is a necessary voice for manifesting both mystical and verbal tension. This is a markedly American world, for in the Puritan way America is made the special ground for the contest of grace, part of the sacred landscape of revelation in which historical and personal event enacts providential meaning. Taylor's poems pass beyond literary artifice to become emblems of transcendent relationships, beyond allegory into the moral, psychological and symbolic intensity that comes to characterize so much of the richest American writing, from Emerson, Hawthorne and Melville through Emily Dickinson and Henry James to William Faulkner.

· V ·

In imaginative prose fiction, there was, however, no comparable voice. Indeed this was long to stay true, and though the novel eventually became a major American form, it was slow to put down roots. But one form of prose story, arising directly out of the Puritan trials in the wilderness, did reach a striking level of creative energy—the Indian-captivity narratives. In the struggles with landscape and climate, and above all in the battles with the Indians, the Puritans found themselves in direct encounter with America. In the providential plan, it was here they would confront Satan in the "howling wilderness" where the Gospel had not yet reached. The Indian-captivity narratives can be read as the record of this story, another form of providential history and annal, but they also became in time a prototype of popular American writing, dominating publication during the last years of the seventeenth century and serving as essential source for much later American fiction.

The ever-present Indian threat haunted all the colonies, and the stories of captivity recorded terrible events. As Cotton Mather said, the settlers felt themselves "assaulted by unknown numbers of devils in flesh on every side," and King Philip's War of 1675–76 brought heavy casualties. The narrative accounts described the ensuing events but drew as well on the essential Puritan myth that shaped perception of the adventure: a chosen people crossing the sea to enter a wilderness peopled with devils, suffering, trial and captivity, learning of the closeness of taint and damnation and seeking redemption in the quest for the new city of salvation. These captivity stories tell of being taken by the Indians, enduring dreadful hardships, witnessing horrors, facing the cruelty of captors toward their prisoners, then of a rescue or escape which restores the narrator and permits him or her to recount these adventures to seek out their providential meaning.

Captivity narratives were stories of trial and persecution endured in the Satanic world of darkness that lay just beyond the covenanted settlement. In the prose of a devout believer, the entire adventure could be shaped into a lived allegory of salvation, not just for an individual but for an entire people. That is the spirit of Mrs. Mary Rowlandson's story, *The Soveraignty and Goodness of God, Together With the Faithfulness of His Promises Displayed: Being a Narrative of the Captivity and Restauration of Mrs. Mary Rowlandson* (1682). Well and carefully written, it was an account of her actual captivity during King Philip's War; it became a prototype, immensely popular, frequently reprinted, much copied. Rowlandson's tale is an adventure story which, as the title suggests, never forgets the experience's transcendental meanings. The Puritan mythos guides her: she links her imprisonment with that of the soul snared by sin and with the countless captivities of the Bible (from the children of Israel to Jonah in the whale's belly); her language echoes that of the Old Testament and she draws on its types. When she calls the Indians "hell-hounds" and their dancing "a resemblance of hell," she means what she says: the Indians are servants of Satan, their celebrations an emblem of spiritual death. Her frequent forced marches parallel the hazardous devil-beset journey all must make through life; her rescue the same unaccountable act of God's mercy that will bring His Chosen People to the heavenly kingdom. The essential Puritan myth asserts itself: the captivity narrative is sermon, moral lesson, revelatory history—but also precursor of later sensationalist fiction and gothic tale.

The apparent reductiveness of these stories should not blind us to the power that Puritan vision could bring to the feel and form of experience. The allegorical level of each narrative provided an entrance by which the power of storytelling could establish itself among a people devoted to serviceable truth and convinced that fiction was simply an elaborated form of lying. Like Bunyan's (almost contemporary) *Pilgrim's Progress,* Rowlandson's approach allows the story of an individual life to be coherently structured and to share the appeal of its scriptural parallels and sources. Within these serious purposes, though, the Puritan writer was—as Defoe would parodically suggest in *Moll Flanders*—free to make a tale as affective and diverting as possible. Rowlandson's captivity account exhibits many qualities we find in the best New England writing. Because God's purposes are displayed in the slightest detail, the language can be remarkably concrete:

On the tenth of February 1675, Came the Indians with great numbers upon Lancaster: Their first coming was about Sunrising; hearing the noise of some Guns, we looked out; several Houses were burning, and the Smoke ascending to Heaven. There were five persons taken in one house, the Father, and the Mother and a sucking Child, they knockt on the head; the other two they took and carried away alive. . . . Another there was who running along was shot and wounded, and fell down; he begged of them his life, promising them Money (as they told me) but they would not hearken to him but knockt him in head, and stript him naked, and split open his Bowels.

This is more than careful observation; it is another application of the "plaine style" striving for accurate representation of observed life. But the limits of the Puritan imagination, the elements of experience their creed made them unable to explore, are also apparent. Mrs. Rowlandson can acknowledge the pull of Indian life and "the wilderness-condition" but must avert her eyes. Native tradition and culture, the complex depths of America's natural world, are not fit subjects for her discourse. The Puritan quest was not to know the land but to redeem it and thereby redeem all of human history.

·VI·

By the end of the seventeenth century, New England was a dense, settled culture, bookish, largely led by its ministers, in relatively close contact with English and European thought. It was also a society confirmed by its own history and the failure of the Puritan Revolution in Britain (in which New Englanders participated) in its redemptive purpose and its sense of living out an elected, providential history on American soil. It was a culture of biblical promise and manifest purpose that deliberately excluded much from without and within—the more Anglican and Cavalier spirit of the twice-deported Thomas Morton of Merry Mount, who would so fascinate Nathaniel Hawthorne and whose *The New English Canaan* (1637) was a highly irreverent account of Puritan piety and self-justification, the antinomianism of the critical religious thinker Anne Hutchinson and the preacher Roger Williams, who managed to get himself exiled both from Plymouth and Massachusetts Bay. Outcast as a dissenter to Rhode Island, Williams was one of the few who tried to see the American Indians on their own terms and made it his apostolic task to live with them "in their filthy smoky holes . . . to gain their tongue." His *Key into the Languages of America* (1643) offered native vocabulary lists and doggerel stanzas which showed how the white man could learn from native culture and native civility:

> If nature's son both wild and tame,
> Humane and courteous be:

How ill becomes its sons of God
   To want humanity? . . .

God gives them sleep on ground, on straw,
   On sedgy mats or board:
When English softest beds of down
   Sometimes no sleep afford.

I have known them leave their house or mat,
   To lodge a friend or stranger,
When Jews and Christians oft have sent
   Christ Jesus to the manger.

If Puritan prose and poetry tell us what the Puritan experience meant for new Americans, the dissenting voices hint at what they excluded. The Indian was only just making his entrance into American writing—as a howling savage for some, a civil child of nature for others like Williams. It was not surprising that Indians, like blacks in the South, remained marginal; not just the Indian wars but the warring relations of the indigenous tribes, the language barrier and the problems of understanding the customs of native culture made contact difficult. In literature as well as society, the Indian was to remain excluded, never really fertilizing mainstream culture as the blacks would eventually do. American nature often lay beyond the Puritan compass as well, largely remaining a place of peril and a "howling wilderness" beyond the safety of the plantation through which the pilgrim passed on his way to the Heavenly City. As many writers since have noticed, one legacy of the Puritan temper was the slow process of American surrender to the land that was America; as Robert Frost put it in the poem he read for President Kennedy's Inauguration, "The land was ours before we were the land's./She was our land more than a hundred years/Before we were her people. . . ." One result of this, William Carlos Williams was to explain in his bitterly anti-Puritan *In the American Grain* (1925), was that the settlers were late to acquire what the Indians possessed naturally, the capacity to "bathe in, to explore always more deeply, to see, to feel, to touch . . . the wild beauty of the New World." What the Puritans denied, then, was what, two hundred years later, Henry David Thoreau accepted, that American nature was the greatest form of instruction the continent offered, that, as Whitman said, the land itself was the greatest poem. While some Puritan nature writing exists, the forest beyond the settlement, rather like the Europe left behind, seemed, as Nathaniel Hawthorne would suggest in "Young Goodman Brown," dangerous and forbidden space, psychologically as well as geographically. The new settlers saw New England as a stage on which their roles in a divine drama were on trial, and their Canaan was a millennial land, not a land of milk and honey. The Indian sense of mystic reverence for the land, of the timeless cycles that separated him from European linear history, had not yet become central to American culture.

Because of such exclusions, much later American writing, and some would say the American imagination itself, revolted against Puritanism. In fact to many later artists the very idea of a "Puritan imagination" would come to seem a contradiction in terms. Hawthorne, one of whose ancestors was a judge at the Salem witchcraft trials, returned with a sense of curious ambiguity to the world of his steeple-hatted Puritan ancestors in *The Scarlet Letter* (1850). He tests the idea of "iron-bound" Puritan society against the world of nature, but discloses as well that the power of the Puritan spirit has not died. Indeed, in the preface, he wonders what Puritanism signifies for his own art, anxiously admitting that his very book would probably seem a crime to his own ancestors:

> "What is he?" murmurs one gray shadow of my forefathers to the other. "A writer of story-books! What kind of a business in life, —what mode of glorifying God, or being serviceable to mankind in his day and generation,—may that be? Why, the degenerate fellow might as well have been a fiddler."

American writers and critics took many generations to come to terms with the implications of Puritanism. In the 1920s, when the modern American arts flowered, fierce debates still raged about the destructive power of Puritan influence: it was frequently held responsible for all that was materialistic, commercial and anti-aesthetic in the American view of life. Critics blamed the Puritan heritage for much that seemed to limit American writing: its heavily allegorizing disposition, its failure to open out to experience or the ambiguity of the symbol, its lack of inclusiveness, its dull response to the world of nature, its rigorous moralism and its Anglo-Saxonism. More recently, a revival of interest in the Puritan heritage has grown to the point of arguing its centrality for the American imagination.

Neither view is entirely true. Even when they glorified their separateness and the virtues of the inner self, American Puritans still owed much to their British forebears and contemporaries. And others, from different origins and with different beliefs, writing later or elsewhere, opened many of the doors of American literary discovery. Yet the Puritans' cosmic, transcendental and providential vision, their faith in an escape from a dead Old World to a redemptive New one—their "exceptionalist" belief in the powerful recovery of history—lingers yet in American culture. So does their belief in the novelty of the story they told and the value of their own "tenth muse." Passionately reasserted as a political aim in the early years of the Republic, repeated with growing confidence in Ralph Waldo Emerson's "American Scholar" oration of 1837, in Herman Melville's rejection of "this leaven of literary flunkeyism toward England" in 1850, again in Whitman's disavowal of the "petty environage and limited area of the poets of past and present Europe" in 1888, and so onward into the twentieth century, the conviction that Americans had a special purpose and would speak it in a special voice was to remain continuous, guiding the vision of American writers long after the devotion to Calvin's doctrines died. The Puritan imagination does not explain the extraordinary variousness American writing was to achieve, but it certainly does not deserve the status of an eternal negative adversary. Puritanism may have set certain limits on the American imagination; it was also one of its essential roots.

CHAPTER

·2·

AWAKENING AND
ENLIGHTENMENT

·I·

The God who sent the Puritans on their errand into the American wilderness did not send all His transatlantic settlers over the water in the same spirit. A Quaker God shaped William Penn's Pennsylvania, a Catholic Lord populated the Chesapeake Bay area of Maryland, an Episcopalian Deity led the way to the abundance of Virginia. Not all the colonists were visible saints; some were entrepreneurs, indentured servants, even convicts. And the land was not only a "howling wilderness" and desert of trials, but a mine, an unexploited source of wealth, a space for social opportunity or social concealment. There were many stories to tell of America, often containing similar elements (a sense of wonder, of freedom, of human novelty or paradisal hope) but with very different intonations. A spiritual or devotional discourse was not the only voice; a language resonating with secular pleasure or more direct commercial cunning might also narrate settlement's historic enterprise, as Captain John Smith had shown.

" 'Tis agreed, that Travellers are of all Men, the most suspected of Insincerity," noted Smith's successor in recording Virginia, Robert Beverly. However, said Beverly in his lively *History and Present State of Virginia* (1705), while Frenchmen incline to hyperbole in such matters, "The English, it must be granted, invent more within the Compass of Probability, and are contented to be less Ornamental, while they are more Sincere." Sincere or not, Beverly well knew the trope within which he was inventing, and it was a large one, nothing less than the trope of the Earthly Paradise itself—"Paradice itself seem'd to be there, in its first Native Lustre." Beverly's account evokes the innocent pastoral already celebrated by Drayton, Raleigh and Marvell, a land where life is propertyless, the noble savages live pleasurably and innocently and the problems are simply those of relating nature to culture. Yet Beverly's is clearly not a seventeenth- but an eighteenth-century mind, concerned with both improving and sustaining the garden of innocent pleasure which is Virginia. His thought, based on values of reason, science and progress, seeks an enlightened pastoral, an intelligent polity; his history tells a story of social growth.

Beverly's Virginia is decidedly not Puritan, yet in New England itself confidence in a theocentric universe was shifting toward a more scientific, rational, empirical curiosity about the nature of the cosmos and of human society. The foundation of the Royal Society in London in 1662, the spirit of Locke, Burke and Newton, the intellectual currents of the age, were introducing ideas that would deeply shape America and in due time help bring it to independent nationhood. Puritanism itself gradually responded to modern scientific study. In *The Christian Philosopher* (1721), Cotton Mather espouses scientific learning: he can assert that "The Works of the Glorious GOD in the *Creation* of the World, are what I now propose to exhibit" since the book of the universe continues to be God's book to be read. But the distance between Mather and a later Enlightenment mind like Benjamin Franklin's nevertheless remains enormous: while Franklin examined in minute detail *what* occurred to see *how* it occurred, thereby increasing the stock of practical human knowledge, Mather's scientific curiosity asked *why* God's nature might behave in the ways it did. "The *Winds;* 'tis an *Angel* moving his *Wings* that raises them," Mather notes. The danger of scientific thought, he warns, is the temptation to atheism that must be "hissed out of the World." Like his ancestors, the world for Mather had been created by a "BEING that must be *superior* to *Matter,* even the *Creator* and *Governor* of all *Matter.*" For his great successor Jonathan Edwards, this was still much the way in which nature must be read.

Yet the spirit of New England was changing as the eighteenth century began. Its emerging secularism is evident in the *Diary* of Samuel Sewall, the most engaging recorder we have of Puritan domestic, social and commercial life. Sewall began as a preacher, turned businessman and finally became chief justice of Massachusetts, a consummate Puritan gentleman. A devout man, he sat as judge at the Salem witch trials but later repudiated his role in the affair—"reiterated strokes of God" causing him to take "the blame and the shame." He als wrote the first attack on slavery in America. His diary, however, portrays an American life of small things in its detailed accounting of the uneasy balance between spiritual aspiration and the petty demands of everyday life. Here we see the scurry of commercial affairs, family life, social contacts, political duties, and learn when Cotton Mather's chimney caught fire. Half-consciously it is a comic record, especially in its account of Sewall's late-life courtship of various widows, "God having in his holy Sovereignty put my wife out of the fore-seat." In a characteristic mixture of spiritual intensity and secular concern, Sewall woos Madam Winthrop with printed sermons and gingernuts, assessing her character and whether or not her clothes are clean. His tone is sometimes pompous, often witty, but he is always a pleasure to read. His significance goes further, however, for he is a figure on the turn: away from the Puritan past, toward the Yankee, commercial, empirical spirit of eighteenth-century America.

The newer spirit in America was more conspicuous outside the bounds of New England. The diarist William Byrd II of Westover, Virginia, was a relative of Robert Beverly—a great landowner and gentleman planter, protector of the Virginian garden, and in many ways the antithesis of his Puritan contemporary Cotton Mather. His library, the largest in the colonies, was nearly twice the size of Mather's and reflected both his rank and his ideals of cultivation. Sent to England for his education like so many of the wealthy, then and since, he learned Latin, Greek, Hebrew, French and Italian. He prepared for the bar at the Middle Temple, learned the tobacco business in Holland, became a member of the Royal Society and made his friends among the courtiers, wits and writers of Augustan England: Wycherley, Congreve, Swift and Pope. He brought the world of Restoration England back with him when he returned to Virginia in 1705 to become a leading political figure and one of America's greatest landowners—he founded

Richmond on his own estate, which at his death covered nearly two hundred thousand acres. He built a great mansion, Westover, and followed the Augustan model of improvement: land development, planned abundance and the managed landscape were his ideals.

Byrd's sense of American life and possibility is cast in terms quite different from those of the Puritan commentators. His world too is, in its way, threatening; he fears disease, disaster and the wreck of his ships, but his nature is no "howling wilderness" or den of devils. Development is hard, but America is a promising garden rising in the hierarchy from barbarism to civilization, nature to art, forest and frontier to tamed landscape. Cultivation in every sense is possible; nature can be balanced between wilderness and artifice as history advances not toward God's millennium but to the plainer achievements of human progress that rest on individual energy and character. Byrd brings us remarkably close to the eighteenth-century American mind that owed quite as much to contemporary Europe as to its seventeenth-century past.

Byrd's writings move in Augustan cadences, turning freely from nature to political events, casting the eye of sophistication on the empirical and primitive world. His three records of Virginia life, *The History of the Dividing Line Betwixt Virginia and North Carolina Run in the Year 1728, A Progress to the Mines in the Year 1732* and *A Journey to the Land of Eden in the Year 1733,* were written for private circulation and not printed till 1841. All are urbane and stylish, often catching Swift's tone as he sends Gulliver on his travels: the desire for colonization is a "Distemper," an "Itch of Sailing to this New World." There is a sharp contrast between Byrd's sophistication and the frontier people he meets as inquiring traveler or surveyor of his colony's boundary line, and backwoods customs on the Carolina frontier excite his sense of comedy. The Indians attract his social curiosity and prompt the observation that their women make excellent wives. As for plantation life itself, that is a responsible Arcadian idyll where the rural gentleman-philosopher may study, think and meditate amid his well-managed lands. The sharpest rendering of Byrd and his times comes from his *Secret Diary* (1709–12)—composed, like Pepys's, in his own code, and discovered and deciphered only in 1941. Here an entire culture comes alive, without any of Sewall's self-scrutiny or pomposity.

The *Diary* is the frank self-record of a powerful political figure and man of commerce who works hard but reads much, entertains considerably but has many family woes, is master over land and slaves yet expresses a modest and rational Christian devotion. "I said my prayers and had good health, and good thoughts, and good humour, thank God Almighty," he notes at the end of many of his days, often adding, "I rogered my wife (lustily)."

Byrd's writing also demonstrates that American nature itself was hard material for the mind to manage. American physical space was vast, its climate varied and often dangerous, its problems of settlement and social organization great. It was neither tamed nor enclosed, neither a garden to work on nor distantly sublime and enlarging to the visual and aesthetic imagination. There were those in Europe, like Buffon in France, who saw the American climate as perverse, a danger to man and his development. Others sought to embrace the special and remarkable wonders of American nature, but the American metaphysic that would merge man and terrain was slow to develop. It was not until the eighteenth century moved toward its end that the idea of America as a promising new pastoral came to accommodate its Revolutionary meaning. Another Frenchman, J. Hector St. Jean de Crèvecoeur, who came steeped in the ideals of Rousseau, expressed them in his *Letters from an American Farmer* (1782), a powerful demonstration of how a new nature and a new social order might generate a new kind of man and close the great circle of civilization on American soil. This was the theme that Thomas Jefferson turned to in his one book, *Notes on the State of Virginia* (1784–85). In Jefferson's post-Revolutionary times, Crèvecoeur's rural metaphysic became a vision of an ideal classical polity where the new free farmer and new libertarian institutions found expression in an extraordinary and openfrontiered landscape, there to administer, according to the highest eighteenth-century ideas, the heroic pastoral of the New World.

· II ·

The eighteenth century was a period of major change in American ideas and ideals, a change which did not so much displace the millenarian impulses so deeply associated with the American continent and American settlement as refashion them in response to the intellectual and scientific questions of the Age of Reason. In America, as elsewhere, the Reformation world of Aristotle and Ramus gave way to the Enlightenment world shaped by Newton and Locke; philosophy turned from rigid theology toward natural science; the values of Deism and moral naturalism, liberalism and progress increasingly became the appropriate ways to interpret American experience. The English-speaking colonies strung out along the Eastern seaboard were growing ever more settled, more heterodox and more open to new ideas not only from Europe but from each other. America's map was enlarging, its sense of being a rising empire increasing as its interior became an object of exploration and curiosity, the number and size of its cities expanded, its professions and mercantile development grew. Americans were gradually discovering the social and scientific complexity of their New World. The Puritan inheritance was being moderated and changed by the new thought and the new social order; the great religious awakenings of the new century were not simply attempts at reviving the old inheritance but energetic efforts to give new meaning to rapidly changing times.

All this is evident in two remarkable American minds that flourished in the eighteenth century, Jonathan Edwards and Benjamin Franklin, two men who between them seemed to realize and sum up the changes of American thought and the variety within it. Born within three years of each other, the two are often seen as representing the contrasting principles of eighteenth-century American life—one the idealist, the other the materialist; one the Puritan preacher working in New England and on the frontier, the other the man of political activism working to influence the affairs and the direction of the Western world; one the speculative thinker who was eventually to be thought of as an American Aquinas, the other the polymathic man for all seasons, the printer and politician, scientist and inventor, whose flexible, ranging intelligence could turn readily in any direction his curiosity led him. In these terms, they do indeed seem to represent opposite principles in the American mind—an older metaphysical Puritan strain, looking back to the past, a new spirit of Yankee mercantile practicality and ingenuity, looking forward to the future. The contrast is significant, but not complete. It is perhaps truer to say that new and old were, in different ways, combined in both, and that both embodied fundamental American continuities they passed on to the future.

Edwards's foremost purposes were clear: to make Puritanism viable for the eighteenth century and re-establish its main doctrines on a sound philosophical basis. He planned a summa, a *History of the Work of Redemption,* but it was still unwritten when he died at 55 from a smallpox inoculation undergone to demonstrate to his Princeton students his confidence in science. His theological purposes are perhaps best suggested by *A Careful and Strict Enquiry, into the Modern Prevailing Notions That Freedom of Will Is Supposed to Be Essential to Moral Agency, Virtue and Vice, Reward and Punishment, Praise and Blame* (1754). The title might well recall his mentor, Cotton Mather, but where Mather had drawn on secular scholarship to buttress his orthodox theology, Edwards went further, responding directly to contemporary Deism and experimental science. As a child he had recorded his observations "Of Insects" and "Of the Rainbow" with a precise notation of data that was to characterize his later assimilation of Newton; by his mid-teens, he was studying Locke's *Essay Concerning Human Understanding* and making notes on "the Mind." The result, for his sermons and theological writings, was both a vivid awareness of physical phenomena and a recognition of human subjectivity; for Edwards, both bore directly on questions of God's grace and spiritual regeneration. His *Treatise Concerning Religious Affections* (1746) and his own story of "awakening" in the *Personal Narrative* (ca. 1743) raise many of the Reformation questions that had concerned first-generation Puritans, but he brought a new emotional insistence to the recording and justifying of the affective force of faith. This emotional power charged his sermons and helped spark the Great Awakening of religious energy which spread from Maine to Georgia in the late 1730s, a revivalist fervor he sometimes condemned but nevertheless acknowledged as a response to the genuine inflowing of grace.

Edwards was, in short, a Puritan whose open-minded study of doctrine led him to the psychology of subjective experience—and so to anticipation of the transcendental Romanticism of the next century.

He was an American millennialist reading signs and types for a coming American regeneration of mankind. Scientific discovery simply added to the typological evidence:

> The late invention of telescopes, whereby heavenly objects are brought so much nearer and made so much plainer to sight and such wonderfull discoveries have been made in the heavens, is a type and forerunner of the great increase in the knowledge of heavenly things that shall be in the approaching glorious times of the Christian church,

he could say in *Images or Shadows of Divine Things,* one of the most powerful illustrations we have of the Puritan typological imagination. But Edwards's typology can embrace as well the experience of intuition and the individual soul, indeed, we might say, of that antinomian heresy for which the Puritans had earlier condemned Mrs. Hutchinson and the Quakers. Nature itself becomes a symbolic system with man its interpreter.

> I believe the grass and other vegetables growing and flourishing, looking green and pleasant as it were, ripening, blossoming, and bearing fruit from the influence of the heavens, the rain and wind and light and heat of the sun, to be on purpose to represent the dependence of our spiritual welfare upon God's gracious influences and the effusions of His holy spirit. I am sure there are none of the types of the Old Testament are more lively images of spiritual things.

Indeed, like the secular Platonism of the Renaissance, Edwards's form of Puritanism opens up a world of interpretative significance to the artist of close observation and imaginative sensation and helps explain the later welcome European Romanticism would receive in America. The symbolistic, transcendental American mind owes much to Edwards. It is his spirit that leads to Ahab's cry in *Moby-Dick,* "O Nature, and O soul of man! how far beyond all utterance are your linked analogies! not the smallest atom stirs or lives in matter, but has its cunning duplicate in mind"; to Thoreau's insistence that the world exists to supply us with tropes and figures; to Emerson's, that "Every natural fact is a symbol of some spiritual fact."

Franklin would seem to have little to do with any of this. "What then is the American, this new man?" J. Hector St. Jean de Crèvecoeur asked in the most familiar passage of his *Letters from an American Farmer;* he answered that

> *He* is an American, who, leaving behind all his ancient prejudices and manners, receives new ones from the mode of life he has embraced, the new government he obeys, and the new rank he holds. . . . The American is a new man, who acts on new principles; he must therefore entertain new ideas, and form new opinions.

Of this new, self-created American type, Franklin seems the supreme example. Born in Boston, son of a chandler and soap maker, he, like Edwards, heard Cotton Mather's sermons. But after meager schooling, drawing his education mainly from the books he read as an apprentice printer, he ran off at seventeen to Quaker Philadelphia, spent two years in London—where he wrote a rationalist pamphlet called *A Dissertation of Liberty and Necessity* (1725) to argue that the individual is not free and therefore not morally responsible—and then returned to Philadelphia to open a highly successful printshop. It was the polymathic side of Cotton Mather, the side that led him through the sciences from natural observation to medicine, that Franklin followed. Indeed the Boston spirit never left him; he remained always Puritan in his self-scrutiny and his desire to edify. But his was the Puritan conscience wholly secularized; absorbing the Deism of his day, he became a man for whom the spiritual questions of his forefathers had turned to questions of ethics, self-management and public service. His very consciousness of self and his determination to master rather than suffer worldly events came from those forefathers, but his rise to public success and his eventual status as the country's first internationally acknowledged statesman reveal how far colonial life had shifted from the guiding vision of the "Pilgrim Fathers" to the historical expansion of the civilization they planted. Franklin was, indeed, the new man, the American as modern, who self-consciously acquired the qualities necessary for the successful creation not only of his own but the colonies' destiny.

Franklin belonged to an expanding new age of American culture, an age of travel, newspapers, bookshops, scientific and philosophical societies, magazines, theaters and universities. He compiled and printed what became one of the most familiar of all American publications, *Poor Richard's Almanack* (1733–58), an annual broadsheet of practical farming, social advice and home-spun wisdom ("Honesty is the best policy"), founded America's second magazine, *The General Magazine and Historical Chronicle,* wrote from his youth onward for the press and devoted himself to inventions and institutions to serve the public weal—the Franklin stove, the lightning rod, the first library, street paving, sweeping and lighting, the American Philosophical Society, the University of Pennsylvania, a city hospital, a new kind of clock. His writings ranged from popular texts to scientific publications over an extraordinary range of interests and in most experimental fields; he was elected to the Royal Society and awarded its gold medal.

Franklin's best-known book, *The Autobiography,* written between 1771 and 1788, published in 1791 and 1818, was thus not simply a personal narrative or even a classic story of self-help and individual progress, but a central document of the evolutionary growth and the intellectual motion of America itself. He wrote it in troubled times, the times of his own greatest importance, international fame and influence—the first part when he was in England in 1771, in the immediately pre-Revolutionary years, the second after the Revolution in 1784, when he was American Minister to France, the third back in Philadelphia in 1788. By then the elderly international statesman and one of the prime forgers of the new nation, its Declaration of Independence and Constitution, was now a "citizen of the world" with much to look back on: his own growth a pattern for the growth of the nation itself.

The Autobiography is one of those summary texts of obvious public importance, though Franklin initially began it in the manner of Lord Chesterfield, as a manual of private guidance for his natural son.

Having emerged from the poverty and obscurity in which I was born and bred to a state of affluence and some degree of reputation in the world, and having gone so far through life with a considerable share of felicity, the conducing means I made use of, which with the blessing of God so well succeeded, my posterity may like to know, as they may find some of them suitable to their own situations, and therefore fit to be imitated.

When the Revolution broke the story off, friends urged its continuation; Franklin (who may fairly be called one of the world's first public relations experts) incorporated their letters:

> "What will the world say if kind, humane, and benevolent Ben. Franklin should leave his friends and the world deprived of so pleasing and profitable a work; a work which would be useful and entertaining not only to a few, but to millions? . . . I know of no character living . . . who has so much in his power as thyself to promote a greater spirit of industry and early attention to business, frugality, and temperance with the American youth,"

wrote one. Another directly linked Franklin to America's meaning as an "efficacious advertisement" of the nation's character: "All that has happened to you is also connected to the detail of the manners and situation of a rising people."

Franklin not only carefully sustains such an identification, but he meticulously establishes its roots in his family's Puritan past. He takes his story back three generations, to Ecton, Northamptonshire, in England, where his family were Protestants and dissenters who traveled to New England in 1682, "where they expected to enjoy their mode of religion with freedom." His upbringing was nourished on Mather's *Essays to Do Good* and Bunyan's *Pilgrim's Progress,* and both feed his own book. But Puritanism has become secularized. Franklin carefully dramatizes his move to Philadelphia to emphasize the space between his own Poor Richard's "unlikely beginnings" and his later wealth, success and influence; the older Calvinist mode of spiritual growth is now adapted to worldly purposes, to a materialist "Pilgrim's progress," for service to God is now service to man, and morality an issue of social utility. It is a tale of a quest for "moral perfection" which is also social achievement. Appropriately it has its failures and backslidings —hence the famous charts he devised to record his progress (later to be imitated by Scott Fitzgerald's Jay Gatsby). He seeks to acquire "the *habitude* of the thirteen virtues," from Resolution ("Resolve to perform what you ought; perform without fail what you resolve") and Frugality ("Waste nothing") to Industry ("Lose no time; be always employed in something useful") and Humility ("Imitate," he asserts comfortably, "Jesus and Socrates"). He noted on his elaborate daily tables his failures in any of these virtues: "I was surpriz'd to find myself so much fuller of faults than I had imagined; but I had the satisfaction of seeing them diminish."

The Autobiography is also the tale of Franklin's life seen *as* a book. To the end, he liked to call himself "B. Franklin, printer," to regard his mistakes as "errata," his task as the making of a "character," his business the finding of a "style" of writing and of life. A main story of the book is his forging of a discourse leading to worldly success; from that discourse he in turn constructs a fictive being, none other than Ben Franklin, man of the world, representative American and example to us all.

> As Prose Writing has been of great Use to me in the Course of
> my Life, and was a principal Means of my Advancement, I shall
> tell you how in such a Situation I acquir'd what little Ability I have
> in that way,

he announces. He recounts how as a child in Boston he and "another bookish lad of the Town" were found by his father disputing with each other—a habit, he notes with characteristic wit allied to edification, that "Persons of Good Sense, I have since observ'd, seldom fall into . . . except Lawyers, University Men, and Men of all sorts that have been bred at Edinborough"—and his father points out "how I fell short in elegance of Expression, in Method and in Perspicuity. . . . I saw the Justice of his Remarks, and thence grew more attentive to the *Manner* in writing, and determin'd to endeavour at Improvement." The source of his lesson is Addison's *Spectator,* a great favorite in America; he thinks "the Writing excellent, and wish'd if possible to imitate it." He makes summaries, sets them aside, then attempts to re-create the essays from notes, finding that, when compared with the originals, "I wanted a stock of Words or a Readiness in recollecting and using them." So he tries versifying, "since the continual Occasion for Words of the same import but of different Length, to suit the measure, or of different Sound for the Rhyme," enlarges vocabulary and usage. Discovering his faults and amending them, he becomes what the reader already knows him to be, one of the most acclaimed of eighteenth-century prose writers.

Essentially Franklin's is a classic eighteenth-century prescription for utilitarian prose, edifying and effective, shaped by Royal Society ideas and standards of good sense. It is "the plaine style" updated in the spirit of Cotton Mather, but to a secular end: "I approv'd the amusing one's self with Poetry now and then," he notes, "so far as to improve one's language, but no farther." The task is to create a man of sense and science in a prose age; since,

> when ill-expressed, the most proper Sentiments and justest Rea-
> soning lose much of their native Force and Beauty, it seems to me
> that there is scarce any Accomplishment more necessary to a Man
> of Sense, than that of *Writing Well* in his Mother Tongue.

As Franklin finds his way to wealth and from moral innocence to useful wisdom, the resulting mixture of Puritanism and practicality surely makes *The Autobiography* the most striking book of colonial America—and the first life, we might say, of modern American man. Franklin was to take the story only to 1757, but already it had reached the public figure who is model for his people, the Founding Father in embryo. Rather like the novels of Daniel Defoe, *The Autobiography* can take its place as one of the memorable realist fictions of the eighteenth century, the story of the making of a self through useful employment in the world of things. A tale of adventures tending ever upward, it defines the success we already expect when we begin our reading. And it shows how what Weber and Tawney have taught us to call the Protestant ethic came to direct the energies of the American character, and indeed shape it toward revolution and nationality.

It may seem remarkable that two of the most important prose documents of the American eighteenth century, apart from political statement and controversy, are autobiographies, but in a Deistic age, when, as Pope said, "The proper study of mankind is Man," autobiography becomes an inevitable form. One, Edwards's *Personal Narrative,* is a tale of spiritual awakening, a discovery of divine emotion within the self. The other, Franklin's self-record, is a tale of moral entrepreneurship and consequent social awakening, for the developed single individual and man of sense could identify with nothing less than human progress itself. In their different ways, the stories of both men reveal an essential American transition from the world of Calvinist orthodoxy to the world of the Enlightenment.

· III ·

Franklin was not only scientist, politician and American Founding Father; he was also a literary critic, much concerned, like the other Founding Fathers, with the fate of the arts in the New World. In late life, he was still wondering whether or when the arts would cross the ocean from Britain to the new nation:

> Why should that petty island, which compared to America is but like a stepping-stone in a Brook, scarce enough of it above water to keep one's shoes dry; why, I say, should that little Island enjoy in almost every Neighbourhood, more sensible virtuous and elegant Minds, than we can collect in ranging 100 Leagues of our vast Forests? But 'tis said the Arts delight to travel Westward.

Even as a sixteen-year-old in Boston, writing in 1722 the *Dogood Papers* he provided for his brother's newspaper, *The New-England Courant,* Franklin was looking to literary matters; his paper no. 7 was one of the colonies' earliest pieces of literary criticism. It is a burlesque, offering to answer the "Complaint of many Ingenious Foreigners . . . *That good poetry is not to be expected in New England.*" Such complaints were to continue well into the nineteenth century, often causing great offense, but Franklin's offense is only assumed. He offers to refute the charge by quoting examples from *An Elegy upon the Much Lamented Death of Mrs. Mehitebell Kitel,* of which

It may justly be said in its Praise, without Flattery to the Author, that it is the most *Extraordinary* Piece That ever was wrote in New-England. I will leave . . . Readers to judge, if ever they read any Lines, that would sooner make them *draw their Breath* and Sigh, if not shed Tears, than these following.

Come let us mourn, for we have lost a Wife, a Daughter, and a
Sister,
Who has lately taken Flight, and greatly we have Mist her.

Franklin's extended mockery of such appalling verse displays him at his most witty and entertaining. But this youthful essay is also notable for its urbane, Augustan manner; it is an attack on what a neoclassical age called "Dullness." He is therefore posing as well the preoccupying problem of the arts in eighteenth-century America: were the colonies indeed refined enough to produce the "polished" arts that a civilized age demanded?

Forms of this question were to last long in American thought, but they took a particular shape in the Enlightenment age. Despite men like Edwards, the old millenarian account of providential history was fading as a new cyclical sense of the fate of nations grew from the work of thinkers like Vico and Montesquieu. The new test of culture was progress, and science and the arts were presumed to progress together, evolving in a cycle of development and passing from age to age, country to country, in sequences of ascent and descent. Behind the spirit of British Augustanism was a faith in just such a succession in the course of empire: this is why, in *Windsor Forest* (1713), the greatest of the Augustan poets, Alexander Pope, could conceive of a motion of empires leading from Greece to Rome and Rome to Britain, where refinement, science and patronage reproduced the age of gold. America frequently figured in this plan of things, since empire seemed to move westward as barbarism turned to refinement, nature to sense. In 1726, the British philosopher and theologian Bishop George Berkeley, shortly to visit the colonies, circulated some verses "On the Prospect of Planting Arts and Learning in America" which turned the old Utopian hope into a new principle. They conclude with a prophecy that came to haunt much American thought and writing.

There shall be sung another golden age,
　　The rise of empire and of arts,
The good and great, inspiring Epick rage;
　　The wisest heads and noblest hearts.

Not such as Europe breeds, in her decay,
　　Such as she bred, when fresh and young;
When heavenly flame did animate her clay,
　　By future poets shall be sung.

Westward the course of empire takes its way;
　　The four first acts already past,
A fifth shall close the drama with the day:
　　Time's noblest offspring is the last.

Berkeley's historical drama, echoed by Gibbon, Volney and many others, sees America as the world's youth moving to a rising glory. Once again a millenarian vision, it was cast now in new and progress-oriented terms. The promise of a golden age that would replace European decay and monarchical institutions and call forth its own heroic epic was to obsess the eighteenth century on both sides of the Atlantic. Other British poets, like Addison and Thomson, embellished this Whig theme, linking poetry to politics. Oliver Goldsmith, in *The Deserted Village* (1770), sees in decaying Auburn the decline of the golden age pastoral, the middle ground between barbarism and urban corruption, but the Muse, driven out of Britain by enclosure and the Industrial Revolution, is sent sailing across the seas—to America.

The index of the golden age was a balanced progress, and so in incorporating the neoclassical ideal, the poets of America began to interpret the colonies in the language of heroic and pastoral epic. The rational world view of Deism, the celebration of progress and husbanded nature, the urbane cosmopolitanism of Pope, Sheridan and Addison, came to preoccupy much if not most American writing. But the problem of whether the colonies were yet ready to nurture such an art was a real one. There were no patrons, few great cities, an insufficient educated audience, and the poets were usually first and foremost preachers or lawyers. As early as 1728, in the first literary publication in Maryland, Richard Lewis offered a translation of Edward Holdsworth's *Muscipula* "to cultivate Polite Literature in Maryland." Yet its dedicatory verses confess the difficulty of bringing such "*soft enchanting strains*" to a colony where

> . . . *Here,* rough Woods embrown the Hills and Plains,
> Mean are the *Buildings,* artless are the *Swains:*
> "*To raise the Genius,*" WE no Time can spare,
> A *bare Subsistence* claims our utmost Care. . . .

It might seem that something rougher and less swain-ridden was more suited to the American case. Indeed Ebenezer Cooke's "The Sot-Weed Factor," published in London in 1708 and revised in 1731, is jingling satire about a British innocent who comes as a "sot-weed," or tobacco merchant, to the Maryland backwoods, where the shrewd locals abuse and cheat him. As John Barth's adaptation in his 1962 novel of the same title reminds us, Cooke's is one early eighteenth-century American poem we can take some real pleasure in.

But Romantic barbarism or mock-heroic were not yet American concerns, and there is little to relieve the stiff solemnity of most eighteenth-century colonial verse. Secular epic gets off to a decidedly shaky start in Roger Wolcott's 1500-line *Brief Account of the Agency of the Honourable John Winthrop* (1725), where the Puritan Fathers provoke classical allusions and, persecuted by Aeolus and Neptune, flounder in the same sea of Vergilian pastiche that would drown Columbus in later poems. The aim might be a new art, in a new spirit, but it rarely departed from Augustan polish and the old classical apparatus. In New Jersey the preacher-poet Nathanael Evans admitted that ". . . we are in a climate cast/Where few the muse can relish," but he nonetheless made it his poetic duty to summon the muses to the Schuylkill River, "Where liberty exalts the mind;/Where plenty basks the live long day,/And pours her treasures unconfin'd./Hither ye beauteous *virgins* tend. . . ." Rarely were the Muses summoned as frequently across treacherous waters as now, but they remained curiously English Muses and apparently loath to travel.

The goal American poets were setting themselves, in neoclassic fashion, was imitation of the best British models. One of eighteenth-century America's most popular preachers and poets, Mather Byles, was a nephew of Cotton Mather, but he did not turn to Puritan models for his verses, as his "To an Ingenious Young Gentleman" (1744) made very clear:

> He, wondrous Bard! whose Numbers reach our Shore,
> Tho' Oceans roll between, and Tempests roar. . . .
> O Pope! thy Fame is spread around the Sky,
> Far as the Waves can flow, far as the Winds can fly!
> Hail! Bard triumphant, fill'd with hallow'd Rage,
> Sent from high Heav'n to grace the happy Age:
> For thee a thousand Garlands shall be wove,
> And ev'ry Clime project a laurel Grove;
> Thy Name be heard in ev'ry artful Song,
> And thy loud Praise employ each tuneful Tongue.

Byles set to work to cultivate an American "happy Age," celebrating imitation and assaulting dullness and eccentricity in *Bombastic and Grubstreet Style: A Satire* (1745)—itself an imitation of similar attacks in Britain. "Pope's are the Rules which you, my Friend, receive," he wrote, "From him I gather what to you I give." For others, like Nathanael Evans, the ideal bard might be Cowley, Milton, Gray, Thomson or Goldsmith, but well into the nineteenth century the dominant spirit of American verse would remain imitation and universality, neoclassicism and Augustanism, all in pursuit of what Thomas Odiorne, in 1792, was still, in a poem of this title, calling "the Progress of Refinement." This dependence made eighteenth-century American poetry minor verse with a major theme—the advance of the nation itself. It was a literature of small talents, but one that awaited, or announced, the arrival of the Muses and the moment of epic fulfillment. As contention with Britain increased, the political implication grew clearer: the Muses would bring both poetry and liberty as intertwined strands of a single fabric.

It is hence not surprising that the celebration of native achievement reached its peak in the 1770s, as the veil seemed to tremble. The decade opened with John Trumbull of Yale inviting American poetry to

> Wake from nature's themes the moral song
> And shine with Pope, with Thomson and with Young;
> This land her Swift and Addison shall view
> The former honours equall'd by the new. . . .

A year later at Princeton, confidence was even higher, as Philip Freneau and Hugh Henry Brackenridge indicate in their jointly written "Poem . . . On the Rising Glory of America":

> Hither they [the Muses] wing their way, the last the best
> Of countries, where the arts shall rise and grow
> And arms shall have their day—E'en now we boast
> A *Franklin,* prince of all philosophy,
> A genius piercing as the electric fire,
> Bright as the lightning's flash, explained so well
> By him, the rival of Brittania's sage [Newton].
> This is a land of every joyous sound,
> Of liberty and life, sweet liberty!
> Without whose aid the noblest genius falls
> And Science irretrievably must die.

These were the poets who were to write during the years of revolution and set the path for poetry in the new republic. Trumbull was one of a group from Yale which included Timothy Dwight, later president of Yale, Joel Barlow, who would write *The Columbiad* (1807), and David Humphreys; we now call them the "Connecticut Wits" or the "Hartford Wits," though the links between them diminished as time went on. Freneau became a political journalist and powerful poet, Brackenridge an early novelist. But here, at the start of their careers, they were already sensing that America was on the doorstep of epic, that the arts and politics, science and liberty, were now bound in one revelatory equation. They believed that revolution signaled the coming of the Muses, the dawn of a golden age of liberty, enlightenment and artistic deliverance. The ideal late Augustan epic, the culminating poem, was thus not in verse at all; it was the Declaration of Independence of 1776. Seven years later, its self-evident truths reigned on the American strand. It is less clear that the Muses did. In epic and mock-heroic, the poets of this Revolutionary generation sought to affirm their arrival, to match art to arms and fulfill the regenerative promise of Berkeley. Yet one thing is obvious: if the Muses had come, and the confident promise of Freneau and Brackenridge that "Susquehanna's rocky stream unsung" would "yet remurmur to the magic sound/Of song heroic" was now being fulfilled, then those Muses chose to reveal themselves not in new artistic forms but fully clad in the metrics, the closed rhymes, the aesthetic conventions and the poetic tropes of much earlier British neoclassical writing.

·IV·

Intellectual histories and theories of *Zeitgeist* lead us to expect radical changes in a nation as its destiny unfolds, but frequently what seems a fundamental shift in direction is merely an alteration in the language of discourse. In the early years, the settlers in the new land thought of their experience and shaped their sense of it in biblical images of the garden and millennial fulfillment. The discourse preceding the Revolution of 1776 and the assessment of its meaning that dominated succeeding decades called forth a language of political economy rooted in the statecraft of Greece and Rome, just as later years would turn to metaphors of philosophy and the arts to comprehend themselves, but the underlying concerns sustain a recognizable continuity throughout. The Revolutionary years were in a sense a second birth for the westering people. Once again they asked themselves the meaning of their errand. By now their God seemed distant and content to let them discover His purposes in the task He set before them—the forging of a new nation—and so their recorded thought turns from scriptural analogy to political debate on the rights and responsibilities of citizenship, the limits and proper obligations of governments.

We have seen how Benjamin Franklin tailored his book as he had his public self to fit the idiom of his time. When he set himself to describe his country in 1782, in "Information for Those Who Would

Remove to America," he provided advice Bradford and Winthrop might have offered long before, though his mode is not theirs. "America is the Land of Labour," he writes,

> and by no means what the English call *Lubberland,* and the French Pays de Cocagne, where the streets are said to be pav'd with half-peck Loaves, the Houses til'd with Pancakes, and where the Fowls fly about ready roasted, crying, *Come eat me!*

One class of immigrant is therefore no more likely to make his way in the new nation than he was in the new colonies, the idle aristocrat. People here, Franklin warns, do not ask of a new arrival, "*What is he,*" but

> *What can he do?* . . . The Husbandman is in honor . . . and even the Mechanic, because their employments are useful. The People have a saying, that God Almighty is Himself a Mechanic, the greatest in the Universe; and he is respected and admired more for the variety, ingenuity, and utility of his handyworks, than for the Antiquity of his Family.

Franklin's formulations are themselves artful, and yet, true to his Puritan ancestry, their art serves to drive their import to good purpose. For, just as God's altar needed no polishing in the *Bay Psalme Book,* the new nation provides no encouragement to artists who, like the wellborn they traditionally serve, contribute little to the nation's workaday needs. Few Americans are willing or able, Franklin warns, "to pay the high Prices given in Europe for Paintings, Statues, Architecture, and the other Works of Art, that are more curious than useful." So true is this, in fact, that "the natural Geniuses, that have arisen in America with such Talents, have uniformly quitted that Country for Europe, where they can be more suitably rewarded." This had already proved the case with painters like Benjamin West and John Copley who had gone to train and settle in Italy and London, beginning an expatriate tradition in the American arts that many native writers would follow, from Washington Irving to Henry James and T. S. Eliot. And though Franklin desired to see this situation reversed, he recognized that artistic culture was still in some sense based in Europe.

The arts, then, were not seen as a first need for the new United States. The Founding Fathers—educated men nourished on ideas of Enlightenment and progress, with cultivated tastes and substantial libraries—might envy the European nations their arts, but not the social institutions that traditionally supported them. Their first concern was the health of their new nation. Franklin once said that one good schoolmaster was worth twenty poets; Jefferson thought the novel a "great obstacle" to the education of youth and advised against sending young people to Europe for "cultivation"; James Madison, like Mather before him, argued that "poetry, wit, and criticism, romances, plays, etc., deserve but a small portion of a man's time."

Of central interest in our thinking about the arts in the early republic is a letter sent by John Adams to his wife from Paris in 1780, where he remarks that it would be a "very pleasant Amusement" to walk in the gardens of Versailles or the Tuileries and describe the statuary to her: "instructive Entertainment, improving in History, Mythology, Poetry." But that is not to his present purpose:

> It is not . . . the fine Arts, which our Country requires. The Usefull, the mechanic Arts, are those which we have occasion for in a young Country, as yet simple and not far advanced in Luxury, although perhaps too much for her age and character.

He cannot allow time for temples and palaces, paintings and sculptures; his duty is to learn the science of government:

> I must study Politicks and War that my sons may have liberty to study Mathematicks and Philosophy. My sons ought to study Mathematicks and Philosophy, Geography, Natural History, Naval Architecture, Navigation, Commerce and Agriculture, in order to give their Children a right to study Painting, Poetry, Musick, Architecture, Statuary, Tapestry and Porcelaine.

The paradigm remains a gloss on Bishop Berkeley's vision of civilization's westward march, the course of empire; for, to Adams and the other Founding Fathers, these are the stages through which human development makes its way.

From this perspective, the relatively slim achievement of the early republican years in the polite arts acquires an almost positive tint. The creative energies were there, but they turned elsewhere in a time when the hardships seemed as great as those faced by the first fathers of Plymouth and the Bay Colony. Once again, as in the seventeenth century, language was needed as an instrument of assertion, definition, confirmation—a language of polemic and logical discourse now became the rhetoric of public speech, newspaper editorial, political pamphlet. The quality of such efforts can be measured by their eventual shaping effect on the nation, but they had their own contemporary recognition. "For myself," the elder William Pitt told the British House of Lords,

> I must declare and avow that in all my reading of history and observation—and it has been my favourite study—that for solidity of reasoning, force of sagacity, and wisdom of conclusion under such a complication of difficult circumstances, no nation or body of men can stand in preference to the General Congress at Philadelphia

The Declaration of Independence and the Constitution were major acts of intellectual endeavor, but study of the classics and their rhetoric did more than guide the planners of the new nation; it fostered a love of oral discourse and a faith in the power of public speech to govern sensible men of good will. This tradition remained a powerful one into the nineteenth century, though little noted by historians because its performances, tied to current events, were rarely preserved. But its power can be measured through the decades of popular stump oratory, the speeches of Clay, Benton and Daniel Webster, the extended debates of Stephen Douglas and Abraham Lincoln. Most central for the student of literature, perhaps, is the crucial part it would play in the platform voice that shapes the declamatory verse of Walt Whitman.

Seventy-five years after the Declaration of Independence, a writer for the *North American Review* could insist that

> We are living once again the classic time of Athenian and Roman eloquence, on a broader stage, in larger proportions, with elements of excitement, hopes of progress, and principles of duration, which

never cheered and strengthened the souls of Demosthenes and Cicero.

In the age of Daniel Webster and Edward Everett, the powers of the word were bent toward the preservation of the republic the first fathers had bequeathed, its reification in phrase and image for the generations yet to follow. For Adams, Jefferson, Madison and Hamilton, the task was to "declare the causes which impel . . . separation," to frame a plan of governance, "in Order to form a more perfect Union, establish Justice, insure domestic Tranquillity, provide for the common defence, promote the general Welfare, and secure the Blessings of Liberty to ourselves and our Posterity." The best words of the best minds did not flow in the familiar rhythms of verse or the conventional plotting of narrative fiction. The poetry and story of these exhilarating times appeared in the pamphlets of Paine, the measured celebrations of the Declaration and the Constitution and the remarkable series of newspaper essays which eventually became *The Federalist Papers*.

The pressure of political events induced Franklin to set aside his autobiography in 1771; three years later the same pressure led him to invite Thomas Paine to leave his native England and settle in Philadelphia. Paine had been forced into bankruptcy after publishing *The Case of the Officers of Excise* (1772), an appeal to Parliament for improved wages. He brought the spirit of British radicalism with him, and the situation he found in America ignited his libertarian sympathies. He wrote an impassioned antislavery pamphlet and several feminist tracts, arguing that progress cannot be expected as long as half the population is kept ignorant and encouraged to be venal in order to survive. In 1776 he published *Common Sense*, a pamphlet urging an immediate declaration of independence from Great Britain. Within three months it had sold 100,000 copies and become the central literary document in the Revolutionary movement. "Government, like dress, is the badge of lost innocence," Paine argued; "The palaces of kings are built on the ruins of the bowers of paradise." Any government is justified only so long as it serves the needs of the governed; they in turn are free to choose whatever form brings "the least expense and greatest benefit." Paine eventually pursued his commitment to revolution back to England and on to France, where his *Rights of Man*

(1791–92)—dedicated to George Washington—urged the overthrow of the British monarchy in response to Edmund Burke's *Revolution in France,* but his greatest work may well have been in prompting and sustaining the rebellion of the British colonies in America. Between 1776 and 1783 he published sixteen pamphlets entitled *The American Crisis* which spoke directly to the current military situation. The first is known to have inspired the colonial troops during the dark December of 1776; it was read aloud to all the regiments and passed from hand to hand. Paine's opening words have become his monument in the American national memory:

> These are the times that try men's souls: The summer soldier and the sunshine patriot will in this crisis, shrink from the service of his country; but he that stands it Now, deserves the love and thanks of man and woman.

If Paine's pamphlets embody the voice of the Revolution itself, the sound of the nation's reflections on the governmental structure it hoped would ensure its future can be heard in *The Federalist,* eighty-five letters published in the *New York Independent Journal* between October 1787 and August 1788. Signed "Publius," the articles were the work of Alexander Hamilton, later the first Secretary of the Treasury, John Jay, diplomat and first Chief Justice of the Supreme Court, and James Madison, supporter of Jefferson and, as fourth President, his successor. For his leadership during the Convention, Madison became known as the Father of the Constitution, and he worked tirelessly to secure its adoption by the still-separate states. Since New York's acceptance was crucial to ratification, the letters of Publius offered extended and often eloquent explanations of the unprecedented form of political organization proposed in the new Constitution. From that day until this, *The Federalist* has remained an unofficial appendix to the nation's first effort to write its meaning; its language of deliberation and cautionary promise has become the public language of the country.

Developing that language engaged the foremost minds of the Revolutionary decades: newspapers, pamphlets and political oratory took the place once held by doctrinal tracts, memoirs of conversion and pulpit eloquence. With the Constitution ratified, argument over its interpretation grew and political animosity intensified. What had once been the matter of literature became a contentious political issue—the pastoral ideal of the new nation was now much more than an elegant literary trope. "Those who labor in the earth are the chosen people of God, if ever He had a chosen people, whose breasts He has made his peculiar deposit for substantial and genuine virtue," Jefferson affirmed in his *Notes on the State of Virginia*. He drew from this a clear implication about the nature of the new republic and warned of dangers in manufacturing and large cities: "While we have land to labor then, let us never wish to see our citizens occupied at a work-bench, or twirling a distaff." Hamilton's faction disagreed and looked forward to an age of industrial production—and so the battle for the future history of America grew. In 1819, Washington Irving, as his name suggests a child of the Revolution, born in the year of Independence, published the first American literary folktale, "Rip Van Winkle." In it the old rascal Rip meets Henry Hudson's ghostly sailors, drinks deep, and sleeps a twenty-year sleep in the Catskills. When he returns to his village, he finds an atmosphere of argument, a "perfect Babylonish jargon," and his world turned upside down; he has slept through the Revolution. "The very character of the people seemed changed. There was a busy, bustling, disputatious tone . . . instead of the accustomed phlegm and drowsy tranquillity." Revolution and independence had forged new conditions for American culture. To them the American writer, just like Rip the old storyteller, would have to adjust.

· PART II ·

FROM
COLONIAL OUTPOST
TO CULTURAL
PROVINCE

REVOLUTION AND (IN)DEPENDENCE

·I·

Perhaps the most remarkable thing about the American literature of national construction between the Revolution and the 1820s is not its quality, but the fact that any got written at all. A time of new nationalism, dominated by practical and political issues, is not necessarily a good age for the creative imagination—although many liked to think so. Through these years of the early republic the desire for a "declaration of literary independence" and a "truly American literature" was constantly repeated, but it would not really be until the 1840s that a noteworthy response came, and the issue would persist into the twentieth century. "Americans are the western pilgrims, who are carrying with them the great mass of arts, sciences, vigor and industry which began long since in the east; they will finish the great circle," Crèvecoeur had declared, explaining what it meant to be American, "this new man." At various points—the 1780s, the 1820s, the 1840s—finishing that great circle became a national preoccupation. Figures like Thomas Jefferson, John Adams, Joel Barlow and Noah Webster in the earlier years, William Cullen Bryant, William Ellery Channing and Ralph Waldo Emerson in the later ones, pressed the argument. In an age of spirited political debate, magazines and newspapers arose in quantity to declare the need for a national art, a national science, a national architecture, a national literature and a national language that would be entirely American—consistent with its newness *and* its classicism, its radicalism *and* its traditionalism, its democracy *and* its high religious principles.

The case for an "American literature" was largely made on nationalist principles already developing in the Europe of Herder and Madame de Staël. Much of this sensibility was Romantic, insisting that the arts were born from the spirit of the people, the power of their traditions, their distinctive institutions, their folk and popular past. America itself was a Romantic principle—rich in remarkable landscape, new social feeling, distinctive and forward-looking political institutions, the finest flower of the eighteenth-century Enlightenment. It had Rousseauesque "noble savages," celebrated by the French writer Chateaubriand in *Atala* (1801), it had men of the woods and of nature like Daniel Boone, celebrated by Lord Byron in *Don Juan*. History now belonged to the new Americans, and more than Americans looked for its new expression in the arts. Yet the obstacles were formidable. The history that Americans possessed was, like it or not, in large part European, and the high arts of the nation were still imported from England, France, Germany and Italy, or shaped by Christian and neoclassical traditions. Despite the importance of rising cultural centers like Boston, Philadelphia and later New York, London remained the primary cultural capital. Most American reading came from Britain, not least because without an international copyright agreement American publishers freely pirated British books without bothering to pay their authors. With their moral seriousness, social density and increasing Romantic sensibility, such books satisfied a growing bourgeois American readership. American taste was provincial; in a time of expanding empire, it was also largely neoclassical, as the new public buildings showed. Public themes dominated private ones, offering little encouragement to poetry. There was no clear American aesthetic, no patronage, no developed profession of letters, no certain audience. No wonder the American writers now beginning to appear spent much time complaining about their fate.

Philip Freneau was no Anglophile traditionalist; indeed he was one of the most consistently revolutionary of the Revolutionary generation of poets. Nonetheless when he contemplated the task of the

American writer he saw only disappointment, and in 1788 he sounded a lament that became familiar in American literature:

> Thrice happy Dryden, who could meet
> Some rival bard in every street!
> When all were bent on writing well
> It was some credit to excel. . . .
>
> On these bleak climes by Fortune thrown
> Where rigid *Reason* reigns alone,
> Where lovely *Fancy* has no sway,
> Nor magic forms about us play
> Nor nature takes her summer hue—
> Tell me, what has the Muse to do?

In 1801 Charles Brockden Brown, editor of the important Philadelphia magazine the *American Review and Literary Journal,* and now the acknowledged father of the American novel, expressed similar concern:

> Genius in composition, like genius in every other art, must be aided by culture, supported by patronage, and supplied with leisure and materials. . . . But a people much engaged in the labors of agriculture, in a country rude and untouched by the hand of refinement, cannot, with any tolerable facility or success, carry on, at the same time, the operations of the imagination and indulge in the speculations of Raphael, Newton, or Pope.

Complaints of this kind—of lack of culture, of patronage, of forms and materials—became a familiar American incantation, almost a subgenre of American literature. Often they betrayed a classical vision of the arts, a Golden Age dream of refined artists supported by civilized patrons. Meanwhile in Britain the patron was disappearing, the mercantile publisher emerging, a new form of Grub Street developing and an altered literary taste taking over. Nature—in which America was, it was agreed, sublime—was replacing social subjects in much art. Yet to Americans even nature seemed to require European decay to make it poetic, and quite a few traveled abroad to experience it. In 1828

James Fenimore Cooper (expatriate to Paris for seven years) complained of American "poverty of materials" ("There is scarce an ore which contributes to the wealth of the author, that is found, here, in veins as rich as in Europe"). In 1860, Nathaniel Hawthorne (expatriate to England and Italy) found the secret of romance in the decay of Europe ("Romance and poetry, ivy, lichens and wallflowers, need ruins to make them grow"). As late as 1873 Henry James (expatriate in Britain for most of his life) has an American artist cry in *The Madonna of the Future,* "We are the disinherited of art!"

So a formidable idea grew that an American art was a promise as yet unredeemed. America was, as it were, Romanticism as yet uninscribed, and the poetic and the imaginative had to be hunted elsewhere, one reason for the continuing transit of American literary expatriates back to the Old World they were supposed to have rejected. American literature found itself caught between two contradictory claims: the need for literary independence and republican originality, and the hereditary tie for nourishing contact with the European cultural past. All this fed the contentious literary debates of new America. Do true artists innovate, or do they imitate? Would they emerge from the spirit of nationality, or cosmopolitanism? Should they serve public purpose, or aesthetic and possibly therefore decadent pleasure? Had they a legacy from the past, or must they be born anew in the radical energy of the present? It is no wonder American post-Revolutionary literature had a double tradition of high promises and dark complaints. A poetry furnished with Indian squaws, heroes of the Revolution, prairies and katydids promptly appeared, but it was novel in subject matter, traditional in form. Revolutionary epics—Freneau's and Brackenridge's *Poem . . . on the Rising Glory of America,* Dwight's *The Conquest of Canaan,* Barlow's *Columbiad*—did more to herald literary greatness than achieve it. British magazinists intervened, sometimes vindictively, but often justifiably, assaulting the new "American literature" for its high ideals and its low performances. Americans often retaliated by puffing small talents into large reputations, as new nations do. To dignify the new society, classical forms remained remarkably durable in a public art seeking to represent the moral universality and democratic dignity of American ideals. The persistent call was for an art of historical grandeur, heroism and national celebration, the expression of God's and nature's timeless truths. But the Deistic and moralistic ideals underpinning the new republic did not adjust easily to the subjective spirit of the new Romantic age—which in its full flowering came to America at least a generation late, in the transcendental movement of the 1840s—in large part a revolution of the imagination against the constraints laid upon it.

None of this should surprise us. After all, one aspect of America's founding legacy seemed to insure her literary provinciality more than any other. "As an independent nation, our honour requires us to have a system of our own, in language as in government," declared the patriotic lexicographer and scientist Noah Webster. "Great Britain, whose children we are, and whose language we speak, should no longer be *our* standard; for the taste of her writers is already corrupted, and her language on the decline." For most of his life Webster labored for linguistic independence, often by looking to the past, as when he edited Winthrop's *Journals*. But he looked to the future too, by publishing his *Grammatical Institute of the English Language* (1783–85), which attempted to define distinctive American expression. Part of this became the famous and best-selling *Spelling Book,* his effort to standardize American spelling. Ben Franklin prompted him to write *Dissertations on the English Language* (1789), which celebrated the purity of American style, above all in the prose of Ben Franklin. Involvement in many political and scientific affairs—he was one of the many polymathic minds of the age—did not stop his undertaking as a lifetime's work his *American Dictionary of the English Language* (1828), a subsequent basis of most American dictionaries. Despite its insistence on distinct American spellings and more than five thousand "Americanisms" not found in British dictionaries, it paradoxically demonstrated the complex historical dependence of America's language on Britain and thus displayed the inescapable limits of linguistic freedom. American language was to go its own way, but it was an indebted language, as American arts were indebted arts. There could be no easy solution to the problem of linguistic and literary independence.

·II·

The Americans of the Revolutionary period had no doubt which was the most serious and necessary of the literary arts. Poetry had sounded the promise of the American millennium, poetry had decorated and civilized Greece and Rome, and so poetry was called to its duty now that the nation's moment had come. The Connecticut Wits represented the ideal of public verse. When General Gage declared martial law in Boston in 1776, poetry responded, and John Trumbull's long *M'Fingal: A Modern Epic* (Philadelphia, 1776; extended 1782) became one of the age's most successful, and delightful, literary works. Drawing on the mock-heroic form, scurrilous rollicking style and loose octosyllabic couplet of Samuel Butler's *Hudibras* (1663–78) to turn all events and causes to farce, it concerns a comic Tory squire (his name is drawn from Macpherson's *Ossian*) who is publicly humiliated by an American crowd in his debate with the American Whig Honorius. There is much literary mockery, as in this passage where M'Fingal finds the patriots have erected a flagstaff:

> Now warm with ministerial ire,
> Fierce sallied forth our loyal 'Squire,
> And on his striding steps attends
> His desperate clan of Tory friends;
> When sudden met his wrathful eye
> A pole ascending through the sky,
> Which numerous throngs of whiggish race
> Were raising in the market-place;
> Not higher school-boys' kites aspire,
> Or royal mast, or country spire;
> Like spears at Brobdignagian tilting,
> Or Satan's walking-staff in Milton.

Despite dense topical allusions, there is enough satirical energy and ebullience in *M'Fingal* to make the poem entertaining today. Yet mock-epic was hardly the spirit with which to celebrate the success of the American Revolution. Once the great events were over, the insistent desire of American poets for a true American epic repeatedly expressed itself.

An early attempt was made by Trumbull's fellow Connecticut Wit Timothy Dwight. Dwight was to become president of Yale, a supporter of the study of literature and a Calvinist moral force in the new nation. His aim was Miltonic, to write the American religious epic in his eleven-book *The Conquest of Canaan* (1785). Following the Puritan typological principle, Dwight reads America as the second "blissful Eden bright" and matches the story of Joshua's defeat of Canaan with his country's revolutionary transformation. His moral summons continued in *The Triumph of Infidelity* (1788), warning Americans that Satan—through Catholicism and Deism—was still busy. An important aim of his stilted verse was to show that the structure of British heroic poetry would adapt easily to American themes. This he illustrated in *Greenfield Hill* (1794), a pastoral poem so determinedly derivative that specific eighteenth-century British poets can be attached to each book of it. Another progress-piece, it follows the motion of liberty from Europe's depravity to the American promise of one emblematic Connecticut village. "Shun the lures/Of Europe," Dwight tells us, nonetheless declaring that "Miltonic strains" will "the Mexic hills prolong." A primary source is Goldsmith's *The Deserted Village*—of which Dwight's theme is an extension. Here is Goldsmith in 1770:

> Sweet Auburn! loveliest village of the plain,
> Where health and plenty cheered the labouring swain,
> Where smiling spring its earliest visit paid,
> And parting summer's lingering blooms delayed.
> Dear lovely bowers of innocence and ease,
> Seats of my youth, where every sport could please,
> How often have I loitered o'er thy green,
> Where humble happiness endeared each scene!

And here, twenty-four years later, is the opening of Dwight's second part:

> Fair Verna! loveliest village of the west;
> Of every joy, and every charm, possess'd;

> How pleas'd amid thy varied walks I rove,
> Sweet, cheerful walks of innocence, and love,
> And o'er thy smiling prospects cast my eyes,
> And see the seats of peace, and pleasure, rise. . . .

The landscapes and the sentiments are as indistinguishable as the rhythms, but that is virtually Dwight's point. America not only fulfilled Goldsmith's pastoral ideal; it offered equivalence of talent. And where Goldsmith has to end in despair, Dwight does not, closing with a "Vision, or Prospect of the Future Happiness of America" which depicts the safe transatlantic landfall of the westering Muses.

Such millennial visions became familiar in Revolutionary American poetry. Joel Barlow was another of the Wits, though of more Deistic temperament. His aim was not religious but classical, secular, political, epic. His first attempt was *The Vision of Columbus* (1787), which turns Columbus into an American Aeneas. In prison he is vouchsafed a vision of successive kingdoms and empires, with the greatest empire of all initiating the "interminable reign" of freedom and justice. Ironically, because his theme was great empires, Barlow dedicated the poem to King Louis XVI. But by 1807, Barlow had become a friend of Tom Paine and Mary Wollstonecraft, written against Burke and identified with the French Revolution. The poem needed recasting. He extended it into *The Columbiad* (1807), firmly epic in tone ("I sing the Mariner who first unfurl'd/An eastern banner o'er the western world") but more than an epic, he said, for it was no mere call to arms but a celebration of the worldwide inculcation of American principles and a new, Deistic universal language. Because Barlow does seek to define his principles and articulate the problems of writing an American epic, we can give him place in the line that leads to *Song of Myself, The Cantos* and *The Bridge*. But no very striking poetic gift is on display, for Barlow was less a poet then than a political agent, land speculator and European negotiator for the American government; following Napoleon to Russia with messages, he was to die on the retreat from Moscow. The poem that survives from his French years refuses all eloquence about liberty and universal freedom:

Ye Alps audacious, thro' the heav'ns that rise,
To cramp the day and hide me from the skies;
Ye Gallic flags, that o'er their heights unfurl'd
Bear death to kings, and freedom to the world,
I sing not you. A softer theme I chuse,
A virgin theme, unconscious of the Muse,
But fruitful, rich, well suited to inspire
The purest frenzy of poetic fire. . . .

The poem is *The Hasty Pudding* (1796), an expatriate dream of home cooking about a very American dish, a mock-heroic celebration of the commonplace that Emerson might have recalled when he urged American poets to look to "the meal in the firkin; the milk in the pan":

Despise it not, ye Bards to terror steel'd,
Who hurl your thunders round the epic field;
Nor ye who strain your midnight throats to sing
Joys that the vineyard and the still-house bring; . . .
I sing the sweets I know, the charms I feel,
My morning incense, and my evening meal,—
The sweets of Hasty-Pudding. Come, dear bowl,
Glide o'er my palate, and inspire my soul.

Such liveliness, all too rare in early American poetry, does much to compensate for the over-heavy diet of *The Columbiad*. But elsewhere the weighty, public, neoclassical standard ruled in post-Revolutionary verse; we find it even in the work of two black slave poets, Jupiter Hammon and Phillis Wheatley. Wheatley, in particular, was a remarkable phenomenon. Brought from Africa at the age of eight, sold as a slave in Boston, she was a prodigy who learned English in sixteen months and, more surprisingly, the prevailing conventions of Augustan verse. These conventions scarcely allowed of any private voice or any expression of her own condition. Her work is primarily a display of the complex web of classical allusions and elegant circumlocutions she had mastered:

> While raging tempests shake the shore,
> While Aeolus' thunders round us roar,
> And sweep tempestuous o'er the plain,
> Be still, O tyrant of the main;
> Nor let thy brow contracted frowns betray,
> While my Sussanah skims the wat'ry way.

More ironically, one of her themes is the statutory American Revolutionary one of liberty, as in "Liberty and Peace" (1784), where golden-haired Muses celebrate a freedom that goes unquestioned by the author's own situation:

> Auspicious Heaven shall fill with fav'ring Gales
> Where e'er Columbia spreads her swelling Sails;
> To every Realm shall Peace her Charms display,
> And Heavenly Freedom spread her golden Ray.

The perfect skill with which Wheatley writes the dominant American poem reveals the extent to which poetry was seen as polite accomplishment and public assertion rather than personal revelation. Her skill makes her important in the history of black writing in America; her limits show the confinements against which her successors would later have to struggle.

The only poet of this period who occasionally strikes modern readers as a significant talent is Philip Freneau, a journalist, propagandist and patriot somewhat in the mold of Paine. Often called "The father of American poetry," Freneau is the only poet whose work in range and quality comprises a considerable American achievement between the Puritan writing of Taylor and Bradstreet and the nature poems of William Cullen Bryant. Like Bryant, much of his energy was consumed by his democratic fervor and humanitarian impulses, so much so that it is commonly assumed, in both cases, that much significant poetry remained unwritten while the artist concerned himself with the drama of his time. But this is doubtful, since both Freneau and Bryant suffered the limitations of the aesthetic principles they had inherited from Pope, and both paid an artistic price for the imaginatively impoverished philosophical assumptions which underlay those principles.

While a student at Princeton, Freneau was already serious about a poetic career, writing early imitations of Goldsmith, Shenstone, Pope and the "Graveyard School" of Collins, Young and Gray. (He produced two adaptations of Goldsmith's *The Deserted Village:* "The American Village" and "The Deserted Farm-House.") But whether he employed the armory of Augustan satire to assault British tyranny or echoed the picturesque sentimentalities of the "early Romantics," Freneau never escaped the aesthetic constriction of contemporary Deism. His "The Wild Honey Suckle" (1786) draws a nature sentimentally committed to illustrating the transience of life from birth to death. "The space between, is but an hour,/The frail duration of a flower." And his celebrated "The Indian Burying Ground" (1788) is yet another echo of the Indian as classicism's primitive, nobly and stoically ready in death to continue the life he knew:

> By midnight moons, o'er moistening dews,
>   In habit for the chase arrayed,
> The hunter still the deer pursues,
>   The hunter and the deer, a shade!

Freneau was an accomplished maker of verses, and the passion of his republican sentiments and his love of country pressed his idea of poetry to its very limits. But limited it was, in ways which were to narrow the emotional range and diminish the poetic achievement of several more gifted later writers. Freneau's Indians are actually French *philosophes* in native dress. Their nature is the nature of Deism, the instrument of logical reason hymned in "On Mr. Paine's Rights of Man" (1792): "From Reason's source, a bold reform he brings,/In raising up *mankind,* he pulls down *kings.*" For the Deist, the God of the Puritans had retreated behind the mechanism of his Creation. He was to be known—and He was to act—only through the laws the scientists were to discover by using the instrument God himself provided: human reason. "Know then thyself," Pope had written, "presume not God to scan;/The proper study of mankind is Man." What this could mean poetically is as apparent in Pope's brilliantly versified *Essay on Man*

as it is in Freneau's stilted "Reflections on the Constitution or Frame
of Nature" (1809), "Science, Favourable to Virtue" (1809), "On the
Uniformity and Perfection of Nature" (1815) and "On the Religion
of Nature" (1815). Each is a rhymed essay that asserts a rational
proposition. The limited scope for the imagination may be seen in
Freneau's titles and in the poverty of imagery available to a world view
that must sing of a "Great Frame," "a lovely philanthropic scheme"
or "The parts that form the vast machine." But it is not only the
clockwork universe that hobbled the imagination that would sing its
praise. Its balance and harmony combined a monotony of verse line
with an optimistic view of man that could prove equally monotonous.
Beside the "organ tones" of Milton or the metaphysical tensions of
Puritan believers like Edward Taylor, Freneau and the Augustans
whom he and his fellow Americans imitated can seem deficient in their
grasp of the complexity, the underlying tragedy of much human life.
When Pope banished the quest for meaning from man's concern, he
unwittingly robbed the poet of his fire:

> All nature is but art, unknown to thee;
> All chance, direction, which thou canst not see;
> All discord, harmony not understood;
> All partial evil, universal good:
> And, spite of pride, in erring reason's spite,
> One truth is clear: Whatever IS, is RIGHT.

What such unquestioning optimism might sink to poetically is apparent
in the droning regularity of Freneau's restatement:

> Who looks through nature with an eye
> That would the scheme of heaven descry,
> Observes her constant, still the same,
> In all her laws, through all her frame.
>
> No imperfection can be found
> In all that is, above, around,—
> All, nature made, in reason's sight
> Is order all, and *all is right*.

Freneau, as we have seen, was frankly willing to acknowledge his own limitations and that of the culture he spoke for so passionately in other ways: "An age employed in edging steel/Can no poetic raptures feel. . . ." He admitted, too, that Revolutionary America had gained political but not yet cultural independence from Britain. The American arts would thus go on feeding on the literary accomplishments of the older nation until the strength for native crafting could emerge. What makes this literature hard to read now is not its imitation, which is always present in the arts, but its failure to match what it imitated. The problem was that European forms did not suit the need to write a new nation with new experience, a new science and a new politics on a new continent. As greater talents than Freneau—Bryant and Longfellow, Holmes and Lowell—would demonstrate, the limitations of importing theories and modes of poetry developed far away from the life and natural landscape of the American continent could only constrain the literary imagination. A new conception of poetry would not come until the task had been reimagined from within—and that lay at least a full generation in the future.

The poets who followed Freneau echoed his complaints. "No longer in love's myrtle shade/My thoughts recline—/I'm busy in the cotton trade,/And sugar line," reflected Fitz-Greene Halleck with similar irony. Halleck was a "Knickerbocker" poet, one of a group of writers from a busy and booming New York that was ready to challenge Philadelphia as the center of literary activity during the first decades of the nineteenth century. It was a diverse group who sometimes met to make common cause—Halleck and Joseph Rodman Drake collaborated on the satiric political poems of the *Croaker Papers* (1819), just as Washington Irving and James Kirke Paulding produced the satirical *Salmagundi* papers (1807–8). Augustan wit and satire met Romantic feeling: their heroes included Byron, Shelley and Scott. Drake's "Culprit Fay" (1816) is an American landscape poem set in the Hudson Valley; Halleck made a British tour in 1822 and wrote "Alnwick Castle" and "Burns" (collected 1827), which, like Washington Irving's prose *Sketch-Book of Geoffrey Crayon, Gent.* (1819–20), revealed the attraction European Romantic writers and subjects now had for American authors. But the same great issue of Native Literature concerned them. "Fairies, giants and goblins are not indigenous here," Paulding complained in an essay in the second series of *Salmagundi* (1819), "and with the exception of a few witches that were soon exterminated, our worthy ancestors brought over with them not a single specimen of Gothic or Greek mythology." He also mocked the now ubiquitous Scott in "The Lay of the Scottish Fiddle" (1813), and in his long narrative poem *The Backwoodsman* (1818) he pleaded again for a break with "servile, imitative rhyme" and turned to the backwoods, the "untracked forest world" of frontier Ohio—though his farming hero Basil is suspiciously Wordsworthian. Paulding is more successful in his local historical novels *Koningsmarke* (1823) and *The Dutchman's Fireside* (1831), which can claim a place beside the American romances of James Fenimore Cooper.

As the War of 1812 ended, the issue of native originality grew lively again. In 1818 William Cullen Bryant joined the debate in the *Edinburgh Review,* acknowledging the current limitations of American poetry but announcing a bright prospect for the American arts. Bryant, who was to be the major figure of American poetry for the generation between Freneau and Emerson, represented that promise himself. From a Massachusetts Calvinist background, he had been drawn to poetry as a child, writing rhymed versions of the Psalms and the Book of Job and precocious verses on the Day of Judgment. His first models were Augustan, but he moved through the "Graveyard Poets" to Burns and, especially, Wordsworth. Burns, he said, had entirely transformed the British poetic habit of looking "at nature through the spectacles of books," while Wordsworth had caused "a thousand springs" to gush from his heart—as is evident in his famous poem "Thanatopsis" (1811), the first version of which he wrote at sixteen. Its title means "view of death," and it displays a neo-Wordsworthian communion with nature and a stoical acceptance of return to its elements ("To him who in the love of Nature holds/Communion with her visible forms, she speaks/A various language . . ."). Bryant and his age were moving away from Calvinism and scientific Deism toward Unitarianism; this released a meditative spirit quite new to American writing, which Bryant expressed in measured blank-verse forms. By 1821 his first collected *Poems* appeared, to be followed by a volume in each decade of his long life. From the middle 1820s it was plain that he was America's foremost poet and critic, as well as a major cultural figure. In 1825 he left his Massachusetts law practice to move to New York, now the dominant literary capital, and became the nation's leading newspaper editor, running the New York *Evening Post* for half a century.

Over a long lifetime of writing that reached from what he himself called "infant literature" to the large creative flowering of transcendentalism, and then to the age of conventional Victorian gentility, Bryant represented the middle possibility of an American verse, somewhere between classicism and the philosophic Romanticism of Coleridge and Emerson. He sustained a sure confidence that America offered primary subject matter for poetry; this lay in

> the elements of beauty and grandeur, intellectual greatness and moral truth, the stormy and the gentle passions, the casualties and changes of life, and the light shed upon man's nature by the story of past times and the knowledge of foreign manners.

Poetry he saw as "a suggestive art," yet essentially a moral one: he was a poet of ideal conceptions and generalities, seeking a verse that exhibited "analogies and correspondences . . . between the things of the moral and of the natural world." There was for Bryant no Romantic agony; these correspondences were clear and commonly shared. Nature's meanings were specific and unchanging and awaited didactic affirmation:

> Poetry lifts us into a sphere where self-interest cannot exist, and where the prejudices that perplex our everyday life can hardly enter. It restores to us our unperverted feelings, and leaves us at liberty to compare the issues of life with our unsophisticated notions of good and evil.

When Bryant pictures the natural world—in poems like "The Yellow Violet" (1814), "The Death of the Flowers" (1825) or "To a Fringed Gentian" (1829)—he usually does so with all the concreteness the English Romantic poets displayed. He could depict American nature and scenic complexity far more effectively than Emerson or Whitman ever would, but the vigor of experienced detail is all too often checked by his need to establish a moral universal. One of his most famous poems, "To a Waterfowl" (1815), creates a memorable figure of a bird's lone flight across the sky. Yet he nails it to mediocrity by adding,

> . . . on my heart
> Deeply has sunk the lesson thou hast given,
> And shall not soon depart.
>
> He who, from zone to zone,
> Guides through the boundless sky thy certain flight,
> In the long way that I must tread alone,
> Will lead my steps aright.

Something constrains the full expression of his imagination, the organic fulfillment of his imagery—and keeps him more a pre-Romantic than a Romantic, nearer to Goldsmith or Gray than Wordsworth or Coleridge in their profoundest questioning.

Bryant nonetheless was the cosmopolitan writer America had needed, regularly visiting Europe, yet always turning his eyes back to his own country. He traveled widely in the United States as well, his admirable travel books following the progress of the nation as it massively opened out through exploration, migration and the taking in of new territories to the West. His poetry followed, with a sense of enlarging and nominating utterance, the grandeur of the American scene, its forests, prairies and mountains—as in "The Prairies" (1832):

> These are the Gardens of the Desert, these
> The unshorn fields, boundless and beautiful,
> For which the speech of England has no name—
> The Prairies. I behold them for the first,
> And my heart swells while the dilated sight
> Takes in the encircling vastness. . . .

In poems like this we can see the serious, measured economy of his verse seeking to respond to the vastness and sensation of the new landscape. We also see the difficulty. Conventional speculations about the rise and fall of empires appear; he imagines vanished Indian civilizations and "that advancing multitude/Which soon shall fill these deserts," just as Cooper had in his novel *The Prairie* (1827)—and he crosses the prairie on a very literary "steed."

American nature poems were Bryant's greatest claim to fame; but he was also a social poet—devoted to humanitarian reform, supporting abolitionist principles and, when civil war came, the Northern cause. By then he was internationally famous and, along with Washington Irving, proof that the new nation had a proud role for the serious man of letters. Edgar Allan Poe said of Bryant that "his poetical reputation, both at home and abroad, is greater than that of any other American." When a successor generation emerged during the 1830s in mercantile, Unitarian Boston, now confident it was the nation's cultural center and hub, the leading figures—Henry Wadsworth Longfellow, Oliver Wendell Holmes and John Greenleaf Whittier—shared Bryant's gently Romantic sensibility, his tone of Victorian sagacity, his moral, didactic and humanitarian impulses. These poets, the "Fireside Poets" or the "Schoolroom Poets," dominated mid-century America and shaped the Genteel Tradition that was to influence the literary direction of the entire century.

Yet the American poetic tradition was already beginning to divide, with the deeper and darker Romanticism of Edgar Allan Poe and the transcendentalism of Emerson proclaiming an ambitious new role for the American writer. Emerson's essay "The Poet" (1844) defined the poet as Shelleyan prophet, seer, namer, not "any permissive potentate, but an emperor in his own right." Emerson's poet was the transformer of epochs: "All that we call sacred history attests that the birth of a poet is a principal event in chronology." In "The Poetic Principle" (1850) Poe discarded "the heresy of *The Didactic*" in his quest for supernal Beauty: "Under the sun there neither exists nor *can* exist anything more thoroughly dignified—more supremely noble than . . . this poem which is a poem and nothing more—this poem written solely for the poem's sake." These were ideals Bryant never sought. If a poem like his "Forest Hymn" (1825) displays a pantheism that sees God as "the soul of this great universe," this is certainly not Emerson's Over-Soul. Nor is Bryant's sentimental if melancholic trust in Nature anything close to the world of complex, shifting, troubling challenge that Emerson, Thoreau and Whitman found when they tried to read nature's meanings. The shift from Bryant to the transcendentalists is from one kind of Romanticism to another, from the world according to Locke and Newton to the world according to Kant and the Neo-platonists. As that deeper sense of poetry and the imagination developed, Bryant stayed in the earlier world. Yet for the 1820s he opened a new sensibility, and he remains an interesting, important precursor of changes to come.

· III ·

This domination of the public over the private, the universal over the imaginative, helps explain why, through the early national period and the first quarter of the new century, an epically oriented, public poetry was regarded by the American audience as a central literary form. By contrast, drama and fiction excited far more social suspicion. We usually date the beginnings of American drama from the 1767 Philadelphia production of Thomas Godfrey's *The Prince of Parthia,* a blank-verse drama of passion and violence in the Orient that rests firmly on the conventions of Jacobean theater. This was some twenty-five years before the first American novels appeared. In 1774 the Continental Congress actually banned "plays and other expensive diversions and entertainments," but dramatic performances favorable to each side were presented during the conflict, and both Crèvecoeur and Brackenridge wrote dramatic dialogues to stir patriotic feeling. During the post-Revolutionary years, theater companies and theater buildings increased in number, and more and more plays were written by Americans. As a popular form, American drama was expected to enshrine patriotism, but in fact most of the repertory came from European stock, and many American plays were adaptations of European originals—like *The Widow of Malabar* (1790) that the poet David Humphreys developed from a French source. Of the playwrights who emerged in the early nineteenth century, there were talents of importance—like James Nelson Barker, author of *Tears and Smiles* and *The Indian Princess* (both 1808)—but none of great literary distinction. Most are forgotten, and the evolution of early American theater belongs more to social than literary history.

There was, however, one early American playwright who not only explored the problems of patriotic drama but earned a lasting place in the repertory of the American theater. Royall Tyler fought in the Revolution, entered the law office of John Adams and eventually became Chief Justice of the Vermont Supreme Court; he authored one of America's earliest novels, *The Algerine Captive* (1797). After seeing a New York production of Sheridan's *The School for Scandal,* he wrote *The Contrast* (1787), a comedy that rises above mere historical interest because Tyler so successfully marries inherited convention and native impulse. His motives, he claimed, were patriotic, as he explained in the introductory notes which invite applause for the work,

> independent of its intrinsic merits: It is the first essay of American genius in a difficult species of composition; it was written by one who never critically studied the rules of the drama and, indeed, had seen but few of the exhibitions of the stage; it was undertaken and finished in the course of three weeks; and the profits of one night's performance were appropriated to the benefit of the sufferers by the fire at *Boston*.

Tyler's now famous prologue was itself a patriotic declaration:

> Exult each patriot heart!—this night is shewn
> A piece, which we may fairly call our own;
> Where the proud titles of "My Lord! Your Grace!"
> To humble "Mr." and plain "Sir" give place.
> Our Author pictures not from foreign climes
> The fashions, or the follies of the times;
> But has confin'd the subject of his work
> To the gay scenes—the circles of New-York.

The "contrast" of the title is between foreign manners and follies and domestic plainness. The central character is homespun, rural Colonel Manly, set against the urbane New Yorker Dimple, whose Chesterfieldian chicanery and aped British manners are mocked. So is the devious foppery of Dimple's man, Jessamy, which in classic Restoration comedic fashion is set against the honest, craggy independence of

Manly's servant Jonathan—who later became a familiar type-figure of the Yankee in American humor.

But Tyler's play is not only a celebration of native homespun— a subject he returned to in the letters of his *The Yankey in London* (1809). He challenges as well colonial suspicion of theater, still so strong that for some performances this rollicking comedy was billed as "a Moral Lecture in Five Parts." Tyler acknowledges the dangerous frivolity of some theater, but blames that, too, on Europe— ". . . all, which aims at splendour and parade,/Must come from Europe, and be ready made." Of course his play is quite different:

> Why should our thoughts to distant countries roam
> When each refinement may be found at home?
> Who travels now to ape the rich or great,
> To deck an equipage and roll in state;
> To court the graces, or to dance with ease,
> Or by hypocrisy to strive to please?
> Our free-born ancestors such arts despis'd;
> Genuine sincerity alone they priz'd. . . .

The contradictions here are apparent, for Tyler's is a very mannered celebration of "genuine sincerity." But we may doubt whether the play's "Moral Lecture" drew its audiences in the first place. *The Contrast* lives, on page and stage, because it masters its contradictions and becomes a successful American version of the English Restoration comedy of manners, with a great deal of its wit and style. The tidy heroic couplets are finished, the dialogue has coffeehouse grace, there is a well-balanced five-act structure, and the play's very "playness" is an act of successful creative assimilation from a well-developed tradition. Though, as we have seen, many attempts were made to graft American materials on British stock, *The Contrast* remains an outstanding example of art and entertainment because the task has been done with high imaginative skill. Yet what the play equally dramatizes is the continuing dependence of American drama on European conventions as an inescapable fact.

Serious American theater was never to escape from the weighty authority of European drama: Shakespeare and Congreve, Ibsen and

Shaw, Pirandello and Beckett. American originality was to show itself in more popular forms: vaudeville, burlesque, minstrelsy, the Broadway musical and Hollywood motion picture. The need to face this dependency was acknowledged early by William Dunlap, who both as playwright and theatrical historian was a principal founder of the national theater. His version of the patriotic argument was that what theater measured was the advance of American civilization: "The rise, progress and cultivation of the drama mark the progress of refinement and the state of manners at any given time and in any country." But drama was, he also urged, the most universal, which meant also the most international, of the literary forms. Of the more than fifty plays that he wrote or adapted over his twenty influential years as theatrical manager and playwright, largely in New York, almost half were free adaptations from French, German and Elizabethan sources. His own best play was *André* (1798), a nationalistic piece about the British officer captured by the Americans during the War of Independence and hanged (it was later revived as a musical spectacle with the title *The Glory of Columbia Her Yeomanry*). He produced several pioneering works of American cultural history, among them *History of the American Theatre* (1832) and *History of the Rise and Progress of the Arts of Design in the United States* (1834). Dunlap was one of those rare Americans of his time able to eke out a livelihood in the arts, in his case as man of the theater and, later, as a successful painter of portraits. He also wrote *The Life of Charles Brockden Brown* (1815), thus celebrating a figure as important in the rise of American fiction as he himself was in the rise of American theater.

Dunlap had few successors. Serious dramatic literature was to remain rare in America throughout the nineteenth century; and when in the next century the best American plays were written, they belonged to an age when the demands of literary nationalism were yielding to the stateless forces of aesthetic modernism. As a result, for a hundred years and more after the Revolution, the literary arts in the United States were to be served predominantly by poets and, above all, by novelists.

·IV·

In its detailed empiricism and treatment of commonplace and ordinary life, the novel from its origins has mirrored the experience of the rising bourgeoisie—so much so that we can think of it, in George Steiner's phrase, as the burgher epic. The novel's language is prose, its heroes and heroines are familiar and recognizable and it deals with the concrete, the everyday, the material. In the novel's emergence in Europe as a new and dominant genre, America had played a significant part. For it was in a Renaissance Spain where romantic chivalry was being replaced by the mercantile adventure of New World wealth that Cervantes wrote *Don Quixote de la Mancha* (1605, 1615)—the book that, in its sense of inquiring empiricism, its concern for commonplace life and its parodic relation to the old romances that send the Don into his madness and adventures, can stand as the first of the modern novels. In Britain, the form perhaps acquires firm existence with the mercantile and documentary actualities of Daniel Defoe—two of whose books, *Moll Flanders* and *Colonel Jack* (both 1722), include in their topography of modern entrepreneurial and profitable adventure episodes set in the southern American colonies.

The novel form developed rapidly in several directions in Britain, all of which were felt in American fiction when it eventually began to evolve. For Defoe and Smollett, narrative fiction was predominantly an art of adventures that involved the physical documentation of an expansive, knowable world, a world the practical intelligence could grasp and use. For Richardson it was a sentimental and moral form which looked to the familial, domestic, Puritan virtues to provide a basis for new laws of feeling and social advancement; Richardson was the founder of the sentimental novel, the novel of sexuality and class, social ascent and managed emotion, the love that finds its fulfillment in the well-made marriage. But as the novel developed self-consciously as a genre, it began to question itself through witty inversion. Henry Fielding's *Joseph Andrews* (1742) began as a parody of the sentimentality and sexual opportunism of Richardson's *Pamela* (1740) but became a full-fledged tale on its own, what Fielding called a "comic epic in prose"—as good a definition of the new form as we can find. And

Laurence Sterne's extraordinary *The Life and Opinions of Tristram Shandy* (1760–67), the open-ended book he could conclude only with his own death, parodies the entire new and novel species, challenging its experiential, pragmatic philosophies, its narrative processes and orders and even the very mode of its presentation, the book itself. With Sterne the novel began its experimentally subversive history. By the mid-eighteenth century all these possibilities were available to Americans, but they shared with many in Europe a suspicion of the new form. Its capacity to inflame as well as instruct grew apparent, and its tempting portraits of sexual immorality and European manners made it suspect; Jefferson condemned it, Timothy Dwight was appalled by its social and moral influence, Noah Webster found it dangerous and encouraging to vice. A late eighteenth-century America fed by libertarian sentimentality and Enlightenment philosophies might seem hospitable context for the form. Yet for various reasons—the ready availability of British books, the rejection of the manners, customs and follies the genre seemed dependent on, but above all a mixture of Calvinist and Revolutionary suspicion—the novel in America emerged belatedly, slowly and hesitantly. Not until the radical decade of the 1790s, a decade when, under the impact of the French as well as the American revolutions, the nature of libertarian and sentimental passions came under scrutiny, did interest in the American novel develop.

Even then, the doubts and hesitations were very apparent in the first novels themselves. In a time when the issue of women's roles and women's rights attracted increasing attention, Samuel Richardson's essential theme, seduction, was a concern of many early American novels—seduction by men, seduction by ideas contrary to nature, seduction, especially, by novels themselves. The book usually identified as the first American novel, William Hill Brown's *The Power of Sympathy; or, The Triumph of Nature* (1789), announces its intent "to expose the fatal CONSEQUENCES OF SEDUCTION." A rather thin epistolary work which recounts a typical Richardsonian tale of female libertarian energy going too far and leading to sexual confusion and disgrace, it eventually brings both seduced and seducer to the tomb for repentance. Novels themselves can be a source of danger—unless, like the repentant seducer of the book, they call for virtue, which means the identification of nature with reason, and reason with strict morality. A very similar plot is used by Mrs. Hannah Foster in her much better novel *The Coquette* (1797), purportedly the tale of the seduction of the author's cousin by a son of Jonathan Edwards that ended with death in childbirth. Both books are fictions warning against fictions, protecting themselves against the accusation of imaginative license by insisting they arise from actual situations, as they did. *The Power of Sympathy* is described as "founded on truth," *The Coquette* as "founded in fact." But the book that established this tradition firmly in America—and prepared the way for our popular modern romances—was Mrs. Susanna Rowson's *Charlotte Temple*. Rowson was an influential Briton who emigrated to America; her book was published first in London in 1791, where its theme seemed conventional, but then in the United States in 1794, where it did not, and became a great best-seller. Part of the interest of this otherwise none too interesting work is that it dramatizes the move of its materials across the Atlantic, telling of a pure young British girl encouraged by her soldier-seducer to elope from Britain to the United States, where she, as usual, dies pathetically, and he, as usual, repents.

This plot is virtually reversed in the tract-novel *The Emigrants; or, The History of an Expatriated Family* (1793), written by the radical American Gilbert Imlay. Having fought in the Revolution, Imlay moved to London and France, knew Paine, Barlow and Godwin, and is now most famous for having fathered in Paris a child by Mary Wollstonecraft, whom he deserted. Nonetheless he expressed feminist passions, attacked British divorce laws and attitudes toward women and celebrated in his novel an alluring, romantic, rural America where new family relations and a natural goodness prevail—in Ohio, "those Arcadian regions where there is room for millions, and where the stings of outrageous fortune cannot reach you." Imlay's book is polemic verging on naive pastoral, and it draws only weakly on the emerging spirit of fiction that was stirring the very circles he moved in—where new tensions of reason and feeling, new concerns with the claim of the subjective and the psychological, were generating the gothic novel. In Britain Mrs. Radcliffe's *The Mysteries of Udolpho* and William Godwin's *Caleb Williams* appeared in 1794, and M. G. Lewis's *The Monk* two years later. Not only was fiction recovering some of its origins in romance and the fantastic, but it was also debating the relations of reason and the imagination, the static and the revolutionary. In challenging the Augustan equation of Nature and Reason, it generated an early Romantic change so deep it would reshape the direction of subsequent fiction both in Europe and in America.

Possibly these are the books that Royall Tyler's hero Dr. Updike Underhill finds everywhere in America when he returns after a seven-year captivity in Algeria.

> In our inland towns of consequence, social libraries had been instituted, composed of books designed to amuse rather than instruct; and country booksellers, fostering the new born taste of the people, had filled the whole land with modern Travels, and Novels almost as incredible.

Tyler's preface to *The Algerine Captive* insists on a native fiction to respond to this situation, and, as with *The Contrast,* congratulates his own homespun depiction of American manners. Ironically, however, the main part of the book is Underhill's adventures in Europe, his captivity by pirates in North Africa and the challenge all this poses to his Protestant view of life. Tyler is offering his own version of modern travel and incredible adventure, as if—rather like later authors, such as Melville—America itself is now so plain and unexotic a world that only more primitive societies can offer the earthly paradise he looks for. The sections on America are thus realistic and satirical, but the world beyond can be treated as romance: Tyler's book points to the romance as a form of American fiction. Given America's very nature, the spirit of romance seemed to many of its best novelists well suited to its new order of things. It was thus a crucial fact about American fiction that it came into existence as neoclassicism turned toward Romanticism and the values of reason and as managed sentimentality moved toward the disturbances of an era of imagination and feeling. That difference from the European novel in chronological and intellectual origin is one reason for the distinctive character of the American fictional tradition.

There can be no doubt that that tradition starts with the work of Charles Brockden Brown, the Philadelphia magazinist, who in an early essay, "The Rhapsodist," urged the powers of intuition to take us beyond sense impressions, "in order to form a rational conception of the present life and our own resemblance to the phantom of a dream." Brown was very much a mind of the 1790s, a late eighteenth-century libertarian with doubts, alive to the contradictory claims of reason and feeling, sincerity and imagination, sense and sensibility. Like William Godwin, the British radical whose *Caleb Williams* deeply influenced him, he saw the ambiguity of the natural moral self his contemporaries celebrated. New scientific theories, new ideas of women's rights, new libertarian questions, ran through Philadelphia at the time, and Brown responded in narratives which treated strange mental states and inner disorders which matched parallel achievements in the British and European gothic tradition. At the century's end, he produced a remarkable group of novels, four of which—*Wieland* (1798), *Ormond* (1799), *Arthur Mervyn* (1799, 1800) and *Edgar Huntly* (1799)—are especially notable tales of troubled reason, fed with Faustian anxieties. Leslie Fiedler, who has written well on Brown, observes in late eighteenth-century gothic fiction the radical's mixture of desire and fear—desire for new knowledge and feeling, fear of a door that might open into the darkness of insanity and self-disintegration, a landscape of collapsing faith, weakening authority and parricidal emotions where minds pass by way of reason to the terrible and perverse, the unfamiliar, the estranging and the grotesque. The psyche becomes implicated, forced ever onward by boundless human desire, irrationally filling with ambiguous reflections and refractions that match the labyrinths and ruins of an unnatural outward world.

It was into this world that Brown was drawn, and he made it central to the tradition of American fiction, as successors like Poe and Hawthorne acknowledged. He knew perfectly well that the topography of that world belonged in Europe, where gothic itself came from. Europe was the seat of those old crimes, hermetic societies, dark forests, ancient castles, strange manuscripts and Piranesian ruins. But American nature had its own grotesqueries, so he undertook the project of transatlantic conversion he describes in the preface to *Edgar Huntly*:

America has opened new views to the naturalist and politician, but has seldom furnished themes to the moral painter. That new springs of action and new motives to curiosity should operate; that the field of investigation opened to us by our own country should differ essentially from those which exist in Europe, may be readily conceived. The sources of amusement to the fancy and instruction to the heart that are peculiar to ourselves are equally numerous and inexhaustible. It is the purpose of this work to profit by some of these sources; to exhibit a series of adventures growing out of the condition of our country.

This was the now statutory declaration, save that Brown is not merely claiming to explore American conditions with an American imagination, but pointing that imagination firmly toward gothic: "Puerile superstitions and exploded manners, Gothic castles and chimeras, are the materials usually employed for this end," he continues, but "The incidents of Indian hostility, and the perils of the western wilderness, are far more suitable; and for a native of America to overlook these would admit of no apology." Hence *Wieland* is subtitled *An American Tale.* Like several of his stories the plot arises among European mysteries and hermetic secret societies, but here the gothic landscape moves from East to West, as the older Wieland leaves Germany for America's vastness and an untried, rootless nature where established moral meanings are no longer secure.

An important part of Brown's interest, and his importance for later writers, is the way he invests the American landscape and cityscape with a new ambiguity. In Brown's writing the uncertain, untracked space of American topography, currently being explored in American travel writing, becomes, as in most gothic writing, peculiarly vivid but also peculiarly placeless, its promising garden also a potentially malign wilderness—a view conditioned by naturalists like Buffon, who read nature's degradation in it, and by contemporary American scientists, concerned with its strange and unexpected forms. Brown turned the same vision on the American cityscape, which could be read at once as the place of civilization and also of pestilence, of "perils and deceptions" as great as those of the wilderness. Brown's Philadelphia was now America's greatest city. The yellow fever epidemics that had ravaged it and other cities in the 1790s rage through *Ormond* and *Arthur Mervyn,* which originate America's city fiction much as *Wieland* and *Edgar Huntly* begin its nature fiction. The plagues had raised medical suspicions that American diseases were more terrible than European ones, and they fed Brown's extraordinary American topography, where nature is no longer pure pastoral but has obscure and labyrinthine significance, where cities contain corrupted innocence and dark relations. Brown's estranging nature and estranging city, his awareness of the irrational power they release, would recur again and again in subsequent American fiction; appropriately Melville would call one of his city nightmares *Pierre; or, The Ambiguities.* In such works, deceptions abound, sense impressions and intuitions are unreliable guides and reason and faith are equally unstable, for here identity itself is thrown into doubt.

This is actually a landscape of *inner* space; Brown brings a genuine sense of psychology to the American novel, one of the true contributions the gothic mode gave to fiction. Using the now familiar seduction plot both in *Wieland* and *Ormond,* he creates two complex heroines—Clara Wieland in the first, Constantia Dudley in the second—guardians of sentiment and sympathy who are exposed not just to the male seducer familiar in this kind of fiction but to the seductive new thoughts of the Romantic age. These persecuted maidens are matched with highly elaborate versions of the male manipulator; Carwin in the first novel, Ormond in the second, are seducers whose obsessions are more than sexual. Both are associated with the Illuminati, the European secret society, both seek strange new knowledge, both employ extraordinary stratagems: Carwin uses ventriloquism, Ormond mimicry and disguise. This is heady stuff, and Brown uses great narrative skill to move his stories beyond the domestic scene through the gothic mirror into that other world where identity grows fragile and the commonplace loses its familiarity. In *Arthur Mervyn* and *Edgar Huntly* Brown makes more use of the American environment; Arthur is a countryman from the farm who encounters the deceptions of the American city and Edgar faces his demon in the American wilderness. Both are drawn by "unconscious necessity" into disordered worlds where apparent adversaries turn out to be dark doubles of the self. This was important material for the American novel; sometimes best remembered for his exotic effects—ventriloquism, hypnotism and spontaneous combustion in *Wieland,* somnambulism in *Edgar Huntly*—Brown's more significant contribution was in the exploration of a contemporary psychology that probes beyond the limits of reason into a world made strange. This results in a moral ambiguity new to American fiction, though it would become familiar in Poe, Hawthorne, Melville and the future great succession of the American novel. Suddenly a power of darkness, a sense of mystery, is shown to be secreted in the seemingly benign world of American nature, in plain American democracy and common sense. The innocent Adamic paradise is laden with dark secrets, landscape dissolves into troubled psyche and a note of challenge enters American fiction.

Brown was the father of American fiction because in his work we can sense European literary forms undergoing a sea change, the novel becoming an American genre. While it owed much to European gothic, the American novel is less concerned with society, institutions, manners, classes, and more with the romantic, the melodramatic, what we now call the "fictive." It became a fictional type for a society where imagination was seeking its own new order, where self, nature and institutions were being redefined. When modern critics began seeking the origins of the powerful tradition of American fiction that still serves today, they soon learned to look to Brown. Richard Chase sees his work as a founding source for the American "romance," which would pursue its different nineteenth-century course from the European "novel." For Leslie Fiedler the essence of American fiction is its gothic sensibility and flight from women, domesticity and settlement toward the existential self-discovery of the frontier. R. W. B. Lewis describes a dominant myth of an American Adam who lives in mythic and metaphysical rather than social space. Harry Levin finds in American fiction a rising power of blackness, an underside discovery of the diabolic, the evil, the estranged, while Richard Poirier discerns an emphasis on imaginary and fictive spaces which separate American written worlds from real ones. In the interests of distinguishing an American novelistic tradition, these points have often been overemphasized; modern criticism stresses the centrality of the gothic, grotesque and fictive modes to European writing as well, and the American and European traditions are now seen as profoundly influencing each other. The fact remains that when, as D. H. Lawrence says, we find in America a literature that goes to "the real verge" as much European writing does not, a literature that interrogates American affirmations and challenges naive American dreams, we owe much of this to the labyrinthine pathways opened up by Brown.

Brown actually quarrels less with the heritage of European writing than with the didactic tradition of sentimental American fiction, yet another product of the Puritan imagination to prove influential throughout the nineteenth century. The tradition of Mrs. Rowson would flourish, leaving the line from Brown to occupy the troubling, interrogating margin. But what James Kirke Paulding described as "the blood-pudding school" was not the only method used by American writers to strain the boundaries of the novel. Another Philadelphia writer, Hugh Henry Brackenridge, tried a different course with *Modern Chivalry,* a vast, open-ended novel he serialized between 1792 and 1805 and collected in 1815. Brackenridge was a poet who had collaborated with Freneau, and he began the project as a Hudibrastic verse satire, "The Modern Chevalier," before switching to the method of picaresque prose comedy drawn from Smollett and, in the end, Cervantes—for this is an updated American *Don Quixote,* as its title suggests. The two key characters transported from situation to situation to comment satirically on society and the times are Captain Farrago, bookish, sagacious but sometimes foolish, who acts as Don Quixote, and Teague O'Reagan, the coarse, unlettered, bogtrotting Irish servant, who plays Sancho Panza. The open structure takes this odd couple all around the Pennsylvania "lubberlands" and into Philadelphia's higher culture. They encounter elections, the Whiskey Rebellion, universities and philosophical societies (like Franklin's). Teague embodies the rise of American populism, and is even shipped off to France to show the oddity of American human and animal nature. Brackenridge himself, like many of his thoughtful contemporaries, was split in his attitude toward the new United States, divided as it was between elitist and egalitarian possibilities, democratic hopes and the threat of the mob. The book is so specific to its age that some historical knowledge is needed to read it now, but it does show us that a vivid social and satirical fiction was possible in America.

The quest for a native American novel progressed slowly. It moved from Philadelphia to other Eastern seaboard cities as Boston, Charleston and New York developed mercantile classes with intellectual and artistic as well as economic and political aspirations. The Knickerbocker scene which had nourished the essay and poetry turned as well to the fictional forms, and it found its voice in Washington Irving. The Goldsmithian essays Irving wrote with Paulding as the *Salmagundi* papers established him as a New York wit, but his reputation was made with his "comic history of the city," *A History of New York . . . by Diedrich Knickerbocker* (1809), a work of mock-learning and literary parody much admired for its technical skill and wit by Scott, Byron and Coleridge. Irving's prose was neoclassical, but his sensibility half-Romantic; he was drawn by Scott and Campbell, excelled in inventing comic personae and yet had an appreciative sense of the melancholic and picturesque. His style was a search for a balanced voice that would let him be both American and European, let him comically report his own age yet reach for the "legends" of the past. A youthful Grand Tour through Europe educated him in Romantic sensations; and it was to Europe he returned, after the War of 1812, in an attempt to heal the widening political and literary breach, establish himself in the literary profession and resolve the manifest problems of the American writer.

In 1815 he sailed for Liverpool, settling in Britain first in an attempt to rescue the family business, then to try to live by writing in the world of the English Romantics. Scott received him generously, and at Abbotsford he read the German Romantic folktale writers. The British too were looking back to the Romantic past, as industrialism thrived during the peace that followed Napoleon's defeat at Waterloo. As the Battle of the Quarterlies raged, British magazines mocked American aspirations for an independent literature: "In the four quarters of the globe, who reads an American book?" demanded Sydney Smith. But almost single-handedly, Irving seized the moment and reversed the condescension with the essays, sketches and stories of *The Sketch-Book of Geoffrey Crayon, Gent.* (1819, 1820), *Bracebridge Hall* (1822) and *Tales of a Traveller* (1824), which appealed enormously to British and American audiences alike. Irving cast himself as a romantic traveler who makes his sketches, essays and vignettes, or collects his fables, as he passes from place to place, observing the picturesque and the historical, the ivy-covered ruin, the falling tower, the "mouldering pile." In Romantic fashion, he polarized the activities of the imagination, dividing them between Europe and America. Europe was the past, the poetic, the timeless, the mythical; indeed in a sense it was living Romanticism, a depository of the antique, the exotic, the traditional, "storied association." America was the present, rushing, potential, time-bound, political; it was in a state of literary promise, with its prodigious but still unwritten and unfelt grandeur of prairie, river, mountain and forest. In the center is Geoffrey Crayon, the traveler-painter hunting each nook and cranny that calls forth a sensation and a sketch, turning Europe's Romanticism back on itself by giving European and American readers alike the history they were beginning to crave in an age of rising industrialism and entrepreneurship.

Irving was the American writer as ambassadorial expatriate. In May 1815, he began a seventeen-year European residence that would take him over the landscape of the new Romanticism in Britain, France, Germany and Spain and establish fresh links between American writing and European tradition. His response to this Romanticism was half accepting, half ironic, but it led him toward a historical mythology of American life. In Volney's *Ruins,* translated by Thomas Jefferson and Joel Barlow in 1802 as a radical text, the French writer had associated moldering civilization with political decline. Irving associated it with art itself; the Europe he paints is a timeless human past, stable and engaging, a picturesque paradise rooted in custom and peasant ways and scarcely touched by modern industrialism or expansion. His essays recognize political antagonism and social change but emphasize the need for the imagination as an aid to reconciliation, "looking at things poetically rather than politically." We can sense an element of evasion in this, and he himself admitted this was a "light" Romanticism, not much more than "magic moonshine." But America needed a legendary past, and he went on to collect it from many European sources, working deliberately to construct a new sense of world landscape for the American imagination. He gathered folktales from the Germany of Tieck and Jean Paul (J. P. F. Richter); in Spain, in addition to writing *Legends of the Alhambra* (1832), he rewrote the Columbus legend, thereby providing another triangulation for American experience. The influential American historians of the time—Prescott, Ticknor, Everett— were cosmopolitanizing themselves in the same way, turning to Europe to give the United States a significant history. Irving likewise defined a set of references that would relate the European Romantic past to a fresh American present, providing an imaginative geography that would shape much later American writing, as well as much American tourism.

Most of Irving's writing was about Europe—as if this had become the required material for the American artist seeking to recover the Romantic past from whence art sprang—but he did set a few tales, now his most famous, in the United States. "Rip Van Winkle" and "The Legend of Sleepy Hollow," both in the *Sketch-Book,* have become classics of American folklore. They were in fact conscious endeavors to transport elements of the European folk tradition to American soil and are adaptations of German folktales, transposed to a "timeless," European part of America, the Dutch-American villages of the Hudson River valley, the heart of the American picturesque. He sets them here, as he says in his own voice in "The Legend of Sleepy Hollow," because

> population, manners and customs remain fixed; while the great torrent of migration and improvement, which is making such incessant changes in other parts of this restless country, sweeps by them unobserved. They are like those little nooks of still water which border a rapid stream, where we may see the straw and bubble riding quietly at anchor, or slowly revolving in their mimic harbor, undisturbed by the rush of the passing current.

It is this ahistorical and apolitical sleepiness that, to Irving, offers the possibility of legend, a view he shared with the German Romantics he imitated. Even so, the "passing current" does enter the stories. Rip Van Winkle steps out of society into twenty years of timelessness when, in the Catskill Mountains, he meets the ghostly drunken revelers from Henry Hudson's crew who lull him into a long slumber with a flagon of magic wine. His sleep takes him through the greatest American change of all, the Revolution; and when he returns to his village *its* old sleepiness has gone, replaced by disputation, politics and historical motion. But Irving's theme is not political; what the Revolution frees Rip from is "petticoat government," for his shrewish wife has died. Like Irving himself, Rip can now become a legend-maker, telling tales of the world before the war, transmuting history into myth. Rip makes legends; Ichabod Crane, in "The Legend of Sleepy Hollow," becomes their victim. This classic Yankee entrepreneur chases a rich heiress and her prosperous farm but is, ironically, cheated into seeing a ghost and losing his fortune through the belief in magic he has drawn from "Cotton Mather's history of New England witchcraft."

For an America without a written folk tradition, Irving provided essential material, the stuff of much future tall tale; here were stout Dutch burghers, backwoodsmen, Yankee peddlers, henpecked males and their garrulous wives, male dreams of freedom and space. His tales—he planned one novel but never wrote it—were his main contribution, a durable invigoration of the Romantic and the popular tradition of American fictional writing. But it was European distance that had added glow to his materials, as he found when, in 1832, he came back to America, a fêted author with a great European reputation, to face contemporary American history in the changed world of Jacksonian, westward expansion and commercial speculation. In this world the eastward Grand Tour was being replaced by a Western one which led not to civilized but to natural wonders, an American scene being written in many literary languages. William Bartram's influential *Travels* (1791) had explored American landscape as romantic grandeur. Timothy Dwight's *Travels in New England and New York, 1769–1815* (1821–22) had seen nature as the field of improvement and subjected the regrettable prevalence of forest to the standards of clearing and cultivation. Meriwether Lewis and William Clark had, in their record of adventurous continental exploration, *Journals* (1814), added new language of description and scientific report. John James Audubon was giving an extraordinary narrative and visual record of the birds and animals of the continent. And so this America was now available to Irving's touring, his sentimental associationism, his sense of the sublime.

This native landscape became the theme of his later books, his "Westerns": *A Tour of the Prairies* (1835), *Astoria* (1836) and *The Adventures of Captain Bonneville, U.S.A.* (1837). The first is his Geoffrey Crayon tour to the "untrodden" frontier where the Indians were being driven from their homelands, but the book simply reveals how hard it was to render the West and the prairies—"For which the speech of England has no name," Bryant had written—in the language of the European Grand Tour. Indians romantically became Arabs and gypsies, the unwritten mountains European Gothic cathedrals, and though the *North American Review* praised Irving for "turning these poor barbarous *steppes* into classical land," they remain, for Irving, in a state of curious vacancy. Something of the reason for this is apparent in the other two books, which were commissioned works. This nature is not innocent, but space for entrepreneurship, and Irving was never interested in the paradoxes and contradictions, the present troubles of history. *Astoria* really celebrates New York commercial intervention into the development of the West in its account of John Jacob Astor's monopolizing of the fur trade in the Pacific Northwest, and *Captain Bonneville* is the similar story of the famous soldier-explorer staking claims to American lands. These are minor works, and Irving seemed to know it, returning to Europe again as minister and ambassador in high government posts and doubting the durability of his talent. What these late works show is the difficulty faced by those seeking the tone and shape of American narrative in the opening world of American nature, exploration and mercantilism. They reveal the West not only as a social and political but as a linguistic and literary frontier.

It was a quite different writer who was to take on those social and narrative implications most directly and thereby point the direction to American fictional maturity. James Fenimore Cooper was in many ways Irving's antithesis. He too expatriated to Europe, but came back not to acclaim but to a kind of disgrace for his criticism of his nation. He too applied Romantic standards to American life and moved toward American legend, but his legends never stepped fully outside history or politics. As a child, Cooper lived among the contradictions of American pioneering, the root conflicts between nature and culture, frontier life and drawing-room civilization. His father was a judge, explorer and travel writer, a land entrepreneur and Federalist squire who himself founded, cleared, settled and governed Cooperstown in the Finger Lakes region of the New York State frontier—he claimed to have put more land under the plow than any other American. Cooper grew up there, went to Yale and then to sea, onto America's other frontier where similar growth and development was occurring. He himself became a landowner, a potential rural aristocrat. But marriage and the need for money drove him toward the writing of fiction. Like most of his contemporaries, he was obsessed with the thought that America was a blank sheet, offering virtually no materials or language for literature. In *Notions of the Americans* (1828), written for European consumption, he was to offer his version of the familiar litany about his country's neglect of talent and "poverty of materials":

> There is scarcely an ore which contributes to the wealth of the author, that is found, here, in veins as rich as in Europe. There are no annals for the historian; no follies (beyond the most vulgar and commonplace) for the satirist; no manners for the dramatist; no obscure fictions for the writer of romance; no gross and hardy offences against decorum for the moralist; nor any of the rich artificial auxiliaries of poetry. The weakest hand can extract a spark from the flint, but it would baffle the strength of a giant to attempt kindling a flame with a pudding-stone.

The irony behind this statement is that, when he wrote it, Cooper was well into a career that would encompass nearly all these literary guises; he was to produce over thirty novels whose mass, variety and very geographical as well as literary scope would display the many openings that existed for fictional and imaginative treatment of American society and nature, land and sea frontiers, history and manners. He drew as well on the age's widening range of narrative voices: those of the historian and exploring scientist, those of the satirist and the writer of romance. These voices were so many, and drawn from so many sources, that he looks clumsy to many readers, as Mark Twain demonstrated with ease in his delightful literary parody, "Fenimore Cooper's Literary Offences" (1895). Both his literary simplicity and his superb mythography make us see him today as primarily a writer of boys' books, the originator of many of the essential "Western" motifs of the American popular imagination. Yet to Scott and Balzac as to Gustave Aimard and Karl May, he was a major presence, an originator of modern fictional romance who did not evade the historical and social conflicts that lay behind it. Looking from East to West, Europe to America, drawing room to prairie, Cooper gave America the romantic narrative history it lacked. His discourse drew from the ever-opening record of the land emerging from the explorers and reporters, the historians like W. H. Prescott and George Bancroft who were writing the romantic historiography of the new continent and recovering its Western and Spanish past. The images of pioneers and Indians he created, above all in *The Leatherstocking Tales,* entered not only American but world popular mythography, but unlike Irving's they had a power of social criticism that took them far beyond legend. Despite the opprobrium he eventually suffered, despite his own doubts about the very existence of a sufficient American writing, he was able to unlock the potent, if chaotic, variety of the expanding national narrative of the busy years after 1820.

Cooper began pallidly enough, with a pseudo–Jane Austen, English-set novel, *Precaution* (1820). His allegiance then shifted to Scott, and with *The Spy* (1821) he was the first to show that Scott's form of romance had American application. The tale took him from drawing room to forest, from manners to historical processes, from Britain to America. *The Spy* is set in the Revolutionary War, seen as a time of historical crisis and changing social order in which families and loyalties divide and ideas of right and justice blur. Its central figure is Harvey Birch, an adventurer who resists marriage and socialization in order to withdraw into the natural moral world he forges for himself. Harvey prefigures many of the qualities of Cooper's most famous hero, Natty Bumppo or Leatherstocking, who was to make his first tentative appearance in Cooper's next novel, *The Pioneers* (1823). Cooper gradually found his essential material, shifting away from the sentimental novel toward a form that could be a critique of his own changing culture—which he sees as divided in direction and intention, yet capable of romantic mythography. Leatherstocking was to become a Romantic archetype in several protean forms over the five books in which Cooper explored various moments in his long lifetime. There are two ways of reading the sequence: one in the order of Natty's life, from initiation to manhood in *The Deerslayer* (1841), maturity in *The Last of the Mohicans* (1826), self-chosen obscurity in *The Pathfinder* (1840), degraded elderly isolation in *The Pioneers* (1823) and death on the distant frontier in *The Prairie* (1827). The other, more illuminating, is to follow the order of writing to see how Natty's image and Cooper's view of fiction altered from book to book.

The Pioneers turns on the conflicts of settlement. Set in the upper New York State region where Cooper grew up, it depicts his own father in Judge Temple, who brings civilization, progress and law to

the virgin forest—but also intrusion, property rules, ungainly mansions, corrupt customs and the careless laying waste of nature. As its
title suggests, the book deals not with a single figure but a group of
settlers who display the paradoxes of this conflict; it is first and foremost a comedy of social clumsiness and moral ineptitude. Cooper
introduces Natty Bumppo first as a minor, dislocated figure, a seemingly degraded man dispossessed and disheartened by the new ways
of American life. Yet as the book grows and settlement comes to seem
morally more doubtful, both Natty and his friend Indian John,
Chingachgook—one of the first complicated portraits of the Indian in
fiction—acquire dignity, even a natural transcendence as expressions
of the dying wilderness. In inventing Natty, Cooper had found a prime
subject, that of the alternative possibility secreted *within* the wilderness, an ideal of life beyond legal and social conventions governed by
moral ones in their Romantic essence. The wild huntsman, *Der Frei-
schütz,* who has made his pact with nature and the forest, emerges
from German Romanticism or Rousseauean idealism to take physical
as well as symbolic place as the legendary, untutored new American
born out of the virgin wilderness. "A hero in space," R. W. B. Lewis
has called him, suggesting that he represents a timeless, innocent,
Adamic image of man apart from history, immersed in nature. But
Natty *is* in history, and so the Leatherstocking novels are historical
novels in the sense meant by the Marxist critic Georg Lukács: that is,
they deal with ideological transformations from one order of things to
another, the making of the stages of society.

Thus, like the contemporary Romantic painter Thomas Cole,
Cooper too is preoccupied with the course of empire, the cyclic
moving process of history along the borders where civilization casts
its shadows before. Where he differs from the progress-piece poets is
that he does not regard every new stage as advance. Leatherstocking,
in the novels after *The Pioneers,* thus follows the moving frontier to
experience the conflicts of various historical periods. Meanwhile,
Cooper was interspersing these novels with many others—tales of
the sea-frontier like *The Pilot* (1824), or tales of the Puritan past like
The Wept of Wish-ton-Wish (1829)—which deal with other crises in
the nation's history. In the next Leatherstocking novel, *The Last of the
Mohicans* (1826), he took Natty back to the forested frontier world of

1757 where, in near virgin land, the Indian is being eliminated. This is an often violent adventure story in which Natty recognizes his true position: like the Indians, he is a borderer, a man without a people, the last of his kind. *The Prairie* presents another transformation. By now Cooper had moved to Paris, for his own and his children's historical education. The blank lands of the high plain where the story is set had been acquired from the French by the Louisiana Purchase of 1803; Chateaubriand had romantically explored them for fiction in *Atala* (1801). Cooper now proposed a more European meaning for Natty: he is now the indurate Romantic, the dying old hero falling back like an Indian into the land from which he has emerged. He has become at last a "philosopher of the wilderness," and the book, says the Preface,

> closes the career of Leatherstocking. Pressed upon by time, he has ceased to be the hunter and the warrior, and become the trapper of the dying West. . . . Here he passes the closing years of his life, dying as he had lived, a philosopher of the wilderness, with few of the failings, none of the vices, and all the nature and truth of his position.

Cooper here becomes almost a Romantic prose-painter as he depicts Natty rising from the land like a youth gilded by the setting sun before turning him back toward the inescapable truth of history as we see his declining powers. For he is now ancient and more or less nameless, an almost Wordsworthian figure in a condition of resolution and independence. Here he has come to escape "the wasteful temper of my people" displayed in Ishmael Bush, the predatory Moses in the American wilderness who has come West "to find a place where no man can ding the words of Law into my ears." Bush is a corrupt version of Natty, who sees man not as a beast seeking freedom by instinct, "but he must see and reason, and then conclude." Meanwhile, fulfilling Cooper's social theme, various orders of society and civilization come across the landscape, the new settlers and despoilers, the scientific explorers on their expeditions, the socialized Easterners. But in its bleakness and exposure the flattened high plain mirrors only Natty's condition. His death is both a Romantic transcendence within nature and the end of things, for the historical cycle will now bring institutions, establish law, raise cities, all the while eroding the philosophical and moral import of everything Natty represents. The book combines Cooper's historical and his mythic impulse to unite social narrative and transcendental arrest, thus creating the mixture of temporal consciousness and timeless wonder Cooper contributed to the American fictional tradition.

But Cooper's seven-year expatriation in Paris complicated his social views. He saw the 1830 Revolution which established Louis Philippe as the citizen-king, and he took it as his role to explain American democracy to Europeans, while examining democracy's own history in Europe in novels like *The Bravo* (1832), *The Heidenmauer* (1832) and *The Headsman* (1833). He also wrote international novels whose cultural comparisons gave much offense in America. *The Monikins* (1835) dealt with Leaphigh (England), Leapthrough (France) and Leaplow (America) and attacked Jacksonian leveling. In *Homeward Bound* and *Home As Found* (both 1838), he told the story of his return home. He questions American institutions and manners from the standpoint of an international group of travelers, including urbane Europeans and returning "hadjis." The attacks on his property and opinions that had gathered during his absence explain his satirical assaults on Steadfast Dodge, the fawning newspaper editor, and the ingenious Yankee confidence man, Aristabulus Bragg. Matters were not helped by his essay of dissent from the egalitarian mood of Jacksonian democracy, *The American Democrat* (1838). Cooper's expatriation had taught him to direct his social and moral criticism in acts of courage and challenge to his times that won him enormous unpopularity and the assaults of the press. Nonetheless his work in the 1840s sustained the attack. The "Littlepage Trilogy"—*Satanstoe* (1845), *The Chainbearers* (1845), *The Redskins* (1846)—is a very different version of American history from that of the more famous Leatherstocking sequence. It is a story of American settlement told in terms of developing greed, moral opportunism and growing national decay. But the Leatherstocking tale had not been finished. Cooper returned to the saga once again, telling, in *The Pathfinder* (1840), the story of Natty's drift toward society and domesticity until he discovers that his own Adamic place in the world forbids it, and, in *The Deerslayer* (1841), portraying

the moral anxiety attached to Natty's first act of killing and his consequent acceptance of the pains as well as the rewards of nature. Some
of Cooper's most intensely mythic and Romantic scenes are here. Side
by side, the two sequences show his complexity: the "Littlepage"
novels exemplify his social realism and his sense of history as process,
while these last Leatherstocking books reassert his gift of wonder
before American nature.

No one could call Cooper an exact novelist; his books run away
with themselves, his language moves strangely from scientific notation
to Romantic sublimity, his minor characters are often crude simplifications. As Mark Twain showed, he frequently violates probability.
Yet he is the central figure in the transformation of the early American
novel; the flood of fiction from his imitators largely began the commercial life of American fiction. Suddenly American history was a ready
subject for narrative, and tales of the Puritan, Indian and Revolutionary
past filled the market, competing with the rival flow of sentimental
domestic fiction, largely written by women, which was pouring off the
presses by the 1830s. "How many new writers rose up suddenly, the
moment that their neighbours had made the discovery that there were
such writers—that such writers should be," wrote William Gilmore
Simms, the Southern author who was Cooper's best disciple, in explaining his impact. Cooper had alerted writers to the value of regional
and backwoods materials and thereby widened the narrative landscape;
they were soon exploring different sections of the country and their
different pasts with a detail that would eventually nourish the local
color movement of the post–Civil War period. John Neal wrote novels
of Maine (*The Down-Easters,* 1833) and Catherine Maria Sedgwick,
of Massachusetts (*Hope Leslie,* 1827). The South found its voice in
John Pendleton Kennedy, who explored the Virginian plantations, and
Robert Montgomery Bird, who wrote of the Kentucky border (*Nick
of the Woods,* 1837). Simms himself, the most important of them,
wrote of Carolina, partly to portray contemporary customs, but also
to retell the past, as he did with his best book *The Yemassee* (1835),
a tale of the early wars between the British and the Yemassee Indians
where the debt to Cooper is very apparent.

But the debt to Cooper was not just one of new subjects but of
new forms, as Simms emphasized. What he had initiated was the

American romance, a form permitting an epic enterprise, allowing a vigorous portrayal of American settings, and enabling the creation of an active and ingenious American hero whose skill is tried in "hitherto untried situations." *The Yemassee* was a "modern romance," and Simms explained that this was quite different from the novel: "The Romance is of loftier origin than the Novel. It approximates the poem. The standards of Romance . . . are very much those of the epic." The persuasive conviction of this argument was demonstrated when Hawthorne continued the speculation about the form in his novels and prefaces at mid-century. The term meant almost the opposite of what it means today; "romance" was virtually the antithesis of the sentimental fiction it sought to rival. Nor did its implications point only toward the land frontier or the new regionality and concern with backwoods and rural life. In 1838 Edgar Allan Poe published his one novel, *Narrative of Arthur Gordon Pym,* a sea story which crossed the tradition of sea adventure with the dark symbolism common to romance. Brockden Brown forms a background, for this is a tale of gothic terror, the story of a dark voyage from Nantucket which follows mysterious hieroglyphs into the vast unknown, the empty whiteness that turns from blankness to death. Poe's book was among other things a parody or literary hoax in the genre of sea fiction—a genre that in American fiction must also be traced back to Cooper. The sea story ranged from a form of romance—as in Robert Montgomery Bird's *The Adventures of Robin Day* (1839)—to a form of documentary realism, largely because of the possibilities explored by Cooper. When between 1834 and 1846 the ex–Harvard student Richard Henry Dana, Jr., undertook a voyage as common seaman and faithfully recorded the brutalities of seaboard and West Coast life anonymously in *Two Years Before the Mast* (1840), the book was immediately attributed to Cooper's pen.

In Brown and Irving, the potential of American narrative had clearly appeared. With Cooper, it became evident to all. By the end of his life he stood at the center of a large, multidirectional flow of American writing. These early writers were male and female, sentimentally uplifting or socially critical. They established a curiosity about moral feeling and social representation, historical rediscovery and contemporary social investigation, about land and sea, East and West,

Yankee and backwoodsman, city and country, factual record and gothic invention, that provided the foundations for further development. When Hawthorne turned back to the subject of the Puritans, more than thirty novels preceded him with the topic (one by Cooper), many, like Harriet V. Cheney's *A Peep at the Puritans* (1824), suggesting the anti-Calvinism of the changing age. When Herman Melville wrote his story of another dark voyage out of Nantucket, he had as predecessors not just Poe and the symbolic romance, but Dana, and Cooper's later, more realistic sea fiction (*Afloat and Ashore* and *Miles Wallingford,* both 1844), in fact an already substantial tradition. The spacious landscape and seascape, the testing historical sense, the feeling of moral interrogation and spiritual questing that marks the writing of what we call "the American Renaissance" may have been a slowly won prize. But it did not arise from nowhere, though its writers often emphasized their isolation. It came, in fact, from a busy writing culture that had, after all, emerged out of the hopes and doubts of the Founding Fathers.

CHAPTER

· 4 ·

AMERICAN NAISSANCE

· I ·

The peaking of American literary power just before the middle of the nineteenth century still seems such a novel and remarkable event that it remains the heartland for all discussion of American literature, out of which arises any understanding of the originality of American writing, any sense of a modern or modernist lineage. For Whitman it all began with Emerson: "America of the future, in her long train of poets and writers, while knowing more vehement and luxuriant ones, will, I think, acknowledge nothing nearer this man, the actual beginner of the whole procession. . . ." In 1941, as America entered the Second World War and it became even more important to recognize the strength of American achievement, F. O. Matthiessen completed a groundbreaking study of the major writers—Emerson, Thoreau, Hawthorne, Melville, Whitman—and their culture. But he could find no title to describe the extraordinary episode he had examined. His friend and student Harry Levin proposed "American Renaissance"; that is what Matthiessen called his study, and that is what we call the era still. The term is, however, imperfect; this was not a rebirth but a new beginning, as Emerson insisted and as Matthiessen himself said, observing that the period signaled America's "coming to its first maturity and affirming its rightful heritage in the whole expanse of art and culture." But it was, as he also said, the American equivalent of an Elizabethan Age, when artistic, intellectual and political energy generated a fresh and still commanding time of expression. Hence the term serves us, though what we are observing is actually the American Naissance.

The shape of the period is fairly exact. Its end is clear; it faded with the American Civil War in 1861, though it also raised most of the issues that brought the war about. The start is less precise, but Emerson's *Nature* (1836), with its repudiation of the past and the "retrospective age" and the assertion of a new vision ("I become a transparent eyeball. I am nothing. I see all"), will serve, followed by his oration "The American Scholar" of the following year, for many, then and now, the nation's true declaration of literary independence. Throughout the 1840s an increasingly confident temper was to grow, partly through Emerson's stimulation, in American writing; in 1841 William Ellery Channing spoke of the age's new "tendency in all its movements to expansion, to diffusion, to universality." By mid-century this sense of innovative, intuitional discovery had reached its peak. Over five remarkable years between 1850 and 1855 appeared Emerson's *Representative Men* (1850), Hawthorne's *The Scarlet Letter* (1850), *The House of the Seven Gables* (1851) and *The Blithedale Romance* (1852), Melville's *White-Jacket* (1850), *Moby-Dick* (1851) and *Pierre* (1852), Harriet Beecher Stowe's *Uncle Tom's Cabin* (1852), Thoreau's *Walden* (1854) and Walt Whitman's first version of *Leaves of Grass* (1855). For today's reader, here is the time of the distinctive emergence in America of the poem, the essay, the questing travel tale, the novel and—if we add Poe's work of the previous two decades—the modern short story.

Behind this efflorescence was the fresh, certain spirit, the conviction of historical opportunity being seized by a novel creativity, that came in large measure from Emerson. "There is a moment in the history of every nation," he said in *Representative Men,*

> when, proceeding out of this brute youth, the perceptive powers reach their ripeness and have not yet become microscopic: so that man, at that instant, extends across the entire scale, and, with his feet still planted on the immense forces of night, converses with his eyes and brain with solar and stellar creation. That is the moment of adult health, the culmination of power.

This was what Emerson was acknowledging in, or exhorting from, American thought. It was, especially, New England thought. Though Poe from the South, Melville and Walt Whitman from New York, joined the enterprise, a New England that had somehow reactivated its dying religious heritage was the center. "From 1790 to 1820 there was not a book, a speech, a conversation, or a thought in the State," Emerson said of Massachusetts in his *Journals*; "About 1820, the Channing, Webster, and Everett era begun, and we have been bookish and poetical and cogitative since." This is overstated. Boston had never neglected the ministry or education, the book or the magazine. It had the *North American Review* from 1815, where Bryant printed "Thanatopsis" and where the arguments for national literature raged; Cambridge, across the river, had Harvard, learning, scholarship, and Bancroft and Parkman, Motley and Ticknor, the leading historians. New England was a hub of reform, from temperance and feminism to antislavery, and was central in national politics. Its old Puritanism had been transformed, above all by Unitarianism, which, William Ellery Channing said, showed "The soul is the spring of our knowledge of God," an assumption close to Emerson's. It had close contact with British and European ideas (its writers and thinkers crossed the Atlantic frequently) and was the port of entry for Romanticism, another major source for Emerson. When Alexis de Tocqueville recorded his impressions of America in the 1830s, he found Boston considered itself "the Hub of the Universe." By the 1830s American literature, serious and popular, was already very largely New England literature. The central triumvirate of Longfellow, Holmes and Whittier reigned, along with Dana and Lowell and Channing. It had key women writers, of whom Margaret Fuller and Harriet Beecher Stowe, author not only of *Uncle Tom's Cabin* but also of vivid records of New England life, were most notable. There were the voices of new religion and radical reform, like Orestes Brownson, the early abolitionists and Margaret Fuller, both a transcendentalist and the most powerful mind of the era's feminist movement. And there were the transcendentalists.

Emerson's leading role has made the transcendentalism of which he was spokesman seem central, but perhaps it seems more so in retrospect than it did at the time. It was one of many movements in the air at a point when sects and schisms, religious and philosophical tendencies, stirred New England life and spread abroad to the nation. Utopianism and sectarianism, mesmerism and phrenology, anything that, as Charles Dickens put it, looked "a little beyond," suited the contemporary New England temper. So powerful have Emerson and his circle come to seem that we should not forget that it was in some respects on the dissenting fringe of what Edgar Allan Poe, an outside observer, called "Boston Frogpondium." For most of the century New England represented a more genteel heritage and a more pedagogic one. It was the poetic home of Longfellow, Lowell and Holmes; it was vestigially Augustan, educated, civilized and almost European; it spoke magisterially from pulpits and Lyceum lectures, from magazines and academic groves. Matthiessen's "American Renaissance" was actually part of a broader and more various Naissance; his view has the modern emphasis on talents who were half-tangential to their age. Yes, New England was transcendentalism, but also a good deal more.

· II ·

"Who, except wretched children, now reads Longfellow?" asked Ludwig Lewisohn in 1932, indicating the reversal that had overtaken the author once thought to exemplify the very spirit of the nation's poetry. The modern condescension toward Henry Wadsworth Longfellow is nowhere better prefigured than in some kindly comments made by Walt Whitman on hearing of the popular poet's death. In a materialist, money-worshipping age Longfellow had been a valuable counterforce, Whitman said, emerging as "the poet of melody, courtesy, deference —poet of the mellow twilight of the past in Italy, Germany, Spain, and in North America—poet of all sympathetic gentleness—and the universal poet of women and young people." But Longfellow "is not revolutionary, brings nothing offensive or new, does not deal hard blows." Whitman thus put Longfellow at the opposite extreme from his own ideal of poetry, which he described elsewhere as akin "to outside life and landscape . . . —to the elements themselves—not sitting at ease in parlour or library listening to a tale of them, told in good rhyme." The two views are incompatible, and Whitman has survived and Longfellow has not. The irony is that Longfellow shared similar passions with Whitman on the need for a national literature. While still a student at Bowdoin, Longfellow gave an address on nationalism in literature in which he resolved to provide his country with the native writing the age needed, and he always spoke for a poetry drawing its qualities "from the spirit of a nation—from its scenery and climate, its historical recollections, its government, its various institutions." The broad public aims were similar, but the methods of achieving them were fundamentally different.

Longfellow's way was to prepare studiously for the task—he eventually became professor of modern languages at Bowdoin and then Smith Professor at Harvard. He joined the tide of American scholars who went to European, especially German, universities in the 1820s, spending three years learning several languages and literary traditions. The chief outcome was his book *Outre-Mer: A Pilgrimage Beyond the Sea* (1833), modeled on Irving's *Sketch-Book,* except that Longfellow presents a soulful self, deeply Romantic, engaged in a Goethean voyage of educative sensations, of melancholy and joy and hunger for unity in the eternal. A second journey in the 1830s took him deeper into German Romanticism and the Goethean ideal of the cosmopolitan man of letters, massively learned and endlessly curious, who yet embodies his native cultural spirit. From this came the novel *Hyperion* (1839), based on *Wilhelm Meister,* which depicts Romanticism as a mode of growth where man's immortal strivings are brought within the tragic compass of human limitation. Now determined to be America's popular poet, he published *Voices of the Night* (1839), where the same issues appear in more accessible cadences. Here, in "A Psalm of Life," Romanticism merges with sentimental optimism and moral uplift to give that familiar poem its striving, cautiously spiritual note:

> Let us, then, be up and doing,
> With a heart for any fate;
> Still achieving, still pursuing,
> Learn to labor and to wait.

"Life is real! life is earnest!" intones a confident voice that distills the strenuous moral truths of an earlier time to touch the hearts of countless unsophisticated readers.

With *Ballads and Other Poems* (1841) Longfellow emerged as the nation's balladeer; "The Village Blacksmith" and "The Wreck of the Hesperus" were to become poems every schoolboy learned and remembered. Hawthorne gave him the American subject of *Evangeline: A Tale of Acadia* (1847), and with *The Song of Hiawatha* (1855) he adapted the metrics of the Finnish *Kalevala* to a sentimental Indian legend, America's equivalent to Tennyson's *Idylls of the King*. The *Courtship of Miles Standish* (1858) is perhaps the most successful of his long verse narratives. Evoking his own New England family past, it rejects the militarism of the Puritan Miles Standish in favor of the solid middle-class stability of John Alden, thereby celebrating the choices of Longfellow's own age. He displayed great talent for the shorter ballad as well, which he employed in a traditional way, to record, simply and musically, moments of significance in the national history. "Listen, my children," begins "Paul Revere's Ride" (1861), establishing the storyteller's compact of simplicity, sustained by a metric of musical fluidity:

> A hurry of hooves in a village street,
> A shape in the moonlight, a bulk in the dark,
> And beneath, from the pebbles, in passing, a spark
> Struck out from a steed flying fearless and fleet. . . .

It was all very learnable. "You know the rest," the ballad concludes, and, as intended, horse and rider ride out of the poem and into the nation's folk-memory. In such ballads, Longfellow's aim was to take Irving's intentions with Rip Van Winkle and Ichabod Crane to greater depths, to give America legend, to clothe, in Irving's phrase, "home scenes and places and familiar names with those imaginative . . . associations so seldom met with in our new country."

This was one Longfellow; but there was another, the vastly learned poet and translator whose lifetime project was his translation of Dante's *Divine Comedy* (1865–67), and whose renderings from Spanish or German or Provençal, often the hidden sources of his own poems, would suggest to a distant relative, Ezra Pound, the scope of learning needed by a poet. The sixty-three sonnets posthumously collected in 1907 not only show his mastery of the form but the breadth of his reading, the disappointments of his life, the importance of his friendship with the great minds of Boston like Agassiz and Sumner. One, "The Cross of Snow," beginning "In the long, sleepless watches of the night," deals with the greatest tragedy of his life, his second wife's death from burns. Another, "Mezzo Cammin," observes that "Half of my life is gone, and I have let/The years slip from me and have not fulfilled/ The aspiration of my youth. . . ." The debt to Dante shows in the poems that treat the *Divine Comedy* as a medieval cathedral, with sculptured towers, blazing windows, confessionals that hold forgotten dramas, crypts resonant with old lamentations. The poet becomes a laborer who sets his load down outside the cathedral to pray as the "tumult of the time disconsolate" fades and "the eternal ages watch and wait" in a sonnet that reveals Longfellow's own burdens of personal grief and the service he saw great literature performing as the solacing voice of eternity. It also displays his conception of his own task: to associate American poetry in spirit with great world literature.

Longfellow was remarkably successful. He became the embodiment of American poetry to a more than American public. His fame was worldwide; he was received by Queen Victoria in private audience; his bust stands in Westminster Abbey. The irony is that the moment in history he summoned, the conception of the poet's role he shared with his wide audience, no longer prevails. We have come to value, as Newton Arvin once put it, a poetry of difficulty, "emotionally perplexed, intellectually hard-earned, stylistically dense," so that it is no longer easy to do justice "to poets who 'signified' no more, or not much more, than they plainly stated." Longfellow's way with poetry was to interpret the mysteries of eternity in the conventional moral terms of his own age. Unless our conception of poetry changes significantly, he will never again be thought great. Yet, that said, it is still possible to admire his learning, versatility, skill, musicality and the civilizing role he played in the development of American verse. America's Victorian sage, he came to embody the Genteel Tradition in its moralism and sentimentality. He also represented Boston in its role of intelligent mediator between the achievements of world art and American possibility. When it was put to him that American literature should reflect the sweep of the prairies and the sublimity of the Grand Canyon, he gave, in his interesting portrait-of-the-American-artist novel *Kavanagh* (1849), the balanced, truly Bostonian answer, that a man does not necessarily become a great poet because he lives near a great mountain. He reflected the new Bostonian confidence that it wrote for the world—the confidence that Bret Harte summed up when he said that you could not shoot an arrow in any direction there without bringing down the author of two or three volumes.

But perhaps the fullest embodiment of that confidence was Oliver Wendell Holmes, doctor, dean of the Harvard Medical School and the witty table-talker who sustained the tradition of Augustan urbanity through the entire era of Boston supremacy and frankly declared his Back Bay aristocracy in *The Autocrat of the Breakfast Table* (1858) and its two popular successors. He was a loyal and proud member of what he identified in his novel *Elsie Venner* (1861) as "the Brahmin caste of New England." In his view, the American poet was set to no high task; he denied the poet prophetic power, argued for much of his life that prose and poetry were essentially the same and demanded straight common sense. "Don't write any stuff with rhyming tails to it that won't make a decent show for itself after you've chopped the rhyming tails off." His own poetry was *vers de société,* dependent, as he said, on his facility: "I'm a florist in verse, and what *would* people say/If I came to the banquet without my bouquet?" He could write serious scientific-philosophical poems like "The Chambered Nautilus" (1858), but he was always ready to respond to an occasion, as in his "Old Ironsides" (1830), dashed off to protect the frigate *Constitution* from destruction by the Navy—"Ay, tear her tattered ensign down!/Long has it waved on high." Behind the confident Augustan wit and Bostonian certainty, however, there was a medical reformer and serious rationalist who challenged the Calvinism of his own upbringing by reaching toward a broader humanism.

This was not always apparent. In "The Moral Bully" (1850) he outraged many by teasing the abolitionists and others who

> Turn the sweet milk of kindness into curds,
> Or with grim logic prove, beyond debate,
> That all we love is worthiest of our hate.

But his quality may be more accurately seen in the exactly executed utterance and firm values of the satirical spoof of his Calvinist heritage in "The Deacon's Masterpiece, or, The Wonderful 'One-Hoss-Shay': A Logical Story" (1858). Here a single poem marks the end of an entire intellectual tradition.

> Have you heard of the wonderful one-hoss-shay,
> That was built in such a logical way
> It ran a hundred years to a day,
> And then, of a sudden, it . . .

begins the parable about a carriage built with no weak link so as to last forever, like Calvin's logical theology. But after a hundred years, it

> went to pieces all at once,—
> All at once, and nothing first,—
> Just as bubbles do when they burst.
>
> End of the wonderful one-hoss-shay.
> Logic is logic. That's all I say.

Holmes's strong humanitarian beliefs, his dissent from the doctrine of original sin and his scientific curiosity are apparent in the fine "medicated novels" he wrote in later life: *Elsie Venner* (1861), *The Guardian Angel* (1867) and *A Mortal Antipathy* (1885). Here Holmes is no longer the repository of safe, sure Boston thought, but the adventurous medical man setting the complexities of psychology against the certainties of religion, exploring the Unconscious, multiple personality and the psychotic origins of behavior. This was the more complex and courageous face of Brahminism, prefiguring the dissent of Henry Adams, the experimental spirit of William James and the inquiries of pragmatism.

For a long lifetime Holmes stood at Boston's center during its heyday, amid a vital and glittering literary-social scene which radiated influence to the rest of America and celebrated the commercial prosperity condemned by more radical thinkers like Emerson. Holmes had no regard for the transcendentalists and dismissed them in verse:

> And oh, what questions asked in clubfoot rhyme
> Of Earth the tongueless and the deaf-mute Time!
> Here babbling "Insight" shouts in Nature's ears
> His last conundrum on the orbs and spheres;
> There Self-Inspection sucks its little thumb,
> With "Whence am I?" and "Wherefore did I come?"

By the time he died in 1894, aged eighty-five, the artistic standards of his attitude and generation had been supplanted by fresh European imports, first by philosophic Romanticism—he mocked the tendency as coming from "those dreamily sensuous idealists who belong to the same century that brought us ether and chloroform"—and then realism. The Genteel Tradition he both teased and represented was dying, and the Boston he embodied was no longer the American literary capital. For several generations he had spoken for its mixture of conservatism and reforming humanism, arrogance and culture, autocracy and saving wit. Just before his own death in 1892, his friend John Greenleaf Whittier addressed his last poem to Holmes, praising his optimism and wit and remarking,

> We have grown old together, we have seen
>   Our youth and age between,
> Two generations leave us, and to-day
>   We with a third hold way. . . .

It was an epitaph for an entire, long-lived era of cultural influence and domination they had shared, or perhaps divided between them.

For if Whittier, too, represented the Boston Genteel Tradition, he represented a very different side of it. Even their friendship can seem strange. Holmes was the embodiment of Back Bay hauteur, Whittier a farm-boy from Haverhill, Massachusetts, who held himself closely attached to the New England countryside. Holmes saw poetry as a form of light refinement ("Poetry is not an article of prime necessity, and potatoes are"); Whittier consecrated his verse to "the sacred interests of religion and humanity." Holmes mocked the British Romantics, parodying their ballads in "The Spectre Pig" and "The Mysterious Visitor"; Whittier's mentors were Byron and Scott, his aim to be his nation's popular balladeer. Holmes denied the poet's emotional power; Whittier saw poetry as "the moral steam enginery of an age of action." Holmes associated versifying with urbanity; Whittier confessed to his own lack of artistic education and his rural limitations and discerned in his verse, in "Proem" (1847), "The rigor of a frozen clime,/The harshness of an untaught ear." Holmes was the humanist Unitarian, Whittier the impassioned Quaker. And where Holmes mocked the abolitionists in "The Moral Bully," Whittier became the poet of abolitionism, devoting much of the first half of his writing life to prose and poetry in support of the antislavery crusade led by his friend William Lloyd Garrison. He repudiated his first book, *Legends of New England in Prose and Verse* (1831), as too literary, and from 1833 to the emancipation of the slaves in 1865 the bulk of his poetic output, in volumes like *Poems Written During the Progress of the Abolition Question* (1837) and *Voices of Freedom* (1846), took the form of "trumpet calls" of declamation and invective on the slavery question. If they have little interest now except in the light of the issues they address, they earned him a national reputation. Whittier's consciousness of his own limits was exact, as "Proem" suggests. His was not "the seer-like power to show/The Secrets of the heart and mind." But there was a task, a very Bostonian task, to perform:

> Yet here at least an earnest sense
> Of human right and weal is shown;
>   A hate of tyranny intense,
>   And hearty in its vehemence,
> As if my brother's pain and sorrow were my own.

Today it is the other side of his verse that claims attention, the side he called his "Yankee pastoral" which bequeathed its legacy to Edward Arlington Robinson and Robert Frost. Like Longfellow, Whittier saw legend and ballad as the key to American poetry. His best volumes are *Home Ballads* (1860), *In War Time* (1864), which contains "Barbara Frietchie," *The Tent on the Beach* (1867) and *Among the Hills* (1869).

In these books folk voice and exact observation of nature convey the quality less of literary than popular legend as Whittier's Quaker pietism and conventional sentimentality fade before fresh, personal intensity. His most-read poem, "Snow-Bound: A Winter Idyl" (1866), recalls two days of childhood confinement in a farmhouse after a heavy blizzard:

> And, when the second morning shone,
> We looked upon a world unknown,
> On nothing we could call our own.
> Around the glistening wonder bent
> The blue walls of the firmament,
> No cloud above, no earth below,—
> A universe of sky and snow!

The sense of scene, the vivid local detail, was the nearest an American writer had reached to Goldsmith's *The Deserted Village* or Burns's *The Cotter's Saturday Night*.

The strengths and limitations of the Schoolroom and Brahmin traditions are perhaps best summed up by the career of James Russell Lowell, a decade younger than the others and the most richly endowed Boston Brahmin of them all. A member of one of the leading patrician Cambridge families with an uncle who had founded the mill-town of Lowell, he possessed all the skill and facility, the breadth and learning, that New England could now provide—but also its fatal lack of artistic focus. A man of brilliant gifts, a highly successful journalist and verse-writer, his writing reflects a theoretical aimlessness, the high price paid by those who cannot identify their purpose or how to accomplish it —what the transcendentalists, whom he came to distrust, were succeeding in doing. He was only twenty-two when he published his first book of poems, *A Year's Life* (1841); when, two years later, he followed it with a second, Edgar Allan Poe wrote that Lowell "had given evidence of at least as high poetical genius as anyone in America—if not a loftier genius than any." Five years later, in 1848, his reputation was at its height. In one year he published *Poems: Second Series,* much applauded, though the verses today seem little more than rhymed platitudes and generalities; *The Vision of Sir Launfal,* a Tennyson-inspired poem on the Grail legend; the first series of *The Biglow Papers,* Yankee-dialect prose and verse firmly supporting the abolitionist cause and attacking American aggression in the Mexican War; and *A Fable for Critics,* a long satire on his contemporaries that he printed anonymously—the title page describes it as "By a Wonderful Quiz, who accompanies himself with a rub-a-dub-dub, full of spirit and grace, on the top of a tub."

One stanza both illustrates Lowell's candid self-knowledge and summarizes what his poetic tradition had achieved since the Revolution:

> There is Lowell, who's striving Parnassus to climb
> With a whole bale of *isms* tied together with rhyme;
> He might get on alone, spite of brambles and boulders,
> But he can't with that bundle he has on his shoulders;
> The top of the hill he will never come nigh reaching
> Till he learns the distinction 'twixt singing and preaching;
> His lyre has some chords that would ring pretty well,
> But he'd rather by half, make a drum of the shell,
> And rattle away till he's old as Methusalem,
> At the head of the march to the last new Jerusalem.

The facility, wit and high spirits recall Holmes; the sense of mission indicates how close to the surface earlier Puritan didactic determination remained. Lowell's learning brought him the Professorship of Belles Lettres at Harvard in 1855; his fame made him first editor of the *Atlantic Monthly* in 1857, where he published most of the major figures of the age and sought out and promoted new writers like William Dean Howells. By now he was largely an essayist and critic producing striking essays on European writers. A second series of *Biglow Papers* (1867) showed his continuing involvement in the issues of the Civil War, but Gilded Age America and the declining power of the older patriciate disappointed him as they did Henry Adams. He came to see that he had dissipated his gifts. He had ranged from local vernacular writing to urbane cosmopolitanism, from reflective poetry to polemic, and he had tried many styles. But his wide-ranging curiosity and intellectuality had not produced a distinctive voice or one clearly major work. Lowell had not become the American Matthew Arnold he had set out to be.

There were other forms of success. In later life he was American Minister at the Court of Spain and Minister in London, where he delivered a memorable address on "Democracy." He adopted the social appreciation for Europe and England that for many in his generation was a form of protest against the America of the Gilded Age and an admission of persistent provincial anxieties. In 1873 he wrote that

> I frankly confess that I like England immensely, I find men of leisure at every turn, men who are profound scholars, who think for themselves, with whom interchange of ideas is an inspiration. Where there is one such man in America there are a dozen here. Do you wonder I like it? The contrast is not a fault on the part of the country: it is the consequence of youth and the struggle for material existence.

James and Adams were to develop this sensibility of displacement into a testing analysis of America, an America where after 1865 primary social assumptions that had guided the nation were no longer viable and where a new education and sense of history were necessary. Lowell never crossed this bridge; moreover, the line of American poetry that sustained him had lost its energy, if not yet its reputation, by the Civil War. Like Bryant, Longfellow, Whittier and Holmes, he represented the American tradition but not the American Renaissance. The force of that lay elsewhere, in another aspect of New England which he found raw—in the contrasting and contrary spirit of New England's most original movement, transcendentalism.

·III·

To try to grasp the spirit of transcendentalism is, by definition, to try to grasp the ungraspable—which is precisely what transcendentalism sought to do. What essentially guided its thinking was its dissent from Unitarianism and the Lockean and Newtonian world view that had persisted so powerfully into the American nineteenth century, its celebration of individualism, self and consciousness and its reassertion of an idealistic Neoplatonism that, paradoxically, drew it back again toward Edwards and the Puritan tradition. Its thinking was fed by the spirit of Romanticism as it had developed through organicist philosophers like Kant and Swedenborg, Coleridge and Carlyle, who asserted the power of the imagination, the soul as spirit illuminated by the divine. But it partook too of that cultism and Utopianism that made New England a flourishing center for new sects and faiths and the urgent self-made individualism that seemed part of the essentially Franklinean American temper. In what John Quincy Adams called New England's "bubbling cauldron of religion and politics," where moral urgencies and new revelations grew readily and prophets and solitary thinkers came to seem a natural part of the landscape, transcendentalism spoke to the value of inward spiritual promptings and the need for a private relation between the self and the universe. It was a form of spiritual revivalism that dramatized the searching self at a crucial moment, when the time—the notion itself was intensely American—seemed ripe for total renewal, yet another Great Awakening.

On September 9, 1832, when Ralph Waldo Emerson, descended from a long line of New England ministers and himself the minister of the Second Unitarian Church in Boston, announced his skepticism about the Lord's Supper, resigned his ministry and pledged himself to a personal, noninstitutional form of faith, very few could have known that a whole new era in the history of the American imagination was under way. At the end of that year, Emerson set sail for Europe in a state of mental crisis to reconsider his position; there he encountered the full force of European Romantic, organicist thought, in religion, philosophy, social opinion and poetry. Of that thought, we may fairly say he gave a creative misreading. The link with powerful European intellectual developments is real, but we have only to compare Emerson's thinking as it now began to develop with that of his British friend and correspondent Carlyle to see how the flight from the quotidian marketplace into the abstract, the empyrean and the personal could be differently conducted in an American mind. After Emerson returned a year later, he settled well outside Boston in sleepy Concord, soon to become transcendentalism's capital city. And he now declared himself in his first book, aptly called *Nature* (1836). Emerson's statement of the innocent vision at work in a natural world was meant as a new beginning for himself and all Americans, and that is what it eventually came to seem.

In its argument for a transformed relation between self and the material world, *Nature* was nothing less than a manifesto serving notice that the Enlightenment tradition of Byrd and Franklin, what had become "the corpse-cold Unitarianism of Brattle Street and Harvard College," no longer lived. It had now to be challenged by the insistence that God had made material nature not as a mere commodity but as a hieroglyph of His spiritual world. Nature was not merely a challenge to man's powers of domination and exploitation; it spoke directly to the self, to the individual mind and soul. "To what end is Nature?" Emerson asked; he proposed that it was a scripture, more immediate and more accessible than any written statement, though it called for its scriptor, the "Orphic Poet," who responds to and incorporates its language. Even though he was quickly denounced for his "German insanity," Emerson's radiating conviction began to catch hold of his times, as he had known that it would. By 1838, Harriet Martineau was explaining to her fellow Britons that one could not really know America unless one knew Emerson. In him "one leading quality is to be distinguished . . . modest independence"—"independence equally of thought, of speech, of demeanour, of occupation, and of objects in life." Emerson himself did not embrace what had originated as a derogatory label until his lecture "The Transcendentalist" in 1841 that acknowledged the influence of Kant and asserted that the transcendentalist "believes in miracle, in the perpetual openness of the human mind to new influx of light and power; he believes in inspiration, and in ecstasy." By then this faith was already becoming a movement. From 1836 there was a "Transcendentalist Club" that attracted many New England radical thinkers drawn by Emerson's faith in the self—Bronson Alcott, George Ripley, Orestes Brownson, Theodore Parker, Margaret Fuller and Elizabeth Peabody, who was just about to become sister-in-law to a far more skeptical resident of Concord, Nathaniel Hawthorne.

Independence was the keynote. In 1837 Emerson delivered his Phi Beta Kappa address at Harvard, "The American Scholar." It memorably restated the theme that "We have listened too long to the courtly muses of Europe" and thereby earned its place as America's declaration of literary independence. And it argued that the scholar in his right state is not simply a thinker but "Man Thinking," an active voice of experience. The theme of independence was extended in "Self-Reliance" (1841), which expressed a central doctrine: divinity existed intimately in each natural fact, in each individual self. This was no appeal to the acquisitive individualism of Franklin's Poor Richard, nor to the entrepreneurism of his busy commercial age. Emerson's self is ethically opposed to selfishness; his is a quest for the best self one can imagine to merge in ultimate union with the transcendent Self, what he called "The Over-Soul" (1841). The religious implications are clear: this independence characterizes the believer whose identity rests on foundations not of this society or of this world. Indeed Emerson's essays, sermons and addresses, which came in a great outpouring as he toured the country and spoke his powerful message, can be read as a secularized version of the jeremiad and millenarian utterance. Drawing on his minister's rhetoric and the language of European philosophy and poetry, he challenged his audiences to see through the surfaces of the familiar world to the wondrous redemptive reality beyond, a reality readily available in its pure Platonic essence but sadly hidden by the mask of appearance. Emerson's natural supernaturalism was less a path to the spirit through the world of matter than a sacramentalizing of the ordinary through recognition of the spiritual import of all things.

In this sense, transcendentalism was yet another awakening of the spirit in New England, an indication that the sensibility of Jonathan Edwards still lived on in the new American world. For Emerson, however, as for Bronson Alcott, Orestes Brownson and the others, the meaningful reality of the immaterial world existed in much closer proximity to the material one than the Puritan settlers had held. For the Puritans, the divine plan vouchsafed hints of spiritual truth as it worked itself out providentially through the successive stages of history; for Emerson, the epochal moment was eternally present. Thus the message that now leapt alive from New England's "bar-rooms, Lyceums, committee rooms" to "fill the world with their thunder," as Emerson put it, was in essence apocalyptic. In *Nature* Emerson was already denouncing the age of the retrospective and announcing: "There are new lands, new men, new thoughts. Let us demand our own works and laws and worship." In *Representative Men* (1850) he announced the moment of new power when man extends across the full scale. He called for a world of self-made genius and the geniuses came, as if from his tutelage; he took from his ministerial training the prophetic role and spoke in the voice of revelation about "the infinitude of the private mind." If history as progress and democracy as American principle seemed to support all this, Emerson nevertheless felt it was possible to bypass history, to make mind and self the measure of life. In time his potent equation of the self and the universe came to seem an essential American principle and the originating theme of much of its finest subsequent literature, indebted as so much of it was to Emerson's radiant message.

Yet for all his travels as a lecturer and his massive appeal to thinkers and writers as various as Nietzsche and William James, Walt Whitman, Carlyle and Harriet Martineau, Emerson was fundamentally a private, contemplative scholar, a man who held that "Life consists in what a man is thinking of all day," who appeared in public chiefly because his sense of mission and his need to support himself demanded it. He was not temperamentally suited to lead a movement, and his relations with others, even fellow-transcendentalists, were often distant. Not everyone was persuaded by his energy and his claim to be a representative man; many, like James Russell Lowell, were drawn but finally unconvinced. When he was asked to join those hoping to form a communitarian, transcendentalist, Fourierist Utopia at Brook Farm, near Boston, where even the solitude-loving Nathaniel Hawthorne joined in the experiment for a time, Emerson declined, repeating his conviction that society would only improve when the individual self was sufficiently cultivated. The transcendentalist spirit worked in many ways to change American life in the age of confidence and progress. But it was just this opposition between individual self-reliance and the desire for group action that would finally split the movement, between those like Emerson and Thoreau who followed the path of individual spiritual regeneration, and those like George Ripley, Bronson Alcott, Orestes Brownson and Margaret Fuller who turned to direct social, political and indeed Utopian reform. Transcendentalism was thus to reach into every aspect of American life: education (Alcott and Elizabeth Peabody), religion (Brownson, Theodore Parker), feminism (Fuller), political and social reform (Ripley, Alcott, Thoreau; Brook Farm and Fruitlands). But its place in American literature would be small if it had produced only the essays on these topics that filled *The Dial* (1840–44) or only the verse of Emerson and Jones Very. What enabled this movement to transform American literature was the crucial relationship Emerson saw between his spiritual vision and the nature and social role of the writer.

Here, again, the inspiration can be traced to European Romanticism. But it was not the Romanticism that Irving and Bryant, Cooper and Longfellow shared with Goldsmith, Collins, Gray, Burns and Scott. When Howard Nemerov asserts that great poets are "admirable not because they present values (though they do) but because they *become* values," he is referring to the tradition of *Der Dichter,* the poet as prophet-seer. In "Circles" (1841) Emerson evokes this ideal to attach it to his epochal expectations for literature:

> Literature is a point outside of our hodiernal circle through which a new one may be described. The use of literature is to afford us a platform whence we may command a view of our present life, a purchase by which we may move it. . . . Therefore we value the poet. All the argument and all the wisdom is not in the encyclopaedia, or the treatise on metaphysics, or the Body of Divinity, but in the sonnet or the play.

In "The Poet" (1844) he expands this idea: poets summon true life through the lens of nature, letting us "see trifles animated by a tendency. . . . Life will no more be a noise. . . . Poets turn the world to glass." The poet may seem to create meaning but actually sees through the surfaces that veil it. This stress on seeing, vision, points to one of the many puns transcendentalism used to reconstitute language itself: the poet is a see-er, a prophet who helps us see through our eye, the "I" of our self-reliance that will make the first-person voice of Thoreau's *Walden* and Whitman's *Leaves of Grass* an echo of that transcendent Self, the Over-Soul. Emerson's poet is also epochal and prophetic, "a principal event in chronology." Poetry summons the transitional moment of a new time: "We are like persons who come out of a cave or cellar into the open air," says Emerson. "This is the effect on us of tropes, fables, oracles and all poetic forms. Poets are thus liberating gods." They are, in fact, perceivers of a prior poem, the universe itself:

> The sea, the mountain-ridge, Niagara, and every flower-bed, pre-exist, in pre-cantations, which sail like odors in the air, and when any man goes by with an ear sufficiently fine, he overhears them and endeavours to write down the notes without diluting or depraving them. And herein is the legitimation of criticism, in the mind's faith that the poems are a corrupt version of some text in nature with which they ought to be made to tally.

It is Emerson's notion of earth as text and sacrament that marks the place he holds in American literature: between the Puritans with their providential allegory and the later symbolists. Emerson is a didactic and religious thinker; he quests for fundamental truth. But he refuses to translate the material world into simple allegory. By distinguishing the *fixed* sign—what he calls "mysticism"—from the multivalent symbol, he opens the way to later writers from William James to Wallace Stevens:

> The quality of the imagination is to flow, and not to freeze. . . . Here is the difference between the poet and the mystic, that the last nails a symbol to one sense, which was a true sense for a moment, but soon becomes old and false. For all symbols are fluxional; all language is vehicular and transitive, and is good, as ferries and horses are, for conveyance, not as farms and houses are, for homestead.

The seeds of the underlying belief here—"The history of hierarchies seems to show that all religious error consisted in making the symbol too stark and solid"—may well lie in Coleridge's *Biographia Literaria* (1817) and Shelley's *Defence of Poetry* (1821). But in thus freeing the symbol to resonate in the imagination of the perceiver, Emerson liberated American poetry from the prisons of subject and purpose inherited from eighteenth-century verse. He thereby discredited univocal didactic art and gave Thoreau, Whitman, Hawthorne and Melville a resonant material world which would yield its transcendent significance only to the free play of suggestive analogy. The promise of poetry lay not in its direct statement but its fluid signification, "a new connection of thought":

> Why covet a knowledge of new facts? Day and night, house and garden, a few books, a few actions, serve us as well as would all trades and all spectacles. We are far from having exhausted the significance of the few symbols we use.

The present world, the American world, is thus present to the poet as material awaiting vision and the utterance that allows it to be known.

"I look in vain for the poet whom I describe," Emerson concludes; "We do not with sufficient plainness or sufficient profoundness address ourselves to life, nor dare we chaunt our own times and social circumstances." He knew he was not himself that poet. He published two volumes of verse—*Poems* (1847) and *May-Day* (1867)—and his own prose, as these quotations suggest, has an extraordinary innovative lyricism. But Emerson wrote no masterpiece. *Nature,* his first book, is a lengthy essay, complicated by what emerged as his special vocabulary and his disdain for coherent, systematic argument. Books like *Representative Men* (1850), *English Traits* (1856) and the two collections of *Essays* (1841, 1844) give ample indication of the independence Harriet Martineau recognized, but like his poetry they cannot provide a rounded picture of his thought or its remarkable centrality to America's philosophical and literary traditions. For this, one must turn to the ten volumes of the *Journals* (1909–14, posthumous) where his popular public lectures germinated, and to the disciples who responded to his leadership with lives and work that have continued to make an important contribution to the American character. The lasting significance of public utterances like *The American Scholar* (1837) and the *Divinity School Address* (1838) lay with those who heard or later read them and then altered the way they thought and lived. Emerson essentially bequeaths his task and his nation's need to the genius not yet come:

Time and nature yield us many gifts, but not yet the timely man, the new religion, the reconciler, whom all things await. . . . Banks and tariffs, the newspaper and caucus, Methodism and Unitarianism, are flat and dull to dull people, but rest on the same foundations of wonder as the town of Troy and the temple of Delphi, and are as swiftly passing away. Our log-rolling, our stumps and their politics, our fisheries, our Negroes and Indians, our boasts and our repudiations, the wrath of rogues and the pusillanimity of honest men, the northern trade, the southern planting, the western clearing, Oregon and Texas, are yet unsung. Yet America is a poem in our eyes; its ample geography dazzles the imagination, and it will not wait long for metres.

Emerson published *The Poet* in 1844. One year later, on July 4, the birthday of national independence, Henry David Thoreau began the venture in spiritual independence that led to *Walden.* Ten years later, Whitman published *Leaves of Grass.* Each drew directly on Emerson's thought, and each, like Emerson's Dante, "dared to write his autobiography in colossal cipher, or into universality" to express an America as complex and fluid as the self he evoked, an America whose strong destiny the expansive ambition of Jacksonianism would label "manifest."

Certainly, when Henry David Thoreau began building a cabin near Concord on Emerson's fourteen acres at Walden Pond, many must have recalled Emerson's *Self-Reliance,* and Thoreau himself would see his two-year adventure on the pond's shore as a westward quest for the Emersonian self:

I went to the woods because I wished to live deliberately, to front only the essential facts of life, and see if I could not learn what it had to teach, and not, when I came to die, discover that I had not lived. I did not wish to live what was not life, living is so dear; nor did I wish to practice resignation, unless it was quite necessary. I wanted to live deep and suck out all the marrow of life, to live so sturdily and Spartan-like as to put to rout all that was not life, to cut a broad swath and shave close, to drive life into a corner, and reduce it to its lowest terms.

The only one of the transcendentalists actually born in Concord, Thoreau, after a ministerial training, chose a life of what he called "excursions"—schoolteacher, surveyor, handyman, student of nature. His writing was itself such an "excursion," a journey to the center of life; as he said, he traveled much in Concord. His *Journals* (fourteen volumes, 1906, posthumous), his letters and verses, articles and speeches, and his two published books, *A Week on the Concord and Merrimack Rivers* (1849) and *Walden* (1854), represent the epitome of Emersonian independence. Written with salty Yankee wit, drawing on etymological puns to force us through the appearance of words and things to the only reality that signifies, they show he was a poet to the marrow. He wrote few good verses, but he approached language and the building of a book the way a genuine Romantic poet does. *Walden* is an experience, as well as a description of one. Thoreau insists that we learn from him but rejects any direct attempt to follow his particular path from cabin to pond; he had cabin and pond, we have *Walden*.

Some critics have seen Thoreau solely in the shadow of Emerson's originality, the agent of Emerson's conception; but this easy dichotomy ignores the complexity of his writing. Indeed we have only to compare Emerson's "The Apology" (1846) with Thoreau's prose to see the distance come:

> Think me not unkind and rude
>> That I walk alone in grove and glen;
> I go to the god of the wood
>> To fetch his word to men.
>
> Tax not my sloth that I
>> Fold my arms beside the brook;
> Each cloud that floated in the sky
>> Writes a letter in my book. . . .

Emerson is simply not his own poet; he is still meter-making and fixing the symbol into discursive statement. Thoreau is defining, refining experience. Through successive versions *Walden* changed; Thoreau the naturalist and Thoreau the transcendental scout reporting from the bush disappeared before the artist exercising elaborate tonal and structural control. In fact we cannot take the simplest word of *Walden* for granted. The "I" of the first page is Thoreau the woodsman, the student of society and his own soul, but also Thoreau the artist, manipulating and coloring the woodsman's experience. We look through this "I" as Thoreau looked through his pond—which is indeed a pond but also a mirror to the depths of the soul (and both, he hints, might be bottomless) and to the endless reaches of the heavens overhead. Eventually we come to see all that Thoreau claims for his pond he claims also for his book. His "I" is our "eye," and our gaze will not be true until we find the pond itself lying between the covers of *Walden*.

The book Thoreau describes writing at Walden Pond was not *Walden* but *A Week on the Concord and Merrimack Rivers*. He published this in 1849 in 1,000 copies largely at his own expense. Four years later he was forced to undertake storage of the remaining 706: "I have now a library of nearly nine hundred volumes, over seven hundred of which I wrote myself. It is not well that the author should behold the fruits of his labor?" It has reasonably been surmised that the failure of *A Week* generated the artistic complexity of *Walden*. In no position to publish, Thoreau went on reading sections of his new book to friends and rearranging passages to heighten their effect until publication became possible. Thus, in the book that gradually took shape, the materials of memory were so transformed by imagination that they became parable, or what Thoreau called "scripture." His churchgoing neighbors would have been appalled by the claim, as they were at his familiar reference to the Bible as an "old book" in no way differing from the Vedas. In *Walden,* simple narrative is persistently lifted and transformed by its context. Part of this effect lies in the narrator's own persona—in the complex way his voice colors details with an irony that doubles the freight of each statement or a wit that moves us instantly from beachcomber voice to sage. But equally important is the role assigned to the reader. Most of us are like the text's John Farmer, with commitments and responsibilities which make the path to the pond inaccessible. But that path was for Thoreau's sole use anyway, not for us, and he has abandoned it himself now that it has grown too familiar for his purpose. Yet, by joining John Farmer in the appropriate cleansing rituals and listening for the beckoning sound of the flute (that Thoreau did play), we, too, as poor students and true readers, can visit Walden Pond.

Walden is not a place of total solitude. The railroad runs by it, society is close. Where Emerson was a retiring man and a largely theoretical lover of nature ("Be careful daddy, or you'll dig your leg," his son cried out as he worked in his garden), Thoreau savored the material world, as he did the social one. While Emerson risked his limbs digging his garden, Thoreau stood in ponds up to his nose observing insects and Whitman walked the Manhattan streets hungrily digesting the tangible life he found there. It is in the complex relations between the inward self and the outward world in all its complexity that Thoreau shows his force; he experienced the material world in his very efforts to interpret and thereby transcend it. In many ways a private man ("Take Thoreau's arm?" a friend once said, "I'd as soon grasp the limb of a tree"), his prickly independence drove him to a public life and public actions Emerson could only commit to his journal. The relation between self and community, coming in and going out, the single separate person and the *en masse,* as Whitman put it, were a lasting transcendental question. Thoreau was no communitarian like Ripley or Bronson Alcott, but he engaged the community. An abolitionist, he spoke out for John Brown; when the Mexican War burdened his conscience, he spent a night in jail rather than pay taxes for its support. Like similar events in reformist New England, this act became a symbolic statement: when asked why he was behind bars, Thoreau wondered why any decent man was outside, supporting an unjust state. In another emblematic gesture, he declared his wish to resign from all the institutions he could not remember having joined. The most durable impact transcendentalism made on social action followed Thoreau's "Civil Disobedience" (1849); it guided Mahatma Gandhi's campaign of passive resistance to British rule in India and the tactics of civil disobedience used against racial discrimination and the Vietnam War in the 1960s.

Thoreau was also a poet, often, as in "The Inward Morning" (1842), one of considerable moral power. But he was no more the great poet Emerson was summoning than was Jones Very, the best of the New England transcendentalist poets. Rather, Thoreau was the symbolist Emerson could only describe, seeing simultaneously the thing before him and the spiritual analogue he held equally real. He was the adventurous pioneer who turned woods and pond into a frontier of the spirit. It was left to Walt Whitman to explore that larger mingling of individual and community, those larger passages of travel and expansive motions of American life that would make the United States itself the greatest poem and Whitman its summoned poet. The connection was clear: "I was simmering, simmering, simmering; Emerson brought me to the boil," Whitman would say. When he sent out copies of his *Leaves of Grass,* Whittier threw his into the study fire. Emily Dickinson would not read it: "I . . . was told that he was disgraceful." Holmes wrote in the *Atlantic Monthly* that Whitman's "rhapsodies" were "figures played upon a big organ which has been struck by lightning." But Emerson responded passionately and impulsively, acknowledging the new book with a remarkable letter:

> I am not blind to the worth of the wonderful gift of "Leaves of Grass." I find it the most extraordinary piece of wit and wisdom that America has yet contributed. I am very happy in reading it, as great power makes us happy. . . . I give you joy of your free and brave thought. I have great joy in it. I find incomparable things said incomparably well, as they must be. I find the courage of treatment that so delights us, and which large perception only can inspire. I greet you at the beginning of a great career. . . .

It is tempting to see these three writers as a single identity: Emerson the thinker, Thoreau the bold experimenter in life's living, Whitman the singer and seer. But if this clarifies, it also simplifies, for each man was truly his own. Perhaps they might better be distinguished by their attitude toward Nature, Emerson's great hieroglyph and the primary reference point for almost all Romantic artists. Emerson—despite his insistence that the world was real and not the shadow of ideas—remained closest to philosophical idealism and the spirit of Kant. Thoreau expressed a far more direct contact with the natural world, and his best writing holds on to it with the transcendentalist's characteristic bifocal vision. Whitman always retained a transcendentalist mysticism and a belief in nature as force and source, but the mysterious value of life lay finally in what he directly felt and saw. Words and vision coincided and so his long continuous poem is open-ended and cumulative—a comprehensive, cataloging, unpunctuated "word-book," as he called it, whose omnivorous pages could encompass, as we shall see, the leaves of grass and the leaves of books, stasis and change, the shifting progress of America from rural to urban industrial nation.

·IV·

Today it is clear to us that one essential service Emerson performed for American writing was to release the power of symbolism and thereby transform much subsequent thought and poetry. But he was not the only poetic revolutionary of his time to perform that task; nor was his the only way to perform it. When the French symbolist poets of the middle and later nineteenth century discovered an American source for their sense of art's power, it was not to Emerson they looked but to Edgar Allan Poe—a writer for whom nature provided none of the emblematic security Emerson could find in it. Like Emerson, Poe is a poet of mental adventure; like him, he is in a fashion a transcendentalist, seeing reason pointing the way beyond itself through intuition and imagination. It was the sense of what lay beyond that made Emerson and Poe so different and transformed the entire nature and sensibility of the quest. What to Emerson gave order to Poe gave disorder; where Emerson discerned Over-Soul or cosmic force, Poe saw a more thanatogenic entity, an elusive beauty, a "never-to-be-imparted secret, whose attainment is destruction," as his narrator puts it in "MS. Found in a Bottle." If Emerson's was the affirmative, Poe's was the decadent imagination. Poetry led not to Orphic truth, "new light and power," but into the inverted, labyrinthine world of the imagination which disinvests the concrete world of its materiality while offering no secure and redemptive mystery beyond. From the start, the optimism of American transcendentalist symbolism had its inversion in a poet who suffered neglect and abuse in his lifetime and after it, whose voice has always seemed not only perverse but frequently insecure, yet whose importance is now quite unmistakable.

It was, aptly enough, in posthumous form, in the essay "The Poetic

Principle," published in 1850, one year after his tragically early death, that Poe summed up the principles of his entire writing life. They were symbolist principles:

> We have taken it into our heads that to write a poem simply for the poem's sake, and to acknowledge such to have been our design, would be to confess ourselves radically wanting in the true Poetic dignity and force:—but the simple fact is, that, would we but permit ourselves to look into our own souls, we should immediately there discover that under the sun there neither exists nor *can* exist any work more thoroughly dignified—more supremely noble than this very poem—this poem *per se*—this poem which is a poem and nothing more—this poem written solely for the poem's sake.

Poetic meaning is located in the poem's own composition and utterance, not in an exterior referential truth. In this Poe was wholly out of tune with New England. He did not share its epochal note—"The truth is, I am heartily sick of this life and of the nineteenth century in general," says the narrator of "Some Words with a Mummy"; "I am convinced that every thing is going wrong." And he certainly did not share what he called its "heresy of *The Didactic*," which was one thing that did unite Longfellow and Emerson:

> It has been assumed, tacitly and avowedly, directly and indirectly, that the ultimate object of all Poetry is Truth. Every poem, it is said, should inculcate a moral; and by this moral is the poetical merit of the work to be adjudged.

Neither Emerson nor the Schoolroom Poets could accept Poe's counterthesis, the fundamental incompatibility between beauty and truth. He aimed, on good Romantic premises, to assault the insistent American union of the aesthetic and the moralistic that obstructed the free enterprise of the imagination. To pursue this hazardous enterprise was to celebrate the aesthetic centrality of the individual symbol: poetry was itself and could be nothing else. As for Emersonian Nature, that was both independent of human life and lacking in poetic guidance: "no position can be attained on the wide surface of the *natural* earth, from which an artistical eye, looking steadily, will not find matter of offence in what is termed the 'composition of the landscape.' "

Poe, in short, embraced not Romantic affirmation but Romantic agony, the separation of art and nature. Everything about his short unhappy life must have confirmed him in this attitude. He was, as it happens, born in Boston, very much by chance, for he was the son of a traveling actress. The bohemian background stuck, for though he was to sign his first book of poems "By a Bostonian," that was half-disguise; he would always quarrel with the place he called "Frog-pondium" and thereby tarnish the contemporary literary reputation he would have liked to win there. When his father disappeared and his mother died, he was adopted as an infant in Richmond, Virginia, and so became a Southerner. These origins seem more consistent with his often aristocratic literary temper, especially since we have learned to associate "Southern Gothic" with historical and social pain. But Poe's gothic spirit comes less from a regional awareness than from a perpetual sense of psychic and geographical estrangement. Indeed his writing seems finally to come from writing itself; his works, like those of Brockden Brown, displace their environment, staking all on the fantasizing process and the refinement of the imaginative power up to and beyond the point of hallucination.

Poe's upbringing was that of the insecure gentleman; he had a period of schooling in England, a year at the University of Virginia ending in bad debts, a spell at West Point Military Academy ending in dismissal. He published poems and wrote for magazines and became editor of the *Southern Literary Messenger* in Richmond. Married to his fourteen-year-old cousin Virginia, he moved north to New York in 1837, to edit, write and make a living in the practical world of "our anti-romantic national character." But he had great difficulty in attracting the attention of the American public; it did not help that he despised it. At forty, he was found dying penniless in a Baltimore gutter. Whitman, one of the few at his grave, spoke of his poetry as "lurid dreams." The controversy which had run through his life managed to outlast his death, for his literary executor, Rufus Griswold, maliciously portrayed him as a depraved, neurotic, indeed satanic figure.

In all this he was the exemplary *poète maudit,* with displacement his home. He had always emphasized his own anonymity, obscurity or aristocracy and cultivated confusion about his background and age. He likewise enfolded the source and the very tone of his work in mystery. His poetry and fiction arise from an inwardly constructed and mentally anguished landscape, far from familiarity, nature and society in any conventional form. His poems and stories voyage, but rarely across flat surfaces: they go above, below, down into the maelstrom, out beyond the grave. Reality is not framed; nothing separates the self and what it sees. The egotistical narrators seem psychotic and divided—as Larzer Ziff puts it, "A Poe character is never more insane than at the moment he begins to reason with us," for reason is not the governor of excess. The visual eye opens on terror and deception, what the storyteller of "A Descent into the Maelstrom" (1841) calls "the wild bewildering sense of *the novel* which confounds the beholder." Dream situations and dream functions dominate everywhere. And if for Poe there is an excitement in the American landscape as it opens westward in "The Journal of Julius Rodman" (1840) or to the sea in his one novel, *Narrative of Arthur Gordon Pym* (1838), familiar sources—the maps of reason, travel memoirs, scientific reports or logbooks—turn into journals of obsession. "For the bright side of the painting I had very little sympathy," Pym says of sea narratives,

> My visions were of shipwreck and famine; of death or captivity among barbarian hordes; of a lifetime dragged out in sorrow and tears, upon some grey and desolate rock, in an ocean unapproachable and unknown. Such visions of desires—for they amounted to desires—are common, I have since been assured, to the whole numerous race of the melancholy among men.

Poe began his career with poetry. His sure voice and insistent theme—the systematic search for a supernal beauty lying both beyond and at odds with the phenomenal or noumenal world—is clear in his 1831 volume of new and revised *Poems* with its preface defending "music" and "indefiniteness" in poems like "To Helen" and "Israfel." "With me poetry has been not a purpose, but a passion," he declared in the preface to *The Raven and Other Poems* (1845). By now he was exploring more intensely the extraordinary dislocated and surreal landscape he calls up in "Dream-land," and "ultimate dim Thule," which is "out of SPACE—out of TIME." There was also some greater reaching toward popularity. "The Raven" was widely read—and much parodied—in part because of its insistent musicality:

Once upon a midnight dreary, while I pondered, weak and weary,
Over many a quaint and curious volume of forgotten lore—
While I nodded, nearly napping, suddenly there came a tapping,
As of some one gently rapping, rapping at my chamber door.
" 'Tis some visitor," I muttered, "tapping at my chamber door—
Only this and nothing more."

Similar musicality and strong narrative line mark much of his later verse like "Ulalume," and "The Bells"—which earned him Emerson's dismissal as "the jingle man." These poems are primarily efforts to define the position of the poet and evoke the supernal mysteries of death and the unknown; they all reflect the metaphysical speculation that peaked in his discursive explanation of the universe, *Eureka* (1848). The musicality itself owes its presence to Poe's poetical theory of transcendence, his endeavor to subvert the didactic: beauty being an "*indefinite*" or nondidactic pleasure, it must be achieved through "*in*definite sensations—to which end music is an essential, since the comprehension of sweet sound is our most indefinite conception."

The consistent intention thus remains throughout the pursuit of transcendental beauty:

We would define in brief the Poetry of words as the *Rhythmical Creation of Beauty*. Beyond the limits of Beauty its province does not extend. Its sole arbiter is Taste. With the Intellect or with the Conscience it has only collateral relations. It has no dependence, unless incidentally, upon either Duty or Truth. . . . If our suggestions are truthful, then "after many days" shall they be understood as truth, even though found in contradiction of *all* that has been hitherto so understood.

This is Coleridgean (a poem is "opposed to a work of science by having, for its *immediate* object, pleasure, not truth"), as is, indeed, that constant speculation about the nature of poetry which made Poe a fascinating symbolist theorist and analyst of the creative process. It is characteristic that having written "The Raven," Poe would offer an analysis of its compositional process. "The Philosophy of Composition" (1846) purports to "detail, step by step, the processes" by which the poem "attained its ultimate point of completion." To counteract the usual Romantic image of composition as "a species of fine frenzy," Poe promises

> a peep behind the scenes, at the elaborate and vacillating crudities of thought—at the true purposes seized only at the last moment —at the innumerable glimpses of idea that arrived not at the maturity of full view—at the fully matured fancies discarded in despair as unmanageable—at the cautious selections and rejections—at the painful erasures and interpolations—in a word, at the wheels and pinions—the tackle for scene-shifting—the step-ladders and demon traps—the cock's feathers, the red paint and the black patches, which, in ninety-nine cases out of the hundred, constitute the properties of the literary *histrio*.

The result is an extraordinary view of the writer's workshop that is itself as much a tale of ratiocination as his own "The Murders in the Rue Morgue," a discussion of "The Raven" designed "to render it manifest that no one point in its composition is referable either to accident or intuition—that the work proceeded, step by step, to its completion with the precision and rigid consequence of a mathematical problem."

That "The Raven" was actually written according to the blueprint described is unlikely. The author of "The Philosophy of Composition" is rather another of Poe's manic narrators, like the teller of "The Fall of the House of Usher," trying to order and systematize the processes of unreason. Poe appears to be determining causes and principles from results, though we know they were appropriate principles for him. Thus he argues that because poems depend on intensity of effect, they should be short, "the limit of a single sitting"; hence the "proper" length for his intended poem should be "about one hundred lines. It is, in fact, a hundred and eight." The end of poetry is the contemplation of the beautiful; the highest manifestation of beauty is associated with sadness; "Melancholy is thus the most legitimate of all the poetic tones." To produce it, he "betook myself to ordinary induction," resolved on a reiterated refrain, determined to keep it to one word, chose the bird and the word it would utter, "sonorous and susceptible of protracted emphasis. . . . These considerations inevitably led me to the long *o* as the most sonorous vowel, in connection with *r* as the most producible consonant." Hence a raven monotonously repeating the word "Nevermore." And what was the most universally melancholy topic? Death.

> "And when," I said, "is this most melancholy of topics most poetical?" From what I have already explained at some length, the answer, here also, is obvious—"When it most closely allies itself to *Beauty:* the death, then, of a beautiful woman is, unquestionably, the most poetical topic in the world."

It has not gone unnoticed that the outcome of his entire logic of composition produces one poem and one poem only: the one he wrote. But the importance of the piece is its penetration of the poetic process and its protagonist: the writer himself, in his imaginative quest for meaning and signification.

Here, too, "The Philosophy of Composition" resembles one of Poe's own short stories, the form he began exploring with such originality in the early 1830s. Like his poems, they too record adventures of the imagination, tales in which, again and again, his narrator or narrators press onward, whether as passive wills or apparently rational interpreters, beyond the world of reason toward a dark melancholic beauty close to death, or—in "Berenice" (1835), "Ligeia" (1838) or "The Fall of the House of Usher" (1839)—through an elaborate decadent economy beyond it, to touch the supernal world across the grave. Some are "ratiocinative" tales displaying the logical powers, the exercise of deductive skills that provided the model—with works like "The Murders in the Rue Morgue" (1841) and "The Purloined Letter" (1845)—for the modern detective story. "The mental features discoursed of as analytical . . . are always to their possessor, when inordinately possessed, a source of the liveliest enjoyment," begins the first of these, opening three full pages devoted to an analysis of analysis: "As the strong man exults in his physical ability, delighting in such exercises as call his muscles into action, so glories the analyst in that moral activity which *disentangles*." This ratiocinative narrator is everywhere in Poe's prose and makes it unmistakable. The discrimination of faculties, the competences as well as the consequences of psychological awareness, are a persistent concern. Yet the rational analytical narrator has his adversary, or else is his *own* adversary: in "William Wilson" (1839) the central character is challenged by a double exactly like himself. In the best-known tale of all, "The Fall of the House of Usher," the narrator, a man of reason and analysis, enters a world where veils gradually fall until everything is inverted and even the house follows its mirror image into the tarn.

Poe's "mathematical" or "ratiocinative" intuitionalism consistently uses scientific methodology to quarrel with science. His conception of common sense is not Common Sense, the Lockean heritage; ratiocination is a reformed logic always inwardly in dispute with its scientific aims. In the stories of ratiocination, intuitional logic may order disorder; in the tales of terror, of "the grotesque and arabesque," the reverse commonly occurs—logic and sense face their obverse in mystery, depression of soul, madness or death. They press beyond the borders of the faculties and senses, through new senses of melancholy or dread, through synaesthesia and sensual multiplication toward the transcendent *and* morbid mystery of the beautiful. Such a quest required its own landscape of terror, which came, Poe said, not from Germany but the soul. "I deduced this terror only from its legitimate sources, and urged it only to its legitimate results."

Yet it was, in fact, the Germany of Tieck and Hoffmann, the England of decadent aristocracy and moldering houses, the sinister Paris landscapes of Eugène Sue, that provided the distant settings he needed for tales like "The Fall of the House of Usher," "William Wilson" or "The Murders in the Rue Morgue." Discarding the properties of American space and time, the tales and poems seek an imaginary world in which to function. Thus they, too, refuse that employment of familiar American life Emerson demanded. Here then was an essential difference: for Poe, the imagination held rich symbolizing potential, but it led toward obscurity and solitude. Transcendentalism's natural supernaturalism, its need to sacramentalize the visible and ordinary, was not Poe's way. His heritage stems rather from

Brockden Brown: the imagination needs a landscape all its own to lay bare its own paths of discovery, its primal principles of composition.

If, for modern readers, Poe—the author whose grave went without a tombstone for twenty-six years—now seems the classic writer of American Romantic decadence and the source of an essential tradition in the American imagination, that is belated acknowledgment. If he has subsequently won major recognition in at least three roles—as deep, troubling poet, significant symbolist theorist and major originator of the modern short story—he remained unappreciated in his own day and was long to seem to many Americans a curiously European writer; he was indeed adopted as such by Baudelaire and the French symbolists. Certainly even the best of his poems and stories often seem superficial, though their meanings go deep. Often they are offered to us as hoaxes or literary mysteries; but they also enfold mysteries, leading us into the realms of a hallucination where reason fractures into psychic release and the world breaks open inside and outside the self. One of Poe's most disordered tales is his only novel, *Narrative of Arthur Gordon Pym* (1838). Presented as a hoax, dismissed by Poe himself as "a very silly book," it seems today one of his most significant works. This story of a sea voyage to the last *terra incognita,* the Antarctic, prefigures the obsessive, deranged and melancholic quest of Melville's Ahab, another traveler from Nantucket. Like Melville's tale, it drives deep into the dark vortex of the world, to "the embraces of the cataract, where the chasm threw itself open to receive us." Making its way there through mysteries and hieroglyphs with rich potential for interpretation, it offers no answers. At the end of the journey is the white, blanked symbol of incomprehensible death. One of Poe's most troubling works, *Pym* is also his furthest outreaching toward the elusive, morbid symbol of supernal transcendence so alluring to Romantic artists, despite its dark terror. Emerson is transcendentalism in its clear-glass face, its clarity. Poe is transcendentalism in the dark obscurity which, as Melville was to say, no honest student of life can deny.

CHAPTER

° 5 °

YEA-SAYING AND NAY-SAYING

· I ·

"The age of the first person singular" was Emerson's name for the key period in American culture he so gladly announced and so proudly celebrated. These pre–Civil War decades were an age of the prophet and an age of the poet, and often the two seemed indistinguishable. Ringing transcendentalist sermons like Emerson's statement of new faith in "The Divinity School Address" (1838) or Theodore Parker's "The Transient and Permanent in Christianity" (1841) showed how much the Protestant tradition was changing. Much of the new prophecy came in verse: Whittier's impassioned antislavery poetry, Jones Very's high-toned mysticism (Very briefly believed himself the Messiah returned), Poe's hunger to be the Shelleyan poet, "unacknowledged legislator of the world," were typical of the times. The self rode high, and a title like Whitman's "Song of Myself" was a natural product of the individualism and self-reliance celebrated by transcendentalism. Essential to its appeal was that it spoke of breaking with the past, beginning anew, reaching to the future and the age of untried possibilities; and that discovering sense of self, that new sense of the possible, fit perfectly with the expanding territory and aspiration abroad in the nation. Transcendentalism may have been born in the economic panic of 1837, but it surged in the confident years when America's material face was transforming, its map of land and resources enlarging, its cities growing, immigration booming, industrialism flourishing. The phrase "Manifest Destiny" helped celebrate the incorporation of Oregon, the annexation of Texas, the Mexican War, and the California Gold Rush; and the European revolutions of the 1840s made America a standard of liberty and democracy others sought to emulate.

No wonder that, within and without, Americans acquired new confidence, which their writing expressed. As James Russell Lowell put it:

> They tell us that our land was made for song
> With its huge rivers and sky-piercing peaks,
> Its sealike lakes and mighty cataracts,
> Its forests vast and hoar, and prairies wide. . . .

The times favored epic travel, sometimes inward and metaphysical (Thoreau's "I have travelled much in Concord") or outward and transcontinental. John Charles Frémont recorded *The Exploring Expedition in the Rocky Mountains* (1845) and Edwin Bryant *What I Saw in California* (1848), a literary prospecting of what would become next year's Gold Rush. The travels went, of course, westward—Margaret Fuller's *Summer on the Lakes* (1844), Francis Parkman's *The Oregon Trail* (1849)—but also eastward, in Emerson's *English Traits* (1856), Margaret Fuller's *At Home and Abroad* (1856), Hawthorne's *Our Old Home* (1863). They looked southward to Pacific paradises (Melville's *Typee*, 1846), even at the blankness of Antarctic ice (Poe's *Arthur Gordon Pym*, 1838), or northward to the Arctic (Elisha Kent Kant's *Arctic Explorations*, 1856). The travel-form became an essential type of American narrative as never before, often testing the self in new types of quest on a new continent, a vast land and seascape for the American mind to wander in—one of the fictional heroes of the age would be the wandering Ishmael who tells the story of Melville's *Moby-Dick* (1851). But the continent also raised anxious questions about guilt and sin, not least as Americans looked to the South and saw the spectacle of slavery.

For, as Emerson observed, this was a time when there was scarcely a man or a woman in New England without the plan for a new community in his or her pocket. In the North the antislavery movement spread, and abolitionists launched the Liberty Party. "God's Time is best!—nor will it long delay," pronounced William Lloyd Garrison in his poem "Universal Emancipation" in 1843. Feminism had been a rising movement in the United States from the early part of the century, but now it acquired new energy with the forceful arguments of Margaret Fuller, whose *Woman in the Nineteenth Century* appeared in 1845. Intensely active in transcendentalism, Fuller edited *The Dial* and urged the movement toward historical and political issues. Her groundbreaking discussions of women's intellectual, economic, political and sexual concerns were driven by all of her passion, high intellectual authority and polymathic reading, and they played a fundamental part in changing general attitudes. Feminism was a dominant cause of the 1840s, but in Fuller's case it was part of her general identification with the many movements of an internationally revolutionary decade, when the changing atmosphere of the nineteenth century led to the revolutionary upheavals of 1848 in Europe. Fuller identified above all with the struggle for freedom in Italy, and she began a book on Mazzini. Returning from Italy in 1850, she perished in a shipwreck, the end of a career of unmistakable power.

The new Romantic emphasis on self was often accompanied by an emphasis on society, that on nature by a concern with the state of rising industrial culture, that on yea-saying by a current of interrogation and nay-saying. "I hear the whistle of the locomotive in the woods," Emerson noted in his journal in 1842,

> wherever that music comes has its sequel. It is the voice of civility of the Nineteenth Century saying, "Here I am." It is interrogative; it is prophetic: and this Cassandra is believed: Whew! Whew! How is the real estate here in the swamp and wilderness? Ho for Boston! Whew! Whew!

Emerson was not the only one to see that the age of self-reliance was based on a decade of explosive industrial development, that the material world was not simply pristine nature. The locomotive, the machine in the garden, inserted history into the landscape and process into transcendent things. This the transcendentalists found hard to accommodate, as Emerson concluded in one of his finest poems in 1847:

> Things are in the saddle,
> And ride mankind.
>
> There are two laws discrete,
> Not reconciled,—
> Law for man, and law for thing;
> The last builds town and fleet,
> But it runs wild,
> And doth the man unking.

Though Emerson saw this tension, he held onto his organic equation—self and nature, soul and Over-Soul. Whitman saw it too, but his response was not interrogative but incorporative; he comprehended contradictions, rather than teasing himself with their conflict and ambiguity, and he nominated himself as the voice of the whole "Kosmos" ("I permit myself to speak at every hazard,/Nature without check with original energy"). But though there was, for the optimistic American mind, primal revelation to be had in modern America, and the buoyant self, the first person singular, spread like the locomotive itself across the continent, the need for interrogation and suitable articulation grew. The appropriate form for that was perhaps not the poem but the much more dialogic, interactive form of the novel.

In Europe, pressures just like these were breaking open the form of the Victorian novel as it responded to what Raymond Williams has called "a pressing and varied experience which was not yet history." A newly vivid and obsessively social fiction—Dickens, Thackeray, Mrs. Gaskell wrote it in Britain; Stendhal, Balzac, Flaubert in France; Gogol, Pushkin, Dostoevsky in Russia—was opening out to mid-century contradiction: to cities and their lower depths, to crime and poverty, to crowds, strange impressions, interweaving voices, existential solitude. It bred new grotesquerie, and the new "realism," which became a formal movement in France after 1848. But America was a land of nature; though immigrants now poured in, its cities were not dominant; though industry grew rapidly and the workplace became familiar ground, nature seemed the space to root national identity and possibility. The transcendentalist poem or essay, the travel record or the questing memoir of self seemed the ideal mode of expression, and Emerson himself never favored the novel. Even so, the great fictional drive that ran through Britain and Western Europe in the 1840s reached America, too. By mid-century America was also discovering and writing itself through the novel, above all the novel of Hawthorne and Melville. It was a fiction that appeared far less social than that of Europe: Hawthorne, who professed a distrust of "the Present, the Immediate, the Actual," called it the "Romance," and Melville said in *The Confidence Man*: "It is with fiction as with religion; it should present another world, and yet one to which we feel the tie." But the novels of both were interrogations of the real. What is more, they were also fundamental interrogations of transcendentalism.

Hawthorne and Melville were both skeptical writers, artists of an irony and detachment not always easy to follow yet essential to their literary discovery. Hawthorne lived on transcendentalism's fringes. He himself went to George Ripley's experimental transcendentalist community Brook Farm, found little creative inspiration in wheeling manure and so created the "Blithedale" of his ironic *The Blithedale Romance* (1852). He had Emerson and Thoreau for neighbors in Concord, where he lived at the Old Manse (*Mosses from an Old Manse,* 1846). Melville traveled to transcendentalist Utopias in the South Seas and explored his self-quest there in *Typee* (1846), *Omoo* (1847), *Mardi* (1849). His ship the *Pequod* in *Moby-Dick* (1851) is manned with old Calvinists and new transcendentalists. When he wrote his remarkable, admiring essay "Hawthorne and His Mosses" (1850), he saw Hawthorne, his friend-to-be, as an American as natural as Niagara; but he also identified in the recesses of the older man's writing something central: a "great power of blackness" that derives its force from "its appeals to that Calvinist sense of Innate Depravity and Original Sin, from whose visitations, in some shape or another, no thinking mind is always and wholly free." Melville was also reading his nation's Puritan legacy in himself; as Harry Levin has pointed out, in Hawthorne, Melville, Poe, blackness is a compulsive shade, and it is in their writings we find what we do not elsewhere, the turned-over, darkened face of transcendentalism, or what Melville called the power of saying "No! in thunder."

Today transcendentalism is still celebrated as the optimistic center of the American imagination, the source of its new language and vision; a recent critic, Richard Poirier, has seen Emerson as the great renewer of all literature and language, the philosopher of natural form, an art beyond artifice from which truth will emerge. If so, Hawthorne and Melville represent the testing of this metaphysic; they explore what its great Yea asserts, in texts of such complexity, such difficult reaches of sign and symbol, that we have difficulty not just in reaching to their meaning but with the very way they seek to mean. Melville, in *Pierre* (1852), declared his ideal of novels that "never unravel their own intricacies, and have no proper endings, but in imperfect, unanticipated, and disappointing sequels (as mutilated stumps) hurry to abrupt interminglings with the eternal tides of time and fate." This is a metafictional enterprise, deliberately leading us into the obscurities and uncertainties that contemporary opinion acknowledges as the basic crisis of all reading. Hawthorne and Melville disclose the American enterprise both in its transcendental and imaginative desire, and also in its fragility. Transcendentalists always questioned their literary heritage; they questioned it the more when they looked beyond the novel genre of the past to the discourse of the present. Along with Poe, they required obscurity. Hawthorne sought it by shutting himself away in an upper room of his mother's house in Salem and writing as an author without readers, like the Oberon of his "The Devil in Manuscript" (1835). Melville accepted the role of the rejected author, saying after the failure of *Mardi*: "So far as I am individually concerned & independent of my pocket, it is my earnest desire to write those sort of books which are said to 'fail.' " This was more than a willful obscurity, for it gave America what it lacked and sorely needed, a truly critical literature.

· II ·

It was exactly at mid-century, after his long obscurity, that Nathaniel Hawthorne published his most successful book, America's first undoubtedly great novel. *The Scarlet Letter* is a historical romance that takes as its focus the adulterous love between a Puritan minister and

Hester Prynne, a married member of his congregation, in the Boston of just two hundred years earlier. It is the one novel of Hawthorne's four which does not deal directly with his own time, though it deals with it indirectly: *The Scarlet Letter* is a careful measuring of the historical, religious, literary and emotional distance that separated the Puritan New England of the past from the transcendentalist New England of the present, of the change from the old "iron world" to the world of "freedom of speculation" which Hester, Hawthorne's most remarkable fictional character, embodies. Adultery is the haunting theme of mid-nineteenth-century fiction, but *The Scarlet Letter* is not really a love story. As Henry James, a direct beneficiary of Hawthorne's artistry, later put it: "To Hawthorne's imagination the fact that these two persons had loved each other too well was of an interest comparatively vulgar; what appealed to him was their moral situation in the long years that were to follow." The story starts not with the love affair itself but with its consequence—with Hester standing on Boston's public scaffold, the child of the liaison in her arms, and the red emblem of sexuality, the scarlet letter, the embroidered "A" for Adulteress, emblazoned on her breast. Hawthorne creates a conflict of nature and culture. The act of love that sanctifies itself in nature ("What we did had a consecration of its own," Hester tells the minister, Arthur Dimmesdale, in the forest) is for this culture an act of sin, requiring guilt, confession and penitence. Hawthorne called his book a "romance," but its implications are not entirely Romantic. He celebrates nature, the self that might be recovered from it and the "vital warmth" coming from the "electric chain" of true humanity. But he also acknowledges culture, the world of social existence. The novel is a tragedy of the divided claims made by the natural and the social self.

The Boston of the book is therefore not its only world. To the east is a cavalier, less rigorous social order, in Britain; to the west is the forest wilderness, a place of romantic potential and unwritten space. Yet the gray iron-bound law of Puritan society is the commanding inescapable world of the novel. Here religion and law coincide, and private action is of both public and providential concern. Just as he sets the scarlet "A" against the gray, steeple-hatted world, Hawthorne introduces other colorful emblems: beside the scaffold are both the prison, "the black flower of civilized society," and the wild rosebush, a "sweet moral blossom" betokening "the deep heart of Nature." Hester's daughter, Pearl, comes to signify natural innocence, and the forest seems to promise an Edenic release from fallen guilt and sin. Still, the Emersonian idea of the guiltless new start is not Hawthorne's. Like the Puritans, he could be a moral and providential allegorist, seeing the signs of nature and individual human acts as emblems in the world's sin-laden drama. But he persistently qualifies those meanings. Forced to wear her sign, Hester by her life amends and complicates it, turning the "A" from Adulteress to Able, to Angel, to any of several meanings available to a responsive reader. *The Scarlet Letter* can be read as a work of either allegory or symbolism. In a sense it is a work where allegory is dispersed, freed of fixed moral meanings, and then reconstituted. It is a novel of signs and symbols, concealments and revelations, hidden truths of self and expressed public utterances and confessions—and a book in which the very nature of meaning, of how we express it, what we seek from it, and why we need to do so, is a central concern.

All this is clear from the book's main story—which is not so much that of the remarkable heroine, Hester, as that of Arthur Dimmesdale, an equally remarkable portrait of a man driven by forces both conscious and unconscious from a suppressed struggle for personal morality to an outward confession and assertion. For most of the book Dimmesdale seeks to hide his sin and learn from it, believing in the rightness of his ministry, the value of holding within himself the guilt that makes him human and so capable of understanding his flock the better. The letter that Hester shows, he hides, as he seeks to read himself and not be read by others. But the sign driven inward keeps insistently manifesting itself—on his body in the form of physical stigmata which are seen and interpreted by the vengeful husband, Chillingworth, and outwardly in nature, imprinted on the heavens at night. Yet in neither self nor nature is there resolution; Dimmesdale comes to peace only when he returns to society and the daylight world and stands on the public scaffold where Hester stood, making his election sermon into a deathbed confession.

Hawthorne insisted that this was an "obscure" book, and this is so. His aim was to penetrate and articulate the deepest levels of human psychology, those levels where conscience, guilt and awareness of sin restlessly function. The subject of the book and the preoccupying interest of Hawthorne's writing is the human heart itself in its contradiction, complexity, its vital moral warmth, its need for expression. The Puritan imagination thus interested Hawthorne not just as a historical subject but because it raised the essential moral issues of his writing, indeed of his existence *as* a writer. He returned to it again and again in his stories and essays, finding his own way to write by shifting the Puritan allegorical mode away from its typological, providential meanings to a different level of human perception and artistic endeavor. The result was symbolic creation, where the moral and religious principles behind the initial allegory do not die in reductive translation but become imbued with the strange contradictions of human life; they take on uncertainty, indecipherability, ambiguity. The symbol is pluralized, moving between the public world and that of personal feeling, between the daylight of actuality, history and social iconography and the dark moonlight of the subjective imagination. The red letter functions with just this ambiguity; it is now a hieroglyph planted in the heavens, now a fixed sexual accusation, now a letter over the heart that, taken into the heart, can be transformed, and now an unmanageable psychosomatic secret. It speaks both to the social law in its fixity and to the Romantic lore of self and humanity, where it can change. It remains at no single or fixed level of literalness, nor do the book's other typological images—black and red, light and shadow, prison and flower, image and refraction. Like the letter itself, the book loses its singleness of meaning so that we need to peer vigilantly to fathom its moral, psychological and expressive mysteries.

Is it therefore not surprising that along with *The Scarlet Letter* went another story that Hawthorne had to tell—the story of the book's writing. In his "Custom-House" preface he explores not only the events that led to the writing of the book, but also his own deep, indeed Puritanic, guilt about the very act of creation—we could say that this is one implicit subject of the novel itself. Along with Poe's "Philosophy of Composition," this essay is a central American document both of creative induction and its consequential literary anxiety. Amongst other things, it suggests that his narrative springs from a particular and crucial moment in American thought and writing and from an anxious response to the claims of Romantic sensibility. Hawthorne portrays the

Salem Custom House, a *locus* of contemporary actuality and practicality where he worked as a surveyor, as the place where he finds an ambiguous embroidered letter which starts his imagination and Hester's story. This story rises from his own condition, as a man divided between a past of Puritan guilt and a present of transcendental hope and between his own subjective imagination and the daylight world of community and actuality. Unlike Poe, however, he does not see the imagination as an autonomous power; it too is touched with fallibility and the need to face what he called "the earth's doom," which is the knowledge of our participation in history and the human community. Hawthorne is even prepared to see the symbolic imagination as a form of false knowledge:

> It was a folly, with the materiality of this daily life pressing so intrusively upon me, to attempt to fling myself back into another age; or to insist on creating the semblance of a world out of airy matter. . . . The fault was mine.

In that doubt, Hawthorne was acknowledging his own Puritan inheritance and making it part of his drama. That inheritance was both destiny and stain. And both were within him. So Hawthorne (who himself added the *w* to the family name) must tease out his relation with his own antecedents. He tells us of his first American ancestor, William Hathorne, who came from Cheshire to Massachusetts amongst the earliest settlers in 1630; he has "dim and dusky grandeur," but was also a "bitter persecutor," possessing "all the Puritanic traits, both good and evil." William's son was a judge at the Salem witch trials and was thereby marked with Puritanism's own sin: the witches' blood "may fairly be said to have left a stain on him." Such guilty stains of human nature are everywhere in Hawthorne's work. They even affect and afflict those who, in the present, seek a guiltless new world composed from the transcendental power of the imagination with its image of man and history reborn; at times Hawthorne was one of these himself. Yet it is his doubt that dominates. He imagines how his "grave, bearded, sable-cloaked and steeple-crowned" progenitors would rebuke his concern with art and this obscure act of his imagination—just as, within the art, they challenged Hester's feelings of imaginative independence ("The world's law was no law for her mind"). The Puritans are his adversaries: "No aim that I have ever cherished, would they regard as laudable." But they are also his history and part of his self-doubting consciousness. Not only do they form the subject of the book; they promote the doubt about whether it should even be written, for "Let them scorn me as they will, strong traits of their nature have intertwined themselves with mine."

This self-doubting aspect of Hawthorne, so mystifying to many of his contemporaries, so familiar and modern to us, penetrated deep into the invention and writing of his narratives. Hawthorne was a man who withdrew into imagination and writerly solitude, only to suspect that this withdrawal was a social offense which produced a loss of reality and actuality in his nature. The same doubts are manifest in his view of the form he used, the very American form of "romance" which Cooper and Simms had espoused. Hawthorne explores it not for its promise but for its complexity and contradiction. It was woven, he said, in a moonlit space "somewhere between the real world and fairyland, where the Actual and the Imaginary may meet, and each imbue itself with the nature of the other." In saying this, Hawthorne was teasing at the very spirit of Romanticism and expressing a doubt about the method that was thereafter to enter the self-challenging tradition of American art. Emerson's poet was to be a seer, seeking a clear sign; but Hawthorne's artist is a creature of conscious contradictions, seeking and creating oppositions. Like many modern writers, Hawthorne was an author who would not claim authority.

It was always Hawthorne's disconcerting way to affirm, or rather half-affirm, art and the artist as being at the center of a set of dialectical contradictions—between past and present, selfhood and community, the allegorical and the symbolic, the Calvinist sense of guilt and the new transcendentalist faith in Adamic innocence, the imaginary and the actual, creation and silence. These, as he saw it, were the contradictions of his culture and his life. After the death of his father when he was four, he had grown up in a house of women in a declining Salem where the older families were losing to new wealth and Puritanism was gradually yielding to Unitarianism. He attended Bowdoin College, where he was a classmate of Longfellow, but after leaving in 1825 he retired mysteriously to the confinement of an upper room in his mother's house. His writings there were as hidden as he was. He published an early gothic novel, *Fanshawe* (1828), at his own expense, but he then sought to destroy all copies, and twenty-one years passed before he wrote another long narrative. He produced many tales, but they were published anonymously in ladies' magazines, and it was twelve years before *Twice-Told Tales* (1837) brought him out of obscurity. He then won political preferment and his first public post, in the Boston Custom House between 1839 and 1841, and he also became engaged to Sophia Peabody. He joined the communitarian experiment at Brook Farm, the Fourierist Utopia near Roxbury, but his inspiration and his hopes both failed. It was not until his marriage and the peace of the Old Manse in Concord that his imagination revived and the stories of *Mosses from an Old Manse* (1846) appeared. But income and society were still necessary, and so he took the post in the Salem Custom House that he describes in *The Scarlet Letter*. In 1851, after its success, he could still say that it was only now, "if it even yet be the case, that the Author could regard himself as addressing the American public, or, indeed, any public at all."

Yet the stories of the obscure years had displayed his uncommon talent and laid down his primary themes: the Puritan past and its ambiguous heritage ("The Maypole of Merrymount," "Endicott and the Red Cross," "The Gray Champion"), human sin and guilt ("The Minister's Black Veil," "Young Goodman Brown"), the complex deceitful messages of nature ("Roger Malvin's Burial," "Rappaccini's Daughter"), the dangerous Faustian pursuit of perfection ("The Birthmark," "The Artist of the Beautiful"). Above all they explore the complexities of isolation and the haunting need for the community of the human heart. He wrote to Longfellow that "There is no fate in this world so horrible as to have no share in its joys or sorrows" and fear of loss of contact with the warm flow of human life is everywhere in these stories. Wakefield moves around a street corner and becomes a mere spectator of the life he might have lived ("Wakefield"). Ethan Brand, like Chillingworth, pries into the secrets of another's heart and through intellectual pride commits the unpardonable sin ("Ethan Brand"). The minister who dons a black veil to remind his congregation of the depravity of human nature ("The Minister's Black Veil") suffers the same separation from his community as Goodman Brown, whose inability to accept a morally complex world completely isolates him: "They carved no hopeful verses on his tombstone, for his dying hour was gloom" ("Young Goodman Brown"). In the more frankly gothic "mad scientist" tales there is the same concern with alienation and its destructive effects. Aylmer insists on removing his wife's birthmark, both to reject the world of common imperfection and to demonstrate his own power ("The Birthmark"). And Rappaccini sacrifices his own daughter to his similar scientific obsession with defeating human mortality ("Rappaccini's Daughter").

Not surprisingly, Hawthorne was seen by most of his contemporaries as a moral allegorist. "The deepest emotion aroused within us by the happiest allegory, *as* allegory, is a very, very imperfectly satisfied sense of the writer's ingenuity in overcoming a difficulty we should have preferred his not having attempted to overcome," Poe said of him, adding, "One thing is clear, that if allegory ever establishes a fact, it is by dint of overturning a fiction." Henry James wrote an admiring study in 1879, but read the warning in his work that a moralistic tale ruined both tale and moral. It is certainly true that some of his stories, like "The Celestial Railroad" or "Egoism, or the Bosom Serpent," do come close to being fixed fables, rather than that kind of work that Emerson called "fluxional . . . vehicular and transitive." But Hawthorne often had a way of making his allegorical implications unstable; his world only seems to offer readable meanings. "The young man rejoiced that, in the heart of the barren city, he had the privilege of overlooking this spot of lovely and luxurious vegetation," we are told of the garden in "Rappaccini's Daughter"; "It would serve, he said to himself, as a symbolic language to keep him in communion with Nature." This symbolic language points to deception, however. The barren city remains around him, the garden is not God's nature at all, but Rappaccini's overreaching endeavor to constrain and improve the natural; the symbols to hand are misleading, equivocal. As in many of Melville's tales, such as the remarkable "Benito Cereno," the messages of sense are elusive. Often the stories are about symbolic *ambiguity,* the difficulty of reading signs, the duplicitous nature of most moral assertions and deductions. Hawthorne *has* a moral theme, but it is in tension with itself, disputes itself. He repeatedly exposes the fiction of his fictions, their potential for deception. Hence Emerson's complaint that he "invites his readers too much into his study, opens the process before them. As if the confectioner should say to his customers, 'Now, let us bake the cake.' "

Hawthorne everywhere reminds us that his American fiction belongs not to the world of Common Sense inquiry, but to the shifting metaphysical and metaphoric world of a troubled Romantic sensibility. The form that Brown, Cooper and Simms had initiated and celebrated poses problems that Hawthorne lays before us on the page. "When a writer calls a work a Romance," he declares in the preface to *The House of the Seven Gables* (1851),

> it need hardly be observed that he wishes to claim a certain latitude, both as to its fashion and material, which he would not have felt entitled to assume, had he professed to be writing a Novel. The latter form of composition is presumed to aim at a very minute fidelity, not merely to the possible, but to the probable and ordinary course of man's experience. The former—while, as a work of art, it must rigidly subject itself to laws, and while it sins unpardonably, so far as it may swerve aside from the truth of the human heart— has fairly a right to present that truth under circumstances, to a great extent, of the writer's own choosing or creation.

The prefaces to the four romances contain what reflection on the theory of fiction itself he has left us. In them he regularly distinguishes between his own psychological aim—what he calls, in the preface to *The Snow Image and Other Twice-Told Tales* (1851), "burrowing, to his utmost ability, into the depths of our common nature, for the purposes of psychological romance"—and the verisimilitude of everyday life he associated with the English novel. In "The Haunted Mind" he describes a half-lit region between sleeping and waking, "an intermediate space, where the passing moment lingers, and becomes truly the present; a spot where Father Time, if he thinks nobody is watching him, sits down by the wayside to take breath." Here one might touch the Unconscious: "In the depths of every heart there is a tomb and a dungeon, though the lights, the music, and the revelry above may cause us to forget their existence, and the buried ones, or prisoners, whom they hide." That this is a world of pure fantasy the modern reader, used to psychological fiction, will doubt; it is part of Hawthorne's modernity. But Hawthorne presents it with anxiety because the daylight world of social verisimilitude *did* concern him.

This conflict provides the tension of *The House of the Seven Gables*. One of Hawthorne's most realistic fictions, it deals with contemporary experience and the demands of history as a process requiring commitment to the obligations of the present. One of its central figures is that most supreme of literalists, the daguerreotypist Holgrave, in whom the demands of the present and those of realism coincide. He is Hawthorne's figure of modern man, an image of Emersonian self-reliance who aggressively rejects the past, seeing it lying on the present like a giant's dead body. He raises some of Hawthorne's key questions: has the present the right or power to set itself free from the past? And is true life the life of the material world, or is there another life of the imagination that feeds on things beyond time? Hawthorne's own uncertainties are evident in his portrait of Holgrave:

> Altogether in his culture and his want of culture, in his crude, wild, and misty philosophy and the practical experience that counteracted some of its tendencies; in his magnanimous zeal for man's welfare, and his recklessness of whatever the ages had established on man's behalf; in his faith, and his infidelity; in what he had and what he lacked—the artist might fitly enough stand forth as the representative of many compeers in his native land.

In the year of Emerson's *Representative Men*, it is clear what Holgrave represents; Hawthorne sets against him the Pynchon brother and sister from an older and simpler economy, the two owls fleeing into a world where history is a process—like the train that takes them to the lonely station with its broken church. But Hawthorne suggests reconciliation by bringing together Holgrave and the innocent Phoebe, the democratic present and the hereditary, Puritan past. Holgrave, resisting the temptation to violate Phoebe's trust, throws off the Puritan curse, Maule's curse, which *his* Puritan ancestors have handed down through their "adamant" disregard for the inner life of others.

This conflict of romance and realism became Hawthorne's subject. In *The Blithedale Romance* (1852) the Blithedale community is itself a romance. It is a version of Arcadian pastoral where, as Hawthorne says in his customary third-person preface, his aim was "to establish a theatre, a little removed from the highway of ordinary travel, where the creatures of his brain may play their phantasmagoric antics, without exposing them to too close a comparison with the actual events of real lives." Hawthorne's concern is the fruits of human pride and isolation—shown in the self-insulating zeal of the utilitarian prison reformer Hollingsworth, the overimpassioned feminism of the misled Zenobia (based on Margaret Fuller), the detached voyeurism of the narrator, Miles Coverdale. This is the one book where Hawthorne uses a self-ironizing narrator other than himself; Coverdale, insipid and self-doubting, peering at others from tree branches and through apartment windows, is an unreliable storyteller and a forerunner of the deceptive narrator of many modern novels. He both interprets the story and, as a "Minor Poet," illustrates Hawthorne's theme of destructive separation from the warm life of others. *Blithedale* is a work of disturbed pastoral, of Utopian ironies, an ironic comedy with a tragic outcome.

The quest for the guilt and sin secreted in the American Utopia was one Hawthorne took with him when he sailed to Europe in 1853 to become, through government patronage, American Consul in Liverpool. His characteristic ambivalence is recorded in *Our Old Home* (1863), a nonfictional work largely derived from his *English Notebooks* (1870, 1942, posthumous) which dwells on the traditional claim of England on the American imagination but also on differences—the ordinariness of the familiar American world, the value of American moral clarity and simplicity. Hawthorne explored what Henry James called the "complex fate" of being an American heir to European culture in three English romances, *Septimius Felton* (1872), *Dr. Grimshawe's Secret* (1883) and *The Ancestral Footstep* (1883), all left unfinished at his death. Once again it was only by rejecting government office that he could write, and in 1857 he left England to live among American artists in Rome and Florence. His fourth full-length narrative, *The Marble Faun* (1860), is set in Rome. It is his most aesthetic romance, perhaps his riskiest—the book in which he makes his most intent inquiry into art's dark ambiguities while still suspecting that all such inquiry might be a cardinal sin, part of that dispassionate observation which is art's moral crime. Rome, the city of Catholicism, corruption and art, embodies the book's controlling problem. The "central clime, whither the eyes and heart of every artist turn," it is also crime-haunted and malarial. Holding the Arcadian promise of an unfallen classical world, it is now degenerate and marked with "the smell of ruin and decaying generations." The metaphoric center of all this is Hawthorne's extraordinary creation, Donatello, the "faun" who is brought from a classical and Arcadian world into an age of moral corruption and degeneracy, there to reenact mankind's primal fall.

One of the sadnesses of *The Marble Faun* is that it seems like a farewell to art. By the end of it, rites of innocence and experience have been performed, but the pressing American question of whether man can escape his fall is left unresolved, to pass on to the unfinished questionings of Melville's *Billy Budd, Foretopman* (1924, posthumous). Hawthorne has faced the decadent consideration that art's very power of penetration into the sinful, the corrupt and the unknown brings it into dangerous intimacies. His uncertainty on the outcome enters into the preface, where he reflects for the last time on the difficulties of romance, especially the American romance, written about a country

> where there is no shadow, no antiquity, no mystery, no picturesque
> and gloomy wrong, nor anything but a commonplace prosperity
> in broad and simple daylight, as is happily the case with my dear
> native land. It will be very long, I trust, before romance writers
> may find congenial and easily handled themes, either in the annals
> of our stalwart republic, or in any characteristic and probable
> events of our individual lives. Romance and poetry, ivy, lichens,
> and wall-flowers, need ruin to make them grow.

A strange irony now haunts the catalogue already familiar from Irving and Cooper; America is reconstituted as the land of artlessness, the artist still a stranger, but the very intensity of human knowledge that Hawthorne had pursued through romance is somehow denied to his homeland. Clearly he feared to the end the direction in which full artistic immersion was tugging him. The fears intensified when he returned to the United States in 1860 to find civil war brewing. His abhorrence of war as an instrument of reform made him want to protest; he also felt American innocence slipping away, and with it his own creative powers. Art and reality now disappointed alike; after he died, aged sixty, in 1864, Emerson commented in his journal on the final sadness of Hawthorne's "painful solitude . . . which, I suppose, could not longer be endured."

· III ·

In the event, Hawthorne's part in the extraordinary fictional upsurge of the American 1850s was to extend well beyond the pages of his own work. One year after *The Scarlet Letter* there appeared the fictional masterwork of nineteenth-century America: Herman Melville published *Moby-Dick; or, The Whale* (1851), a novel in whose origins Hawthorne had played a significant part. Its dedication reads

> In Token
> Of my Admiration for His Genius
> *This Book is Inscribed*
> To
> NATHANIEL HAWTHORNE.

Behind this acknowledgment lay a striking connection between the two men. They had met in the Berkshires after Melville had printed "Hawthorne and His Mosses" (1850), where he had declared "great geniuses are part of the times, they themselves are the times, and possess a corresponding color"; his claim for Hawthorne is as sweeping as anything in Emerson, yet another American Renaissance claim for the power of a man, a moment and a nation. The essay's nationalism stems partly from indignation at his century's preference for British authors, a preference Melville himself had suffered: "Let America first praise mediocrity even, in her children, before she praises . . . the best excellence of the children of other lands." Sydney Smith's jibe of thirty years before—"Who reads an American book?"—still rankled. So it is the mighty Shakespeare that Melville sets at Hawthorne's side:

> Some may start to read of Shakespeare and Hawthorne on the same page. . . . But Shakespeare has been approached. There are minds that have gone as far as Shakespeare into the universe. . . . Believe me, my friends, that men not very much inferior to Shakespeare,

are this day being born on the banks of the Ohio. And the day will come, when you shall say who reads a book by an Englishman that is a modern?

Melville's Hawthorne has a "black conceit" that "pervades him through and through," a "blackness ten times black"; a writer of obscurity misunderstood as "a man who means no meanings," he is actually "deep as Dante" with a "great, deep intellect, which drops down into the universe like a plummet." This view of Hawthorne is close to many modern readings of him, but in describing Hawthorne Melville was clearly intent on picturing himself. Hawthorne is "the divine magnet" to whom "my magnet responds," he explained in the admiring, thoughtful correspondence that now followed. Yet his letters to the more famous writer and new friend reveal a fear that his own writing will not be understood. Both the essay and the letters are displays of Melville's own sense of flowering genius, intimations of the grand scale, discursive, dramatic and tragic, of the masterpiece he was planning, testaments to the process of conception and reconception that would take it down to the heart of things: "I feel I am now come to the inmost leaf of the bulb." In fact, as Melville later indicates in his elegiac poem "Monody," the two men's tempers never quite matched—Hawthorne never did wholly share Melville's intensity and tragic sense. After the strained ambiguities of *Pierre* (1852), the friendship began to cool, but it had nevertheless been one of those seminal literary relationships based on a primal shock of recognition. It nourished the essential spirit, the lightness and also the darkness, the symbolic inclination and the philosophical scope of *Moby-Dick*, the one work of Melville's that succeeds in dramatizing an Emersonian scale of vision wrestling in self-questioning irony with the fundamental obscurity of life's meaning.

Perhaps it was this shared sense of obscure meanings, philosophical and social, that brought the men together. Melville had been born in New York City of rooted and distinguished stock: the Calvinist Melvilles of Boston, the Dutch Reform Gansevoorts of Albany. But in 1830, when he was 11, his businessman father went bankrupt and soon died mad from worry and overwork. Melville always saw himself as an economic orphan, a displaced person thrown into a harsh world of alienating social forces. His male central characters usually move from deprivation into some hard rite of passage—the most famous of them all takes the name of the classic wanderer: "Call me Ishmael," begins *Moby-Dick*. Working as bank-clerk, salesman, farmhand, schoolteacher, Melville became an Ishmael. The economic panic of 1837 sent him shipping as a cabin boy on a voyage from New York to Liverpool, the bleak experience behind *Redburn* (1849). His exploration of the American land frontier down the Erie Canal and the Mississippi led to *The Confidence-Man* (1857), and clerking in a New York bank helped with his most Dickensian story, "Bartleby the Scrivener" (1853), with its famous dissent: "I would prefer not to." In 1841 he sailed as seaman aboard the whaler *Acushnet* on a long voyage into the Pacific; when he jumped ship in the Marquesas Islands he found the alternative primitive world he portrayed in *Typee: A Peep at Polynesian Life* (1846), his first book. He joined an Australian ship, where mutiny on board led to imprisonment in Tahiti, the experience behind his *Omoo: A Narrative of Adventures in the South Seas* (1847). It was at sea, in these alternative worlds, that his life began: "Until I was twenty-five," he told Hawthorne, "I had no development at all." A whaling ship and the extensive reading he did while at sea was, he said, his Yale and Harvard.

At first he was successful. Like many American writers, he began, in *Typee* and *Omoo*, with a fictionalized travel-writing very in tune with 1840s American expansionism and the interest in contrasts between social and natural life. He enlarged and embellished his own adventures and added factual material culled from his wide-ranging, haphazard reading to produce a pleasing mixture of fact and fancy. *Typee*, a combination of seagoing experience, travelogue and Pacific adventure in exotic and Edenic circumstances, greatly pleased his readers, and thereafter Melville always feared he would be remembered only as the man who had lived among cannibals in the Marquesas, a public expectation he was indeed never to escape. None of the eight full-length fictions that followed ever matched this first popular success, as Melville grew less willing to provide publishers with what they wanted and what he went on promising them. When, in 1849, he published *Mardi*, we can see what could be called the persistent American weakness for allegory asserting itself. To the theme of travel and adventure, he added metaphysical questioning and a search for life's meaning that would make his work grow ever more obscure. Based on voracious intellectual reading, the book is a long-winded allegory of sea travel, a vast quest for transcendent beauty laced with Swiftian satire and a running dialogue between characters representing philosophy, poetry and history. Today we can read it primarily as Melville's preliminary skirmish with romance, the book that searches for that break in the crust of fictional form that would open the way to *Moby-Dick*.

Mardi did not satisfy contemporary readers, and Melville reverted to more popular books, written quickly for the market created by *Typee* but displaying a grim new realism. *Redburn* (1849) tells of a young American sailor who attempts to retain his Romantic innocence in the face of harsh shipboard conditions and the terrible Liverpool slums. Even his return to America, along with a shipload of Irish immigrants seeking the promise of the New World, cannot lighten the book's somber vision. Melville's early paradises were beginning to dissolve under the pressure of social and personal evil: harsh economics and base poverty, dark modern cities and deluded expectations displace the national optimism. A similar realism deals with Melville's own experience in the warships of the U.S. Navy in *White Jacket* (1850), where he develops his fundamental concern with the conflict between American Romantic naivete and darker experience. The central character's symbolic white jacket is the metaphor for his innocence, isolation and attempted Emersonian self-reliance. He takes his name from it, and he nearly dies in it when he falls from the yardarm into the "speechless profound" of the sea and is tugged down by its weight. That plunge into the dark vortex of experience, the nodal mystery, was to be a mysterious goal guiding the quest of Melville's next and most notable work.

Moby-Dick is a novel that grew only slowly into what it is: surely the best American novel we have had. Melville started it as a factual account of the whaling industry, but it crossed with his reading of Shakespeare, his involvement with Hawthorne, his wish to write a "wicked" book to interrogate the persistent innocence of his age. "This

is the book's motto (the secret one),—*Ego non baptiso te in nomine*
—but make out the rest yourself," he wrote excitedly to Hawthorne;
Ahab uses the same words to give a harpoon a diabolic baptism.
Melville himself described the book as a "botch," but it became a
powerful Romantic Faustian tragedy of man confronting nature and
divine power. Its three central characters are the wandering narrator
Ishmael, the monomaniac Captain Ahab and the white whale itself.
Ishmael, the observer and wry storyteller, gives the book its speculative
and varying narrative voice, indeed voices. Ahab's bitter revenge on a
natural adversary that has not nourished but wounded him provides
mythic struggle, which is as much a battle of intellect and faith as of
action. The whale itself manifests the elusive, complex energy of nature.
So Ahab, that "ungodly, God-like man," setting his need for revenge
against his captain's duty to ship, crew and commerce, becomes a
challenger of the universe, attempting to puncture the pasteboard mask
of the world itself in order to reach whatever power has let the whale
violate his body. That mask conceals something like the Emersonian
Over-Soul, which the novel both invokes and challenges, testing what
Melville saw as the great transcendentalist belief and Thoreau perceived
as its greatest danger: its easy assumption that the cosmos is good.
That benign face of nature is not denied in *Moby-Dick*; indeed it
suffuses the book. Ishmael takes a contemplative and comradely view
of the world's fecundity, as we see in his friendship with the "savage"
Queequeg, in the kneading of the sperm and above all in the undersea
domesticity of the family of suckling whales. That vision undoubtedly
helps secure his salvation as the one survivor from the wreck of the
Pequod: "The unharming sharks, they glided by as if with padlocks
on their mouths; the savage sea-hawks sailed with sheathed beaks."
But the great vortex under the sea which draws us into contemplation
is also a vortex of destruction, and Ishmael, riding at the end on
Queequeg's coffin, on a "soft and dirge-like main," survives alone.

Moby-Dick is a great and also a distinctively American novel, about
the ambiguity and duplicity of transcendental knowledge, the light and
the dark, the dangers of "craving after the indefinite." It takes tragic
form because Melville, here and elsewhere, regards nature as a deceitful
hieroglyph. Indeed, he suggests, the "key to it all" lies in the story of
Narcissus, and the way it matches the lure of the sea:

And still deeper the meaning of that story of Narcissus, who because he could not grasp the tormenting, mild image he saw in the fountain, plunged into it and was drowned. But that same image, we ourselves see in all rivers and oceans. It is the image of the ungraspable phantom of life; and this is the key to it all.

But no key unlocks *Moby-Dick*. Where Hawthorne discovered ambiguity in the space between imagination and reality, Melville finds it in the strange signals of reality itself. In the chapter "The Doubloon," a gold coin is nailed to the mast, a forging of the great circle of the world itself. But when each member of the *Pequod*'s crew steps forward to examine it, he interprets it differently, according to his beliefs, intelligence, age, sensibility and personal nature, doubling and redoubling the doubloon itself. "I look, you look, he looks," mad Pip proclaims; "we . . . are all bats." Appropriately, the book itself constantly multiplies its own language, as it conducts its own narrative and linguistic search for the meaning of "the whale." We hear the language of dusty scholarship, of scientific cetology, of Christian and classical myth and Romantic celebration, of voyaging and adventure, as the prose seeks a sufficient commensurability. If there is no human way to know even a small truth, Melville undertakes to demonstrate, then any and all meaning must remain uncertain. Like any major novel, this one has generated a multiplication of readings and of readers; in fact, modern fiction is filled with Melvillean commentaries. But *Moby-Dick* is, amongst other things, the novel *as* commentary, surrounding its tragic myth of the great Romantic overreacher with a wealth of interpretation of the Great Leviathan, who is both whale itself and the whale as book, each representing "the great gilding demon of the seas of life."

Melville's skepticism about transcendentalism ("He who hath more of joy than sorrow in him . . . cannot be true—not true, or undeveloped," he says in the book) found its perfect form in the vision of large Romantic tragedy. Melville was never to discover himself again to this degree. *Moby-Dick* enjoyed a small success, though one contemporary critic called it "maniacal—mad as a March hare—mowing, gibbering, screaming, like an incurable Bedlamite." But the book that followed, *Pierre; or, The Ambiguities* (1852), lacks a fundamental shape and is an eccentric, ambitious failure. Between 1853 and 1856, however, Melville produced eighteen shorter fictional pieces, some of them minor masterworks. Recalling Melville's visit to Liverpool of November 1856, Hawthorne described his friend discussing "Providence and futurity, and . . . everything that lies beyond human ken." Melville had

> pretty much made up his mind to be annihilated; but still he does not seem to rest in that anticipation. . . . It is strange how he persists . . . in wandering to-and-fro over these deserts. . . . He can neither believe, nor be comfortable in his unbelief; and he is too honest and courageous not to try to do one or the other. If he were a religious man, he would be one of the most truly religious and reverential.

In this special sense, Melville *was* a religious man, and most of his late writing continues his anxious questioning of the visible world's mysterious hieroglyphs. In "The Piazza," Melville's narrator knows that he is spinning a fairy-tale web to escape the world's pain, just as he acknowledges the nest of cankerous worms beneath the lovely blossoms of his Chinese creeper. But in "Benito Cereno," the benevolent optimist Captain Delano does not see the gap between appearance and reality aboard ship, fails to unravel the deceptions of the slave revolt that has turned society upside down. Delano's innocence protects him from harm but also from understanding—the mystery of human nature, the double face of good and evil, the ambiguous complexities of the world's realities. The narrator of "Bartleby the Scrivener: A Story of Wall Street," is similarly benevolent and, wrapped in self-concern, similarly blind to the ambiguities of human existence suggested by the employees in his law office. Wall Street, the law, the tomblike confines of the office itself—all point to a society and a world uncongenial to human life. Bartleby, one-time clerk in the Dead Letter Office and now the narrator's copier of legal documents, has come at last to the ultimate existential denial: "I would prefer not to," he responds to each request, and finally, "I'm not particular" to identify his condition as quintessentially human. In its grotesque urban atmosphere and vision of the superfluous man, "Bartleby the Scrivener" seems kin to

Gogol, Kafka or the Dostoyevsky of *Notes from the Underground.* Melville, that is, was a true nineteenth-century writer of a changing age whose tales deal with a good deal more than what he called "landlessness." His work, like Dickens's, builds a narrative of major transition, from the innocence of *Typee* and "The Paradise of Bachelors" to the industrial power of "The Tartarus of Maids." Even the *Pequod* is as much a floating factory and workplace as an adventuring sailing vessel, and its crew are part of a process of historical change. In *The Confidence-Man: His Masquerade* (1857), another remarkable tour de force, a Mississippi steamboat, the *Fidèle,* sets sail on April Fools' Day and, a true Ship of Fools, becomes a microcosm of the American order. Here the confidence man, a grotesque master of cunning disguise, manifests the mysterious, deceitful "confidence" that makes commercial society work and money function. As the book shows, Melville was himself a mid-century master of the grotesque, like Gogol or Dickens. His grotesque is not simply a mannerism but a way of grasping the absurd realities of an age when prelapsarian innocence must give way to a sense of deceit, guilt and corruption.

Melville is a central figure of American writing prior to the Civil War. But, unlike Poe or Hawthorne, he survived that war, living on till 1891; the great nay-sayer who never won unqualified admiration for his finest books lived out the last twenty-five years of his life in the obscurity and mental agony he had always feared. The war inspired his first book of poems—*Battle-Pieces and Aspects of War* (1866)—and he wrote further volumes in verse: *Clarel: A Poem and Pilgrimage to the Holy Land* (1876), about his ceaseless quest for faith; then *John Marr and Other Sailors* (1888) and *Timoleon* (1891), privately printed in editions of twenty-five copies. The late story *Billy Budd* demonstrates persuasively that he retained his power as a writer of narrative fiction to the end of his life. Here innocence stutters and evil speaks loud as the simplicities of an eighteenth-century world give way to the battleship of nineteenth-century life. Adamic Billy dies at the yardarm, nonetheless stoically affirming the rule of the ship of state and the inhumane forms of society; his legend, Melville says, survived, to be read in many ways. So did Melville's manuscript, left unfinished when he died unknown in 1891 and continuing to haunt readers with its conflicting and unresolved meanings since its recovery in 1924. It remains as well an eloquent indictment of America's inability to recognize and support a major literary talent who now seems to us what he wished to be: his nation's candidate for rivalry with Shakespeare or Milton.

·IV·

In 1849 Melville wrote to Evert Duyckinck, editor of the New York *Literary World* and his mentor and friend, describing his attitude toward Emerson, "this Plato who talks through his nose":

> Nay, I do not oscillate in Emerson's rainbow, but prefer rather to hang myself in mine own halter than swing in any other man's swing. Yet I think Emerson is more than a brilliant fellow. Be his stuff begged, borrowed, or stolen, or of his own domestic manufacture he is an uncommon man. Swear he is a humbug—then he is no common humbug. . . . Now, there is something about every man elevated above mediocrity, which is, for the most part, instinctively perceptible. This I see in Mr. Emerson. And, frankly, for the sake of the argument, let us call him a fool;—then had I rather be a fool than a wise man.

There is much in the biblical figure of the wise fool that characterizes the works of the American Renaissance and the sources of its strength. Its authors belonged to Melville's "corps of thought-divers" who consequently attempted and achieved more than any of their nation's writers had yet done. As he went on to tell Duyckinck, Melville loved

> all men who *dive*. Any fish can swim near the surface, but it takes a great whale to go down stairs five miles or more; & if he don't attain the bottom, why, all the lead in Galena can't fashion the plummet that will. I'm not talking of Mr. Emerson now—but of the whole corps of thought-divers, that have been diving & coming up again with blood-shot eyes since the world began.

Melville was nonetheless prepared to make his distance from Emerson plain: where Emerson assumed a beneficent energy in the world, Melville felt uncertainty and frustration. "This 'all' feeling," he wrote to Hawthorne in 1851,

> there is some truth in. You must often have felt it, lying on the grass on a warm summer's day. Your legs seem to send out shoots into the earth. Your hair feels like leaves upon your head. This is the *all* feeling. But what plays the mischief with the truth is that men will insist upon the universal application of a temporary feeling or opinion.

The "all" feeling was familiar in America, and it was soon to find its poet. Four years after this letter, Walt Whitman published the first version of his *Leaves of Grass* (1855), that work of cosmic inclusion which accepts the unity and beneficence of the All with an affirmation far more akin to Emerson's "Brahma" than to the skepticism of a Poe, Hawthorne or Melville.

The "all" feeling, the ideal of large embrace, is the guiding principle of *Leaves of Grass*. Its first preface expressly asserts it. Anonymous save for its daguerreotype of a bohemianized Whitman—named only once in the poems as "Walt Whitman, an American, one of the roughs, a Kosmos"—it offers to respond to the democratic American present in the spirit of the "equable man" who encompasses everything and sees eternity in each man and woman. Whitman casts himself as the poet into whom everything poured—the massive and varied continent, the democratic spirit, "the general ardor and friendliness and enterprise—the perfect equality of the female with the male," "the large amativeness—the fluid movement of the population—the factories and mercantile life and laborsaving machinery." America was itself the greatest poem: "Of all the nations the United States with veins full of poetical stuff most need poets and will doubtless have the greatest and use them the greatest." Over Whitman's lifetime, the dream, like the poems in the successive versions of the book, grew ever more complex, but even when he found that he was not "used the greatest," it was never entirely lost. The 1855 edition of *Leaves* was a slim volume, twelve untitled poems in ninety-five pages, some set in type by the author himself. Among them were the first versions of his finest, later called "Song of Myself," "The Sleepers," "I Sing the Body Electric" and "There Was a Child Went Forth." For the next three decades, Whitman worked this same book like a landscape garden, shifting and changing, revising and deleting, developing mass and detail, dramatizing his own complex self, but above all incorporating—with that famous all-accepting, physical embrace.

Gradually, as edition followed edition, the original poems grew and major new poems began to emerge. The 1856 edition boldly added to its spine Emerson's warm salute celebrating the beginning of a great career, one of the most notable of all acts of literary acknowledgment: "I find it the most extraordinary piece of wit & wisdom that America has yet contributed." It also added "Song of the Broad Axe," "Crossing Brooklyn Ferry" and "The Song of the Open Road." The 1860 edition introduced "Starting from Paumanok" and "Out of the Cradle Endlessly Rocking," as well as the sexually explicit Calamus and Children of Adam poems that mark a change of direction from mysticism to personalism, from democracy to physical "adhesiveness." Whitman's ideal of democratic universalism was deeply strained by the Civil War of 1861–65, which challenged and in many ways broke the optimistic transcendentalist spirit. But the war ultimately intensified Whitman's identification with the nation and its people. In Washington he entered into the horror of the wartime bloodshed by visiting and working in hospitals, calling himself a "wound-dresser" and sharing the lives of the young men forced to enact their country's quarrel. He wrote his later prose account *Specimen Days* (1882) and the cycle of war poems *Drum-Taps* (1865) in the light of this experience, identifying with the historical momentum of the times and the deaths of "beautiful young men"—"everything sometimes as if blood color, & dripping blood." Above all, his identification with Lincoln was total. The President's death and state funeral drew the poet into a process of complex incorporation: of death with life's flow, of a hero with his nation and people, of Whitman himself with Lincoln, the people and the nation. Whitman's lament for the dead leader, "When Lilacs Last in the Dooryard Bloom'd," is one of the finest elegies in the language. With *Drum-Taps*, it, too, merged with the ever-growing *Leaves* in the edition of 1867.

The war changed things, and so did the Gilded Age. Whitman was no longer the mystical bohemian radical, but the "good gray poet."

His early hopes changed to the serious doubts that afflicted most intelligent Americans in the period of careless industrial growth that followed the Civil War. Whitman made his opinions plain in the prose of *Democratic Vistas* (1871), lamenting a spectacle of depraved greed and base acquisitiveness. A logic of despair was perhaps appropriate, but others, like Henry Adams, expressed it, not Whitman. Though everything seemed less simple than before, the westward flow toward human happiness less inevitable and democratic spiritualization less certain, Whitman's fundamental trascendent assertion remains: life is good, with America the vessel appointed to carry it forward into the future. Thus to the edition of *Leaves* in 1871, the year of *Democratic Vistas*, he added his poem of westering transcontinentalism and democratic world unity, "Passage to India." There were to be three more editions, in the centennial year of 1876, in 1881 and, in 1892, the "Deathbed Edition." They incorporated change and recorded an altered national destiny, the bloodiness of war, the shifting motion of history. Yet the essential structure remained the same. The open-ended and never-punctuated leaves remained persistently affirmative—man is divine, the self true, the world good. The continent America was filling would eventually manifest its destiny in a perfect commonwealth that would reshape the world. And the *Leaves* would live as he had meant them to, as procreative leaves of the life force itself.

Leaves of Grass could thus be the massive open poem that nonetheless always retained its essential principles and its essential structure. Edmund Gosse, one of Whitman's many British admirers, once described the *Leaves* as "literature in a condition of protoplasm. . . . He felt acutely and accurately, his imagination was purged of external impurities, he lay spread abroad in a condition of literary solution." That was the aim and the novelty. At the heart of its subsequent widespread influence on the twentieth century was its capacity to incorporate all, and although its essential task was mystical, it was also realistic, that of amassing and cataloging. A subjective poem of self, it is also confidently epical in its absorption of the past and celebration of the future of a people. Whitman's aim was preemptive. He offered himself—and has ultimately been accepted—as the nation's Homer, Vergil and Milton, singing the song of the nation as a song of a particular self. This was a new song, both a way of seeing and being, a unifying song compounded of ego and society, people and landscape, male and female, death and life, personal sensation and historical destiny.

In both his radical poetic theory and his politics, Whitman sought to merge his opened-out self with his country and her place in the march of history by a transcendent and transcendentalist act of the ego—and thereby become an Emersonian representative man, prophet and seer. The "Walt Whitman" who stands bearded in his broad-brimmed hat and stares confidently out from the frontispiece of the first edition is a seer whose visionary words are intended to be large and long-lived. Similarly the poetry is a shocking break with the private intonation of traditional lyric poetry. "I CELEBRATE myself," begins the lengthy "Song of Myself":

> Shall I pray? Shall I venerate and be ceremonious?
> I have pried through the strata and analyzed to a hair,
> And counselled with doctors and calculated close and found no
>   sweeter fat than sticks to my own bones. . . .
>
> Divine I am inside and out, and I make holy whatever I
>   touch or am touched from;
> The scent of these arm-pits is aroma finer than prayer,
> This head is more than churches and bibles or creeds. . . .
> I dote on myself . . . there is that lot of me, and all so
>   luscious. . . .

By 1867 he could add to the poem:

> One's-self I sing, a simple, separate person;
> Yet utter the word Democratic, the word *En-Masse*.

The operative public recitative of the frank, tasteless ego, what he himself called the "barbaric yawp" he sounded across the rooftops, becomes universal; it can embrace society itself.

The space between that representative ego and the private man can still baffle Whitman's biographers. Born of a modest, barely literate Long Island family, Whitman had eight brothers and sisters, two of them imbeciles. With only five or six years' formal schooling, he took to the trade of Franklin, Twain and many other American writers: setting type for a printing house. After some schoolteaching, he turned to journalism—reporting, reviewing, editing—eventually becoming an editor of the Brooklyn *Daily Eagle* in 1846, to resign in 1847 because the paper was too conservative on the slavery issue. There was a period of "loafing," out of which the first *Leaves* came, but he was never to support himself with his verse. He held a government post for a time but lost it when a superior discovered the sexual explicitness of his poetry. During the Civil War, he spent long hours nursing and comforting the wounded of both sides; and he eventually—after a paralytic stroke in 1873—retired in a wheelchair to Camden, New Jersey, where for twenty years he continued his revisions of *Leaves* and reminisced for the adoring disciples who now clustered about him. His book claims that "who touches this touches a man," yet neither the book nor the facts really clarify the actual Walter Whitman. Specificity was one of his standards; his poems seem acts of frank description derived from the hard details of his actual life. But as often as not he was distorting, inventing, coloring the facts to flesh out the changing fictive character of the all-embracing "I," the persona he invented for *Leaves:* "Walt Whitman, an American, one of the roughs, a Kosmos,/Disorderly fleshy and sensual . . . eating, drinking and breeding,/No sentimentalist . . . , no stander above men and women or apart from them . . . no more modest than immodest."

Like Milton's blindness, Whitman's life, with its frustration and final physical incapacity, mocked the heroic mission he had undertaken as the nation's epic bard, its articulating public voice. But everyone must live with the gap between what he is and what he would like to be; part of Whitman's greatness—like Milton's—was his ability to project the larger-than-life self he could imagine into the voice of his poetry. Whitman's "I," which in the end *becomes* the poetry and the poet's supreme creation, is a recognizable product of American oratorical tradition, a *spoken* or chanted ego. As he tells us in "A Backward Glance . . . ," his 1888 meditation on his conception of the *Leaves* and its high national function, it had its literary sources. He was an early and avid reader of the Bible, Shakespeare, Ossian, Scott and Homer, knew Greek and Hindu poets, the *Nibelungenlied* and Dante.

Goethe's autobiography showed him a man unafraid to portray the universe in terms of himself, and Carlyle and Hegel reinforced Emerson's stress on the representative man and his heroic role in cosmic consciousness. All this crossed with the apparently contradictory mission of finding an aesthetic formulation that would merge the poet with the ordinary life of the folk. The result was a democratic epic: "Endless unfolding of words of ages!/And mine a word of the modern, the word En-Masse." Moreover, this voice of the self, voice of the mass, voice of the destined future, voice of the all, must also be the voice of the All, the Over-Soul. "I speak the password primeval . . . I give the sign of democracy;/By God! I will accept nothing which all cannot have their counterpart of on the same terms." His aim was to solve the problem of writing an epic in democratic America: the fundamental desire behind the poem was, he tells us,

> a feeling or ambition to articulate and faithfully express in literary or poetic form, and uncompromisingly, my own physical, emotional, moral, intellectual, and aesthetic Personality, in the midst of, and tallying, the momentous spirit and facts of its immediate days, and of current America—and to exploit that Personality, identified with place and date, in a far more candid and comprehensive sense than any hitherto poem or book.

For his contemporaries, this Adamic aim was particularly evident in one notable aspect of Whitman's "I": its unabashed physical corporeality. His is, he said, "avowedly the song of Sex and Amativeness, and even Animality." This was one thing that divided him decisively from the transcendentalists. Thoreau understood his transcendental aims, but not this: "it is as if the beasts spoke," he said. Emerson strolled with him one day on Boston Common trying to persuade him to soften his explicit sexuality; Whitman made it clear that he not only would not, but could not, compromise. "Nature was naked, and I was also," he wrote in *Specimen Days* (1882), the late book where he painfully sought to reconcile the divisive elements of commercial, Gilded Age America and to question the cultural Genteel Tradition that it nourished. The naked sexual self is central to his desire to include everything, from birth to death, dark city street to wide countryside, rich life and poor, men and women, in his work. Like the spear of grass itself, sex expresses the life force that drives the poetry onward:

> Tenderly will I use you curling grass,
> It may be you transpire from the breasts of young men,
> It may be if I had known them I would have loved them;
> It may be you are from old people and from women,
>   and from offspring taken soon out of their mothers' laps,
> And here you are the mothers' laps. . . .

> O I perceive after all so many *uttering tongues:*
> And I perceive they do not come from the roofs of mouths
>   for nothing.

Like Emerson's ideal symbol, Whitman's grass-blades, the uttering tongues of the writing and the central figure in his title, resist narrow signification. But a crucial implication is the phallic one of irresistible creativity, Thomas's "force that through the green fuse drives the flower." Grass is life itself, speaking beyond and behind death, common everywhere and to all, endlessly vital, tirelessly procreative. So were his own leaves to be, as they continued in unending growth and inclusiveness from edition to edition. By modern standards, his sexual frankness and homoerotic implication is tame; it is nevertheless important to recognize that his embrace and ejaculations are meant to evoke the surge of nature's continuous renewal, while his indiscriminate mergings of men and women, self and nature, are his signs of divine love.

These stratagems bred hostility for Whitman by setting him firmly in opposition to the decorum of the Genteel Tradition. Whitman mourned this, but it was what he had calculated. "Establish'd poems, I know, have the very great advantage of chanting the already perform'd, so full of glories, reminiscences dear to the minds of men," he observed in "A Backward Glance O'er Travell'd Roads"; "But my volume is a candidate for the future." His aim was essentially avant-garde; he was a radical and a new kind of symbolist. Though he appeared to literalize the world about him by granting it linguistic place in his poems, he insisted on his aesthetic novelty and above all, in symbolist fashion, on "the image-making faculty, coping with material creation, and rivaling, almost triumphing, over it." Proposing a new relation between observing poet and what he observes, his aim was experimental—as was America's. He always felt that his *carte de visite* was to the coming generations and not alone to his own:

> One main contrast of the ideas behind every page of my verse, compared with establish'd poems, is their different relative attitude towards God, towards the objective universe, and still more (by reflection, confession, assumption, &c) the quite changed attitude toward the ego, the one chanting or talking, towards himself and towards his fellow-humanity. It is certainly time for America, above all, to begin the readjustment in the scope and basic point of view of verse; for everything else has changed.

This was the spirit of Ezra Pound's later determination to "Make It New." With it, Whitman made himself central to the legacy of nearly every later American poet of scale, for the multivalent imagery he cultivated posed long-term questions of the relation in America between symbol and reality, ego and epic. That fertile tradition of the expansive and incorporative American poem that haunted so many twentieth-century American poets—Pound with *The Cantos,* Hart Crane with *The Bridge,* Wallace Stevens with *Notes Toward a Supreme Fiction,* William Carlos Williams with *Paterson,* Charles Olson with *The Maximus Poems*—took its rise and guarantee from Whitman's faith in the open assimilative poem, ever in process of creative renewal in its reach toward the future.

·V·

"The proof of a poet is that his country absorbs him as affectionately as he has absorbed it," Whitman wrote in the early confident days of his 1855 preface, only to find how long it would take before reciprocal absorption would indeed begin to develop. It is one of the ironies of American literature that the later nineteenth century should produce two major poets who would prove to be the genuine antecedents of most serious modern American poetry, yet that, of those two, one should be a public poet who virtually lost the public he so confidently addressed, while the other was so private that scarcely any of her poems appeared in her own lifetime.

Emily Dickinson so shunned public disclosure that most of her verses imply a total inwardness, a refusal to share in the collective utterance of the world; there is no ideal of chanting or talking here, rather a universe of rugged inward meditation and drama that takes on expression but no clear social form. Indeed, to set Whitman and Dickinson side by side seems almost a breach of propriety—though one way of understanding modern American poetry is to say that many of its poets did just that. Yet this quiet resident of Amherst, Massachusetts—where Calvinist and Unitarian traditions mingled in doubt and uncertainty—is so private and subtle where Whitman is so public and garrulous, her poems are so brief, tight and oblique where his expand, circle, ramble and repeat, that many forget they were contemporaries. Did they in any way know of each other? She was told his book was disgraceful and never read it. He might just have known of her, but her "letter to the World/That never wrote to Me" was not ever really mailed. Seven of her poems appeared, anonymously, during her lifetime, but the remaining works, close to eighteen hundred of them, did not come to light until after her death. They were published in 1890, just before Whitman died, but it was not until the 1920s that they were fully acclaimed, and not until 1958, when Thomas H. Johnson edited them, that a satisfactory edition and full impression was possible. Only then was it fully clear that these enigmatic short lyrics were the work of America's greatest poet. As with Edward Taylor, another part-Puritan spirit before her, her poetry was a metaphysical and moral secret which might never have been fathomed.

This was because, although she did now and again try to publish, for Dickinson the writing seemed a satisfying secret, sufficient to itself. The continent she sang was that of Emerson's inner self, and her vocation was the liberation of—in Emerson's phrase—a private chicken coop. We know that she read Emerson and heard him lecture and that he had some effect on her. We also know the people she met and corresponded with, but there biography virtually ceases to illuminate her or her verse. There is no egotistical sublime here, no dramatic self on show and no trascendentalist outreach. Rather there is an inreach, a guiding concept of privacy and selfhood which creates a metaphysical distillation from its own being. We need only look to some of her famous opening lines—"The Soul selects her own Society," "I dwell in possibility," "Renunciation—is a piercing Virtue"—to feel the pained self-anatomizing, the willed self-enclosure, which is the field of her verse. Unlike Whitman's, her poetry articulates a life carefully hidden, even from the Puritanism and Evangelicalism of her Amherst neighbors and of her own family. With few forays out, the sum of her life was conducted in her father's house. Even here she kept her distance. As she said of her family in a letter to her one literary mentor, Thomas Wentworth Higginson: "They are religious—except me—and address an Eclipse every morning—whom they call their 'Father.' "

Even this remark is oblique. Dickinson is religious, but her world of faith seems homemade. She knew very well the painful erosion of belief that was taking place among the orthodox who surrounded her, the troubles that marked the transition from Calvinism to Unitarianism, and she felt this in her own conscience and consciousness. But although the subtly rewritten iconography of Christian discourse provided her essential material and transcendentalism evidently stirred her, neither provided her with a solution to the agonized experience of life, nor did the optimistic spirit masking the divisions of her age ever color her spirit. The years of the Civil War saw her most concentrated poetic work, but the war itself did not impinge directly on her poems— though we may speculate that it had something to do with the doubt and horror they so often express. The Emersonian vision is there, too. The artist becomes the spider of her poem, who "holds a silver Ball,—/In unperceived hands" and rears "supreme/His theories of light." Her poet sings the inner self, but also searches in vain for the truth outside—for "Not unto nomination/The Cherubim reveal." Poetry is thus as devious as the meaning of the universe. When she sees Truth, she must tell it all, but "tell it slant . . ./The Truth must dazzle gradually/ Or every Man be blind."

Hence not only the themes of Emerson but the devotional intricacies and metaphysics of a John Donne or George Herbert appear to lie beneath her poetry. Yet no single familiar artistic convention seems to match the slanted truth of her verse. She writes with condensation, with tight formal control and hymnlike construction, but there is also fragmentation. Whitman broke with the metric of stresses, turning to free-verse forms that roll rhythmically and to "bare lists of words" that work through reiteration to amplification, while dashes and dots imply incompleteness, language's pressure otherwise limiting what pushes to be said. A similar struggle with the limits of traditional discourse breaks open Dickinson's verse, which rejects conventional punctuation and completed phrasing, employs dashes for pacing, and thereby creates ambiguity and multiplicity. Where Whitman used lists, she scattered alternative words about her manuscripts—synonyms, close pairings or rival locutions that keep the poems incomplete so that final print seems to imprison them. This is doubtless deliberate, part of the method of "circuit" which she celebrates. Apparently simple or even naive perception takes on extreme tension that holds contradictions in balance. In this sense, too, she seems a metaphysical poet. One of the most powerful of all her contradictions is between the banal and the momentous, as in the familiar "I heard a Fly buzz when I died," that subtly disturbing poem wherein

> I willed my Keepsakes—Signed away
>   What portion of me be
> Assignable—and then it was
>   There interposed a Fly—
>
> With Blue—uncertain stumbling Buzz—
>   Between the light—and me—
> And then the Windows failed—and then
>   I could not see to see—

Dickinson's reclusive nature so masked her intense dedication to the discipline of her craft that confidants like Higginson mistakenly thought she was unable to reach the smooth rhymes and rhythms of Tennyson or Longfellow. And yet for today's reader, no single sampling can adequately represent the range of play and speculation that explodes in the tiny cosmos of her individual poems. There are several

Emily Dickinsons: a poet of wit, the creator of the riddling, sometimes overcute description of the snake, "A narrow Fellow in the Grass" who brings "a tighter breathing/And Zero at the Bone—" and the railroad—"I like to see it lap the Miles—/And lick the Valleys up." There are the wry reflections on death, that dominant preoccupation where the wit functions doubly, not just as a voice of condensation but as the extreme, postmortal source of her meditation—"Because I could not stop for Death,—/He kindly stopped for me." And there are poems of vision, of mystical experience—"Better—than Music! For I—who heard it—/. . . 'Twas Translation—/Of all the tunes I knew—and more. . . ." There are transcendental poems of nature and poems appalled at nature, where the vision recalls the doubtful questioning of Melville or the icy abyss of Poe. In "I tried to think a lonelier Thing/Than any I had seen," the only hope she can imagine for one "Of Heavenly love forgot" is another poor soul to touch in mutual pity. "The Soul has Bandaged moments—/When too appalled to stir," she suggests. Despite occasional respite, the "moments of Escape—/When bursting all the doors—/She dances like a Bomb, abroad," she faces unflinchingly the loss of such gay freedom,

> The Soul's retaken moments—
> When, Felon, led along,
> With shackles on the plumed feet,
> And staples in the Song,
>
> The Horror welcomes her, again. . . .

these things, she concludes, are "not brayed of Tongue."

These were certainly not frequently brayed of tongue in nineteenth-century America. We are hearing here the accents of the modern world, a world of doubt, of Kurtz's "the horror" that Emerson, Thoreau or even Whitman could not or would not imagine. This world could grow cold and harsh, as in "It was not Death, for I stood up,/And all the Dead lie down," where living comes to seem "like Midnight, some—"

When everything that ticked—has stopped—
And Space stares all around—
Or Grisly frosts—first Autumn morns,
Repeal the Beating Ground—

But, most, like Chaos—Stopless—cool—
Without a Chance, or Spar—
Or even a Report of Land—
To justify—Despair.

Traditional faith yields for Dickinson and the America of her age, and ours, to present doubt, as in this extraordinary short poem:

I reason, Earth is short—
And Anguish—absolute—
And many hurt,
But, what of that?

I reason, we could die—
The best Vitality
Cannot excel Decay,
But, what of that?

I reason, that in Heaven—
Somehow, it will be even—
Some new Equation given—
But, what of that?

The Emerson of "Experience," "Politics" and "Fate" had explored the flaws in his own special optimism and felt the anguished strain of acknowledging death as inescapably part of his affirmation of life. In "Out of the Cradle Endlessly Rocking," Whitman had sought to make death the source of beauty by turning the sea into an eloquent mother of natural motion who whispers "the low and delicious word death." But it is Dickinson who fully distilled the darker Janus-vision of her age against the grain of a culture that called its popular poetry increasingly toward sentimentality. It is this Janus-vision that made her seem so contemporary to the modernist poets of the next century.

They responded as well to her insistence on the discipline and formality of art, the craft by which the words are placed rightly on the page. In consequence her reputation grows daily as one of the best of America's writers, a writer in whom the legacy of nineteenth-century Romanticism turns toward the complexities of twentieth-century Modernism.

· PART III ·

NATIVE AND COSMOPOLITAN CROSSCURRENTS: FROM LOCAL COLOR TO REALISM AND NATURALISM

CHAPTER

·6·

SECESSION AND LOYALTY

·I·

When Nathaniel Hawthorne observed in his 1860 preface to *The Marble Faun* that "No author, without trial, can conceive of the difficulty of writing a romance about a country where there is no shadow . . . , no picturesque and gloomy wrong, nor anything but a commonplace prosperity in broad and simple daylight," he wrote on the eve of a conflict that would shatter his America forever. Almost every European traveler to America, from Alexis de Tocqueville to Charles Dickens, had seen a shadow, a gloomy wrong, a monstrous contradiction at the heart of American claims to freedom, democracy, equality. A year later, that wrong—slavery, "the peculiar institution" —would plunge the nation into the world's first modern war and threaten to divide it beyond mending. Melville's "Benito Cereno" (1856) had presciently pictured American innocence staring blindly at its own tragic secret. In New England almost every writer—Emerson, Thoreau, Whitman, Bryant, Lowell, above all Whittier—had responded to the abolitionist cause; meanwhile in the South nearly every writer had written with equal passion and religious certainty in support of a culture that saw slavery as essential to its economic and social survival. When the conflict came, it shattered and transformed American culture. Before the war had ended, Hawthorne died in depression and an entire era of American writing came to a close.

The Civil War was fought for a complex of reasons, but chiefly Abraham Lincoln's need to maintain the Union as a whole, against

Southern claims to the right of secession. "My paramount objective in this struggle is to save the Union," the President asserted to Horace Greeley, the influential abolitionist editor of the New York *Tribune,* in August 1862:

> it is *not* either to save or destroy Slavery. If I could save the Union without freeing any slaves I would do it; and if I could save it by freeing some and leaving others alone I would also do this.

But the rising surge of Northern abolitionist sentiment and the growing argument about the spread of slavery into the West had already made slavery the main *casus belli*. By 1862 Lincoln had already prepared the Emancipation Proclamation that would free the slaves and change black American destiny. In the popular mind in both camps, the abolition or extension of "the peculiar institution" was the issue—a fact that had much to do with the power of books—and of one book in particular.

"So this is the little lady who made this big war!" Lincoln said to Harriet Beecher Stowe, author of two prodigiously popular novels that could be fairly said to have altered the course of the nation and created international feeling on the slavery issue. Stowe was one of the many women writers who largely dominated American popular literature, shaping general taste and moral sentiment. The daughter of a famed Northern Congregationalist preacher, Lyman Beecher, the wife of another minister, the sister of six more, she felt all the moral force of the abolition issue. She had never lived in the South and did not know slave life at firsthand, though when she lived and ministered in Cincinnati she had contact with many fugitive slaves fleeing North. She turned her sentimental and moral mode of writing to the subject of slavery in *Uncle Tom's Cabin,* which first appeared as a serial in a Washington antislavery weekly from 1851 to 1852, increased in length as interest grew, and then came out as a book in 1852. It had extraordinary impact; it sold more than 300,000 copies in the United States in one year and a million and a half worldwide, making it one of the greatest international best-sellers ever, the best-known American novel—a book, said Emerson, that "encircled the globe." Holmes and Whittier praised it; when, in 1868, John William De Forest described the nation's search for "the Great American Novel," he made it a prime contender. George Eliot, George Sand, Tolstoy and Henry James all honored it, though less for its art than its moral power. Stage versions increased its impact, while often turning it toward minstrel humor—to which, in fact, its more comical black characters owed something. Motifs from the book—Eliza crossing the ice—or characters like Topsy ("I 'spect I just grow'd") became general folklore. Songs, poems, plates and busts illustrating the book appeared everywhere. Stowe followed it with the story of a slave rebellion, *Dred: A Tale of the Dismal Swamp* (1854), an equally interesting, if less well known, novel. She also published *The Key to "Uncle Tom's Cabin"* (1853) to show that she had drawn extensively on abolitionist materials and slave narratives for the "truth" of her story.

Preachy, moralistic and overdramatic, *Uncle Tom's Cabin, or Life Among the Lowly* is nevertheless a remarkable book. Stowe had no doubt about its virtue; it was, she claimed, a Christian book, written by God Himself, with her as merely His scribe. With such authorship, it was inevitably a work of certainties rather than ambiguities. The old Puritan theme of God's American intentions recurs in Congregationalist guise: the novel's driving energy stems from His accumulating wrath at the wrongs slavery does to fundamental laws of love, family and true feeling. Stowe brought vivid powers of representation to the didactic social and moral themes of the book. She knew just what she was doing: "There's no arguing with *pictures,* and everybody is impressed with them, whether they mean to be or not," she said. The book's best sections are, in fact, those which picture living human beings who are thought of, bought and sold as things, and not those concerned with the famous Uncle Tom, the long-suffering slave who was to become the stereotype of black fortitude and, ultimately, humiliating passivity. Stowe's difficulties are understandable; she was not close to black life and the black had not become a rounded character for fiction. The real strengths of the book are in its social portraiture and its use of sentimental techniques for serious purposes. Feminist critics have celebrated the novel as offering an alternative to the literature of moral ambiguity or male adventure, for creating a "matriarchal vision" emphasizing the values of love, culture and morality over instrumental values. Along with Stowe's other work, including her tales of New England domestic life like *The Minister's Wooing* (1859), *Oldtown Folks* (1869) and *Poganuc People* (1878), it affected the tradition both of the moral tale and of local-color writing, and it certainly has helped bring women writers of succeeding generations toward the center of American fiction and has helped give confidence to their themes, subject matter and moral emphasis.

But like all books that change the world and shape popular feeling, its influence was also problematic. *Uncle Tom's Cabin* unquestionably established black life—a white version of it—as a subject for an American fiction that had essentially neglected it. It provoked innumerable counterversions from the South—no fewer than fourteen proslavery fictions of contented black slave life appeared in the next three years alone. For black writers, however, it had more complex and longer-lasting impact, as its motifs and themes, versions of black speech and black character, above all its image of pious black humility, shaped future fiction, popular culture, even the movies. Over the generations black writers have therefore felt compelled both to draw upon it and to struggle against it. James Baldwin wrote of black writers working within the "cage" of the book, and recent black novelists from Richard Wright (*Uncle Tom's Children,* 1940) to Ishmael Reed (*Flight Into Canada,* 1976) have continued the struggle to break loose from its images. The difficulties of the fight for black expression were already evident in the very slave narratives on which Stowe drew. The classic example, a powerful and deeply felt reversal of all the conventional images of slave existence and sensibility, was *The Narrative of the Life of Frederick Douglass, An American Slave* (1845). Douglass wrote his own account of escape from slavery, but there were many more which often had to be written with white assistance; most slaves had been denied the possibility of reading and writing. Yet another key slave narrative, used by Stowe, was by William Wells Brown (1817–88), who fled slavery, became active in the cause of abolition and went to England, speaking on its behalf. He there produced the first black novel, *Clotel; or, The President's Daughter* (London, 1853). About Jefferson's daughter by his slave housekeeper, this powerful work deals with sexual exploitation, miscegenation and the humiliations of the slave auction; Brown later extended his story to cover the Civil War itself. Brown, an educated mulatto, clearly faced the problem of black representation, which he solved by making his central character near-white. His novel is also evidently influenced by Stowe's book, which he warmly praised and which helped secure him an audience. Not surprisingly, later black writers criticized this dependence and his failure to get closer to slave speech, social existence and sensibility. But Brown's still interesting novel shows how hard the problem was. The full representation of the black in fiction would have to wait, till the turn of the century and beyond.

Much the same could be said about the depiction of the Civil War itself. This was the largest crisis the nation had faced. It marked the fracturing of its unity, the moment of greatest change in its history. Yet none of the major writers of its generation came close to it, in either language or actual experience: Henry James was kept from battle by his "mysterious wound," Mark Twain was away in the West, William Dean Howells was a consul in Italy, Walt Whitman was not a participant but a hospital visitor and wound dresser, Emily Dickinson was, as always, a recluse. When Edmund Wilson wrote *Patriotic Gore: Studies in the Literature of the American Civil War* (1962), he was struck by the relative absence of literary expression. Wars, he concludes, are no time for *belles-lettres*. What they produce is polemic, speeches, sermons, reportage, soldiers' songs and popular battle hymns and verses like "John Brown's Body," Julia Ward Howe's "Battle Hymn of the Republic" and Daniel Decatur Emmett's "Dixie," which rallied the combatants in the conflict. As Emerson said near the start: "All arts disappear in the one art of war." But wars are often followed by a major burst of creativity reflecting the wartime experience, as happened after the First World War. There was important literary expression, especially in verse—Whitman's *Specimen Days* (1882) and *Drum-Taps* (1865), eventually to form part of *Leaves of Grass,* Herman Melville's *Battle-Pieces* (1866), war poetry by Henry Timrod and Sidney Lanier, whose verse was deeply marked by his Southerner's experience of a Northern prison during the war. Various novels followed, like John William De Forest's *Miss Ravenel's Conversion from Secession to Loyalty* (1867), Albion Tourgée's *A Fool's Errand* (1879) and works by Thomas Nelson Page and George Washington Cable. Yet direct trace of the great crisis on the novel was not strong. It seemed Whitman was right when he said, "The real war will never get into the books."

De Forest, with his strong battle scenes, was the first realist to record the conflict, though with a clear message of healing. Ambrose Bierce's sensitive and macabre war stories come a good deal later, while perhaps the greatest novel about the immediacy of the battlefield did not appear for thirty years, from a writer born six years after the conflict ended who said he reconstructed the experience from the football field— Stephen Crane's *The Red Badge of Courage* (1895). The major impact of the war on Southern fiction had to wait even longer; some interesting novels appeared during Reconstruction, but the great treatments came in the twentieth century, with Ellen Glasgow and William Faulkner, who found in the conflict of mercantilism and feckless chivalry a modern and a universal theme.

The notable changes came not in what was written about but in ways of writing. Few wars have been as fully recorded by the direct participants in memoir and annal, as the upheaval forced language toward a new realism to undermine old myths, ideals and faiths. An old eloquence died to be replaced by a new plainspokenness, the note of Lincoln's great speeches. The war destroyed two social orders, both justified by the same God: not just the "race of stately planters" and their Southern feudalism, but the old entrepreneurial democracy of the North. What replaced them was a modern, imperial, industrial nation-state. When the South capitulated to end the war and Reconstruction came, the dominant voices stressed the need for healing and recovery, for a return to the gospel of national expansion, progress and Manifest Destiny. Walt Whitman, who had tended wounded troops, recorded the horror of death and suffering in his war poetry, but his essential theme was to be, more than ever, reconciliation:

> But now, ah now, to learn from the crisis of anguish,
>   advancing, grappling with direct fate and
>   recoiling not,
> And now to conceive and show to the world what your
>   children en masse really are. . . .

"During the secession war I was with the armies, and saw the rank and file, North and South, and studied them for four years," he wrote in 1881. "I have never had the least doubt about the country in its essential future since." In *Miss Ravenel's Conversion from Secession to Loyalty,* John William De Forest follows the course indicated by his title; the book moves from realistic reporting of wartime pains toward "a grand, re-united, triumphant Republic." Albion Tourgée's *A Fool's Errand* is a bitterly critical record of war and Reconstruction in the South by a Northern-born writer who was wounded in battle and settled in North Carolina. George Washington Cable defended the civil rights of blacks in the postbellum South but eventually turned toward softer regional romance. Indeed, as industrialism spread, the memory of the Old South actually became a myth which Northerners accepted and cherished. "Make [your Southern heroine] fall in love with a Federal officer and your story will be printed at once," advised one Southern romance novelist, Thomas Nelson Page.

In a time for healing, the idea of national progress was the balm. Westward expansion diverted attention from the conflict of North and South to the ever-enlarging new lands that were prompting vast population movement. Attention shifted as well toward the development of industry and technology which had helped cause and mechanize the war and now provided the energy of Reconstruction. Before the war, Walt Whitman's open-ended verse had celebrated the transcendental self. After it, in a sweeping imperial surge, it celebrated the transcontinental self passaging westward to India, a modernizing self turning toward new inventions, technologies and industries. Whitman's ever-expanding and wandering ego undertook to utter a nation in its imperial phase, taking on geographical and industrial enlargement. For several decades the two processes seemed parallel; then, as we can see from Whitman's verse, they began to divide as it grew apparent that the nation had two contrary images of itself—one as an ever-westering pioneer land based on nature and space, the other as an urban nation where immigrants labored in great factories while the skyline pushed ever higher. In 1869, when a golden spike was driven at Promontory Point, Utah, to mark the completion of the transcontinental railroad joining the two coasts, it seemed a celebration of the opening West. More fundamentally, it was a celebration of the industrial motors driving America forward that would draw that West into a vast modernizing process which made America, by the century's end, the world's leading industrial nation.

The twenty-five years between the end of the war and the 1890s, when the frontier officially closed, were the period of the most profound changes America had yet seen. This was America's Victorian period, celebrated in a series of great exhibitions like the Great Exhibition held in London in 1851 to proclaim the Victorian and the technological age. In 1876, a hundred years after the Declaration of Independence, the Centennial Exhibition held in Philadelphia put American mechanical achievement on display, a mass of technological wonders like Thomas A. Edison's telegraph and Alexander Graham Bell's telephone. The spread of new land was matched by industrial innovation, the migration of national population by a massive increase in the scale of immigration, the emergence of new states and territories by the bursting upward energy of high-rise shock cities like Chicago. Industry, technology, capital investment and the growth of trusts led to the amassing of great personal fortunes, a new kind of wealth and power. The "Wild West" no sooner opened than it became a place like any other, already developing its "Buffalo Bills" and its place in popular mythology and national nostalgia. In 1893 came the World's Columbian Exposition in Chicago, the dynamic city that tied West and East into a single, interlinked, modern economic and social system. The historian Henry Adams, scion of one of the oldest American families, already feeling himself displaced by the new wealth and new politics, visited the massive display housed in over four hundred buildings. With the hum of the large electric dynamo in his ears, Adams recognized the proliferating processes and "energies quite new" that expressed the aggressive capitalism and political management destined to displace abstract thought and all traditional educations, including his own. The old order of Jeffersonian agrarianism had turned into an advanced industrial society, a unified process—but also a multiverse running beyond intellectual comprehension and control.

·II·

Predictions of these developments had already appeared in the writings of the American Renaissance, even though in this new America many prewar authors and works were to be forgotten. Thoreau and Emerson had constructed their "nature" and their idea of the transcendental self in part as adversary to a world devoted only to material systems. Melville and Hawthorne posited a fundamental conflict between the pastoral world of mythicized history, the history of ideal nature, and the timebound world of the practical and the mechanistic; both perceived the changes in consciousness that would be required by the new cities of iron and alienation, Hawthorne in *The Blithedale Romance* (1852), and Melville in *Redburn* (1849), *Pierre* (1852) and "Bartleby the Scrivener" (1857). Melville's *The Confidence-Man* (1857), about the masquerade of trust on which capitalism depends, is a work of deep modern awareness. Like the transcendentalists, the novelists of American "romance" did not fail to perceive the directions of American development; in fact, they often saw more deeply into its implications than their successors. Yet the sense of national change was so great that in a few years their work seemed distant and remote. When Henry James wrote his study of Hawthorne in 1879, he described him as a distant ancestor from a thinner soil and a more innocent time. And so it was that the only influential reputations to survive the war were those of the New England Schoolroom Poets celebrated by the Genteel Tradition whose domination would endure to the end of the century.

The survival of the Genteel Tradition was ensured by the authority of its critics, among them Edmund Clarence Stedman, an important anthologist and an influential voice in the "new ideality" that guided the postwar age. When Stedman looked around him in his *Poets of America* (1885), he saw his own time as an interregnum. Great American poets lay in the past, above all Longfellow, Whittier, Holmes and Lowell, who demonstrated that the genius of America revealed itself in high moral principles. Their very accessibility made them American; they set the standard for judging a present of proliferating, debasing literary commercialism and divisive sectionalism. Emerson was admitted to the pantheon, but held to be overfond of "woodnotes wild." Whitman was judged valuable for his commitment to literary democracy, but found guilty of a "lack of spirituality." Stedman reflected his age and its desire for a solemn moral literature; he felt that the challenge of his day was to relate "ideality" and the spirit of realism when what Americans craved were "the sensations of nature and cosmopolitan experience." Poetry, Stedman had to admit, was thus far losing in importance as the task was assumed by novelists, who "depict *Life* as it is, though rarely as yet in its intenser phases."

Depicting life as it is became the preoccupation of the newer American novelists. John William De Forest had set the tone in a manifesto-essay of 1868 titled "The Great American Novel." De Forest called for a novel that provides a "picture of the ordinary emotions and manners of American existence," a picture, he says, never yet fully drawn. "The Great American Novel" must avoid the "subjective" spirit of Hawthorne's romances ("only a vague consciousness of this life") and the expatriate withdrawal of the writer who "neglected the trial of sketching American life and fled abroad for his subjects." And though he admitted America was still a "nation of provinces," regional or cameo writing would not really serve, either. The need was for a novel of closely observed detail and broad social significance. In this, De Forest was urging the claims of the new realism that was already finding expression in the work of writers like William Dean Howells, Henry James and Mark Twain who in different fashions were to draw the developing realistic methods of Europe deep into American fiction. Realism of social subject had become a dominant characteristic of the European novel from the upheavals of 1848 onward. Flaubert and the Goncourt brothers urged the need to open literature to a full range of social concern; George Eliot in *Adam Bede* (1859) argued the importance for fiction of "all those cheap common things which are the precious necessaries of life." These and other authors, like Turgenev and Tolstoy, pointed the way for the new American writers too, for as William Dean Howells declared after acknowledging the importance of European developments, realism was characteristically democratic and therefore implicitly American, an art of the dramas of ordinary existence and the "life of small things." In the United States it could be an expression of optimism and even of ideality, for it was, Howells said, about "the more smiling aspects of life, which are the more American." Taking what was familiar and local in American experience, the methods of realism could create a democratic universal. This was very much Whitman's aim in poetry, where catalogues of things are to merge into wholeness through his poetic *"En-Masse."* The new realism was particularly relevant for the novel, that most realistic of all the literary forms. The older lineage of romance did not die, but in a material time it became displaced toward popular fantasy; it was realism in its various languages that became the exploring and innovative discourse of the new American writing.

This was due in part to the accelerated widening and spreading of American life. "Write of what you know! Write of your very own!" urged Edward Eggleston, author of the popular dialect novel *The Hoosier Schoolmaster* (1871) about a youthful Indiana schoolmaster struggling through the rough frontier years before the war. One of many books from the "Middle Border" of America, its new preface in 1892 explained Eggleston's intentions:

> It used to be a matter of no little jealousy to us, I remember, that the manners, customs, thoughts and feelings of New England country people filled so large a place in books, while our life, not less interesting, not less romantic, and certainly not less filled with humorous and grotesque material, had no place in literature. It was as though we were shut out of good society.

Regional writing, he said, "had made our literature national by the only process available," for "the 'great American novel,' for which prophetic critics yearned so fondly twenty years ago, is appearing in sections." Looking back from the 1890s, Eggleston recognized that an important development in American writing lay in its escape from East Coast domination and its turn toward sectional narratives and poems. Nourished by the *couleur locale* tradition of Hugo and Mérimée, Maria Edgeworth and Bulwer-Lytton, it drew also on the more directly American influences that came from travel writing, dialect humor and frontier tall tale. Many things encouraged this regional spirit in writing: the domination in book-length publication of European authors (not until 1891 did American writers acquire the protection of an international copyright law), the emergence of mass periodicals as a market for short fiction, postwar curiosity about disparate sections of the country and a growing nostalgia for simpler times and tales of an ever-more-strange past.

The concern of this writing was to capture the peculiar flavor of regions and districts, dialects and customs, dress and landscape. It reached from the New England of Harriet Beecher Stowe, author not only of *Uncle Tom's Cabin* but of accurate evocations of Massachusetts life in *The Minister's Wooing* (1859), *Oldtown Folks* (1869) and *Poganuc People* (1878), through O. Henry's metropolitan New York, to the South of the Georgia writer Joel Chandler Harris, who created Uncle Remus, George Washington Cable, who captured Creole life in *Old Creole Days* (1879) and created a dense panorama of Louisiana in his novel *The Grandissimes* (1880), and Kate Chopin, with her outspoken novel of female repression, *The Awakening* (1899). It treated the "Middle Border" of America as its mixed ethnic groups moved from frontier to settled agriculture in the work of Edward Eggleston and E. W. Howe, author of *The Story of a Country Town* (1883). But above all, literary regionalism explored the West. When Bret Harte, the writer from Albany, New York, who had traveled to the goldfields and mining camps of California, published the stories of *The Luck of Roaring Camp* in 1870, he won acceptance for an entire new realm of discourse by bringing into literature a world of drunks, rogues and vagabonds, described with an emotional and vernacular freedom that challenged the moral strictures of the Gilded Age and prepared the way for the greatest master of the entire genre, Mark Twain, who followed it to worldwide popularity.

What was important about regionalism was not only that it opened up new parts of the nation's life and geography for literature, but that it also introduced new languages for the rendering of American experience, several drawn from popular comedy: the powerful dialect humor of George W. Harris's Southern tall tales in *Sut Lovingood: Yarns Spun by a "Nat'ral Born Durn'd Fool"* (1867), and Joel Chandler Harris's exploitation of Negro plantation stories in the *Uncle Remus* tales which began to appear in the 1870s. Popular humor flourished in the work of stage and newspaper performers like Charles Farrar Brown ("Artemus Ward"), Henry Wheeler Shaw ("Josh Billings") and David Ross Locke ("Petroleum V. Nasby"); they passed on their arts to Samuel Langhorne Clemens—who chose in the same manner to call himself "Mark Twain." Extravagant tall tale could turn to bleak irony, as it did in the work of Ambrose Bierce, the writer from California whose macabre battle tales prefigured the work of Stephen Crane and whose mischievous mockery of hypocrisy and gentility in *The Devil's Dictionary* (1906) anticipated H. L. Mencken. Poetry too became regionalist. The best-known poet of the West, Joaquin Miller, won international reputation for his *Songs of the Sierras* (1871). The diplomat John Hay, a friend of Henry Adams, collected the vigorous dialect poems of the *Pike County Ballads* (1871). The most popular poet in America toward the end of the century was James Whitcomb Riley, the "Hoosier Poet" from Indiana, whose local dialect verse, in volumes like *The Old Swimmin'-Hole* (1883), sentimentalized rural life and whose "Little Orphant Annie" tugged the national heartstrings.

It was part of the strength of this regional tradition, which became universally popular during the 1870s, that it not only called up and often sentimentalized an American past that was fading, but also gave expression to the as yet unvoiced and radical, thus introducing new aspects of American life—the immigrant experience, the black experience, the experience of women—and pointing the path toward social criticism and naturalism. The work of Harriet Beecher Stowe and her successors, like Mary E. Wilkins Freeman in her grimly detailed portraits of New England life, *A Humble Romance* (1887) and *A New England Nun* (1891), fostered a feminine sensibility far different from the sentimentality of the mob of scribbling women who had so annoyed Hawthorne. In Maine, Sarah Orne Jewett explored her decaying seaport world in *The Country of the Pointed Firs* (1896) with extraordinary literary finesse; in New Orleans Kate Chopin created her analytical studies of women's suffering, *At Fault* (1890) and *The Awakening* (1899), with a skill and power that has only lately been recognized. When Willa Cather wrote her memoir *Not Under Forty* in 1936, she acknowledged Jewett and this tradition as a source for her own writing, and it had its impact on the work of other central twentieth-century women authors, like Edith Wharton and Ellen Glasgow. William Faulkner, that preeminent modernist regionalist, recognized that "my own little postage stamp of native soil was worth writing about"; we can see a similar indebtedness to these exploring antecedents in the work of Carson McCullers, Eudora Welty and Flannery O'Connor.

Writing the identities of regional life undoubtedly brought extensive new possibilities into American literature, but its challenge was always to cast local experience onto a universal scale, as Kate Chopin vehemently argued when she disputed with the "veritist" regional writer of the Middle Border, Hamlin Garland:

> Human impulses do not change and can not so long as men and women continue to stand in the relation to one another which they have occupied since our knowledge of their existence began. It is why Ibsen will not be true in some remote tomorrow. . . . And, notwithstanding Mr. Garland's opinion to the contrary, social problems, social environments, local color and all the rest of it are not *of themselves* motives to insure the survival of the writer who employs them.

While she may have been wrong about Ibsen, Chopin was right about the literary problem. Subject matter alone is never sufficient to insure literary quality, and realism quickly fades into document unless it displays aesthetic awareness and complexity. Howells sought to resolve this difficulty by linking the local to the national and thereby to the universal. But it was also possible to reverse the quest by seeking aesthetic complexity and artistic cosmopolitanism as a way to discover the nature of a serious realism.

We might say that Mark Twain took the first of these paths and Henry James the second. As the American literary heritage was growing more regional, it was also growing vastly more international. For James, it was the destiny of the American writer to be cosmopolitan. The rise in American expatriation after the Civil War was not due only to dissent from American commercialism and opportunism; it was also a response to artistic hunger for more complex literary awarenesses and forms. Even the regionalist spirit had its European sources; writers like Joaquin Miller, Ambrose Bierce, Bret Harte and Mark Twain spent considerable time in Europe, and Howells himself, who attacked "literary absenteeism," was greatly tempted to stay on in Venice. As American writers in the aftermath of the war confronted the land spread of the nation and the new cityscapes, the conflict of moral faiths and material processes, nostalgic reminiscence and radical changes, they began to encounter the complications of modern art.

·III·

No writer sought to give voice to the conflicting resources and directions of American culture in the post–Civil War period more fully than
the author who took to himself the humorist's name of "Mark Twain."
Samuel Langhorne Clemens had begun his literary career by going
West, lighting out for the territory like his most famous hero, Huckleberry Finn. During the war he had divided his sympathies, even
serving briefly in the Southern army, for his parents were Southerners
who had moved from Virginia into the slave-holding lands of the
Louisiana Purchase and settled in Missouri. But the Scott-influenced
line of Southern chivalry did not finally tempt him (in his later writing
he both employed it and devastatingly mocked it) and the West became
his answer. His instincts were entrepreneurial; his father was a speculator always dreaming of a fortune. Samuel had grown up in Hannibal,
on the Mississippi riverbank, at a time when the river was still the
nation's great north–south turnpike, the crossroads of slavery and
abolition, a gathering place for Western passages. This prewar Mississippi Valley life was to become his best material and acquire a
pristine innocence, but it was always charged with the nation's changes
and tensions. His first instinct was to live on the river, and, as he was
to explain in *Life on the Mississippi* (1883), he followed this instinct
to the point of becoming, in 1859, a licensed steamboat pilot. But he
had also worked as a printer's apprentice on the local newspaper that
was edited by his brother Orion, and when he went West it was as
much a journalist as a prospector. He did prospect in Nevada but
joined the Virginia City *Territorial Enterprise*, where he began to draw
on the Southwest humor tradition and adopted a humorist's pseudonym from the river life he had left behind him.

His early writing owed much to the tall-tale tradition of Augustus
Baldwin Longstreet, whose *Georgia Scenes* (1835) lay behind much
contemporary dialect humor. But there were also "Artemus Ward"
and "Josh Billings," and then, when he moved on to San Francisco,
the work of Western writers like Bret Harte and Joaquin Miller. A
Western tall tale, "The Celebrated Jumping Frog of Calaveras County"
(1865), gained him a national reputation, and so in 1866 he decided

to move to the East, being drawn, he said, by "a 'call' to literature, of a low order—*i.e.* humorous." Twain's relocation signaled the start of his remarkable synthesis of the elements of post–Civil War American writing as he undertook to link the local-color and Western tradition of his early work with the social, intellectual, commercial and industrial spirit of the decades he himself helped name the Gilded Age. His materials were always to lie in the world of the West and the rural Mississippi Valley of the period before the war; but the essential conditions and primary spirit of his writing were to come directly from the rapidly changing world that was to follow it. The prewar world was agrarian, the postwar world industrial; the prewar world he knew was based on black slavery, the postwar world he would come to explore depended increasingly on wage slavery. The world of the river frontier was the world of innocent, individual morality; the world of the new industrial and urban frontier was the world of the Genteel Tradition. Twain's eastward voyage in 1866 was a journey into the deepest changes of his own contemporary culture.

His great gift was his humor, which was not simply a comic tactic but a vernacular clarity and moral skepticism which he could deploy against respectable Eastern pretension and moral convention. In 1867, already an established writer, he left New York with a group of well-off and pious Easterners drawn by the "tide of a great popular movement" on an extensive steamer tour to Europe and the Holy Land. Americans were looking with new veneration and *nouveau riche* innocence toward European culture and the past. Travel facilities were improving, passages growing more quick, and many could afford to look at, and collect, art. Twain's comic report on the voyage, *Innocents Abroad* (1869), mocks not so much European customs, culture, religion and art ("when I had seen one of these martyrs I had seen them all," he wrote, summing up the Old Masters in a famous phrase) as innocent American veneration of them. But Twain was an innocent himself; his difference from his fellow passengers was that he could offer the clarity of Western skepticism, a "splendor of gay immorality" they did not share. Innocence thus becomes a form of realism, a perspective that could be turned on America itself. After the great success of *Innocents Abroad,* Twain wrote *Roughing It* (1872). Like Irving and Cooper before him, he looked from East to West, evoking the mining camps and pioneers he had left behind in a voice that mingled Eastern literariness with vernacular extravagance. But it was what came next, the articles of "Old Times on the Mississippi" (eventually *Life on the Mississippi*), that staked out his essential resources—Mississippi Valley life in its heyday before the war. In one sense this was idealized, picturesque material, and he partly treated it as such. But he also offered a new realism: the river was not just a landscape but a workplace, and a dangerous one, with deceits and snags he had plumbed himself in his training as a riverboat pilot.

Twain was writing of the past, but his career was becoming one of the great success stories of American letters. He became an energetic Eastern businessman, promoting his product through the new market in subscription sales and as a powerful stage performer. He married into a wealthy coal-owning family and moved to Hartford, Connecticut, where he reigned as both luminary and licensed rogue in the Nook Farm group. His writing and reputation acquired the respectability he wanted, even as he chafed against it. Philip Rahv once set Twain as a typical Western "redskin" writer against the Eastern "palefaces," but there was a paleface in him, too. An entrepreneurial go-getter himself, he understood the shifting history of his time, as his first novel, *The Gilded Age* (1873), written in collaboration with Charles Dudley Warner, showed. The book confronted the present, looking at the period 1860–68 as one which

> uprooted institutions that were centuries old, changed the politics of a people, transformed the social life of half the country, and wrought so profoundly upon the entire national character that the influence cannot be measured short of two or three generations.

A deeply revealing book, it portrays the age as a great gold rush where land and city alike are packed with fortune hunters. Its great comic invention is the confidence man Colonel Sellers, a latter-day portrait of the indefatigable huckster that Cooper, Melville and Charles Dickens, in his one American novel, *Martin Chuzzlewit,* had seen as an important American type. What is apparent is that, despite the satire, there was a Colonel Sellers in Mark Twain himself. For literature now was a form of hucksterism, a capitalist enterprise in which copyrights were patents and the age encouraged literary mass production (Twain thought of sending a fellow humorist to South Africa to collect material for a diamond mines *Roughing It*).

Literary contradiction flourished in the Gilded Age, and—like Whitman in his own way—Twain manifested it. The critic of American society was also its celebrator, the times of moral flux and corruption were also times of national greatness and expansion. Never quite sure whether to enjoy or condemn, Twain developed two warring voices: that of the boyish comedian, that of the bitter satirist. As the bad boy of American genteel culture he found himself able to identify with Tom Sawyer in *The Adventures of Tom Sawyer* (1876), an evocation of his Mississippi boyhood life and a classic boy's tale of a romantic adventurer enjoying treasure hunting, infant loves and secret games just beyond the gaze of the adult world. In the end, Tom is the bad good boy, but a deeper challenge lay secreted in the story in the figure of the more independent and anarchic Huckleberry Finn, for whom return to genteel life after the adventures are over is far less easy. It took Twain much trouble and many pauses in the writing to dig out Huck's deeper story. He did not publish *The Adventures of Huckleberry Finn* until 1885, a boy's book that is far more than a Boy's Book, the book with which, said Ernest Hemingway in another famous act of literary affirmation, American literature really starts. The book's greater depth and its extraordinary intensity do not simply come from the fact that Huck, the dirty child of nature whose escape from the Widow Douglas and "sivilization" is so much more than a boyish prank, is a deeper hero. It is not simply due to Twain's sharpened sense of evil and social pain, nor his fuller vision of the deceptions, gullibilities and feuds of that "sivilization." It is not even that he confronts here the stain of slavery by presenting in Nigger Jim not a stage black but a round human being. When Huck and Jim commit themselves to following the course of the elemental river downstream, this commits Twain too into following the course of a mythic natural power to which not only they but their inventor—and his readers— must respond.

Twain described *Huckleberry Finn* as "a book of mine where a sound heart & a deformed conscience come into collision & conscience suffers defeat." That defeat was possible, of course, because of the change in American history between the time of the story and the time of its writing: Twain knew that his audience would feel that Huck does right when he decides to do "wrong"—"what's the use you learning to do right when it's troublesome to do right and ain't no trouble to do wrong, and the wages is just the same?" Huck asks, explaining his decision not to return Jim to slavery. Yet the book still challenged its genteel audience because it is not religion or social responsibility that brings Huck to his decision; it is a simple and natural innocence beyond civilization. Twain's generative decision was to tell the story in Huck's first-person, dialect voice, with all the unreflecting simplicity that this enforced. In a marvelous comic conspiracy, therefore, we must read the book in naivete and wonder. Huck has no complete vocabulary for what he does; his tone of spoken innocence voices the clear-seeing eye of childhood which can question and upturn so many social values by failing to comprehend them. The great moral climax of the book—Huck's "All right, then, I'll go to hell"—is possible because the domain of the raft has become a special world of human intimacy where a fundamental human bond develops between the tattered, instinctive white boy and the superstitious, equally instinctive black slave. The drifting river transforms their journey into an intuitive, mythic quest, and in the process Huck's dialect becomes a serious and capacious literary language.

It remains nonetheless a comic language; Huck never really discovers conscience. Nor, as the author's warning note at the beginning reminds us, is his the only dialect in the book. Twain's is not just a story of nature but society, the society of the mercantile, often urban central river where the great technological steamboats work, as do the Melvillean confidence men, the King and the Duke, exploiting innocence for gain. At the end Tom Sawyer reappears and returns the tale to Twain's favorite form, burlesque; most readers agree in disliking the last part, seeing it as a weakening of the story's moral intensity. Even the familiar ending, where, in one of the most often remarked gestures in American literature, Huck decides he cannot return to "sivilization" and chooses to "light out for the Territory," is not quite what it seems. This is still Tom's plan: its aim is to have "howling adventures amongst the Injuns," not celebrate moral independence. Twain leaves us uneasy even with Huck; he refuses to affirm that Huck has discovered a new conscience. It is rather the conscience below the conscience, the freedom of comic play itself, that Twain celebrates. That is why he can seem to us both the author of one of America's greatest books, a novel that through its vernacular realism, its self-creating voice and its childlike naturalness in the face of moral challenge freed American fiction for the future, and a writer riven with contradictions. He was never to repeat this triumph and was entirely happy to bring both of these heroes back for boyish, burlesque adventures in later books written for money. Nor is it clear whether he himself believed in Huck's "sound heart." When Tom Sawyer announces toward the end that Jim is "as free as any creature that walks this earth," we cannot be sure just what that freedom amounts to.

Nor could Twain, for in the best of the books that came after *Huckleberry Finn* he shows increasing doubt about the possibility of asserting any natural independence or true innocence in the post-Darwinian era he lived in. Sometimes his optimism rose and he celebrated the age of democratic technology; sometimes he despaired of man's enslavement to machine. He sometimes saw potential for growth in human nature, at other times a dangerous power that struggled to impose religion, reason and morality over chaos. All this ambiguity of feeling is present in his fantasy *A Connecticut Yankee in King Arthur's Court* (1889), set in the feudal past of sixth-century Camelot, that popular resort of the Victorian gothic imagination. The book starts as a celebration of American entrepreneurship and Yankee ingenuity in the person of Hank Morgan, the Connecticut machine shop superintendent and inventor, who says: "So I am a Yankee of the Yankees—and practical; yes, and nearly barren of sentiment, I suppose—or poetry in other words." Transported by a blow on the head to King Arthur's court, he becomes a Promethean apologist for democracy and technology. In this dark place of monarchy, snobbery and ignorance he is, he says, a modern Robinson Crusoe, bringing the benefits of contrivance and efficiency to the savages. The slaves are freed, superstition overthrown, the benefits of the bicycle and modern advertising are introduced, as they had been to modern America. Twain's friend William Dean Howells called the book an "object-lesson in democracy." Yet this is to miss the dark implication of the ending. For it is not simply modern science and enlightenment Hank brings to Camelot. The story ends in a fantasy of terrifying superiority and then a massive holocaust of violence and technological murder, a dark prediction for the future.

By now Twain was America's leading writer: "the Lincoln of our literature," said Howells. His fame was international and his assaults on the Genteel Tradition had an impishness that spared him the hostility Whitman met. He was engaged in every kind of ambitious venture, but in the early 1890s the structure collapsed. His entrepreneurial activities turned to failure as a result of investment in technological projects like the Paige typesetting machine, which wouldn't. He went bankrupt. Family deaths and the promptings and commands of his humor—which often seemed to him like a demonic possession—added to his pessimism. And so did his growing intellectual doubts. His ideas were not systematic, but he had read Darwin, Haeckel and Lecky, the modern determinists. He came to see man as an absurdity, the world as a mechanism set going by a cruel Creator. He undertook to pay his debts with *Pudd'nhead Wilson* (1894), which, not surprisingly, "changed itself from a farce to a tragedy while I was going along with it." He turned once again to the Mississippi Valley of his youth, but sees it now through a darkened vision. The plot comes, as so often in Twain, from fairy tale, the old prince and pauper plot he had used before of two infants exchanged in the cradle. But here one child is free, the other a slave; one a person, the other property. The book observes the absurdity of slavery, where a touch of black blood makes the child a chattel, and makes Roxana, the black mother who contrives the exchange to protect her child, a remarkable heroine. But the dark irony is that there is no freedom to set against slavery. Both children are trapped by the lives they have learned and, in failing to find any effective moral or social identity, show the worst marks of their origins. Identity becomes no more than the fingerprint Pudd'nhead Wilson, the book's aphoristic sage, uses to unravel the murderous tragedy that develops.

Like Melville, Twain was to devote all his late work to this pessimistic vision, revealing, behind the popular humorist, a dark satirist responsive to the rising determinism that was turning optimistic American thought to doubt and self-questioning. "The Man That Corrupted Hadleyburg" (1899) is the story of an apparently virtuous town corrupted by money lust. "The Mysterious Stranger"—completed in 1906, but published posthumously in 1916—sums up Twain's sense of man's absurdity in a story of Satan's appearance in a medieval Austrian town to explain that mankind is part of a "grotesque and foolish dream," a toy in a Creation devised to ridicule the idea that men progress, act morally or really exist at all. In *What Is Man?*—privately printed in 1906, published in 1917—he argued similar views: man is a machine, moral and mental faculties are automatic products of temperamental impulses and man is therefore "entitled to no personal merit for anything he does." The sense of cosmic irony and human solipsism that informed his work up to his death in 1910 was a revolt against the innocent, flamboyant writer America asked him to be. He had himself remarked that the secret source of humor was not joy but sorrow; the bitter satirist in him now exploded, showing him beset to despair by the intellectual anxieties of his times. As with any popular author—and he was the first of the major American novelists to *be* really popular—critics since have left us with widely different versions of his qualities. Some saw him as the comic democratic sage, the quintessentially humane American writer. Others saw him as a sensibility defeated by the blandness of American culture, a satirist who yielded to materialism and gentility: "Twain paid the price of caving in," said Sherwood Anderson. For others like Henry Nash Smith, it was exactly his double consciousness that made him a great writer—the pull between an instinctive realism and a genteel aspiration, between progress and nostalgia, that forced him to experience the inner contradictions of his age.

Certainly Twain expressed his age and its changes, not only in material and social conditions but in belief. Reflecting on his friend's career in 1901, William Dean Howells saw him as the Westerner who had been forced to face, but also challenge, a world in which the natural and the primitive were being made obsolete:

> The inventions, the appliances, the improvements of the modern world invaded the hoary eld of his rivers and forests and prairies, and while he was still a pioneer, a hunter, a trapper, he found himself confronted with the financier, the scholar, the gentleman. . . . They set him to thinking, and, as he never was afraid of anything,

he thought over the whole field and demanded explanations of all his prepossessions—of equality, of humanity, of representative government, and revealed religion. When they had not their answers ready, without accepting the conventions of the modern world as solutions or in any manner final, he laughed again. . . . Such, or somewhat like this, was the genesis and evolution of Mark Twain.

Twain knew and wrote of an America that grew from the pioneer, pastoral, yet slavery-stained world of the 1830s and 1840s through the war, and then onward into the deep uprootings of 1860s technology and social Darwinism where a new image of nature replaced the Western myth he had begun with. These changes he explored, comically, nostalgically and with affection until the pain and sense of corruption broke out in the heroic refusals at the end. Like Dickens, his talents were half-instinctive; he was a popular writer, not an author of fine controls. He had the ranging eye of comedy, from farce and burlesque to satire and dark irony, and comedy's doubt about the sureness of human identity and the deceit of social institutions, its pleasure in imposture and anarchy. This was, moreover, *American* comedy with its angle of simplicity and native amazement, always ready to mock, though often almost ready to be charmed by, rank, pretension, manners or status. Like Whitman, his lasting gift to American writing was a native voice. As T. S. Eliot said, he was one of those seminal writers who, by escaping false structures and bringing language up to date, change the tradition for all their successors.

·IV·

Howells's portrait of Twain as a regionalist from the American past challenging the transformations of the present suggests one reason why these two men, the most celebrated writers of their time, became such close friends. For Howells was a believer in the novel—the novel as a serious form of social attention, not a species of romance. His argument for fiction's centrality dominated literary debate in the Gilded Age—for his voice sounded from the editorial chair of the authoritative *Atlantic Monthly*—and his views had much to do with the fact that, from the war to the century's end, it was the novel and not the poem that was the central expressive form. The genteel Fireside Poets of Boston wrote on; Emily Dickinson sustained the tight aesthetic economy of poetry in her privacy. There was Whitman's aim of representativeness and amplitude: "Chants of the prairies,/Chants of the long-running Mississippi and down to the Mexican sea,/Chants of Ohio, Indiana, Illinois, Iowa, Wisconsin and Minnesota" and of catalogued attention and response to social change: "Immigrants arriving, fifteen or twenty thousand in a week." But such lines were almost a description of fiction's aims, and there were those who saw Whitman's loose, endless declarations as nothing more than prose in pieces. "The art of fiction has in fact become a finer art in our day than it was with Dickens or Thackeray," Howells claimed, writing now of his other eminent friend, Henry James. By "finer art" Howells meant a more precise and detailed art, an art responsive to social necessity. For Howells insisted that America was no longer to be written as timeless myth, a state of nature, a Hawthornian "romance," but as a changing social mechanism very much in process that required the detailed understanding of the new novel.

Howells saw both American society and American literature crossing a great divide, and some version of this vision haunts the best American writing of the Gilded Age. It explains the conflict of modern process and nostalgia in Twain and the theme of American innocence forced to encounter modern experience in the work of Henry James. It is evident in Howells's own fiction. In his most famous novel, *The Rise of Silas Lapham* (1885), the move from an innocent, independent prewar economy to the corrupting world of postwar corporations and mergers brings moral crisis to his simple paint manufacturer Lapham. Howells was spokesman for a change in stylistic assumptions which were direct responses to deep changes in national experience. Behind him was the large imaginative universe we call Romantic; its American geographical locus was largely New England, and its essential spirit optimistic-libertarian. Beyond would be the imaginative universe we vaguely call Modernist, its geographical locus commonly bohemian or stateless, and its essential spirit one of experiment prompted by crisis. But between is the major movement we call Realism. Like the others, it was an international movement, but it had, as Howells saw, its special

American application. Its geographical locus was the place of change—the altered farming community, the new practices of business and politics, the modern city, the changing region; its pieties were increasingly those of skepticism and science. It was not one tendency but many, ranging from local-color regionalism, that extension of the geographical and empirical reach of American literature that Howells firmly supported, to wider-ranging novels of social process or political corruption—Twain's and Warner's *The Gilded Age,* Henry Adams's *Democracy* (1880), John Hay's *The Breadwinners* (1884), Hamlin Garland's *A Spoil of Office* (1892). The writing of realism could express social nostalgia and idealism, but would move also toward progressive or populist indignation and scientific materialism. In helping America understand itself in historic time as a society in the forefront of modernizing change, it expressed the logic both of American conditions and the American mind with its "peculiarly matter-of-fact" quality, as Thorstein Veblen put it, and its moral pragmatism. This was the understanding of reality Howells came to represent, both as critic and novelist.

William Dean Howells was a Midwesterner from Martin's Ferry, Ohio, and grew up, like Twain, in an atmosphere of printing and journalism. A campaign biography of Abraham Lincoln provided him with funds for a trip to Boston, where he had an almost dreamlike welcome from Hawthorne, Holmes and Lowell. They greeted him as the representative literary Westerner with what Holmes actually described as a "laying-on of hands." The book on Lincoln also won him the substantial political reward of the American consulship in Venice. Here he spent the crucial years of 1861–65, so that along with his two major contemporaries Twain and Henry James he too missed the war. Europe tempted him, and his first novels are set there. But he steadfastly rejected the rising fashion for what he called "literary absenteeism" and insisted instead on dealing with the immediate, ready material of contemporary American change. Back in Boston, he secured his apostolic succession by joining the *Atlantic Monthly;* by 1871 he was its editor and influential tone-setter, the Dean of American Letters. Supportive to his contemporaries, he administered critical reputations, became the temperate voice of literary change and set out to balance New England's "idealizing" tendency with the "realizing" spirit of

New York and the West. Realism—the "only literary movement of our times that seems to have vitality in it"—became both his cause and the method of his own writing. Romanticism, he granted, had worked to escape the paralysis of tradition and widen the bonds of sympathy, but it was now exhausted. It remained for realism "to assert that fidelity of experience and probability of motive that are the essential conditions of a great imaginative literature. It is not a new theory, but it has never before universally characterized literary endeavor." Its moment had come: as both the dominant tendency in the Europe he never ceased to be conscious of and the controlling emphasis of George Eliot, Turgenev and above all Tolstoy, whose methods and socialistic principles he admired, it was equally the best way to express the new America.

Howells was always to see himself neatly placed between his two friends, Mark Twain and Henry James. James was, he said, the leader of the "new American school," but he was too dependent on aestheticism and on Europe; it was Twain who was "the Lincoln of our literature" and the man of "western sense." Between the two (who did not like each other's work), Howells mediated; never the experimentalist that James was, he was nevertheless a formalist who could only watch with admiration Twain's divine amateurishness. He had his own formula for success in postwar American culture, a culture of those who, like himself, had "risen": he spoke middle-class morality back to itself as common sense and confirmed the nation's confidence in its contemporary mass and solidity. His interests were extensive and flexible; his books assimilated moral observation, politics and reportage with a capacious curiosity. They are often spoken of as "photographic"; Henry Adams began the metaphor, in an admiring review of *Their Wedding Journey* (1872). His first novel, it is a work of common American detail done, like so many American novels, in the simple form of the travelogue as we follow a honeymoon couple to their classic, picturesque destination, Niagara Falls. Plot, he said, was "the last thing for which I care"; his stories developed through vignette and a luminous vigor of the commonplace. Howells had the good novelist's gift for selecting just those elements in a situation which bring it home and suggest forthright veracity.

Many of Howells's novels—he produced something like a novel

a year, of varied quality—are slight, but he is perhaps the most undervalued of nineteenth-century American authors. He was a middlebrow writer, close to the Genteel Tradition and to many its very personification. Yet at best his books display a detailed social attention combined with a moral acuteness rare in America; as Lionel Trilling once said, the novel of manners and morals, so familiar in Europe, is uncommon in the United States. "Don't despise the day of small things!" says the lawyer Atherton in *A Modern Instance* (1882), one of his best books. The "day of small things" was what Howells himself never despised, and his books link personal and national experience so carefully that all small experience has larger consequence, all private lives and values acquire a subtle illustrativeness, and the domestic and local standard becomes a sufficient measuring-rod for the largest issues of existence. This was, he claimed, his Americanness, and American realism could deal with plainer problems and brighter things than European—after all, what was "peculiarly American" was the "large cheerful average of health and success and happy life." Recording American life in its smallest, newest details and qualities, he could, he believed, see it with a special clarity. His books therefore create a feeling not just of the familiar, but of the *worth* of the familiar: what is ordinary can redeem us. If one part of his realism was a realism of presentation, a fidelity to the commonsense material world, another part was his realism of judgment, his commonsense morality.

This, certainly, could lead to simplicity. His works have a Norman Rockwell spirit of detailed innocence, and he too recognized his photographic flavor—he was, he said, using the American "snap-camera" to focus small groups, happy scenes, rural society, street life. His moral realism could indeed seem pious and separate him from the naturalist writers who came after him and whose work he acclaimed with generosity and warmth. The dark determining secrets behind the real, the problems of social stress and strife which now began to rock American life, only slowly penetrated to disturb his writing. As both his age and his books developed, however, he too began to see desperate forces at work in America and increasingly came to doubt how "smiling" the face of the American commonplace really was. Indeed, in his work, as it took on larger political themes and Utopian questions, we can see how the values of domestic moral individualism were coming under threat in corporate America. Howells found himself pushed toward socialism and to yet larger subjects, as other writers, too, were being pushed. *Annie Kilburn* (1888) deals with the immigrant poor and working-class experience. Then came the harsh social contrasts that rocked New York City and challenged its indifferent capitalists in the novel with which he greeted the troubled 1890s, *A Hazard of New Fortunes* (1890), and the social—and socialist—criticism of his Utopian romance *A Traveler from Altruria* (1894). Here he pursued the rigorous social questioning of books like Edward Bellamy's *Looking Backward* (1888) and Ignatius Donnelly's *Caesar's Column* (1891) which test the American present against the promises and dangers of an imagined future.

His two best works are novels of this transition. *The Rise of Silas Lapham* (1885) develops his recurrent theme of the moral or Western parvenu trying to understand American society and American Society, the web of classes. Lapham has discovered a source of paint and gone into business in the "Poor Richard" way, making money through his own energy and resourcefulness. But he returns from the Civil War to find a new era of business, "The day of small things was past," and he is stretched beyond his moral means. Though his paint business thrives and he becomes a "Solid Man of Boston," an early case of the businessman as public hero, he is lost in a world too big for him. He aspires to upper-class status and polish, but he encounters Gilded Age corruption in the new corporatism; he overextends and is drawn into shady dealings and speculation. The image for this is the big house he is building in Boston. The house burns down and he instinctively renounces his speculation, finding that it has threatened his domestic life. His financial fall is his moral rise; he is taken back into the world of his family and small things—the heartland of Howells's fiction.

But Howells also arrays the forces *against* this solution, for American society was indeed displacing the men of small things. Progressivism and sociology alike showed that life in modern cities was not always subject to moral control, and newer, younger writers were seeing around them a world not of traditional culture and morality but of iron forces in society and human biology that "really" determined existence. Howells had attempted to reconcile through realism two essential American traditions: the tradition of "rough" democracy, represented by Emerson, Whitman and to some degree Twain, which looked to the self and the West to bring forth a brave New World, and the Genteel Tradition, which asserted the power of society and culture as real forces and looked eastward to the Old World. But he found this meditation was doomed to fail.

Howells was outraged by the hanging of seven anarchists following the Chicago Haymarket Riots of 1886. As the conflicts between capital and labor grew, he was no longer sure that smiling American life *was* coming out all right in the end. *A Hazard of New Fortunes* (1890) is a transitional book in more than one way, for it explores his own decision to leave genteel, moral Boston for competitive New York City, a decision that forced on him a rereading of American culture. New York in this troubled novel is seen as a city of social tension and strikes, poverty, tenements, Darwinian competition. His new portrait of the capitalist, Jacob Dryfoos, presents a man who no longer possesses ethical inner guidance but functions according to the "lawless, godless" rules of social Darwinism. His central character, Basil March, acknowledges the "economic chance-world we have created" where men struggle bloodily, "lying, cheating, stealing."

Society was no longer a bright moral stage where life is illumined by its own virtuous center; it demanded a new kind of novel and a more determinist and sociological vision to grasp it. In the essays of *Criticism and Fiction* (1898) Howells restated his realist credo:

> We must ask ourselves before anything else, is this true?—true to the motives, the impulses, the principles that shape the life of actual men and women? This truth, which necessarily includes the highest morality and the highest artistry—this truth given, the book cannot be wicked and cannot be weak; and without it all graces of style and feasts of invention and cunning of construction are so many superfluities of naughtiness.

It is a credo which lends support to the new naturalist generation that did not idealize and humanize but defined an American life of human ironies, underclasses, social conflict and Darwinian struggle. Howells backed Hamlin Garland, Stephen Crane, Frank Norris and Abraham Cahan, the new literary voices. He also backed the new muckrakers and social critics, from Henry Demarest Lloyd, whose attack on the Standard Oil monopoly was given a whole issue of the *Atlantic,* to Thorstein Veblen, whose work of ironic social analysis, *The Theory of the Leisure Class* (1899), was a superb dismantling of the laws of "pecuniary emulation" by which many Americans sought to live. In turn, these writers recognized his influence and importance, and he remained a literary power to his death in 1920. He had indeed guided a new era in American writing—but into far less smiling places than he could ever have anticipated in 1865.

·V·

In 1867, Mark Twain had found himself joining the tide of a great popular movement:

> Everybody was going to Europe—I, too, was going to Europe. Everybody was going to the famous Paris Exposition—I, too, was going to the Paris Exposition. The steamship lines were carrying Americans out of the country at the rate of four or five thousand a week in the aggregate. If I met a dozen individuals during that month who were not going to Europe directly, I have no distinct remembrance of it now.

But Twain was not the only observer of these new innocents abroad, these older patricians distrustful of the new wealth and the new politics or else the representatives of that new wealth hungering for the reinforcement of older culture—as if to reverse the massive tide of immigration from Europe flowing onto American land and into American cities, they went by the steamerload to a Europe that increasingly became a cultural and social romance. In *The American* (1877), Henry James tells a story almost the reverse of Twain's, the romance of the rich Western American, Christopher Newman, who tours Europe, finds that "what he had been looking at all summer was a very rich and beautiful world, and that it had not all been made by sharp railroad men and stock-brokers," and, not just looking but discovering, learns that both innocent and deep stories contain their deceptions and cor-

ruptions. James is usually seen as Twain's outright opposite—the paleface to his redskin, as Philip Rahv once put it. And certainly, though
both men were voices of the new realism, they were realists of contrasting hue. Twain threw himself into America's chaotic postwar materialism and became the voice of its confusions and contradictions,
its hopes and nostalgias; James followed realism into elaborate moral,
psychological and aesthetic complexities, seeking to penetrate beneath
their surfaces and discover those means in consciousness and form by
which we give, in Roland Barthes's words, "to the imaginary the formal
guarantee of the real." Twain, like Whitman, opened American writing
to a freer voice; James opened it to a deeper art, art as a quest for
knowledge of self and the wider world.

Like Twain and Howells, James was conscious of growing up in
an America undergoing enormous and fundamental changes. He was
raised in New York City and Cambridge, Massachusetts, in the world
of "the busy, the tipsy and Daniel Webster," but in a very special
enclave of it: the James family, almost a country in its own right. Henry
James, Sr., his father, was a man of means, a Swedenborgian and a
friend of Emerson's who adopted the tradition of transcendentalist
idealism and once said he preferred spiritual to natural existence. The
heritage of New England moralism shaped the son—the doing of
"simple and sublime" things that his sculptor in *Roderick Hudson*
(1876) celebrates. His father had regularly taken his children to Europe
for their "sensuous education"; not only Europe but that sensuousness,
the hunger to apprehend experience through consciousness, remained
with the novelist son throughout his life. He was kept out of the Civil
War through an "obscure hurt" sustained fighting a fire. He studied
law at Harvard but then turned to writing; his first tales appeared in
the Boston magazines as the war ended. He sought to establish himself,
as did most American writers, with the travel piece, writing of America
but also of England, France and Italy, the three essential European
parishes of the novels that would follow. He visited Europe between
1869 and 1870 and from 1872 to 1874, returning each time to "do
New York" but steadily opening up the eastward map which he felt
was as central to the American heritage as was that to the West.

In 1875 he collected his travel pieces as *Transatlantic Sketches*
and his tales under the apt title *The Passionate Pilgrim and Other Tales,*

tales that lay down many of the essential themes that would serve him for his novels and draw on and amend a symbolic international geography already part-established by Irving and Hawthorne. The title tale treats the familiar subject of an American claimant in England, which Hawthorne had also used; "The Last of the Valerii" and "The Madonna of the Future" contrast American innocence of vision with Italian beauty and decadence and also consider the American artist's quarrel with his own country; "Madame de Mauves" concerns an American fortune allying itself with a French title, as would *The American*. His first novel published as a book, *Roderick Hudson* (1876), is the story of an American sculptor's need to drink the cup of experience and leave Puritanic America for the decadent "golden air" of Italy, a tale that implicitly comments on *The Marble Faun* by Hawthorne, an author to whom James remained clearly indebted. It is a romance, but a skeptical one, skeptical, too, about the very idea of Europe *as* a romance, by insisting on social and psychological verisimilitude and the value of experience, "the real taste of life." As in most of James's early novels, the large mythology persists, drawing on the old literary polarities: innocence and experience, ordinary American life and the rich art of Europe, plain present and dusky deep past. James suggests that the romantic and innocent American will always risk defeat in Europe's ambiguous, social and often tainted air while enlarging his or her knowledge and vision. At the same time the innocent and unencumbered American "balloon of romance," as a kind of fiction, would need to be made more profound and grainier by incorporating some of the experiential, moral and social subtlety, the denser registration of life, to be found in the great European novels.

In the centennial year of 1876, when Americans at the Philadelphia Exhibition were gazing in amazement at the new technologies, the telephones and typewriters they would be using in quantity just a few years later, and when speeches announced the spread of American territory and "the vast profusion of our wealth," James was making what he called his "choice." That year he was back in Paris with the leading novelists of his age, Flaubert, Daudet, the Goncourt brothers, Maupassant, Zola, Turgenev, admiring their fierce literary honesty while gradually coming to distrust their aestheticism. He moved on to London, and at the end of the year decided to settle there for good:

"My choice is the Old World—my choice, my need, my life." He selected London, his "murky Babylon," as

> on the whole the most possible form of life. I take it as an artist and a bachelor; as one who has the passion of observation and whose business is the study of human life. It is the biggest aggregation of human life—the most complete compendium of the world.

It was, in short, the most strategic location for one whose essential posture was that of watcher and observer and whose conviction was that art arose from the texture of the culture on which it drew. James was soon assuring Howells that it was on "manners, customs, usages, habits, forms" that the novelist lived, that it took complex social machinery to set the novel into motion, that America was too divided between the material and the abstract. Howells disagreed: it was the American want of such things that made the opportunity of its writers so interesting. Precisely this question haunted James thereafter. Nonetheless, with many doubts about "giving up" and "payment," he began the expatriation that would last his lifetime. So began, too, his full commitment to the "international theme" that would dominate most of his subsequent work and which he would take to ever more elaborate levels of refinement and complexity.

James's choice was not a rejection of his American heritage—indeed he saw himself claiming that heritage as a right to cosmopolitanism, for he was, he recognized, "more of a cosmopolitan (thanks to the combination of the continent and the USA which has formed my lot) than the average Briton of culture." As he wrote in 1888 to his brother William James, the philosopher, psychologist and expounder of American pragmatism whose thought was greatly to influence him,

> I aspire to write in such a way that it would be impossible to the outsider to say whether I am at a given moment an American writing about England or an Englishman writing about America (dealing as I do with both countries), and so far from being ashamed of such an ambiguity I should be exceedingly proud of it, for it would be highly civilized.

For Henry James the essential principle of fiction was contrast, and no contrast was greater than that encountered "when we turn back and forth between the distinctively American and the distinctively European outlook." Commenting on the American writer who had shaped him most, he observed in his study *Hawthorne* (1879) that Hawthorne lacked roots, wanted soil for his fiction, but also that he possessed the American "joke": the realization that social forms and densities were not everything. This indeed would become the heart of James's fiction, the persistent probing both into and beyond the material world, the probing that has historically been so deeply American. He was always to retain the Adamic conviction that self is in some sense prior to social formation and circumstance, the pragmatist's presumption that perception and experience are not commonsense matters but formative crises of consciousness, an idealist belief that knowing reality is always a pursuit, an endless aesthetic and social quest which the novel, with its roots in both myth and density of detail, embodies. That American quest for reality among the murky depths of Europe, its buildings, social practices, ancestries and hieroglyphs, would drive his fiction persistently toward new types of inquiry, so that his work as a whole becomes an elaborate search for the sufficient impression and the significant form—and finally an essential foundation of all modernist fiction.

Like his brother William's philosophy or his friend Henry Adams's history writing and *Education,* James's work is thus essentially a search for knowledge in a world so massed and yet so evanescent that it demands intense self-awareness from its observer. In its earlier forms, James's explorers enact the need of the "free" but materialist American self to encounter what it knows least of: history, society and the complexities of art. In *The American* (1877), the emblematically named Christopher Newman is the modern American hero as Western millionaire businessman, a "commercial man" with an easy but concerned morality whose optimism is confronted with dusky Old World expedients. We see him "stepping forth in his innocence and his might," longing for a new world which now can only be the Old. Like most of James's central figures, he begins as an observer and becomes a discoverer, adjusting his Western physicality and his Puritanism to a growing aesthetic and experiential need. But as is usual in James, such desire is also financial and sexual; Newman's "program" is to buy himself a "first class" wife and link new American wealth with established social distinction. Thus James's international theme concerns transatlantic exchange in more than one sense: the plot of the American "romance" of Europe includes the intricate embraces of money. Newman's quest fails in a melodramatic European deception, and when James, late in life, wrote his preface to the book for the New York edition of 1907, he confessed it was an "arch-Romance."

Through the late 1870s James complicated his concerns. *The Europeans* (1878) brings two socially experienced Europeans to the plain Puritanic light of New England; *Daisy Miller* (1878) tests a young American girl's complex innocence in the decadences of fever-infested Rome; *Washington Square* (1880) looks through many refractions of irony at the New York City of James's youth, much as *The Bostonians* (1886) would explore posttranscendentalist Boston in the new age of "the woman question." But his finest early novel is undoubtedly *The Portrait of a Lady* (1881), the story of Isabel Archer of Albany, New York, the free young girl determined "to see, to try, to know." Set in motion through three European countries—a green-lawned England, a socialite France, an aesthetic Italy—she endures as an emblem of hope until the money that is to set her free becomes her downfall. Entrapped by two scheming American expatriates, the materialistic Madame Merle and the sterile, metallic aesthete Gilbert Osmond, she marries him, refuses to leave him and is consequently "ground in the very mill of the conventional." The tale can be read in the tradition of George Eliot, the line of the English social and moral novel that balances against the needs of the individual self the claims of society —and its moral exactitude is an essential part of its power. But in the conflict between the two versions of self expressed by Madame Merle and Isabel it is very American:

> "There's no such thing as an isolated man or woman; we're each of us made up of some cluster of appurtenances . . ." [says Madame Merle]. "I know a large part of myself is in the clothes I choose to wear. I have a great respect for things! . . ."
>
> "I don't agree with you . . ." [says Isabel]. "I don't know whether I succeed in expressing myself, but I know that nothing

else expresses me. Nothing that belongs to me is any measure of me: everything's on the contrary a limit, a barrier, and a perfectly arbitrary one."

Though Isabel must ultimately face the fact that there is more to life than the Emersonian unconditioned self, James preserves her as a transcendent character, for this is a novel of apprehending psychology. In his preface he explains his decision to "place the centre of the subject in the young woman's own consciousness," thereby identifying her angle of vision with the untried spirit of the discovering imagination itself. We follow the workings of her thought and feeling as she engages the life she knows she cannot separate herself from: "the usual encounters and dangers . . . what most people know and suffer." She becomes the very essence of character in fiction as she suffers contingency and knowledge. The question of how we apprehend reality and derive morality and experience from it (Isabel's question) is paralleled by the question of how the artist apprehends, creates an impression, positions himself beside discovering characters, composes form and creates the illusion of life (James's question).

If, then, the novel is a social form, creating the "illusion of reality," and a moral form, expressing "felt life," it is also an aesthetic, self-knowing form, a managed and composed impression. There is an *art* of fiction, which James increasingly concerned himself with in the stories and literary criticism he wrote in the 1880s. His two big novels of the period depart from the "international theme" to detail an age of alteration, gathering masses, increased political activity, changing modern cities. *The Bostonians* (1886) deals with the way in which the city of transcendentalism was riven by a conflict in sexual relations through the rise of feminism; *The Princess Casamassima* (1886) is a turbulent city novel about anarchism in London. The books were not well received, though they are fine works of modern culture-reading, and James began to feel he had fallen on "evil days." For a time he set the novel aside altogether, only to suffer disappointing failure as a playwright. For him as for Twain and Howells, the early 1890s were a bleak period, when, as his brother William said, the world seemed to enter a "moral multiverse" of growing fissure between consciousness and the material or realistic world. But like the best writers of the 1890s, James responded to the sense of crisis with a new art, self-consciously made, at odds with the rising popular audience whose expectations seemed to limit the novel. His new methods were apparent in *What Maisie Knew* (1897), a work of impressionist psychology. As the title suggests, it is a fable set in consciousness—the "small expanding consciousness" of the young girl Maisie, with its "register of impressions" as she seeks to understand what is happening in the adult (which is also the adulterous) world around her. Similar sexual secrets are hidden in the labyrinths of *The Turn of the Screw* (1898), but here the ghost-story form obscured the obscurities and made this one of his most popular late works.

But his finest novels were yet to come. Around the turn into the twentieth century—the century when, he said, the novel would come at last to self-consciousness—he produced his founding novels of Modernism: *The Sacred Fount* (1901), *The Wings of the Dove* (1902), *The Ambassadors* (1903), *The Golden Bowl* (1904). In them the international theme returns, but as a matter for total reconsideration. *The Ambassadors,* the story of Lambert Strether's attempt to discover what has happened to his compatriot Chad Newsome in Paris, is the most accessible. It appears to restate James's earlier moral theme: "Live all you can; it's a mistake not to," Strether is told by Little Bilham in the Paris where Strether has learned to perceive his own American limitations. But what Strether eventually learns is the more consequential ability to *see,* to master "the impression, destined only to deepen, to complete itself," to recognize the limits of consciousness. Strether is the only one of James's late characters to reach so far into understanding and coherence. Most of the late novels are about the "cracks in things"—as in *The Golden Bowl,* where the international theme is recast and the aesthetic and the mercenary, the contemplative and the acquisitive, mingle in the central symbol of the flawed bowl, itself suggesting not only social emptiness but the necessary incompleteness of art itself. These books capture an increased sense of the disorder and contingency of modern European society, a new awareness of the flaws in the sought object and an admission of the epistemological incompleteness of perception, patterning, composition. Society becomes suspect, an object of dangerous knowledge; the "thickness of motive" James had always associated with Europe begins to dissolve; aesthetic awareness no longer promises clear moral realization.

Like his brother William, Henry eventually came to see through the hard material surface of the modern world to the discrepancy between consciousness and the matter it implied, and he became a severe challenger of his own earlier realism and an experimental Modernist. Europe, he said, "had ceased to be romantic to me"; a visit to America in 1904 showed him there too a world of Mammon towers and hotel civilization which had lost its light expectancy. Like Henry Adams's *The Education of Henry Adams,* his *The American Scene,* printed in the same year, 1907, displays a massed modern world outrunning comprehension and perception, yet charged with material energy and power. When the First World War came, he expressed his sense of the rising unreality of reality to Hugh Walpole: "Reality is a world that was to be capable of this." Yet he pledged his support for the British cause by taking out British citizenship just before he died in 1916. In his lifetime, and since, there have been many who criticized him for his "literary absenteeism" and his withdrawal from his nationality. But in his poet's quarrel—not just with Gilded Age America but with the direction of modern history—he was not alone. Many who stayed at home—Melville and Whitman, Howells and Twain— displayed their inward expatriation, showing themselves increasingly alienated from their times, their audience and the confident illusions of material progress. Others followed James on the path of expatriation, temporary or permanent: Bret Harte, Howard Sturgis, Bernard Berenson, Stephen Crane, Henry Harland, Edith Wharton, Gertrude Stein—some seeking Europe's "civilization," others the radical bohemia of art for its own sake, the path of experiment. James himself had sought both: social Europe, the Europe of the past, and aesthetic Europe, the Europe of artistic innovation. As perhaps his most cunning admirer, Gertrude Stein, was to see, there were two Henry Jameses —the nineteenth-century realist allured by Europe, and the twentieth-century Modernist who set American writing free to tell the story of the nation's new era.

CHAPTER

· 7 ·

MUCKRAKERS AND
EARLY MODERNS

· I ·

In Europe, at the start of the 1890s, the age was swept by a fundamental change of mood: a fresh spirit for a millennial decade. Ibsen and Zola, Schopenhauer, Nietzsche, Bergson and Freud were transforming mental response to the modern—it was a key word of the decade—in much the same way that scientists and technologists like Marconi and Röntgen, Diesel and Benz, Pasteur and Curie were transforming the physical universe and creating a climate of discovery. Old certainties faded; the old Norwegian playwright Ibsen was reported as saying, "The great task of our time is to blow up all existing institutions—to destroy." For the following twenty-five years, until this explosive attitude found its eventual expression on the battlefields of the First World War, the transformation continued. It was commonly agreed, not just in America but in Europe too, that in this transformation the United States would play a historic role. Yet, as the 1890s began, there was little about the surface appearance of American literary culture that suggested the great upheaval of the new was taking place. William James, the Harvard psychologist-philosopher-pragmatist, did publish *Principles of Psychology* in 1890, which displayed the same interest in a new subjective science of consciousness that men like Henri Bergson were exploring in Europe.

James portrayed human consciousness struggling for pragmatic self-definition in what he called the modern "pluriverse," and he went on to offer a new metaphor for the processes of mind. Thought, consciousness, was not a chain of linked segments: "A 'river' or a 'stream' are the metaphors by which it is most naturally described," he said—his "stream of consciousness" phrase had rich implication not only for the changing language of perception but for the twentieth-century novel. And, at much this time, the great historian Henry Adams, already feeling displaced in a world that no longer needed his eighteenth-century values or nineteenth-century education, did recognize the undisciplined energies of a new age of exponential acceleration and did acknowledge the dissolution of earlier intellectual orders. Indeed he was to subtitle his account of this new pluriverse, the extraordinary third-person ironic autobiography *The Education of Henry Adams* (1907), "A Study in Twentieth-Century Multiplicity."

Yet in most departments of American intellectual life and culture it seemed that the Genteel Tradition went on—idealistic, polite, cultured America surviving despite both the changing directions of Western thought and the commercialism, materialism and vulgarity of the age. Its leading figures were old, and several would die before the decade was done. But critical opinion supported it, and even the increasingly bitter Howells and the impish Mark Twain came to seem part of it. In an age that has since been described as "the end of American innocence," it lived on, right up to American entry into the First World War, a sharp reminder of the division in American culture between ideal and mechanical processes—and the social irrelevance of the arts. The American philosopher George Santayana assessed the tension between the world of thought and art and the world of historical change in his famous lecture of 1911, "The Genteel Tradition in American Philosophy":

> The American Will inhabits the skyscraper; the American Intellect inhabits the colonial mansion. The one is the sphere of the American man; the other, at least predominantly, of the American woman. The one is all aggressive enterprise; the other is all genteel tradition.

Indeed at the dawn of American multiplicity, the Genteel Tradition rode high. Its literary critics like Edmund Clarence Stedman and Thomas Bailey Aldrich felt that the times were not ripe for innovation but were made for taking stock. "For the first time we have an absolutely free and democratic Republic, extending from sea to sea," Stedman said introducing his *American Anthology* (1900). "It is a fitting moment for this historical survey of the stages through which we have reached the threshold of an assured future." But when he had looked back, in the earlier *Library of American Literature* (1888–90), ten large volumes of readings from colonial times to the present, he did not see the tradition we would celebrate today. There was, in effect, no American Renaissance. The literary past defined and celebrated by Stedman and his generation, the reading of the nation's identity they sanctioned, was—as Longfellow had described it—a branch of English literature. Its major authors were Irving, Cooper and Bryant, Longfellow, Whittier, Holmes and Lowell. All came from the cultured, semipatrician intelligentsia of the East and North, all pleased Boston-led literary taste, all were white and male. Yet for a whole generation the most energetic writing had had far more populist backgrounds and expressed a vaster nation and the regions and fresh sources within it—the farms, small towns and, increasingly, the new urban melting pots.

This new writing had become much more than local-color regionalism. The settlement of the frontier had been an enormous national task, an act of making culture grow on arid plain and prairie. But according to the census of 1890 the land mass was officially filled from coast to coast, the frontier no longer open. The new frontier was the city, where immigrants in massive numbers from Southern and Eastern Europe joined internal migrants driven off the land by the agricultural depressions of the 1880s. America was now a continent webbed by railroads and modern communications with rising urban conglomerates, surging industry, commerce and technology. Towering skyscrapers rose, great department stores appeared, the yellow press spread everywhere. Beneath the general patina of wealth and social aspiration, the massive changes of post–Civil War America were becoming apparent in every walk of life. The automobile, the telephone and electric street lighting, the bright streetcars and elevated railways, all the sophisticated embellishments of urban America were turning the rural American from Jeffersonian hero into rube. As the United States became a great commercial empire ruled by multimillionaires like Rockefeller, Frick, Carnegie and Morgan, scandals and massive fortunes, from oil, railroads, steel, money itself, dented the gospel of pure individualism and generated passion for reform. American industrial achievement and output were now outstripping those of Great Britain and Germany combined, making America the world's leading technological power. But the social unrest that ravaged Europe in the 1880s reached America too; strikes and riots revealed the conflict of mass and class, poor and rich, new money and old.

Some of this sense of conflict had already made its way into what was now beginning to be called "muckraking literature," the new reporting and fiction that had been emerging since 1879—the year Henry Adams published his bitter novel *Democracy* about the corrupt new political order, and Henry George printed his powerful social tract *Progress and Poverty* which saw the two elements of the title proceeding hand in hand. Thereafter in the work of authors like Rebecca Harding Davis, Henry Demarest Lloyd, Edward Bellamy, Ignatius Donnelly and many more, we can see a rising note of progressive critical indignation growing out of the age of capitalism, industrialism and political conflict and displayed alike in fiction, journalism and polemic. Thorstein Veblen's ironic *Theory of the Leisure Class* (1899) would introduce the phrase "conspicuous consumption" to the language, and Lincoln Steffens's *The Shame of the Cities* (1904) would make investigative journalism an American tradition. By the 1900s "muckraking" would become a critical flood urged along by many of the leading writers. From the end of the 1870s on it was starting to become clear that what Newton Arvin has called "the apparently placid interval" between the upheavals of the frontier and the ravages of new industrialism was over. The 1890s was a cultural fulcrum, when the religious, social and moral faiths of an older America began to shift toward a twentieth-century vision.

· II ·

Like similar exhibitions in Buffalo and St. Louis, or the Paris Exhibition of 1889 dominated by Eiffel's great modern tower, the Chicago World's Columbia Exposition of 1893 brought together many of these competing energies and tensions. Set in the shock city where the new skyscrapers rose, it displayed the vast scale of American technological progress and called on the arts to celebrate the new era: the motto of the exposition was "Make Culture Hum." The historian Frederick Jackson Turner came to speak on "The Significance of the Frontier in American History," explaining that the frontier was the cornerstone of American national character—but acknowledging its era was over. The writer Hamlin Garland came and declared, "Here flames the spirit of youth. Here throbs the heart of America." As he later recalled, "Far from being a huge, muddy windy market-place [Chicago] seemed about to take its place among the literary capitals of the world." He shared that belief with the poetess laureate of the exposition, Harriet Monroe, who later worked to make it reality by starting, in 1912, her famed little magazine *Poetry,* which carried many writers both of a Midwestern and of the Modern movement and where Carl Sandburg celebrated the city as "Hog Butcher for the World,/Tool Maker, Stacker of Wheat." Midwestern writing would flourish over the next twenty-five years with such writers as Henry Blake Fuller, Sherwood Anderson and then Carl Sandburg, Edgar Lee Masters, Vachel Lindsay and later still Ernest Hemingway. Yet only a small part of this was joyous American celebration. In the exposition year of 1893, Fuller published his realist Chicago novel *The Cliff-Dwellers,* set in the business skyscrapers dominating a city where "all its citizens have come for the one common, avowed object of making money." Chicago was not only the frontier city of the past but the commercial megalopolis of the future; when Fuller wrote romances, as he did, he chose Italy as a more appropriate setting. Theodore Dreiser acknowledged Fuller as the founder of the modern American city novel and an influence on his *Sister Carrie* (1900)—in which Chicago appears as pure magnetic force, a driving modern dynamo where artistic values and all the old standards of genteel morality have virtually no place.

The new city was a new subject, but more than a subject; it provided verbal expression for a new attitude toward life, remote from the genteel vision. Life would no longer be interpreted by the classic moral counters, the traditional liberal codes. In their early writing, Twain, Howells and James had espoused a moral liberalism that sought to give some animating intention to the social and material world they so exactingly explored. But the traditional morality of a Howells, the Romantic ideality of a Whitman, the discriminating cultural intelligence of a James no longer seemed to offer entry to the experience witnessed by the younger writers of the 1890s. They reached toward the material mass and American aggressive enterprise, in search not just of the "facts" but of the iron laws behind them that "really" determined existence—the biological constitution of man, the impersonal machinelike operations of society, the functions of evolutionary process.

These young writers of the 1890s came from the emerging American worlds they drew on in their writing—Garland from the economically depressed prairie of the Wisconsin and Iowa Middle Border of *Main-Travelled Roads* (1891; revised 1893), Frank Norris from the Chicago of *The Pit* (1903), Theodore Dreiser from the Ohio German-immigrant stock lured to the city of *Sister Carrie* (1900) and *Jennie Gerhardt* (1911), Stephen Crane from the Methodist upbringing he rejected for the New York tenement bohemia of *Maggie* (1893). Norris's McTeague, Crane's Maggie Johnston, Dreiser's Carrie Meeber and Jennie Gerhardt, Harold Frederic's Theron Ware, the new raw businessmen and salesmen, the immigrant workers, the disenchanted ministers, the rural and urban proletariat—these were new people in literature, found in new environments like the modern tenement, the industrialized stockyard, the sweatshop, the department store, the skyscraper, the commercial trust. Their world—and this was a charge that would be turned against their authors—was not one of culture or ethical scruples, manageable by conscience and moral judgment. The traditional sequences of fictional plot—human beings fulfilling sensible and rational lives against a worthy backdrop of fortunate social reality or benevolent nature—are displaced by an image of man as small figure in a deterministic system which ironizes by ignoring him in an irresistible evolutionary process wholly indifferent to individuality. Norris explored the naturalist's *bête humaine;* Crane, in "The

Open Boat," portrayed nature as "indifferent, flatly indifferent";
Dreiser observed in *Sister Carrie:*

> Among the forces which sweep and play through the universe,
> untutored man is but a wisp in the wind. . . . As a beast, the forces
> of life aligned him with them; as a man, he has not yet wholly
> learned to align himself with the forces. In this intermediate stage
> he wavers—neither drawn in harmony with nature by his instincts
> nor yet wisely putting himself into harmony by his own free-will.

The new vision had several sources. In *On Native Grounds* (1942)
Alfred Kazin argues that it was engendered locally and grew "out of
the bewilderment, and thrived on the simple grimness, of a generation
suddenly brought face to face with the pervasive materialism of industrial capitalism." It "poured sullenly out of the agrarian bitterness,
the class hatred of the eighties and nineties, the bleakness of small-
town life, the mockery of the nouveaux riches, and the bitterness of
the great new proletarian cities." It had "no center, no unifying principle, no philosophy, no joy in its coming, no climate of experiment."
This assessment is only partially true: there was both a philosophical
component and external influence as well. In 1891 in Paris the French
novelist Paul Alexis produced what is now one of his most famous
works—a five-word telegram that read: "Naturalism not dead. Letter
follows." It went to Jules Huret, a French journalist investigating the
fate of a movement influential in European writing, painting and drama
from the 1870s, naturalism. Alexis was a disciple of its leading figure,
Émile Zola, who had explained its implications: art was both a workshop task and a form of documentary discovery in which "the study
of abstract, metaphysical man is replaced . . . by the study of natural
man, subject to psycho-chemical laws and determined by the effects
of his milieu." By the 1890s, naturalism was under threat in Europe,
prosecuted in the courts and press for its "foulness" and gradually
displaced by more aestheticized, avant-garde ideals of decadence,
impressionism, intuitionalism—an art less concerned with the objective
recording of a so-called "scientific" reality than with subjective apprehension, the first arts of "Modernism." But in America naturalism
had a special appeal as a way of interpreting material change and

systematically recording the processes that were altering the nation. For two decades, versions and variants of naturalism dominated until European Modernism began to be felt in America and provide powerful opposition.

The writers of the 1890s were, both in Europe and America, a consciously transitional generation that broke free of Victorianism and the American Genteel Tradition. They felt themselves standing at the end of one era and about to enter another. As Garland put it in his appropriately titled *Crumbling Idols* (1894): "We are about to enter the dark. We need a light. This flaming thought from Whitman will do for the searchlight of the profound deeps. All that the past was not, the future will be." In America, these writers were the first to articulate an age shaped by the harsh impact of modern industrial life and the scientific ideas emerging to interpret it. Their idea of reality was "cultureless," a material, phenomenological affair invested with the contingency following man's alienation from thing. Finding past accountings incomplete as they contemplated the proliferating social, psychic and sexual energies and changes at work, theirs was predominantly an age of scientized realism, of naturalism, and hence largely an age of the novel and the short story. True, there was an aesthetic or bohemian movement, in authors like Henry Harland, James Gibbons Huneker, Lafcadio Hearn, Stuart Merrill and Richard Hovey, which took the path toward symbolism and art for art's sake. But this usually led out of America altogether, as often as not toward Paris. There was some important poetry: that of Edward Arlington Robinson, the somber poet from Maine who brought naturalism to his stoic, vernacular verse in *The Torrent and the Night Before* (1896) and *Captain Craig* (1902). And Stephen Crane's *The Black Rider and Other Lines* (1895) showed him to be a poet as well as a storyteller with a voice for the cosmic irony that presided over the decade:

> A man said to the universe:
> "Sir, I exist!"
>
> "However," replied the universe,
> "The fact has not created in me
> A sense of obligation."

But it was above all the short story and the novel that expressed the nation's changing sense of itself and—despite entrenched genteel critics—directed the writing of the decade and led it firmly toward the twentieth century.

Cosmic irony was very much a note of the 1890s and many of its stories end in tragedy. This was the spirit of the dark fables of Ambrose Bierce, whose macabre *fin de siècle* tales were collected in *In the Midst of Life* (1892). And it was the spirit of Stephen Crane's stories, like "The Open Boat" or "The Blue Hotel." Crane's own life was tragically short: he died of tuberculosis at the age of 28. His brief writing life more or less spanned the decade which his novel *The Red Badge of Courage* (1896) now seems to dominate. His literary career began with the "city-sketches" he wrote when he broke with his religious upbringing and settled, scandalously, in the bohemian poverty of New York City. These led to *Maggie: A Girl of the Streets* (1893) and its companion piece, *George's Mother* (1896), set in the tenements of "Rum Alley," a Darwinian world where life is lived in the urban jungle. In his presentation copies of *Maggie* he wrote that the book intended to show "that environment is a tremendous thing in the world, and frequently shapes lives regardless," and the book's naturalist bias is clear. It retells the familiar sentimental tale of a good girl from a poor background who, soiled and discarded by her lover, is forced to become a prostitute, the victim of the genteel accusations of others. But Crane draws not a moralistic but a naturalist lesson. "I'll fergive her, I'll fergive her," cries Maggie's hypocritical mother at the end, but she is simply attempting to apply a sentimental code to a world of amoral energies and misfortunes, the world of the modern city where survival depends only on strength and fitness. Maggie lies outside this world—"None of the dirt of Rum Alley seemed to be in her veins." This intensifies her pathos but also exposes her to fatal misfortune, since she falls between the forces of genteel hypocrisy on the one hand and evolutionary vitalism on the other. *Maggie* is naturalism, but its mock-heroic style, high irony and careful literariness make it a form of impressionism as well.

This is the mixture that shapes the novel which won Crane international reputation and the high artistic regard of Henry James, H. G. Wells and Joseph Conrad, *The Red Badge of Courage*. Here he shifts from one fundamental naturalist setting, the city, to another, the battlefield. He was too young to have known the Civil War, but he had, he said, got his sense of the rage of conflict from the football field, "or else fighting is an hereditary instinct, and I wrote it intuitively." The times witnessed wars and imperial adventures, and many of the writers of the decade like Norris and Crane were to work as war correspondents in the Spanish-American conflict of 1898. Crane sets his story in the past, but this could well be called the first novel of modern warfare, a novel of war as inexorable machine, fought between mechanical corporate masses in a neutral natural world where Emersonian self-reliance counts for nothing. Beneath the panoply of armies and flags, the human agent is ironized, distanced by force, subjected to incomprehensible, terrifying experiences of which he can possess only elusive and partial knowledge. Consciousness requires a new mode of perception and the artist a new strategy of presentation. Thus *The Red Badge* has two perceivers. One is Henry Fleming, "The Youth," whose ordered consciousness is displaced by the motions of war and of instinct, and whose traditional processes of apprehension become instantaneous, sudden, intuitive, his mental mode impressionistic, even cameralike—"His mind took a mechanical but firm impression, so that afterward everything was pictured and explained to him, save why he himself was there." The other is the artist himself, who must also generate image from contingency, form from chaos, find a "hidden long logic" for his story and so become not simply the realistic reporter but the conscious, explicit interpreter of things.

The Red Badge is a novel of an age greatly preoccupied with "reality." War is presented as reality at its most extreme, as an assailing world aggressively assaulting consciousness and existence itself. Henry goes into battle hoping to be a Romantic hero, but Crane deliberately omits all indication of a moral or political purpose in his Civil War and simply emphasizes its experiential nature. The novel confines itself to the experience and impressions of one simple young private over two days of hard fighting as he loses his desire for heroism and experiences cowardice, adapts to the corporate mass and realizes nature's basic indifference, but then strangely achieves his red badge of courage, his initiatory wound, in the confused instinctual economy of battle. At the end we are told that he comes to feel at home in this world, and the book is usually read as the story of his initiation into manhood. But the novel's thrust is far more ironic. The world he discovers is not for him: it belittles the self until he finds he is "a very wee thing." Heroism and cowardice are not acts of will but the functioning of instincts. His wound is not so much an initiatory rite of passage as a touch from the nihilistic world, and his bravery is as ambiguous as that of Joseph Conrad's weak heroes. *The Red Badge* can be doubly read: as a work of naturalism, as it largely was in the United States, or as a work of experimental impressionism, as it was when, at the end of his short life, Crane moved to England and found himself admired for what H. G. Wells called "the expression in art of certain enormous repudiations."

But what was "real" and what realism actually *was* in the American 1890s was argued endlessly. "In advocating veritism," Hamlin Garland declared, "I am not to be understood as apologizing for the so-called realists of the day. In fact they are not realists from Howells's point of view. They are indeed imitators of the French who seem to us sex-mad." Garland was well-read in scientific determinism, like so many of his contemporaries, but in his belief in the potential strength and moral competence of the individual self he was less than fully naturalistic. His novel *Rose of Dutcher's Coolly* (1895) treats the period theme of the growing up of a Western farm girl and her emancipation in, once more, Chicago. But Rose is no Carrie Meeber; when tempted by stirring sensuality, she is "rescued" "by forces within, not laws without." Garland's best work was in the short stories of *Main-Travelled Roads* (1891; 1893) and *Prairie Folks* (1893) where he could use a lyrical impressionism to bring out the essential contrast of his work: between the prairie world of the Middle Border and the new city. Though he could write bleakly about it, his city is largely a place of emancipation and wonder; it is in rural life that the laws of naturalism prevail, both in the unchanging drudgery of enslavement to the land, and in the changing, ever-more-harsh cruelty of economic process. In several of the best stories—"Up the Coulee," "A Branch Road"—an individual who has seen wider horizons and hopes returns to "the old place" to find the cost of his freedom has been the entrapment of others. But if Garland sees rural life as lost life, he also invests the broken farmsteads of his changing world not just with harshness but lyrical value, and its people not just with brutality and fatalism but stubborn individualism—a "warm soil" lies hidden in their hearts. This contrast, this sense of a need for psychic liberation and this lyrical impressionism would, two decades later, pass into the tales of Sherwood Anderson's *Winesburg, Ohio* (1919), which link this poetic form of local color with technical and aesthetic experiment inspired by Gertrude Stein.

The writer most firmly and systematically committed to naturalism was Frank Norris—who had studied art in Paris and returned to the University of California bearing Zola's yellow paper-covered works. He dismissed the realism of Howells as "teacup tragedies" and saw naturalism as "a form of Romanticism," a form of great modern drama encompassing "the vast, the monstrous, the tragic." Norris urged the importance of exploring "the unplumbed depths of the human heart, and the mystery of sex," and admired Zola's novels of purpose which set in motion a social hypothesis or a dominant passion—love, hate, greed, sexuality—to follow its fatal destiny. His *McTeague: A Story of San Francisco* (1899) is the purest example of Zola-esque naturalism America would produce. Naturalism, he said, meant placing life above literature—"the honest, rough-and-tumble, Anglo-Saxon knockabout that for us means life." It also meant a basic kind of evolutionary analysis that assumed the *bête humaine* and the war of the "higher" and "lower" parts of human nature, so he projected an underworld of powers and instincts which became for him the truth about life; not until Dreiser (whom, as an editor at Doubleday, Norris discovered) does an American novelist reach so far in portraying man's "victimization" by instinctual processes and the universal energies which suggest a life force at work in the world, indifferently using and abusing man. Norris was to introduce two forms of naturalism into American writing: a psychological naturalism in *McTeague* and *Vandover and the Brute* (1914, posthumous) and a sociological naturalism in *The Octopus* (1901) and *The Pit* (1903), the first two volumes of "a big epic trilogy," the "Wheat trilogy," he never completed—for, as he was about to go to Europe to collect material for the third volume, *The Wolf,* he too died young, from peritonitis, at the age of thirty-two.

McTeague is the story of an oxlike Sweeney Agonistes, an atavistic dentist from the California mining camps who goes to San Francisco and is sexually awakened by a patient, Trina, of careful Swiss peasant background. Norris develops the story melodramatically; naturalism here is not simply the documentary instinct he brings to his portrayal of San Francisco immigrant and poor life, but also the fatalism that links every apparent good fortune to a system of dark inevitability. Gold, the California metal, dominates; McTeague wants a gold tooth to hang outside his parlor, and the wealth of gold is what Trina most desires. Her win in a lottery precipitates misfortune, turning her peasant frugality to base avarice and his native brutality into drunkenness and violence. *McTeague* is, like *Vandover,* a story on the period theme of degeneration and the brute double that lies beneath apparent civilization. Despite his insistence on the difference between "higher" and "lower" instincts, Norris, pursuing the "black, unsearched penetralia of the mind," is led—without benefit of a Freudian vocabulary —into the world of unconscious forces and the complexities of psychological life. McTeague finally kills Trina after the deterioration of their marriage and ends in the desert of Death Valley, handcuffed to the corpse of the bounty hunter who has pursued him and whom he has killed. Large forces dominate Norris's world, as inexorable as anything in the work of his contemporary Thomas Hardy. Hence the book's comment on McTeague and Trina:

> Their undoing has already begun. Yet neither of them was to blame.
> . . . Chance had brought them face to face, and mysterious instincts
> as ungovernable as the winds of heaven were at work knitting their
> lives together. . . . [They] were allowed no choice in the matter.

But Norris's appetite for experience and scale, his hunt for life itself, led him toward a naturalism of yet more epic reach. It would concern the largest economies of force, the vastest laws of supply and demand, the most universal energies—much like the history of Henry Adams or Brooks Adams. He found his subject in the cultivation, distribution and consumption of the wheat which functioned both as energy principle and as the basis of capitalist economy. In naturalist fashion, *The Octopus* is based on an actual scandal, the conflict between the farmers of California's San Joaquin Valley and the Southern Pacific Railroad in 1880 as the railroad tightened its stranglehold on the regional economy by manipulating freight rates. Norris moves through individual tragedies and corrupt politics to vaster chains of causality, seeing ranchers and railroads alike in the grip of yet larger forces, cosmic laws of nature, the ever-working machine, of which the wheat itself is the center, the fundamental naturalist symbol. At the end of the book "*the WHEAT remained,* untouched, unassailable, undefiled, that mighty world-force, that nourisher of nations, wrapped in Nirvanic calm, indifferent to the human swarms, moved onward in its appointed grooves." The novel concludes in powerful, vague abstractions that transcend all the characters' sufferings and pains—"the individual suffers, the race goes on"—and Norris emerges as a biological evolutionist with a dual commitment: a writer of radical, progressive indignation and a cosmic fatalist, mystically believing in some harsh yet ultimate "good."

It is tempting to read *The Octopus,* a very powerful book, as a protest novel leading the way to the muckraking fiction of the progressive years of the century's first decade. It is certainly a precursor of works like Upton Sinclair's *The Jungle* (1906)—the novel about the abuse of immigrant labor in the Chicago stockyards that led to reform of the food-packing laws. It is likewise tempting to read *The Pit,* where Norris takes the wheat story on to Chicago and the wheat-trading pit of the Board of Trade, as one of the first modern novels to challenge the values of American business. Larzer Ziff claims it as "the first profound business novel because it rightly examines the psychic consequences of the commercialization of American life." Again Norris shows himself a local pessimist and a cosmic optimist. For him, determinism can be both a gospel of human victimization and a gospel of hope. As Santayana was to say:

We are part of the blind energy behind Nature, but by virtue of that energy we impose our purposes on that part of Nature which we constitute or control. We can turn from the stupefying contemplation of an alien universe to the building of our own houses.

Charles W. Walcutt once aptly described American naturalism as "a divided stream" that expresses both determinist pessimism and transcendentalist optimism. This was one reason why naturalism in America proved so adaptable. Biological inevitability produces the brutal fate of McTeague but also the indifferent life-giving energy of the wheat. In Jack London's works, understanding the laws of the pack can produce Nietzschean mastery and the authorial superman, Jack London himself. New confinement is also new freedom, for the world that works beyond individual destiny can also emancipate individual or race from the debilitating past.

Nonetheless, we may also read in Norris that concern with lost aesthetic and sensuous emotion which was part of the 1890s in America as well, a concern which finally helped lead American writing *away* from materialist realism. The revolt of the aesthetic against the Puritanical was the subject of Harold Frederic's tale of a small-town minister from New York State, *The Damnation of Theron Ware* (1896). And it served as centering theme for another fine novel of the decade, Kate Chopin's *The Awakening* (1899), the book where she confidently displayed herself as far more than the local-colorist of Creole and Cajun life she had so far seemed to be. A vivid evocation of New Orleans polite and Creole life, *The Awakening* is also the disturbing story of Edna Pontillier, six years married to a wealthy businessman who lives solely for "getting on and keeping up with the procession." She becomes discontented with her life of money, fine clothes and furnishings, her status as her husband's valuable possession, and she leaves his home. She recognizes her love for Robert, with whom she has an innocent friendship, succumbs to the attentions of Arobin, but then decides there is no way to fill the emptiness in her life and so ends it by surrendering to the waters of the Gulf of Mexico. The gulf sounds throughout the story, with its murmur "like a loving but imperative entreaty," as it "invites the soul to wander for a spell in the abysses of solitude, to lose itself in mazes of inward contemplation." Her first "awakening" comes when Robert teaches her to swim in its waters; the sexual implication of this led to contemporary disapproval and later modern and feminist interest in the book. Yet to read it solely as a Victorian woman's futile attempt to break society's bonds confines Chopin's book to the "problem novel" she sought to transcend. This is certainly a tale of women's changing self-perception—Edna's husband attributes her vagaries to "some sort of notion . . . concerning the eternal rights of women." But in resolving "never again to belong to another than herself" and casting off "that fictitious self which we assume like a garment with which to appear before the world," Edna confronts the wider ambiguities of Emersonian self-discovery. She is caught between self-realization and existential inner solitude, between a sense of human divinity and regression. This is her tragedy and the book's compelling mystery.

The Awakening—dismissed in its day as "gilded dirt," rightly praised now as "the first aesthetically successful novel to have been written by an American woman"—is a reminder that 1890s writing is often a transitional writing that allows the unexpressed to express itself, lets the repressed be spoken. The immigrant and the Jewish-American novel began to find voice; Abraham Cahan published his story of a Russian-Jewish immigrant who becomes a sewing-machine operator in the harsh city, *Yekl: A Tale of the New York Ghetto* (1896), and opened a new tradition. Now, too, black experience began to find shape in literature. Up to the 1890s, the most powerful writing by blacks had taken the form either of slave narratives—above all the majestic *Narrative of the Life of Frederick Douglass* (1845)—or, like the art of the American Indian, found expression in song or oral folktale. Those who had written—Phillis Wheatley, William Wells Brown, Harriet E. Wilson and others—had found it hard to break the impress of white convention. The poet Paul Laurence Dunbar, born in Ohio, knew slavery only by hearsay, but he set himself "to interpret my own people through song and story, and to prove to the many that after all we are more human than African." With collections of dialect verse like *Lyrics of the Lowly Life* (1896), he became the first black poet of reputation. Even so, he could hardly escape the limited poetic of the time, and his work, though moving, often remains close to the dialect verse of white writers like Stephen Foster and James Whitcomb Riley. He also wrote novels: *The Uncalled* (1898), using a white protagonist to tell a personal story of a minister's rejection of religious faith, and *The Sport of the Gods* (1902), the first novel to handle black Harlem life in detail. But the author who best anticipates future achievements is Charles W. Chesnutt, also from Ohio, whose stories in *The Conjure Woman* and *The Wife of His Youth* (both 1899) and novel, *The Marrow of Tradition* (1901), dealing with political violence against blacks, made him the first important black fictionalist. In both writers, the griefs of slave life are left behind as they begin to explore the contemporary tensions of the "new negro" in white society. Thus they lead the way to the debates about black consciousness that would develop between Booker T. Washington's remarkable memoir *Up from Slavery* (1901) and the more militant polemic of W. E. B. DuBois's multigenre book *The Souls of Black Folk* (1903) and continue into the "Harlem Renaissance" of the 1920s.

As the new voices sounded during the 1890s the Genteel Tradition began to fragment, and by the time the century turned there was evidence of a vigorous modern mood. It did not yet have the flamboyance and challenge of the European movements of the opening years of the century; it was heavily wedded to the spirit of naturalism—a naturalism that was, however, by no means a flat statement of reality but an innovative struggle to perceive it and understand it, thereby questioning moral values, dominant social assumptions, social and political power, the limits of literary form. The new mood reaffirmed the Romantic sense of the arts as experimental, reaching to the future, distrusting the conventional values of the prevailing culture. It opened ways forward, but in two contrasting directions. One was toward a literature of reportage, prolixity, social intervention, a writing that insisted on the power of the material and the exploration of fact. The other was toward an art of omission, trusting little to its subject matter and everything to its form. One was the path toward naturalism as documentation, the other the path toward aestheticism. Naturalism's promise lay in writers like Norris, Dreiser, Jack London, Upton Sinclair; aestheticism found its heroes in Stephen Crane, Ambrose Bierce, new bohemians like James Gibbons Huneker, Lafcadio Hearn, Richard Hovey and Bliss Carman. One of these, the former realist Henry Harland, went to London to become editor of the decadent bible *The Yellow Book*. But bohemia, the land of art itself, still seemed a European location, though in the following years New York, Chicago and San Francisco began to offer their versions of this model of aesthetic paradise. As they said at the Chicago World's Fair, culture in America was indeed beginning, if quietly, to hum.

· PART IV ·

MODERNISM
IN THE AMERICAN
GRAIN

CHAPTER

·8·

OUTLAND DARTS AND
HOMEMADE WORLDS

·I·

"So the Twentieth Century came it began with 1901," wrote Gertrude Stein, prophetess of the new, in *Paris France* (1940), as if not everyone had noticed; and indeed not everyone had. For it did not come everywhere or in the same way. Stein observed that the British had had the nineteenth century and the twentieth would be one too many for them; the French, with their taste for the eternal, had difficulties too. America, with its special gift for progress, *was* the twentieth century, though it would have to go somewhere else to make it happen, in fact to France. At times Stein sounded like Senator Beveridge, who, as the century turned, announced: "The twentieth century will be American. . . . The regeneration of the world, physical as well as moral, has begun." At others she sounded more like her artistic contemporary Ezra Pound, who described turn-of-the-century America as "a half-savage country, out of date" and went to Britain. In the strenuous Rooseveltian age, the truth for the moment was that, however assertively American an American writer felt, the best place to carry forward that assertion was probably abroad. At the start of the century, the American arts had almost no artistic confidence, no certainty of direction or guiding tradition, no strong aesthetic feeling and no pride in the creative past. As James Gibbons Huneker said, the United States was a land of bathtubs, not bohemia. And, as Van

Wyck Brooks could still complain in 1915, "Human nature in America exists on two irreconcilable planes, the plane of stark intellectuality and the plane of stark business" which forced American artists into one of two postures: inward exile or outward expatriation. Close to the beginning of the century, Henry James revisited the United States, setting down his unhappy record of its modern mass in *The American Scene* (1907). Writing his memoirs, he recalled how the American who refused to sacrifice to the "black ebony god of business" had so often experienced what he called the "American complication; the state of having been so pierced, betimes, by the sharp outland dart as to be able ever afterwards but to move about, vaguely and helplessly, with the shaft in one's side." The shaft, of course, was the claim of European experiment that so powerfully influenced the rediscovery of the American arts.

The thought waves stirring artistic innovation across Europe that would prove so important to American writers, artists and intellectuals were both potent and yet still remote. Most of the American writing up to the second decade of the century was both practical and popular, or populist, though it carried the sense that this was an age of revolutionary ideas. Yet, as the modernist revolution developing in the European arts made clear, the crisis and the promise of modern forms was far more complex, radical in far more fundamental ways. As the nineteenth-century synthesis shattered, as the tradition collapsed and the underlying value systems that had shaped centuries of art were challenged or dissolved, the whole basis of artistic enterprise had, it seemed, to be re-created. This was the radical adventure of Modernism, and it dominated European artistic endeavor in the years between 1900 and the Great War. It was a time of movements, radical artistic theories, a time for what the German critic Wilhelm Worringer called abstraction. The new movements multiplied, and they awarded themselves abstract and aggressive names: cubism and postimpressionism, expressionism and futurism, acmeism and constructivism, imagism and vorticism. Americans were there as it happened and played major roles. Gertrude Stein, from 1903 an expatriate in Paris, was a stimulus to cubism and tried to find its equivalent in fiction; Ezra Pound, equally active in London, stirred the lively literary scene there into a comparable spirit and played a central part in starting the English-language movements of imagism and vorticism. Other Americans were influential, not the least of them T. S. Eliot, who bridged the space between the British and American traditions. But this was not, or not yet, American literature, which on native grounds took a slower path toward the modern revolution.

In muckraking times, the heritage of naturalism prospered, becoming both more central and more commonplace in the work of writers like the adventurous and incredibly popular Jack London, the politically influential Upton Sinclair and the many investigative journalists, such as Lincoln Steffens and Ida Tarbell, who expressed the critical spirit of populism and progressivism in a time of reform. Speaking for the unspoken, often expressing strong radical theories, they turned critical language into a dominant literary discourse—and seemed for a time to be the voice of the modern itself. The literary power and the radical energy of which the tendency was capable became evident in Theodore Dreiser's *Sister Carrie,* an ambitious novel that merged American innocence and deep social experience. Born to German immigrants in Wabash, Indiana, and speaking German at home, Dreiser found that his path into literature became a tale of struggling self-discovery. After moving to Chicago and journalism, he published his novel, with the support of Frank Norris, in 1900. It had a difficult career, for its publisher virtually suppressed it and forced changes on its text. And indeed it was clear that it contained a deep affront; for Dreiser, naturalism was no literary device (though he had literary pretensions), nor was it an abstract philosophy (though he had philosophical pretensions, too). *Sister Carrie* is a novel written by an author who takes naturalism entirely literally. A plain tale of contemporary urban life and the very material terms under which it is lived, it tells the story of the Darwinian ascent of Carrie Meeber, a totally ordinary girl who leaves her Midwestern hometown, is captured by the amoral magnet of Chicago, loses her virginity and then uses her body and her energy to win economic and social success—a plot that offended all the moral idealism of the day, yet has the ring of practical truth.

Sister Carrie won its early reputation in Britain, and only slowly was accepted as what it is, an American classic. Today it can be seen as a fundamental myth of modern displacement, filled with the detail of the changing modern world. Carrie's first seducer, Drouet, is an American prototype, the traveling salesman or "drummer," a new naturalist character. She is lured to him by his expensive clothes, bulging wallet, free and easy manners and above all by the social prospects he offers. She is not drawn primarily by sexual temptation; in fact the true seducer is the city of Chicago itself. It is "a giant magnet," a "wonder," and it has "its cunning wiles, no less than the infinitely smaller and more human tempter. . . . Half the undoing of the unsophisticated and natural mind is accomplished by forces wholly superhuman." *Sister Carrie* displays the power of this material super-world and the way it replaces conventional moral and social values. Carrie eventually rejects Drouet for Hurstwood, whose calf shoes and gray suits are more sophisticated and who stimulates her into further aspiration. This leads her onward again; sex is her American education, drawing her at last from material obsessions to aesthetic curiosity, and she turns to a young man who teaches her to read. Each stage of her development is understood by Dreiser; she becomes engrossed in each and every situation, material and sexual, until it loses its magic and is set aside. Despite the many large generalizations about human nature Dreiser offers, there is never any irony, for society is always real, a fabric of growing energies in which the individual is eternally immersed, a force field in which new lives are lived. Things, clothes and goods speak to Carrie, with what Dreiser calls the "voice of the so-called inanimate." Even the human mind is a modern machine. When Hurstwood stands in front of his office safe, wondering whether to steal its contents in order to possess Carrie, his consciousness is represented as an existential mechanism, a "clock of thought." As Richard Poirier has said, Dreiser's characters—here and in the later novels he produced into the 1940s—always merge in a common bondage to "the humming, soaring vistas of the city with their evocations of mysterious promise," drawn by no personal factors or human sympathies but by "the non-personal forces that fill the yearning eye with steel and concrete, that manipulate time by the pulsations of manufacture and money-making."

Dreiser was the great original of modern American naturalism, and *Sister Carrie,* published appropriately as the century turned, expressed its lasting force. His book remains a classic work of naturalist expressionism, superior to all the conventional naturalism of the day simply by force of his personal identification with the material world he explored. But meanwhile naturalism was to become the convention of American writing, shaping the practice of everything from journalistic exposé to the popular tale of adventure. Americans deprived of much of their moral history now saw a process-ridden or Darwinian world about them, and the writers responded. Dreiser himself had trained as a journalist, and it was the writer-journalists who guided the "muckraking" spirit that dominated the early twentieth century and its ascendant progressive feeling. In the mid-1890s *McClure's Magazine* had already become a central expression of this tendency, and the paper was soon filled with the work of important writers testing the world of trusts, city ghettos and political corruption. Lincoln Steffens, author of one of its most powerful exposés, *The Shame of the Cities* (1904), became an editor (so, later, did Willa Cather), recruiting many of the newer writers; "I could not pay them much in money, but as an offset I promised to give them opportunities to see life as it happened in all the news varieties," he said. The muckraking impress became central to American fiction, exemplified above all in the novels of Robert Herrick and Upton Sinclair. Sinclair's *The Jungle* (1906), described by Jack London as "the *Uncle Tom's Cabin* of wage-slavery," represents the best of this powerful genre. First and finally a savage diatribe against the Chicago meat-packing yards, the killing pace of factories and the squalid and deprived ghetto life of immigrant workers, it displays the progressive indignation of a radical era in American thought. Sinclair begins the book powerfully, exploring the arrival of optimistic Eastern European immigrants in the promised land. But as his story grows, we can see, rather too plainly, his polemical intent, for he forces his human material into misfortune and thence toward a radical outcome clearly aimed at social reform in the society beyond the book.

The radical reportage of the early 1900s represents the hopes of an America that saw a Utopian political future which the century has not confirmed, though its critical vision should not be forgotten. The classic case is Jack London, a Nietzschean socialist who represents the restless side of the modern American mind. London was a popular writer, famed for his tales of the Klondike, like the stories of *The Son of the Wolf* (1900). But his political energy drove him to explore society's underside as well, not least in *The People of the Abyss* (1903), an account of the poverty of London's East End. But more famous than his revolutionary works were his stories of the evolutionary struggle in the wild—*The Call of the Wild* (1903), *The Sea-Wolf* (1904), *White Fang* (1906)—where he explored what he called "the dominant primordial beast." The fifty books London managed to produce (often by buying his plots from other writers) earned him over a million dollars before his early death; he was able to turn his revolutionary Marxism into a capitalist triumph. Writing in the Rooseveltian era of rugged individualism about the laws of the pack and the tribe, the life of the wilderness, the sea and the jungle, he celebrated endurance, courage and Nietzschean energy. Even his radicalism was in tune with the popular mood. His stories turned easily from intolerable work conditions or strikes to racist tales about the Yellow Peril, or from children's adventure fables to eventful apocalyptic novels like *The Iron Heel* (1907) about a totalitarian future America. Always beyond the adventures was the adventurous Jack London himself, the former hobo who had been everywhere and done everything. He presented himself directly in the serious and autobiographical *Martin Eden* (1909) and by implication in all his courageous, superhuman leaders of the pack who master "this chemic ferment called life," learn the ferocious ways of nature and come to a leader's understanding of force. He turned naturalism into a romantic popular and populist celebration—away from a philosophy of despair or ironic victimization toward a celebration of will and vitalism. He is still read by the young as an exciting storyteller and in the former Soviet Union as one of America's foremost radical novelists.

Naturalism also made itself felt in the less popular, more serious writing of the times. The work of Edith Wharton marks a moment in American fiction when the accumulated social transitions of the century made the novel of society and manners on the European model possible in the United States. Born and brought up as a debutante in a patrician New York that aped European manners but whose traditional social standards were giving way to new wealth, new frivolity, new customs of the country, she had a ready subject to hand. "Fate had planted me in New York, with its fashionable stiff upper class, its money and status oriented world," she noted, adding that such material was as suited to tragedy as that articulated by the social realists and naturalists. The tragedy came from her sense of social and sexual imprisonment and her fundamental awareness of the discrepancy between civilization and the harsh economic laws on which its privileges were founded. Her own society marriage was unhappy; she was disquieted not only by the direction American society was taking but by her own role as commodity and sexual victim within it. She turned to writing and followed her friend Henry James into European expatriation, settling in Paris in 1907. There were those who read her work as being essentially Jamesian, and she certainly shared his and Henry Adams's sense of the cultivated American mind being driven steadily into ironic detachment—this is the theme of her late backward glance over the Gilded Age society of her growing up, *The Age of Innocence* (1920). But her social knowledge was far more precise than James's, and her sense of imprisonment and the limits set on self-expression greater. She shared his finesse but had a sexual anger all her own.

Wharton's novels portray social existence doubly, as tragedy and as material for satire. In her most powerful book, *The House of Mirth* (1905), Lily Bart comes to know herself as "the victim of the civilization which had produced her," the "highly specialized product" of a society that needs specimens of beauty, fineness and delicacy for economic exhibition. Lily is a woman of some moral scruples and civilized aspiration. Her tragedy is her discovery that behind the world of morality and society are the rules of sexual trade:

> It certainly simplified life to view it as a perpetual adjustment, a play of party politics, in which every concession had its recognized equivalent; Lily's tired mind was fascinated by this escape from fluctuating ethical estimates into a region of concrete weights and measures.

Arrayed against the promises of cultivation are the naturalistic conditions of economic determination; the conflict leads to Lily's death. The underlying naturalist principles are even clearer in *Ethan Frome* (1911), the story of a New England farmer who is kept in emotional and physical imprisonment after he had sought to escape a loveless marriage. But it was social imprisonment in the world of class and commerce that finally interested Wharton, and in *The Custom of the Country* (1913) tragedy is replaced by satire. The "custom" is divorce, the new fashion of the age, which Undine Spragg, who has no moral anxieties, uses for her social promotion. Undine understands what more delicate and cultivated Wharton heroines do not, that the "instinct of sex" is a "trading capacity" and that one sells oneself at the highest going rate. Undine is an upper-class Carrie Meeber, who uses society while manifesting its underlying laws.

Aristocratic decline in a society in transition acquires additional intensity in the novels of Ellen Glasgow. For Glasgow was a Virginian and her theme the collapse of the elite classes in the South. She deals directly with the Civil War in her early *The Battle Ground* (1902), but the bulk of her novels are set in the postbellum world where the social order must transform itself and shed its illusions. With this theme she set the scene for what was to become the Southern Renaissance, that major growth of Southern fiction and poetry that was to develop through writers like William Faulkner and Robert Penn Warren, Carson McCullers, Eudora Welty and Flannery O'Connor. Like Wharton, Glasgow was essentially a novelist of society and manners, a devastating observer and satirist in a world where serious codes have been defeated by economic laws and can produce only static and absurd behavior. As the Old South became the new South, she recorded the process with growing irony until, in later works like *Barren Ground* (1925) and *Vein of Iron* (1935), her vision of life as a realm of suffering and endurance reaches its peak. She once called herself a radical in conservative times, a conservative in radical times; the reformed South she sought was not what history gave, but her rejection of nostalgic sentimentality made her into a rigorous and serious novelist. The hard laws of human survival form the common theme of her varied books, and those who understand the necessary stoicism are the women for whom life is no romantic comedy but a world of pain.

Perhaps the most striking interfusion of social manners, moral scruples and the dark world of unyielding nature is to be found in the work of Willa Cather. She, too, was Virginia-born but went at the age of nine to Nebraska, still to some extent pioneer land. This meeting between the novel of form and culture in the tradition of Flaubert and

Henry James and the western world of pioneering and immigration provided the essential materials of her fiction. In *O Pioneers!* (1913), *The Song of the Lark* (1915) and *My Ántonia* (1918) she explored pioneer experience in the landscape of Nebraska, the Midwest and Colorado; her energetic, resourceful heroines express a vitalism she celebrated in books that evoke a prairie aristocracy pursuing an idealistic and spiritual life in a harshly material world. That growing material harshness becomes the subject of her lesser-known yet remarkably subtle novels of the mid-1920s, *A Lost Lady* (1923), *The Professor's House* (1925) and *My Mortal Enemy* (1926). Reacting against an enervated culture and an arrogant commercialism, she looks back to the primitive roots of culture itself, to the ancient western civilizations whose historical vitality was now being dissipated. She then turned to making legend of American settlement in two novels of early spiritual pioneering supported by her Catholic faith: *Death Comes for the Archbishop* (1927), set in New Mexico, and *Shadows on the Rock* (1931), set in Quebec. Like Wharton and Glasgow, Cather was a delicate formalist looking past society to a world of force beyond it; like them, too, she is notable for how she finds in the endurance of women a way of redeeming the naturalist division of nature and culture.

The formal precision of these three illustrates how naturalism in America was changing, a change that is apparent in the fate of Dreiser's career. His *Sister Carrie* had announced the new century as an age of compelling material forces in which old moral codes were at best irrelevant; in displaying through Carrie's evolutionary desire an amoral means of dealing with these new challenges, his book caused outrage. When, in 1911, he returned to fiction with *Jennie Gerhardt,* another tale of a woman in whom desire defies convention, the shock was less apparent. And when he began his "trilogy of desire," a story about a vitalistic millionaire (part-based on the Chicago traction magnate Charles Tyson Yerkes), his portrait of Frank Cowperwood, a man of massive commercial and sexual energy triumphing in the Darwinian world of business, seemed a glorification of American possibility. The first two volumes, *The Financier* (1912) and *The Titan* (1914), are frank celebrations of Cowperwood's superhuman powers; only the posthumously published *The Stoic* (1947) suggests reservations and reminds us that Dreiser became a Marxist in later life. By the 1920s the conviction that material acquisitiveness was corroding American life was growing, as Glasgow and Cather also showed. In his powerful later novel, *An American Tragedy,* Dreiser offered a darker vision that dramatized the tawdriness of the American dream. Carrie's potent modern energy had taken her from poverty along a spiral of ascent to fame and the suspended animation of her rocking chair. Clyde Griffiths's not dissimilar dreams take him through the contradictions of American society to the electric chair, a victim of chance and system.

The method of *An American Tragedy* remains naturalism. Researched and documented, amassed and massive, its story founded on an actual murder case, it lays its claim to truth in its very density. When it appeared in 1925, however, naturalism was being challenged by a Modernist symbolism. The change taking place can be illustrated by a novel on a similar theme published the same year: Scott Fitzgerald's *The Great Gatsby.* Both are tales of the American Dream gone wrong; both turn on figures who seek to enjoy the success American society seems to promise; both characters construct a dream with women at their emblematic centers; both these dreams lead to tragedy and death. But *An American Tragedy* identifies with the victim alone, as an object of our compassion. Clyde is made a representative figure for whom life is a struggle. Ironically, his rewards come to him just too late; when the chance comes to make a wealthy marriage, he already has made a poor mill-girl pregnant. He takes her on a photographic expedition in a boat and naturalist fate strikes. The boat rocks, the camera strikes her, she drowns. The bulk of the bulky book examines the naturalist implications: if man is the product of conditions, circumstances and accident, is he to blame for the crime with which he is charged? Dreiser turns the question into indictment by taking the story into the complex legal arguments of the law courts and the death cell to relate his sense of naturalist ambiguity to a passionate concern with injustice. *An American Tragedy* is ultimately a protest novel which points backward to earlier naturalism and forward to the social protest fiction of the Depression 1930s.

The Great Gatsby, however, transforms its naturalist materials just as Gatsby himself magnificently transforms his own past and social reality. We know little that is literally true about him. Also a story of a careless, materially privileged society built on a sterile world, the book generates, through Gatsby, an extraordinary illusion. Gatsby's easy corruptions are hidden in his own glow and justified by his love for Daisy and the timeless dream he hopes to fulfill with her. Gatsby is a dandy of desire who seeks to transform money into love, time into an endless instant of contemplation, the clock into dream. He floats, in his "ineffable gaudiness," on the everlasting American dream, while beneath him a confusing, surreal record of economic and social facts unravels. His existence is supported by the moral tolerance and reticence of the narrator, Nick Carraway, who records the modern world through the shifting flash of fashions, the sensuality of clothes, the motion of traffic, the jumble of parties, the contrasts between the landscape of wealth and the ashheaps of a wasteland economy. Contemporary social disconnection passes by under the indifferent billboard eyes of Dr. T. J. Eckleburg, the book's impassive divinity. Gatsby's surreal dream meets defeat as an "ashen, fantastic figure" destroys him under "amorphous trees." Two worlds of modern writing here intersect: the apocalyptic world of modern sterility and fragments and the transcendent world of the symbol where time can become myth. The tension lasts into the famous ending where Fitzgerald re-creates the American Dream of a wondrous pastoral America, but also the world of the modern history which has displaced it. If *An American Tragedy* is a naturalist tragedy, *Gatsby* is a symbolist one. Setting the two books side by side, we can sense that a literary revolution has divided them into disparate ways of articulating the terms of American life. A fundamental change has occurred in fictional notation and in underlying assumptions about the nature of literary language itself.

· II ·

No one ever set out more deliberately to produce such a change than did Gertrude Stein. She asserted her place in history unabashedly: "I was there to kill what was not dead, the Nineteenth Century which was so sure of evolution and prayers," and nothing compelled her more than the desire to be a modern genius. She was born in Allegheny, Pennsylvania, of educated and cultivated German-Jewish immigrants who took her regularly to Europe as a child and were wealthy enough to give their precocious daughter an education at the Harvard Annex, now Radcliffe College. Here she learned, from William James and others, that in the 1890s a new climate was emerging and that the evolutionary, determinist neo-Darwinian view of nature and the individual and nature was giving way to a freer, more complex vision. Along with Peirce, Royce and Dewey, James was emphasizing that the relation between mind and object can never be static but must be understood as part of developing flux. Conclusions can never be fixed once and for all but are constantly under "pragmatic" test; consciousness manifests our transitivity of being and is best seen as a Heraclitean "river or a stream"—with this he substantiated one of the most fundamental of Modernist epistemological metaphors. Stein's initial training was in experimental psychology and medicine, and she took her interest in automatic writing, the rhythmic tropes of memory, the collectivities of consciousness with her when she moved to Paris in 1903 with her brother Leo, an art collector and very much a Harvard aesthete. Intending to continue her experiments in the form of imaginative writing, she settled, almost by accident, in the center of the postimpressionist and then the cubist experimentation which would so revolutionize twentieth-century visual art. Both Steins were responsive and interested, acquiring Cézannes, Matisses and Picassos; partly as a result of her experiments in verbal psychology, she set out to do like things in literature.

She had brought with her a novel in progress, *Quod Erat Demonstrandum* (posthumously published in 1951 as *Things As They Are*). Between 1904 and 1906 she took a late Flaubert text, *Trois Contes,* and undertook to create a "new composition" with it—a product of the "new space–time continuum" that she, like Henry Adams, that other prophet of modern consciousness, dated from the modernizing turn into the new century and saw as especially American. The book that emerged, *Three Lives* (1909), she claimed as "the first definite step away from the Nineteenth and into the Twentieth Century in literature." As the debt to Flaubert suggests, the work contains naturalist and behaviorist elements, but also a high aestheticism. Its subject is the limited lives of three servant girls, and she used, in her portrait of the black girl Melanctha, what she called "the continuous present" to display Melanctha's way of perceiving. As Stein put it, "there was a marked direction of being in the present although naturally I had been accustomed to past present and future, and why because the conception forming around me was a prolonged present." This was a crucial step. Reinforced by the example of cubist painting and her recognition of the "future feeling" hidden in the work of Henry James, she moved toward a form of abstraction—toward tropic repetition and against the realist noun, direct chronological ordering of narrative and "remembering" as the recording device of fiction. She sought to displace conventional narrative past tense with a "continuous present" and approached, in short, the spatial form and the narrative devices and assumptions, the displacements and estrangements central to fictional Modernism.

This method she now tried in her one large novel, *The Making of Americans,* written between 1906 and 1908 but not published until 1925 when her most famous literary pupil, Ernest Hemingway, helped transcribe it. It attempts in nine hundred pages to write a nonsequential history of America by following the rhythms of repeated experience within one single immigrant family, her own—a form of verbal cubism. The artworks she had acquired were now taking on increasing analogical significance for her work—as is evident in *Tender Buttons* (1913), the book that, appearing around the time the Armory Show introduced postimpressionist painting to America, brought her importance home to her compatriots, or to some of them. Consisting of short prose lyrics, its collagelike constructs function by word association and reject realistic or naturalistic notation. Like her novel, they derive from a principle of contemporaneity rather than developing sequence, for it was her aim to turn temporal or historical perspectives into spatial structures. She was convinced that she lived in a world of totally transformed relations, a new scenario of consciousness ("the composition in which we live makes the art we see or hear," she said, adding that everyone had become contemporary with Modern composition). Above all it was Americans who knew that, but they still had to find the *aesthetic* of the Modern, to discover the changed task of the arts. Although her intentions were, as she always insisted, American, she needed the art movements of Europe to direct them and provide her with an experimental climate. As she was to say of the American expatriates who in considerable numbers were to follow her on a similar quest: "Of course they all came to France a great many to paint pictures and naturally they could not do that at home, or write they could not do that at home either, they could be dentists at home."

Stein's importance and her limitations can be seen by comparing her with her foremost contemporaries. Though she retained many elements of naturalism, she was also naturalism's antithesis, insisting that the importance of the Modern lay not in its subject but in its method, its poetic. The conflict of the aesthetic vision and the contemporary social subject that so concerned Edith Wharton or Willa Cather did not concern her: a rose was a rose was a rose. She had little interest in examining the historical forces *behind* the new composition; so, unlike the other Modernist writers with whom she is often compared, unlike Joyce or Proust, she does little to locate or explore the crisis of perception her form would appear to enact. At a time when single unitary reality no longer seemed available, her devotion was to the nature of sensation and relation within the work itself. This implied not only the dissolution of plot, character and mimesis, but also of a rigorous control of material through authorial consciousness. "Begin over again—and concentrate," she told Ernest Hemingway when, after the First World War, she became mentor to an entire new generation of American writers of fiction. Yet in a sense her own work does *not* concentrate or seek the condensed emotion, the kinetic impersonal center sought by so many of her contemporaries. She celebrated the dismissal of the noun and the paragraph and ignored the sentence—producing abstraction; Hemingway, learning his distinctive lesson from her, reached almost the opposite conclusion by insisting on the perfection of the "true sentence" and the hard noun. "It is flattering to have a pupil who does it without understanding it," she said of him, yet his "misunderstanding" became central to modern American fiction.

In the years before the First World War, Stein constructed a remarkable if often bewildering bridge between American writing and the most experimental aspects of French painting; in the years after it, her flamboyant personality, her wealth, her active part in the expatriate scene of Paris in the stylish and agonized 1920s, all helped make her a major influence. Few writers have ever had such impact on their successors. By 1913, when it was obvious that a new and "modern" generation of writers and painters was coming to birth in an America just beginning to accept the avant-garde, and when Stein was at last gaining American fame as the literary wing of the Armory Show, Sherwood Anderson, just starting to write, turned to her *Tender Buttons*. He found a bareness of composition, a rhythmic prose, a concern with language in its own right vital for "the artist who happens to work with words as his material." Anderson in turn influenced Hemingway and Faulkner; during the 1920s the expatriation of an important part of an entire literary generation turned her Paris apartment into a place of aesthetic pilgrimage where writers absorbed the advice, the literary education and the artistic milieu she could offer. It became apparent that she represented a major aspect of European Modernism, a great "revolution of the Word," and though European writers and artists were often cynical about her Barnumlike style of promotion, she passed on much of value to Americans, arguing that the Modern movement was especially crucial to the natural experimentalism of the American arts. With the appearance of *The Making of Americans* in 1925 and of her striking critical essay "Composition as Explanation" in 1926, her own best work was over. But plays, operas and memoirs continued to appear in profusion. Works like *The Autobiography of Alice B. Toklas* (1933), celebrating Stein as a genius and written not by her companion but by Stein herself, and *Everybody's Autobiography* (1938) capitalized on her public reputation but at best largely display her great powers as a wit. She nevertheless remained the figurehead for an experimental attitude more and more American writers and readers were ready to acknowledge. If the best American prose from around 1913 moves toward a stronger sense of its own modernity, to a fracturing of naturalistic surface and a new and more profound attention to the word as such, that has much to do with the merger of European experimentalism and distinctive American preoccupations forged by Gertrude Stein.

Stein was not the only experimental American writer of her generation to turn to the new arts of Europe in order to begin over again and concentrate and so discover a new basis for American writing. The depressed state of poetry was readily apparent to many in the United States around the turn of the century when the modest gifts of Trumbull Stickney and his friend William Vaughn Moody, a bitter lyric poet and poetic dramatist, seemed the best available. There was discussion of French symbolism, which had transformed the European verse of the 1890s, and some American poets addressed themselves to its spirit, but usually by flight: Lafcadio Hearn to Japan, Stuart Merrill and Francis Vielé-Griffin to Paris, Henry Harland to London to edit *The Yellow Book*. Interest gradually grew as Ezra Pound, T. S. Eliot, John Gould Fletcher and Conrad Aiken all acknowledged the impact in America before 1908 of Arthur Symons's book *The Symbolist Movement in Literature* (1899). Attention turned to the Decadence and *Les Fleurs du Mal,* to Verlaine, Mallarmé and Laforgue, to W. B. Yeats and Ernest Dowson and to the accelerating transition from Victorianism. As students at the University of Pennsylvania between 1901 and 1905, Ezra Pound and his friends William Carlos Williams and Hilda Doolittle began discussing the possibility of a revitalized American poetry and concluded that they had no native models to turn to. They disagreed about their next step, with Williams believing that the solution lay in America and a return to native speech and Pound increasingly looking to the path of expatriation. Soon the energetic, spectacular troubadour was in London, busily bullying compatriots and British alike into seeing him as the main spokesman of an incipient American poetic revolution.

For all that is flawed and idiosyncratic about him, Pound is one of the great modern poets and a fundamentally important critic. His importance lies not just in his own poetry at its best—the poems of *Canzoni* (1911) and *Ripostes* (1912), *Homage to Sextus Propertius* (1918), *Hugh Selwyn Mauberley* (1920) and of his early *Cantos*—or in critical essays on matters ranging from how to read and the spirit of Romance to the critical interpretation and promotion of his greatest contemporaries, but also in his general influence and guidance. Pound began in the languid spirit of the Decadence, but he knew all the time that he was fighting for a new poetry and a new interpretation of all the literature and culture of the past; his idea of the modern revolution, his "Risorgimento," changed many times, and finally it became politically disastrous. His expatriate career ended in tragedy when his lifetime interest in the interaction of the arts and economics led him to support Mussolini and consequently face a charge of treason. Yet Pound was always intensely American. Cruelly, but accurately, Gertrude Stein portrayed him as the classic American village atheist and cracker-barrel philosopher: "A village explainer, excellent if you were a village but if you were not, not." Born in Hailey, Idaho, Pound always bore the trace of his Western origins, not least in his populist attitudes toward money and credit. He spent most of his youth in Philadelphia, first visited Europe at thirteen, and in 1906, perhaps recalling his distant kinsman Longfellow, took his master's degree in comparative literature. Pound began as a Romantic, his model the bohemian troubadour, and he lost his teaching post in Indiana for his eccentricity. His poetic interests spread, from Rossetti, Swinburne and Browning, who dominate his earliest poems, to François Villon, Provençal poetry and Lope de Vega. These came to mingle with attraction to symbolism and the *japonisme* and impressionism of Lafcadio Hearn, Whistler and later Ernest Fenellosa that created an enduring interest in Oriental literatures, in the Japanese Nō play and haiku, in the Chinese ideogram. But the American debts were deep, above all to Walt Whitman, with whom, as he would explain, he had a long love-hate relationship:

> He *is* America. His crudity is an exceeding great stench but it *is* America. . . . He is disgusting. . . . Entirely free from the renaissance humanist ideal of the complete man or from Greek idealism, he is content to be what he is, and he is his time and his people. . . . And yet I am but one of his "ages and ages encrustations," or to be exact an encrustation of the next age. The vital part of my message, taken from the sap and fibre of America, is the same as his.

> Mentally I am a Walt Whitman who has learned to wear a collar and a dress shirt (although at times inimical to both).

Pound was not content to be what he was. In 1908, disillusioned with American poetic provincialism and seeking a vast education in *Kultur,* he left for Europe, pausing in Venice to publish his first volume of poems, *A Lume Spento* (1908), a deeply Swinburnian volume, dedicated "to such as love this same beauty that I love" and filled with ideas of Decadent fragility. But then he settled in London, which, he explained in a bitter attack on cultureless America, *Patria Mia* (1913), illustrated "the futility of all art except the highest." Like Stein in Paris, he was fortunate in finding himself surrounded by an atmosphere of artistic revolt, for London had been filling with movements, European and homegrown, what Wyndham Lewis called "titanic stirrings and snortings." Pound saw a "new school of arts" forming and joined in enthusiastically. For these experimentalists the line inherited from Romanticism and Victorianism was exhausted, and even Decadence had died of its own fragility. No longer public orator or spiritual aesthete, the poet had to be an avant-garde adventurer. In reaction to the lyricism, personality and "slop" of Romanticism, a harder form of verse was evolving—"Let us agree to call it classicism," said the poet-philosopher T. E. Hulme, whose verse Pound encouraged. This "new poetic" came from many sources: the residue of the Anglo-Irish symbolist revolt of the 1890s, particularly as evidenced in the work of W. B. Yeats; the hard intellectual wit of Donne and the Metaphysical poets; the more ironic aspects of French late symbolist poetry in the work of figures like Laforgue and Corbière; the brevity of the popular Japanese forms of haiku and tanka, which stimulated Pound's interest in the ideogram; the philosophy of Wilhelm Worringer, emphasizing the abstraction of art, and of Remy de Gourmont; and the impact of many current European movements, from *unanimisme* to Italian futurism.

In London Pound found two essential literary communities he sought to unite. One drew together British and Irish writers—Yeats, Hulme, Wyndham Lewis, F. S. Flint, D. H. Lawrence, Edward Storer, Ford Madox Hueffer (later Ford), James Joyce, himself expatriated to Trieste. The other was an expatriate community of American poets—Hilda Doolittle, Robert Frost, John Gould Fletcher and, after 1914 and most importantly, T. S. Eliot. Hilda Doolittle, an old friend, shared some of Pound's ideas and moved toward a Modernist classicism; she published her first volume, *Sea Garden* (1916), in London. Frost wrote in a different spirit. He had farmed in New Hampshire before moving to London and was closest to British nature poets like Edward Thomas. But he also possessed a darkened Emersonian vision, a sense of human irony close to William Vaughn Moody's, a stoicism like Edward Arlington Robinson's; there was an uneasy melancholy and bite in his Romanticism that Pound recognized as American, and so he helped him publish his remarkable early volumes *A Boy's Will* (1913) and *North of Boston* (1914) in London. But it was T. S. Eliot—born in St. Louis of New England stock, educated at Harvard by Irving Babbitt and George Santayana, a philosopher who turned to poetry to evade the family tradition of public service—who was to prove the crucial figure. He had seized on the importance of the Metaphysical poets and Laforgue; he "has actually trained himself *and* modernized himself on *his own*," Pound wrote to Harriet Monroe, editor of the Chicago magazine *Poetry,* urging her to publish "The Love Song of J. Alfred Prufrock" in 1915. This extraordinary work, begun in America and finished in Munich in 1911, was indeed, with its hard modern irony, its sense of contemporary sterility, its fragmentary method and *vers libre,* the exemplary modern poem—Pound was to describe it as sufficient justification for the Modern movement in poetry. Eliot was also a major critic whose doctrines of "impersonality" and the "objective correlative" derived from modern argument and fitted with those of Hulme, Worringer and others who now impressed Pound as well as with the ideas of Pound's "Imagism." Like Pound, Eliot was laboring to reconstruct the literary tradition and redeem the "dissociation of sensibility" he found in most verse. With the striking new idiom he offered in his ironic early poems and the radical transformation of theory he presented in criticism, he exactly answered Pound's needs, and their complex and often troubled relationship became the seedbed of much Anglo-American poetry.

The literary movement that developed between about 1912 and the end of the 1920s in London had links and parallels with the extraordinary outburst of poetic activity that was taking place in America in the work of poets like William Carlos Williams, Wallace Stevens and Marianne Moore. Here too Pound was a prime mover. A remarkable assimilator of the experimental ideas and techniques of others, he was also an innovator who followed out each stage in the evolution of the "new poetic" not just as condenser and promoter but as maker. Without him, it seems totally unlikely that two disparately formed traditions—the British and the American—would have come temporarily together in a volatile mixture that would completely radicalize them both. An excellent if flamboyant translator and impersonator, Pound in his own verse moved rapidly from late Romanticism and Decadence to Modernism. The early troubadour pieces and Browninglike dramatic monologues gave way to a tougher, harder, more classical modernity in *Personae* (1909) and *Canzoni* (1911). Sentimental female figures from Pre-Raphaelitism and Decadence still hover here—Romantic apparitions that suggest the evanescent splendor of beauty, the ideal, the symbolic. In fact they are figures for a unity that Pound, like many of the great symbolists, would eventually find in the very form of the poem itself, in the instant complex of language and image. Pound's critical evolution shows similar development. Though *The Spirit of Romance* (1910) seems to seek a Romantic revival, he increasingly described the task as "classical," the essential recovery of what Van Wyck Brooks in America was calling "a usable past," the selective sense of tradition that would overcome gentility and provinciality. Increasingly it would prove that even in America there was such a past, to be found through bypassing the Genteel Tradition. But for Pound and Eliot the answer was "cosmopolitanism," based, as Henry James had said, on the American gift for assimilating other cultures. Eliot argued in his essay "Tradition and the Individual Talent" (1919) that tradition was not simply inherited; it had to be earned and possessed by great labor. That meant recovering the great moments and meanings not just of European but of classical and Oriental civilization, distilling the focus of creation, the impersonal nature of poetry and seeing the poet as the radical agent of culture and the measuring edge of language. In the modern crisis of language and poetry lay the heart of the modern crisis of culture, for the relative vitality of language revealed the validity or the worthlessness of culture itself. Both Pound and Eliot acknowledged this sense of crisis; and for Pound it was the artists, "the antennae of the race," who had to resolve it.

This entailed for the modern artist an avant-garde responsibility, a break with mediocre social values and the commercialism of culture, an urgent enterprise in Making It New. The new poetry also required a new criticism, a changed version of aesthetics and cultural definition. Art had to respond to discoveries in science, psychology and philosophy, to fundamental issues of language and cultural structure. The artist was in every sense a critic, of culture, of artistic heritage, of the kind of creative past that would construct a civilized present. This was another reason why the task of poetry and the task of criticism went hand in hand, reforming the bases of literary argument. In this Eliot's was clearly the greater mind, the more philosophically acute and exact, the more judicious in interpretation; Pound's was the richer, the more various, the more concerned with action and discovery. Pound was an arch organizer—Ford Madox Hueffer saw him as a kind of Baden-Powell, always trying to get artists under canvas—who promoted major writers like Frost, Eliot and James Joyce, constantly visited Paris to gather news of fresh movements, took an active part in the international literary scene and commandeered whole sections of literary magazines on both sides of the Atlantic to promote what he most admired. Later Pound and Eliot diverged, Eliot to become a British writer and a close associate of the Bloomsbury group, Pound to continue his expatriate wanderings and his dreams of a contemporary cultural transformation in Paris and then Italy. But between 1914 and 1920, when they were working most closely together, they transformed the entire scenario of Anglo-American poetic Modernism.

So, as Stein pursued her prose revolution of the word in Paris, Pound, closely aided by Eliot, fought the poetic revolution of the new in London. His first major enthusiasm was imagism, reputedly founded in a Kensington tea shop when he persuaded Hilda Doolittle to start signing her poems "H. D. Imagiste," sometime in 1912. Pound was convinced that London needed a "mouvemong" on the French model, expressing the new post-Romantic and post-Victorian aesthetic he recognized developing around him. His genius was to attach names and manifestolike ideas to a congeries of tendencies already coming into existence, though imagism was undoubtedly his creation, based on a half-willing group of participants whose aims were comparable but hardly the same, drawn together around the force of his personality and the excitement of the moment. Doolittle's talents were as a delicate poet of modern classical subjects and as a lyric feminist; Joyce and D. H. Lawrence, whom he also managed to involve, were heading in very different directions. But movements were indeed in the air, the avant-garde was becoming alert on both sides of the Atlantic and in Britain and America "little magazines" were springing up to advance the new experimentalists and their underlying tendencies. Pound hastily constructed a lineage, going back to 1908 and T. E. Hulme's call to find "beauty in small dry things." He included Hulme's slight poetic output in his 1912 collection *Ripostes* and formally announced the movement in Harriet Monroe's *Poetry: A Magazine of Verse,* which started that year to express the explosion of artistic energy in Chicago—and to which he appointed himself foreign correspondent. In the March 1913 issue, he and the British F. S. Flint announced "Imagisme" and declared its essential principles for creating a "harder and saner" new poetry:

> Use no superfluous word, no adjective which does not reveal something. . . .

> Go in fear of abstractions. Don't tell in mediocre verse what has already been done in good prose. . . .

> Don't imagine that the art of poetry is any simpler than the art of music. . . .

Imagism was to become a central theory of twentieth-century poetry primarily because it concentrated a general Modernist direction into a reasonably clear set of precepts. The overall intention was summed up in the "Retrospect" Pound added to spell out guidelines for anyone who wished to understand modern verse:

> In the spring or early summer of 1912, "H. D.," Richard Aldington and myself decided that we were agreed upon the three principles following:
> 1 Direct treatment of the "thing," whether subjective or objective.
> 2 To use absolutely no word that does not contribute to the presentation.
> 3 As regarding rhythm: to compose in the sequence of the musical phrase, not in the sequence of a metronome.

Broadly, imagism is a neosymbolist theory. Stressing the concreteness of literary language and the responsibility of the poet *for* language, it defines the image as "that which presents an intellectual and emotional complex in an instant of time." Unlike allegory, the imagist symbol does not confer coherent fixity of meaning; refusing to use symbol as ornament or a figure for something other than itself, it aims for concretion and the immediate release of poetic energy. A formalist doctrine, it makes language prior to reality; as a later adherent, Archibald MacLeish, rephrased it, "a poem should not mean but be." Imagism struggled against Romantic shimmer and haze, the bland indefinite in poetry and its dependence on exterior facts or forces. What was universal in art came not from some power *beyond* language—the absolute, a priori quasireligious "Over-Soul" of the transcendentalists, for example—but from language's own combinative and kinetic powers. Similarly the poet was no longer Whitmanian visionary or cosmic assimilator of the universe attempting to comprehend the all in the self. He was the ironist, the doubting skeptic, Wallace Stevens's comedian of perception or the blind seer of Eliot's *Waste Land* ("I Tiresias, though blind, throbbing between two lives,/Old man with wrinkled female breasts . . ."). Thus poetry lost its narrative qualities, its naive descriptions, its broad Romantic abstractions and its prophecy. It acquired the hard, edgy, impersonal, post-Romantic skepticism of Modernity.

Despite all the quarrels and variations since, there are still good reasons for believing that the major line of inquiry in twentieth-century Anglo-American poetry started here. Most of the significant poets of the time were engaged with aspects of what Pound was trying to concentrate. In 1914 he edited his remarkable anthology *Des Imagistes* with its gifted group of contributors: "H. D.," James Joyce, D. H. Lawrence, William Carlos Williams and more. Yet signs of divergence were already evident. The British and Irish writers were going in different directions from the American. Two major figures, Eliot and Stevens, were absent. The most minor of the poets, Amy Lowell, was soon to mount a takeover bid, carrying imagism off to the States, where she produced three more imagist anthologies (which Pound dubbed "Amygisme"). The search for the poetic supreme fiction bred personal quarrels, political disputes and different reactions to a world terribly darkened by world war. For Pound the key question was how to achieve the symbolist transfiguration of form he desired, the "bust through from the quotidian into the 'divine or permanent world.' " He looked to the method of "super-positioning," an energetic juxtaposition of disparate elements generating kinesis. His two-line poem "In a Station of the Metro" (1916) illustrates the technique:

> The apparition of these faces in the crowd;
> Petals on a wet, black bough.

The two elements—the faces, the petals—are parallel, neither prior to the other. The poem thus uses neither simile nor conventional metaphor where *this* is illuminated by being called *that*. The image-collision occurs simultaneously, to produce the concentration and pictorialism of Chinese ideogram or Japanese haiku. Pound claimed to have caught "the precise instant when a thing outward and objective transforms itself, or darts into a thing inward and subjective." For him this was the essence of modern poetic energy, uniting thought and object, inward and outward, and generating both symbolic vision and form.

Yet there were great problems in taking this kind of concentration onward, beyond the short poem, the thought-feeling complex in an instant of time, and beyond the friendly agreements of 1912. Pound himself joined Wyndham Lewis in vorticism, redefining the image as "a radiant node or cluster . . . what I can, and must perforce, call a VORTEX, from which, and through which, and into which ideas are constantly rushing." Vorticism, a neofuturist tendency which linked poetry and cubist-influenced semiabstract painting, produced the magazine *Blast* to demand a transforming modern explosion in the arts. It found its terrible equivalent in the World War which put the mechanical modern energies it celebrated to horrifying use, killed some of the key figures involved and left the rest conscious of a crisis in human history and civilization more profound than any they had anticipated. Yet war in many ways justified the Modern movement in which Pound was so central, putting a final end to Romantic celebration and Victorian historical optimism. Many young American writers, from Pound and Stein to Hemingway, Dos Passos, Faulkner and Fitzgerald, were involved in it or suffered from its direct impact. Pound himself directly expressed his historical dismay and at the same time made his farewell to London in the bitterly satirical *Hugh Selwyn Mauberley* (1920): "There died a myriad,/And of the best, among them,/For an old bitch gone in the teeth,/For a botched civilization." He interrogated the collapse of culture in *Homage to Sextus Propertius* (1919), a translation-adaptation of the Roman poet, and began the lifetime epic called *The Cantos.* But the culmination of the modern method and the modern mood, with its intense sense of personal and cultural sterility, came in T. S. Eliot's *The Waste Land* (1922), which Pound edited down to a third of its original length and which Eliot duly dedicated to him as *il miglior fabbro* (the better craftsman).

Modernism flourished amongst the generation of the 1920s, but directions also began to diverge and multiply. Pound moved on to Paris, which was to become the experimental laboratory for young "lost generation" American writers, while Eliot remained in London and became a British citizen. Meanwhile in the United States the Risorgimento that Pound had been pleading for seemed to be occurring. Critics like Randolph Bourne and Van Wyck Brooks had been urging a radical view of the literary past, assaulting "puritanism" and calling American writers to their own critical responsibilities. Avant-garde movements and magazines emerged to draw on the "modern tradition" defined by Stein and Pound. Pound himself increasingly acknowledged American artistic origins by announcing an angular pact with the one nineteenth-century American poet who had constructed an avant-garde poetry entirely out of his own world-encompassing American self. In 1913 in *Poetry* Pound made his declaration: "I make a truce with you, Walt Whitman—/I have detested you long enough./ . . . We have one sap and root—/Let there be commerce between us." Pound's cosmopolitan, free-form project, *The Cantos,* "a poem including history," an "endless poem, of no known category," is a kind of objectified *Song of Myself.* It joins, as Roy Harvey Pearce has said, the continuity of American poetry as none of Pound's earlier work does by embracing Whitman's sense of the poet as his own hero, struggling to fashion a relation between self and the elusive world of culture and history beyond himself, and finding that struggle means a challenge to all existing modes of expression. Pound remained an imagist, using the techniques of superpositioning and fragmentation to make an epic poem designed to distill the *"paideuma,"* the essential complex of ideas that constitute the core of any culture. The quest took him through explorations of Homer's Greece, Confucius's China, the Medici's Italy and the America of the Adams family and of Roosevelt, examining the structural interaction of politics, economics and artistic energy, seeking those central moments in human history when it transfigures into myth and secular time achieves artistic coherence. "This is not a work of fiction/nor yet of one man," Pound says in *Canto 99,* still far from the end of his lifetime quest. In fact the great quest-tale—founded, like his friend James Joyce's *Ulysses,* on Homer's *Odyssey*—led to personal and to cultural tragedy. Assaulting twentieth-century debasement of coin and word, looking for the enlightened leader, Pound moved to Mussolini's Italy and made fractured radio broadcasts for the Axis during the Second World War. So the poem takes us to a guarded cage in Pisa, where Pound was held under military arrest, and through St. Elizabeth's mental hospital in Washington, D.C., where for many years he was held unfit to plead to treason charges, before coming to final self-doubt and recrimination. The long run of *The Cantos* (1925, 1928, 1934, 1937, 1940, 1948, 1959, 1968), reaching to *Canto 118,* is still not properly edited, and it dissolves into incompleteness, dismay and silence that records a vision sadly different from that of Whitman's open-ended *Song of Myself,* a dark fulfillment for one still potent line of American Modernism.

No serious poet writing in English could avoid the implications of the imagist revolution, the new tasks for poetry it implied, the artistic crisis and artistic possibility it defined. In 1917 T. S. Eliot published the poems, *Prufrock and Other Observations,* and in 1920 the essays, *The Sacred Wood,* that established him as a leading figure of the postwar scene. It was in 1922, however, that the Modern movement exploded in Europe with publication of Joyce's *Ulysses,* Rilke's *Sonnets to Orpheus,* Yeats's *Later Poems,* Pirandello's *Henry IV,* D. H. Lawrence's *Fantasia of the Unconscious,* Oswald Spengler's *Decline of the West*— and Eliot's *The Waste Land,* the most powerful poem of the decade and the summation of both its war-weary spirit and recent poetic developments in the English language. Eliot's poem owed a great deal to Pound, as he acknowledged, and it used imagist methods. Even so, it pointed another way from Pound. Deeply indebted to the French symbolist tradition of irony and to the Eliot doctrine of impersonality, this five-part work distills what we now know was a personal psychic crisis into a vision of a wasted world of lost religious faith and total cultural decline, of clinics and breakdowns, sterile sexual liaisons and futile entertainments, of Babylonish cities of degeneration where all faces are blank and where commerce dominates. It was a poem of "fragments shored against my ruins," a quest for feeling, faith and prophecy in an age that felt itself cut off from history and meaning. Based on the root myth of the parched and sterile land which awaits the intervention of the Fisher King, it deals at once with historical, spiritual, religious and psychic crisis. The faint hope of redemption at the end, in fact, pointed Eliot's path toward what was to come. In the complex poetry of *Ash Wednesday* (1930) and the long meditative poems of *The Four Quartets* (1943), he moved through memory and desire toward tradition and religion.

Eliot's was not basically an American tradition, as he indicated by taking British citizenship—much as his British inheritor W. H. Auden later took American citizenship in a complex exchange of traditions. Eliot did acknowledge his native ancestry, not least in *The Dry Salvages* in *The Four Quartets,* but he had genuinely cosmopolitanized himself. *The Waste Land* owes little or nothing to the emerging American line of Emerson and Whitman, nor do the religious and meditative poems of his later work. For this reason, Eliot's influence on other American poetry, though it was profound in the 1920s and again after the Second World War, remains ambiguous. While recognizing his monumental imperative, William Carlos Williams complained bitterly in his *Autobiography* (1951) that "Critically Eliot returned us to the classroom just at the moment when we were on the point of escape to matters much closer to the essence of a new art form itself—rooted in the locality that should give it fruit." In the self-ironizing figure of J. Alfred Prufrock, the tired dandy who can only watch life from a distance, Eliot had mocked the confident role of the Romantic poet. In insisting on the separation of the man who suffers and the mind which creates, he had repudiated all Whitman-like inclusiveness, the union of the single separate creature and "the *En-Masse.*" In the Janus-faced figures of Tiresias and the cardplaying Mme Sosostris of *The Waste Land,* he had questioned the poet as the prophetic visionary with an unambiguous truth to assert. And in the Henry Adams–like cultural dismay and despair he expressed, he made the poet a bleak reader and critic of culture rather than a creative optimist. Both Williams and the somewhat younger Hart Crane felt the need to challenge this skepticism and despair, though in verse forms and techniques that sprang from imagism and the concept of the modern poem represented by *The Waste Land*.

For the generation of American poets arising around and after 1912, the task was to come to terms with the conception of poetic modernity encapsulated in imagist ideas. In the November 1915 *Poetry*, Wallace Stevens, another poet who had followed the path through ironic dandyism and the influence of French symbolism, published "Sunday Morning." Set on the Christian Sabbath, it is a highly stylized dialogue between the poet and a woman who questions her religious faith yet still feels the need for a spiritual life and for "some imperishable bliss." The poem suggests that although old moral and religious certainties have faded, the imagination can still respond to the "ambiguous undulations" of the world and find its transcendental occasions:

> Deer walk upon our mountains, and the quail
> Whistle about us their spontaneous cries;
> Sweet berries ripen in the wilderness;
> And, in the isolation of the sky,
> At evening, casual flocks of pigeons make
> Ambiguous undulations as they sink,
> Downward to darkness, on extended wings.

Stevens's poet of the modern secular imagination, seeking for "fictive things"—ultimately for a supreme fiction—was touched by current philosophical contradictions and the sense of poetic and imaginative deprivation. But he is more like the Europeans Rilke or Valéry in believing that a twentieth-century philosophical poem can be constructed, that the crisis of modern history can be healed by poetic acts of perception and creative imagination. In "Anecdote of the Jar" (1923), the human agent "placed a jar in Tennessee," and "The wilderness rose up to it,/. . . no longer wild." Stevens, the Hartford, Connecticut, insurance executive, is essentially a contemporary aesthete constructing a role comparable to that claimed by cubist painters. It was appropriate that to define the modern poet, he took for a later volume a Picasso title, *The Man with the Blue Guitar*.

Stevens's poetry represents a bridge between a French and European tradition and an American condition particularly shaped by American nature. Other poets were even more determined to assimilate those elements of Modernism that would settle with least fuss into the American landscape, what William Carlos Williams called "the locality that should give it fruit." Williams was a friend of Pound's and dedicated a volume to him; he was unquestionably part of the same international Modernist thought world. But he resisted expatriation and the tradition of social dissent and cultural dismay that went along with it. He wanted imagist things—a concentrated poetry in which meaning was focused on and in objects, "the thing itself," and on the relationship of the imaginative faculty to them. But he also wanted this "hardness" to be balanced by Whitman's wide Romantic acceptance and his celebration of the "procreant urge" in all things. Williams wanted imagism without the apocalyptics, as did Hart Crane when he finally brought his long poem *The Bridge* (1930) to the point where all the images of urban sterility he locates in Manhattan are transcended by the Romantic completeness he is finally able to assign to the span of the Brooklyn Bridge, that American Romantic-mechanical achievement. It soon became evident that American poetry was dividing between *two* Modernist traditions, the cosmopolitan and the native, the despairing and the hopeful.

By the beginning of the 1920s, it could be asked whether the Modern or Modernist movement in America really owed its origins to the artistic adventures of Europe, or whether it had a native, natural birth in what Hugh Kenner calls "the homemade world." The truth is, of course, that great artistic revolutions, large innovative periods in the arts, normally arise in a climate of cosmopolitanism; this one certainly did. But what stirs in the international melting pot is then often amended and nativized to suit national traditions and sensibilities— even though these traditions and sensibilities are themselves amended by the process. The Modern movement afforded to American writers the possibility of rediscovering and reconstructing their sense of that native tradition, of looking at their forms, their artistic assumptions and above all their national past in a different way. Some of them, like Eliot and Pound, took a European or even a global view of the traditions of the new. Others returned to native soil and looked afresh at the American heritage. Stevens sought to make his poem "the cry of its occasion," exploring American sites by placing jars in Tennessee. Williams reviewed America's literary stock back to the Puritans, trying to Whitmanize Modernism; Whitman, he said, had always declared that

> his poems, which had broken with the dominance of the iambic pentameter in English prosody, had only begun his theme. I agree. It is up to us, in a new dialect, to continue it by new construction on the syllable.

In metric, subject matter, aesthetic intention and social attitude, Williams and others sought to relandscape the Modern movement, to fit it to the American place and moment. So, while Pound and Eliot helped point the general direction of Western poetry, Williams, Stevens, Frost, Moore and later the objectivists took the American line forward, only to find it merging readily with the legacy of Emerson and his contemporaries. This path eventually created a new poetic authority for American verse; by the 1950s it represented a main force in international modern poetry. In the novel, likewise, the line that linked James to Stein and then Stein to Anderson, Hemingway and Faulkner gave fiction an innovative and experimental tradition that was in turn to refresh the literature of Europe. In theater, the influence of Ibsen, Strindberg and Maeterlinck would revivify the American drama of Eugene O'Neill and Elmer Rice, and that would duly pass lessons back to modern European drama. If the Modern movement was initially a very European affair, it had always had American participants whose role, influence and dominance increased steadily. In the difficult political age that developed in Europe, they became ready and necessary hosts to the tradition of the new, which began to look ever more westward. Whether outland or homemade, American writing began to take key place in the vigorous ferment of Western twentieth-century literature.

CHAPTER

·9·

THE SECOND FLOWERING

·I·

According to most of the memoirs, somewhere in the short span of years between 1912 and 1914 the entire temper of the American arts altered: Pound's Risorgimento seemed at last to dawn, America's cultural coming-of-age occurred and writing in the United States became unmistakably modern. The salons of Mabel Dodge Luhan—prophetess of the new, early psychoanalysand and radical hostess—brought artists like Alfred Stieglitz and D. H. Lawrence together with political left-wingers like John Reed and Big Bill Haywood. In her aptly titled four-volume autobiography, *Movers and Shakers* (1933–37), she recalls that

> it seems as though everywhere, in that year of 1913, barriers went down and people reached each other who had never been in touch before; there were all sorts of new ways to communicate as well as new communications. The new spirit was abroad and swept us all together.

Sherwood Anderson and Harriet Monroe, Margaret Anderson and Alfred Kreymborg and many more cultural commentators and participants agreed. "The year 1912 was really an extraordinary year, in America as well as Europe," wrote Floyd Dell, the novelist and playwright who started in Chicago's bohemia and moved to New York's to edit the radical new politico-literary magazine *The Masses* (later *The Liberator*).

> It was the year of the election of [Woodrow] Wilson, a symptom of immense political discontent. It was a year of intense woman-suffragist activity. In the arts it marked a new era. . . . It was then plans were made for the Post-Impressionist [Armory] Show, which revolutionized American ideas of art. In Chicago, Maurice Browne started the Little Theatre. One could go on with evidence of a New Spirit come suddenly to birth in America.

It was clear that by 1912 the radical change in the arts that had been sweeping across Europe was finding its way into America. In fact the new tendencies had been developing there for some years. The avant-garde spirit of the prewar years was not entirely an affair of American expatriates in Europe. From 1905 Alfred Stieglitz promoted the newest French and German art movements through his Photo-Secession Gallery in New York City. H. L. Mencken, throughout the 1920s the scourge of the American "booboisie," was one of many who had been celebrating the antirationalist and intuitionalist spirit of Nietzsche and Bergson. Freud's American visit of 1908 indicated the growing importance of psychology and psychoanalysis, and the views of George Bernard Shaw, Dostoyevsky and D. H. Lawrence made their impact on young American minds. Many of the new ideas coming from Europe proved useful sticks for beating a Genteel Tradition which, as George Santayana argued in 1911, was now being repudiated:

> The illegitimate monopoly which the genteel tradition had established over what ought to be assumed and what ought to be hoped for has broken down. . . . Henceforth there can hardly be the same peace and the same pleasure in hugging the old proprieties.

Similar ideas were alive in political thought where an old progressivism was moving toward anarchist and syndicalist ideas. In the singular year of 1912, political radicalism peaked in America, with all the presidential candidates offering versions of a Progressive ticket and the socialist Eugene V. Debs polling a million votes. This was, it seemed, an avant-garde moment in American life, as political and artistic radicalism joined hands and the bohemias of New York and Chicago were energized by fresh political, artistic and psychosexual awareness. In 1913 the Armory Show toured New York, Chicago and Boston to display side by side the painting of the American naturalist "Ashcan School" and the postimpressionist works of Cézanne, Picasso, Matisse and Duchamp, while through Walter and Louise Arensberg's New York salon (1914–21), poets and painters maintained their contact with cubism and dadaism and the waves of the new continued to reach the American shore with regularity.

Not every innovation was fully assimilated; much of the experiment, particularly its political spirit, would not survive the war. But for a time these fresh currents engaged an America of rising intellectual opportunities and intensifying artistic preoccupations convinced that nineteenth-century values were increasingly obsolete. Avant-gardes exist to shock, yet in some ways the shock was less intense in the United States than in Europe; the new styles and attitudes often seemed yet another facet of the social and mental change accompanying technological developments everywhere apparent. The most notable impact was on American arts and architecture, on the subsequent direction of American style and on the future of Modernist experiment. Little magazines and reviews began appearing in great numbers: political magazines like *The Masses* (1911) and *The New Republic* (1914), literary magazines like *Poetry* (1912), *Others* and *The Little Review* (1914) that presented remarkable new talents confidently exploring bold new forms. On the European model, experimental theaters, like Maurice Browne's Little Theatre in Chicago and the Provincetown Players of New York and Cape Cod, offered work by Eugene O'Neill, Edna St. Vincent Millay and Floyd Dell. The Washington Square Players staged both European experimental drama and new plays by John Reed, Zona Gale and Susan Glaspell; and from 1919 the Theatre Guild began its contribution to the transformation of American drama. In fiction, James's late novels and the work of Gertrude Stein offered an equivalent artistic radicalism that was to be taken up by many of the younger novelists after 1913.

The changes went deep, suggesting to many an end of the provincialism that had seemed to limit the free development of American culture for so long. During his visit to London in 1914, Van Wyck

Brooks contemplated the growth in his country of a new sensibility. The book he wrote there, *America's Coming of Age* (1915), was in effect his "American Scholar" address to his generation. Calling for an era of independent, creative living, a rejection of the irrelevant past and present to embrace a freshly assertive future, Brooks followed Santayana and Charles Eliot Norton in assaulting the Genteel Tradition of the post–Civil War era; like Mencken, Randolph Bourne and Harold Stearns, he rooted that tradition in what he too easily labeled "Puritanism"—he identified everything Anglo-Saxon as colonial and insisted that America's future lay in a natively based cosmopolitanism. Brooks's Romantic expressionism was hostile to the classicism of "New Humanists" like Irving Babbitt and Paul Elmer More who had so profoundly influenced T. S. Eliot. Their opposed views would shape critical debate for more than a decade, but they agreed in their antagonism to contemporary American philistinism and in their concern with recovering what Brooks called a "usable past," a cultural and literary legacy to nourish and sustain the redemptive initiatives of the present. Brooks's quest for viable literary tradition led him eventually to the enormously popular "Makers and Finders" sequence of books (1936–52) on the heritage of American writing. But his principal achievement came earlier, when his was the leading voice of the pioneering optimism that dominated the years from 1912 to 1917, the first phase of American Modernist experiment.

That mood was not to last. American entry into the war in April 1917 divided the radicals and weakened the progressive spirit. By 1914 Henry James, near his life's end, had recognized the cultural implications of the war:

> The plunge of civilization into this abyss of blood and darkness by the wanton feat of those two infamous aristocrats is a thing that so gives away the whole long age during which we have supposed the world to be, with whatever abatement, gradually bettering, that to have to take in all now for what the treacherous years were all the while really making for and *meaning* is too tragic for any words.

The horrors of mechanical warfare and mass slaughter, the disintegration of European empires and the rise of Bolshevism in Russia,

Wilson's failure to win American support for the League of Nations —everything conspired to alter the national temper irrevocably. The Red Scare of 1919 signaled new intolerance toward radicalism, while the election of Warren Harding in 1920 showed the American voter, according to H. L. Mencken, "tired to death of intellectual charlatanry" and turning "despairingly to honest imbecility." The First World War had a tragic impact on aesthetic sensibility, especially among the young American writers or would-be writers who served in Europe, either as combatants or as members of the various ambulance corps. It imprinted itself across the writing of the 1920s and had much to do with the atmosphere of Spenglerian gloom and decadent anxiety which haunted that period. Scott Fitzgerald's Amory Blaine, in *This Side of Paradise* (1920), missed the war, as his creator just did, but has "grown up to find all gods dead, all wars fought, all faiths in man shaken." For many American writers, the war marked a cutoff point from the past, an ultimate symbol for the dawn of modernity. In the new mood of nihilism and decadence, the spirit of aesthetic revolt nevertheless survived despite the waning of political radicalism. Indeed political disarray and continuing acquisitive commercialism confirmed artists and writers in their suspicion that the national culture was Puritanical, repressive and indifferent to the arts, and so they continued the revolt of bohemia and the large-scale expatriations and experiments of the 1920s—until the bubble of the Jazz Age, for Fitzgerald "the greatest, gaudiest spree in history," burst in the economic crash of 1929.

Thus the two generations of 1912 and 1919, so close in age, so divided in experience, launched a major era of American writing, an era during which, as Fitzgerald, that responsive interpreter of stylistic history, put it, "something subtle passed to America, the style of man." The major careers that dominated American writing into the 1950s started then and so did the modern tradition. The prewar generation was largely founded in the poetry of Pound and Eliot, Frost and Doolittle, Wallace Stevens, William Carlos Williams, Marianne Moore, Conrad Aiken, Carl Sandburg, Edgar Lee Masters. In theater there was Eugene O'Neill, in fiction Gertrude Stein, Sherwood Anderson, Willa Cather and Sinclair Lewis, in general ideas Brooks, Randolph Bourne, Babbitt and More, Mencken and Walter Lippmann. The postwar generation included Fitzgerald, Ernest Hemingway, John Dos Passos, William Faulkner, e. e. cummings, Thornton Wilder, Kenneth Burke, Edmund Wilson, Archibald MacLeish, Ring Lardner, Hart Crane, Robert E. Sherwood and Elmer Rice. The later emphasis shifted decisively toward the novel, so that by the end of the 1920s both American poetry and American fiction were established on a radical course. Taken together the work of these two generations over the years from 1912 when the first promise came of the American Risorgimento that would, Pound promised, "make the Italian Renaissance look like a tempest in a teapot," through to 1929 when the Great Crash collapsed not just the American boom but the postwar global economy can be regarded as one of the major ventures of modern literature. It was all, said Malcolm Cowley, a "Second Flowering," comparable only to the great age of the American Renaissance just before the Civil War. Certainly by the end of the 1920s, it was no longer possible to regard American literature as a provincial literature, a subbranch of British writing, or deny it a dominant role in the evolution of the Modernist arts. As America had emerged from war not a debtor but a creditor nation, so too had its culture.

The main realization of this achievement was concentrated in the decade of the 1920s. As with the American Renaissance, the sheer magnitude of this creative explosion is best suggested by a simple roll call. The year 1919 was that of Pound's *Homage to Sextus Propertius,* of Sherwood Anderson's cycle of linked short stories *Winesburg, Ohio,* which did for a small Midwestern town what James Joyce had done for Ireland's capital in *Dubliners,* James Branch Cabell's mannered novel *Jurgen,* sign of a rising mood of decadence, Willa Cather's *My Ántonia* and Eugene O'Neill's first play collection, *The Moon of the Caribbees.* The year 1920 saw Edith Wharton's late novel *The Age of Innocence,* Sherwood Anderson's *Poor White* and one of the first of the war novels that would dominate the decade, John Dos Passos's *One Man's Initiation—1917.* Sinclair Lewis published *Main Street,* which prefigured the new decade by satirizing the transition of the old pioneer West into dullness, boosterism and vulgarity that thought small-town main street the center of civilization. *Main Street* shared the best-seller lists with a first novel by another Minnesotan, F. Scott Fitzgerald, whose *This Side of Paradise* caught the flamboyantly decadent spirit of youth in a postwar age. Ezra Pound published *Hugh*

Selwyn Mauberley, T. S. Eliot *Poems* and his critical collection *The Sacred Wood* and William Carlos Williams his surreal prose poem *Kora in Hell.* The year 1921 saw Dos Passos's war novel *Three Soldiers,* Fitzgerald's collection of stories *Flappers and Philosophers,* Marianne Moore's *Poems* and Eugene O'Neill's play collection *The Emperor Jones.*

The event of 1922 was unquestionably the appearance of Eliot's *The Waste Land,* which coincided in publication with the second part of Oswald Spengler's *The Decline of the West,* James Joyce's *Ulysses* and W. B. Yeats's *Late Poems.* In the United States Fitzgerald published *The Beautiful and Damned,* its very title suggesting "the touch of disaster" that Fitzgerald would find in all the stories he now told. Carl Van Vechten's mannered *Peter Whiffle* appeared, and Sinclair Lewis produced his best-known novel, *Babbitt,* a sociological-satirical portrait of a Regular Guy from Middle America who belongs to all the clubs, is obsessed with new mechanical gadgetry, devotes himself to the cult of business but suffers a vague sense that something important is missing from his life. That vitalistic essence is also the theme of Eugene O'Neill's play collection *The Hairy Ape,* and its absence in contemporary American culture the subject of Harold Stearns's collection of critical essays by leading critics, *Civilization in the United States*—which in effect concluded that there was none and advised young artists to seek out artistic Europe. The year 1923 showed that the advice was being taken: in Paris the enlarging American expatriate community was generating its own magazines and small presses from which came William Carlos Williams's poetry collection *Spring and All* and *Three Stories and Ten Poems,* the first book of Ernest Hemingway. A small press might well have printed—so little did it sell—Wallace Stevens's first gathering of poems, *Harmonium;* e. e. cummings displayed himself as a poet of imaginative typographical experiment in *Tulips and Chimneys.* Williams also produced in this year *The Great American Novel,* a small book travestying the everlasting ambition indicated in the title; but D. H. Lawrence's *Studies in Classic American Literature,* the first book by an Englishman fully supportive of the experimental history of American writing, did much, along with Stuart Pratt Sherman's *The Genius of America,* to assure American writers that they did indeed have a usable past. Elmer Rice's *The Adding*

Machine showed that America had an expressionist drama, and Jean Toomer's *Cane* signaled the beginnings of the Harlem Renaissance of black writing.

The year 1924, when Calvin Coolidge became President, was not among the richest literary years, though it saw publication of Robinson Jeffers's poetry in *Tamar and Other Poems,* Marianne Moore's *Observations* and a first book of poems by a virtually unknown writer, *The Marble Faun* by William Faulkner. The year 1925, however, was an *annus mirabilis* that displayed the experimental spirit now at work in all its wide variety. Theodore Dreiser's *An American Tragedy* was a monumental naturalist document, but it was F. Scott Fitzgerald's *The Great Gatsby* that Eliot called "the first step the American novel has taken since Henry James." In Paris Gertrude Stein published *The Making of Americans,* her lengthy cubist novel. Begun around 1906–08 and copied out by Ernest Hemingway for his literary education, it was her contribution to the Modernist revolution of the word that preoccupied Montparnasse in the 1920s and 1930s. Stein's influence was apparent in Sherwood Anderson's *Dark Laughter,* his most experimental novel, another lament for lost vitalism and the book Hemingway would parody the next year in *Torrents of Spring.* Equally experimental, in an expressionist mode, was John Dos Passos's city novel *Manhattan Transfer,* while Hemingway himself came to full notice with *In Our Time,* a collection of linked, hard-edged stories which portrayed the collapse of older confident American ideas among the World War's stockyard piles of corpses. With Willa Cather's *The Professor's House,* Ellen Glasgow's *Barren Ground* and Sinclair Lewis's *Arrowsmith,* the more traditional American novel also showed its strength. In poetry, too, a major project appeared in Pound's *XVI Cantos;* Eliot published *The Hollow Men,* his dance of despair, and *Poems, 1909–25,* e. e. cummings *XLI Poems,* H. D. (Hilda Doolittle) her *Collected Poems,* Robinson Jeffers *Roan Stallion* and William Carlos Williams *In the American Grain,* his endeavor to recover from the national past a fertile iconography and myth, the materials of a mature American literature.

The year 1926 continued this extraordinary acceleration of experiment and emerging talent. With history and politics, naturalism and realism in question, the momentum of the times pointed firmly in an avant-garde direction—a search for stylistic alternatives to cultural nostalgia, an aesthetic release from the naturalistic view of art, an encounter with the new, exposed conditions of contemporary life. Hemingway's *The Sun Also Rises,* with its famous epigraph from Gertrude Stein, "You are all a lost generation," distilled the essence of the postwar expatriate revolt while William Faulkner's *Soldier's Pay* portrayed the decadence of the postwar world in America. Hart Crane published his first volume of poems, *White Buildings,* and Langston Hughes his *The Weary Blues,* merging jazz rhythms with black themes. The year 1927, the year of Lindbergh's flight, saw the execution of Sacco and Vanzetti—which began to rally intellectuals back toward politics—and Ernest Hemingway's *Men Without Women,* some of his finest short stories, William Faulkner's second novel, *Mosquitoes,* and Conrad Aiken's experimental text *Blue Voyage.* In 1928 came William Carlos Williams's *A Voyage to Pagany,* dedicated to Pound, as well as Ben Hecht and Charles MacArthur's play *The Front Page* and Eugene O'Neill's *Strange Interlude.* The year 1929 saw two major developments in the work of William Faulkner: *Sartoris* began the Yoknapatawpha sequence, while *The Sound and the Fury* told the story of the Compson family in four voices to begin a phase of experiment with time and consciousness. With Ernest Hemingway's *A Farewell to Arms,* the decade's major war novel appeared; another wildly ambitious writer, Thomas Wolfe, produced his prolix celebration of American genius in *Look Homeward, Angel.* Theatrical expressionism flourished in Elmer Rice's *Street Scene* and O'Neill's celebration of machine mysticism, *Dynamo.*

With the crash of October 1929 the whole remarkable episode seemed to end and the "Twenties" were over. But in 1930 came Hart Crane's attempt at the modern summative American poem, *The Bridge,* the first volume of John Dos Passos's attempt at the summative American novel, *The 42nd Parallel* (which opens *U.S.A.*), William Faulkner's *As I Lay Dying* and *Sanctuary,* and T. S. Eliot's *Ash Wednesday.* In this year, too, Sinclair Lewis became the first American writer to win the Nobel Prize for Literature, a recognition, as he acknowledged in his speech, less of his own writing than of the recent extraordinary achievements of his American contemporaries. The 1930s brought attacks on stylistic experiment from both right and left, and the Modernist movement seemed over in a time of pressing social troubles. The tags of decadence and despair stuck: Malcolm Cowley's *The Second Flowering* is subtitled "Works and Days of the Lost Generation." There had actually been two generations whose work had interfused to remarkable effect, interlocking the experimental formal and social optimism of the first with the Spenglerian disillusion and historical pessimism of the second. If they were initially, some of these writers, lost, they found themselves artistically with remarkable speed. It was as if the relatively apolitical climate of the 1920s and the social banality of what cummings called "the epoch of Mann's righteousness/the age of dollars and no sense" stirred them toward aestheticism, experimentalism, expatriation and avant-garde inquiry, while the driving, often disturbing changes of their transitory era prompted a search for new styles that would reconcile the Modernist word to the modernizing war-wounded world. By the end of the 1920s, the results seemed as much part of the native climate as the radio and the Ford automobile. A fundamental change of forms had occurred; it paralleled the achievements of European Modernism but had its own distinct timbre, even its own affirming vision. Nor did the achievement seem foreign, as the writers for the American future rediscovered a usable American literary past, an experimental tradition that helped them accommodate and nationalize the modern need to rename the world into a fresh and vital existence.

· II ·

From the first, the nature of Modernism in the United States was to be a matter for passionate debate. When Harriet Monroe started her new Chicago magazine *Poetry: A Magazine of Verse* in 1912, she set on it an epigraph from Whitman: "To have great poets there must be great audiences, too." But this was nowhere near avant-garde enough for Pound, whom she wanted to recruit as her foreign correspondent. "Are you for American poetry or for poetry?" he wrote from London, adding:

> If I can be of any use in keeping you or the magazine in contact with whatever is most dynamic in artistic thought, either here or

in Paris—as much of it comes to me, and I *do* see nearly everyone that matters—I shall be glad to do so.

He conceded that some boosting of *American* poetry was valid, "provided it don't mean a blindness to the art," since "Any agonizing that tends to hurry what I believe in the end to be inevitable, our American Risorgimento, is dear to me." What Pound disputed was where the poetic stuff of that renaissance was to come from; it would certainly not develop from dependence on past models, or sentimentality, or collusion with genteel audiences. His own contributions to the magazine were, like everything else he did, a form of education, a study session in the international sources of Modernism:

> I think if our American bards would study Remy de Gourmont for rhythm, Laurent Tailhade for delineation, Henri de Régnier for simplicity of syntactical construction, Francis Jammes for humanity, and the faculty of rendering one's own time; and if they would get some idea of intensity from Tristan Corbière (since they will not take their Villon in the original) there might be some hope for American poetry.

But this was not where Harriet Monroe drew her hope for an American poetry. She was an old poetic hand who had been appointed Laureate of the World's Columbian Exposition in Chicago in 1893, where her "Columbian Ode" was declaimed to the accompaniment of brass bands. One of her aims for *Poetry* was to encourage a native epic that celebrated the building of the Panama Canal. Her dispute with Pound, conducted in the pages of the magazine both as an argument and a competition in editorial choices, can stand as the formative quarrel of modern American poetry.

What made *Poetry* so central was that it coincided exactly with a set of major poetic changes that the magazine was eclectic enough to capture. The rubbish was considerable: Monroe offered the magazine as "a green isle in the sea, where beauty may plant her garden," and Joyce Kilmer's "Trees" was a find she celebrated with pride. Yet Pound provided W. B. Yeats, D. H. Lawrence, H. D., T. S. Eliot and the declaration of imagism while a native generation of American poets—William Carlos Williams, Edna St. Vincent Millay, Sara Teasdale, Vachel Lindsay and Carl Sandburg—found its way to her magazine. In 1914, when Monroe instituted a competition for a war poem, she received a group of Paris-set verses from "Peter Parasol." The poems did not win but some appeared in the magazine, and Wallace Stevens's poetic career began. Eliot's "Prufrock" appeared there, though only after Pound had rejected Monroe's view that it ought to "end on a note of triumph"; in November 1915 Stevens published his seminal speculation on faith in a secular world, "Sunday Morning." But Monroe's deepest satisfactions lay elsewhere—in the late work of Edward Arlington Robinson, the nature verse of Robert Frost, the free-verse Chicago poems of Carl Sandburg, the chants and ballads Vachel Lindsay based on "American" rhythms from hymns and folk songs, the gloomy local portraits of Spoon River by Edgar Lee Masters and the Red Indian pieces of Lew Sarett. These favorites led her assistant editor, Alice Corbin Henderson, to rebuke W. B. Yeats after he had told those at a *Poetry* dinner in Chicago that they were too far from Paris:

> Mr. Lindsay did not go to France for *The Congo* or for *General William Booth Enters Into Heaven.* He did not even stay on the eastern side of the Alleghenies. . . . He is realizing himself in relation to direct experience, and he is not adopting to his work a twilight zone which is quite foreign to him, as it is, generally speaking, to the temperament of the nation. He is working out his salvation in his own way. It will be his salvation at any rate, and therefore worth more to him than if he trundled in on the coat tails of English and French credentials, and much more worth while to the nation.

For a time, until Pound broke with the magazine and turned his attention to the rival Chicago venture *The Little Review, Poetry,* like the Armory Show, dramatically revealed two different versions of the modern. One drew on the cosmopolitan inheritance, with its decadence, symbolism, critical questioning of modern culture and quest for a new supreme fiction; the other stood on native ground, Emerson and Whitman, local color and progressive romantic confidence. Both lines were to prove crucial to American poetry and indeed became most forceful when they began to interact with each other. In the years up to 1920, it seemed that the major representatives of the native line were Vachel Lindsay, Carl Sandburg and Edgar Lee Masters. All were Illinois-born voices from the land of Lincoln and all expressed the Chicago spirit Monroe sought to print. Whitman lay behind them, but not Pound's Whitman, the poet of new forms; theirs was the affirmative, chanting, all-embracing democrat whose poetry was popular and populist hymn. Lindsay acknowledged some affinities with imagism, but his "General William Booth Enters Into Heaven" ("To be sung to the tune of 'The Blood of the Lamb' with indicated instruments"), printed in *Poetry* in 1913, was an attempt to catch the collective sound of mixed races, creeds and personalities forging the onward, singing progress of humanity. He was a defiant populist, a celebrator of small-town virtues who took his vigorous rhetoric from the tent-meeting and the hayride. His innovations lay in the beat of popular song, the Whitmanesque "yell" and the voodoo voice ("Mumbo-Jumbo will hoo-doo you," he declared in "The Congo: A Study of the Negro Race") as ways to merge popular culture and art. But although his experiments were, in the end, naive and limited, they helped change the voice of American poetry and for that he is remembered.

The true Chicago poet was Carl Sandburg, whose "Chicago Poems" appeared in *Poetry* in 1914. His free, loose-line verses sing the railroads and the stockyards, the people of the streets and the facts of poverty, with a warm affectionate energy. Where Lindsay opposed the modern city, Sandburg celebrated it and its people: "The People, Yes," he declared. Nature and city merge with each other, as in "The Skyscraper" where "the sun and the rain, the air and the rust" all "play on the building and use it." Yet he retained a rural simplicity which, like Lindsay's, was finally outrun by the larger cosmopolitanism of the 1920s. By contrast, Edgar Lee Masters offered the darker voice, drawing on the stoicism of Edward Arlington Robinson and above all on Robinson's practice of naturalist portraiture ("Miniver Cheevy," "Luke Havergal"). Masters's *Spoon River Anthology* (1915) consists of some two hundred or so such portraits. Their characters have two things in common: all belong to the same Illinois small town and all are dead, speaking their sad stories from beyond the grave. As in his friend Sherwood Anderson's *Winesburg, Ohio,* the short-story sequence which clearly shows Masters's influence, the small town is here no place of virtue or moral strength; these are tales of meaningless marriages, accidents and disease, unsung songs of individual ineptitude and economic exploitation. Though Masters seeks in his epilogue for a Whitmanian wholeness, it is the sense of blighted lives that survives. Yet what Dreiser, Anderson and these three poets confirmed was that there really was a "Chicago Renaissance" which was playing its vigorous part in the nation's literary development.

But in the pages of the same magazine far larger talents were declaring themselves. One was Robert Frost, who had worked in a mill, studied at Harvard, then farmed and taught in New Hampshire. Frost learned his own lessons from Edward Arlington Robinson. He had, however, become an expatriate, moving to England in 1912 and farming in Buckinghamshire. He was not really part of imagism; indeed his closest associations were with the British "Georgian School" of nature poets, especially Edward Thomas. Even so, Pound supported him, not only getting his first two books, *A Boy's Will* (1913) and *North of Boston* (1914), into print in London but affirming him for painting "the thing, the thing as he sees it." These were remarkable early volumes, immediately generating sufficient reputation for his return to America. Frost had somehow found both his voice and his needed subjects very quickly. The subjects were drawn from nature and simple, as the titles declared: "Mending Wall," "After Apple-Picking." The voice had a shrewd, grainy vernacular tone with a stoical moral wisdom to it, and it never changed greatly thereafter, through the many volumes of lyrics, dramatic monologues, duologues, political poems and verse plays that Frost would produce over a long lifetime after he returned home to New Hampshire. The voice would make him seem almost innocent of technique, and consequently he has a double reputation. For many he was the plain, popular rural sage, a moral sentimentalist, a poet of the rural heartland, an individualistic democrat who spoke publicly for private values and was admired by President Kennedy. But for others, like the critic Lionel Trilling, he was the great poet of contemporary tragic vision, evoking a "terrifying universe" of exposure and emptiness, the romantic vacancies of modern secular life.

If Frost is a major Modernist poet, it is precisely because of this latter dimension of his work. An essential development in the history of twentieth-century poetry has been a coming to terms with the withdrawn legacy of Romanticism, the fading traditional claims of panthe-ism and transcendence. The poet is thus returned to him- or herself, the word to vacancy, the symbol to disconnectedness. Frost often seems to suggest that the old tradition of nature poetry is recoverable; a major part of his verse is, after all, based on seasonal or natural lessons drawn from a natural world that seems to contain human significance. Frost strikes this pose, yet what he finds in nature—the harsh lives, the rugged New Hampshire settings, the relation of farmer to neighbor—breeds skepticism about ideas of wholeness or fulfillment. Nature's mystery is present, but it is not Emersonian. As in the poem "Design," it may be "the design of darkness to appal" or there may be no design at all. The famous "Stopping by Woods on a Snowy Evening," from the volume *New Hampshire* (1923), is a poem of division between human promises and obligations and the white mystery of nature. Yet the whiteness is itself ambiguous in its meaning, as is apparent in another poem from the same volume, "For Once, Then, Something." Here, looking down a well, the speaker seeks to read the obscure meaning there, the image beneath the water. He does see "Something more of the depths—and then I lost it":

> One drop fell from a fern, and lo, a ripple
> Shook whatever it was lay there at bottom,
> Blurred it, blotted it out. What was that whiteness?
> Truth? A pebble of quartz? For once, then, something.

The vernacular roughness of Frost's lines is more than pure pop-ulism; it is a skepticism of vision that gives him the curious and dis-tinctive metaphysical control of his best poems. An image, word or construction is turned and teased as he as speaker tests and retests himself. One of the key questions for the poets of Frost's generation was whether a Whitmanian or Emersonian Romantic posture was re-coverable in the modern urban and secular world. Frost gives us little of that world as a place, but he responds to its poetic condition. Like Wallace Stevens, though with demotic skepticism rather than philo-sophical abstractness, he is concerned both with the difficulty of finding meaning in the thing perceived and the danger of unacknowledged self-shaped perception. His poetic utterance asserts meaning's potential yet confesses to its own anxiety. The figure he summons at the end of "The Oven Bird" looks remarkably like a personified representation of the problems of the modern poet:

> The bird would cease and be as other birds
> But that he knows in singing not to sing.
> The question that he frames in all but words
> Is what to make of a diminished thing.

Frost's answer seems interestingly contradictory. The very act of personification claims a Romantic availability of natural symbols, just as the rhyming verse suggests the continuing accessibility of a traditional lyricism. Yet the symbols reveal a diminished access to insight, a reduction of poetic potential, as the vernacular pressure on the lyric voice demonstrates the need for a new discourse. Frost's response is a kind of caution and canniness in theme and in form—a knowing in singing not to sing.

For other poets, the challenge to redefine the imaginative process and the Romantic symbol in a post-Romantic world pointed the way to new aesthetic experimentation. This, indeed, was just the problem imagism had sought to pose, and it was the problem which every considerable poet in America after 1913 felt the need to face. Pound and Eliot had questioned the organicist inheritance from the British, European and American Romantics which had already reached a crisis in late nineteenth-century symbolism. Pound's idea of the kinetic image-vortex or ideogram and Eliot's doctrine of poetic impersonality had sought to focus poetic activity on the functioning of language itself and away from the radiating Romantic sensibility of the poet. That was why the questing enterprise of *The Cantos* and the ironic fragmentation of *The Waste Land* took their places at the center of serious modern poetry. Nonetheless there were those who, equally modern, wanted to displace cosmopolitan despair and chaotic dispersion and replace them with American optimism and a vision of wholeness. One such poet was William Carlos Williams, who as a medical student at the University of Pennsylvania met Pound and Hilda Doolittle and like them began to write youthful poetry in imitation of lush late Romanticism. He visited Pound in his London expatriation but rejected that path: "I knew I could not live as Pound lived, and had, besides, no inclination to experiment," he explained in his *Autobiography* (1951). Instead he chose to settle himself for life as a general practitioner in his own hometown, Rutherford, New Jersey, and tried to grow what Hugh Kenner has called "home-made" poetry there; neighboring Paterson with its polluted waters and industrial wastes became his primary poetic cityscape. Yet he too was going the way of imagism. In 1913—the year he published his first significant volume of poems, *The Tempers*—he contributed to Pound's *Des Imagistes* anthology, and the work he now printed in *Poetry* and Alfred Kreymborg's lively *Others* showed how close he was to its aims: concentration and objectification through the rejection of emotion and the dislodging of the "poetic," the search for "hard" images and poetic energy generated by the poem itself from the process and instant of its making.

When Williams's volume *Al Que Quiere!* appeared in 1917, he thus seemed a prototypical imagist. But in the preface to his next book, *Kora in Hell: Improvisations* (1920), he declared his quarrel with Pound and Eliot, describing them as "Men content with the connotations of their masters." In 1922, when *The Waste Land* appeared—that poem of the evanescent international city as a *mélange adultère du tout* with its images of fragmentary sterility amongst the rootless, stony rubbish— Williams saw it as the great poem it was, even though he complained that it was a setback to the development of poetry. He was primarily offended by Eliot's lack of Americanness and his enactment of the poem within the universe of tragic world culture; for Williams's own fragments were not shored against ruins. Yet for all his emphasis on the American voice and the locality that bore poetic fruit, Williams consorted with experimental, expatriate developments right through the 1920s. Many of his books were printed by the small presses of expatriate Paris, and in 1924 he visited the experimental scene there— though showing equal interest in James Joyce and the sale at the Bon Marché. Nonetheless he persisted as a counterweight to cosmopolitanism: Modernism *was* necessary, but it could be gotten better from 9 Ridge Road, Rutherford, New Jersey, than anywhere else, and not from an irrelevant "classicism" but from a recovered Romanticism.

This was the aim of the volume *Spring and All* (1923), which starts with a series of declarations on the all-powerful imagination and its need for a new compact with reality. It asserts the guiding value of the great American poet of new forms, Whitman, as well as that of postexpressionist painters like Juan Gris who show that "the illusion once dispensed with, painting has this problem before it: to replace not the forms but the reality of experience with its own." Hence poems, like paintings, "must be real, not 'realism' but reality itself." Typical of the path Williams was taking was "By the Road to the Contagious Hospital," where the pictorialist, object-centered method is directly invested with Whitmanian ideas of "the procreant urge," or generative creativity. The poem ends, "One by one objects are defined—/. . . the profound change/has come upon them: rooted, they/grip down and begin to awaken."

This procreant rooting of poetic materials went with the case for localism, his attempt to be what he called in the title of his next book *In the American Grain* (1925). He wanted art to reach fresh force, as the precise thing was touched by the imagination and made open to fusion and incorporation. His Americanness has something to do with this. His own background was part-European (an English father who never took American citizenship, a mother from Puerto Rico, a half-European education), but like Twain, Lardner and Dos Passos, he believed in the power of distinctive American speech to give writing a new dialect and form, "words washed clean" by American voicing, things seen anew through the American gift for wonder. If history was indeed darkening, as he came ever more to suspect, it could be recovered by a going "back to the beginning." That was the aim of *In the American Grain,* a prose recovery of the best past of the American imagination and its unique sense of things and nature. He compared early responses to the new land, the difference between Puritan distrust of America as "devil's territory" and the wonder felt by explorers like Columbus and Cortés. He compared Cotton Mather's "Wonders of the Invisible World," which saw the Puritans embracing "voluntary Exile in a squallid, horrid American desart," with the spirit of men like Daniel Boone or the missionary Père Rasles, who sought to incorporate to himself God's visible world, implying that

All shall be included. The world is a parcel of the Church so that every leaf, every vein in every leaf, the throbbing of the temples is of that mysterious flower. Here is richness, here is color, here is form.

In the American Grain was Williams's *ABC of Reading,* his endeavor to construct an American *paideuma* pointing not toward despair but to transcendental possibility.

From this point on, Williams's poetry and prose were to function in counterpoint to the developments of Modernism in Europe. His prose work *A Voyage to Pagany* (1928), dedicated to "the first of all of us, my old friend Ezra Pound," was in fact a commentary on the gains and losses of European expatriation. Williams was driving toward the idea of a Modernist epic born from localism, from American experience and the loose vernacular line or "variable foot" based on the rhythms of distinctively American speech. As he was to put it:

A minimum of present new knowledge seems to be this: There can no longer be serious work in poetry written in "poetic" diction. . . . Speech is the foundation of the line into which the pollutions of a poetic manner and inverted phrasing should never again be permitted to drain.

In the early 1930s he aligned himself with the postimagist group of American poets called the objectivists, Charles Reznikoff, George Oppen and Louis Zukofsky, and supported their insistence that all associational or sentimental value should be dropped from verse. He contributed to their *An "Objectivists" Anthology* of 1932 and increasingly insisted that "No symbolism is acceptable. No symbolism can be permitted to obscure the real purpose: to lift the world of the senses to the level of the imagination and give it new currency." In the world of the Depression, of poverty, starvation and bread lines, descriptive documentary writing received renewed attention; Williams employed the form in his *Life Along the Passaic River* (1932), an important step toward the epic poem that was growing in his mind. With *White Mule* (1937) he began an experimental novel trilogy, but the logic of his endeavors all came clear when the long poem *Paterson* appeared in four volumes between 1946 and 1951 with a fifth volume, really a coda on its writing, added in 1958.

Paterson's importance, and the reason for its influence on many postwar American poets, is undoubtedly that it was Williams's answer to *The Cantos*. As Pound's ambitious epic went on, the possibility of bringing it to unity had grown more remote, and his political involvement drove his plan for the new *paideuma* ever more adrift. After the tragedy of the Pisan prison cage and his period in a Washington mental hospital, Pound offered in 1962 the poignant confession of *Canto 116*:

> . . . My errors and my wrecks lie about me.
> And I am not a demigod,
> I cannot make it cohere.

But *Paterson* is a poem determined to cohere, and within the demanding, testing world of the imagination. Like any modern epic, it was made of profusion and confusion, of images and episodes which were, as Williams said, "all that any one man may achieve in a lifetime." The perception of *Paterson* is disjunctive but not in the fragmentary way of *The Waste Land,* the shoreless sea-questing of *The Cantos,* nor even in the reconstitutive, overarching spirit of Hart Crane's similar endeavor, *The Bridge*. In Williams's culminative long poem,

> man in himself is a city, beginning, seeking, achieving and concluding his life in ways which the various aspects of a city may embody—if imaginatively conceived—any city, all the details of which may be made to voice his most intimate convictions.

But no generalized, cosmopolitan city, no "unreal city" like *The Waste Land*'s, would really do. Like Faulkner, Williams turned to the shapes and secrets of his own local landscape. He verbally constitutes neighboring Paterson, at once place and person, from its varied American history, from its contemporary industrial debasement, its polyglot population, its trees, rocks and water. The "filthy Passaic" which runs through it is his river of inseminating consciousness, his version of Joyce's Liffey as it passes over the motion-in-stasis of the Passaic falls into the fertilized male-and-female world beyond.

Paterson is in its way a Postmodern poem, which is why it could pass on lessons to later poets as varied as Allen Ginsberg and Charles Olson. Like *Leaves of Grass,* its aim is unitary, a total creative immersion, a floating in the procreative. Williams knew that with its fragmentation and multiplication it would otherwise have been a poem of disconnected ruins, isolated symbols or crude allegorical myths, like earlier Modernist epics. "I wanted to keep it whole, as it is to me," he said. He tried to do this through what he called "a mathematics of particulars" which would transfer the plural into the one, the local into the universal, the fictive into the transcendental. Whether *Paterson* does effectively cohere, thereby healing Modernist fragmentation, is something readers will go on debating. Coherence is itself one of fiction's fictions which the imagination so celebrated for its making seeks to guarantee. In the end, as with most fictions, the weight of our interest falls on the making, not on the conclusions that can be drawn from it. But for the poet, as Williams set out to confirm finally in "Asphodel, That Greeny Flower" (1955), the two elements were inextricable because "Only the imagination is real!" Williams, the family doctor from Rutherford who had seen so much dirt, so many births and so active and sensual a creation everywhere around him, had taken that as a hard reality to confront; the lifetime lesson taught the triumph of the imagination. When Wallace Stevens prefaced Williams's *Collected Poems, 1921–1931* (1934), he made a surprising but accurate judgment: "he is a Romantic poet. This will horrify him." Williams was indeed a Romantic poet, or rather a Romantic antipoet who strove to reconstitute the ordinary as a Romantic principle.

Stevens always conceived his own task in Romantic terms, as one wherein the imagination informs and is informed by reality. This, in a post-Romantic age, requires, he said, "an uncommon intelligence" and an instinct for the genuine. He said this not directly about himself but about Marianne Moore, another of the crucial explorers who pointed the direction of American poetry and gave it a sense of coherent endeavor. Women's poetry and its mode of perception had been from the start an essential part of imagism. H. D. had been the first named "Imagiste" and the method had been seized by Amy Lowell. But it was Miss Moore who grasped the poetic possibility it raised most forcefully with that stipulated "uncommon intelligence." Her work showed no large epic themes and her output was never great: against the 400 poems of Stevens's collected work, her *Collected Poems* (1951) contained some seventy pieces. But, like Stevens, her one major subject was the nature of poetry and the complex relation of reality and artifice, a subject to which she attended with careful wit and a great capacity for meditation within verse. She was born in St. Louis, like T. S. Eliot, who identified her as "one of those few who have done the language some service in my lifetime," and like him she became one of the important modern editors, editing the revived *Dial* from 1925 to 1929. Her early poems appeared both in *Poetry* and the London *Egoist*. Through the efforts of H. D. and Bryher (A. W. Ellerman), her first volume, *Poems,* was published without her knowledge or approval in London in 1921; her first American volume, *Observations,* appeared in 1924. Like Williams, she acknowledged an "appetite for the essential"; like Williams, but with a good deal more wryness, she sought to adapt imagist methods to American conditions (her early poem "England" both celebrates and questions her own "languageless country" where letters are written "in plain American which cats and dogs can read!").

But a late poem has the Stevens-like title "The Mind Is an Enchanting Thing," and like Stevens she was always very much a poet of the mind. Her poem "Poetry" (1921), which went through several versions, still remains her best-known piece. It faces the postimagist question: what is the basic relationship between poetic emotion and real things? She asked for poets who were "literalists of the imagination," for poems which would present "imaginary gardens with real toads in them." Poetry was a mode of delusion, but

> if you demand on the one hand,
> the raw material of poetry in
> all its rawness and
> that which is on the other hand
> genuine, then you are interested in poetry.

Moore's interest in poetry recalls Dickinson's, although Moore was in her twenties before her forerunner's work was widely known or appreciated. Both poets worked the spaces they identified as belonging to them as women and both have been called "poets' poets" for their verbal precision and formal experiment. Like Dickinson, Moore never married (she is said to have mourned Eliot's marriage in 1957) but although she led a quiet life in New York, she knew many of the writers and artists of her time and pursued diligently her career as an innovative poet. Pound, David Kalstone has remarked, "worked with the clause, Williams with the line, and Stevens with the word"; Moore worked carefully with individual stanzas, then duplicated them meticulously: "I tend to write in patterned arrangements, with rhymes . . . to secure an effect of flowing continuity." Modest subjects—animals, features of the landscape—are treated with technical subtlety not always apparent to the casual reader. But Moore has helped shape a generation of younger writers, most notably Elizabeth Bishop, Randall Jarrell, Richard Wilbur and Robert Lowell. Her careful mosaics of fragments gleaned from a lifetime's close observation are among the era's major exhibits of art embodying the simultaneous seeing and saying of perceived experience.

For Wallace Stevens—that ironic, self-skeptical modern Romantic —the limits of the imagination in the secular contemporary world were the enduring subject of his artistic attention. The result was a poetry of originating meditation which made him the one natively American poet among his generation who—as a thinker about, and a thinker *in,* poetry—can seem genuinely comparable to Yeats, Eliot or Valéry. There have been those (like the critic Yvor Winters) who have felt Stevens reached the state and stuff of the imagination all too easily, with a ready hedonistic gaiety and a want of real human experience; to them Williams's grainier and more rootedly experienced poetry seems the better, a founding form of liberation for the century's American poetry. But Stevens was the poet of poetry as intelligence and that rare thing in America, an essentially philosophical poet, which is to say that his poems endlessly engage us with abstract conceptions of "imagination," the "real" and "poetry" itself as a fictionalizing, naming and world-constructing enterprise. We can find his achievement concentrated for us in three books—*Collected Poems* (1957), *Opus Posthumous* (1957) and *The Necessary Angel: Essays on Reality and the Imagination* (1951). Here are more than 400 poems and much prose devoted to the end which he declared as his own, consideration of "the theory of poetry in relation to what poetry has been and in relation to what it ought to be." They display a quest that runs from the mood of 1890s decadence to the preoccupation with the fictive that drew so many after the Second World War, a quest for what Stevens called the supreme fiction, in a postreligious world where, he said, "After one has abandoned a belief in God, poetry is that essence which takes its place as life's redemption." It was Stevens's sense of the imagination's restorative force that made his poetry Romantic; he had, he said, "a feeling about the world which nothing satisfies except poetry."

Stevens began, in fact, as a Paterian Decadent and a dandy: "The novelty of the poet's radiant and productive atmosphere is the morality of the right sensation," he once said. The few student poems he published in the *Harvard Advocate* drew for tone on the more flamboyant symbolists like Verlaine and Laforgue and display what Samuel French Morse calls "an interest in the comic irony of the quotidian and a glance at the grotesque." Stevens studied law in New York, practiced at the New York bar until 1916, then joined the Hartford Accident and Indemnity Company, where he would remain an executive and finally a vice president for the rest of his life. But when in 1914 he approached *Poetry* magazine, the serious and reticent lawyer masked himself as the poetic aesthete "Peter Parasol," author of a mannered and high-toned poetry which insisted on its flamboyance and novelty, its comic bravura. It has always been easy to mistake Stevens's seriousness. The early poetry in particular, collected in his first volume *Harmonium* in 1923, with its bright languages, its hoo-hoos and ay-tay-tums and its stylish systems of consonance and alliteration, made him look to some a bright, balletic but finally trivial poet like Edith Sitwell. He had a taste for fanciful poetic personae: Peter Parasol soon appeared in his own poem as a Parisian dandy bemoaning the shortage of female beauty in the world, and there would be the "Emperor of Ice Cream," the "Comedian as the Letter C," the "Sleight-of-Hand Man," the "Man with the Blue Guitar." Titles came from French poetry and from paintings, especially cubist paintings. In Decadent fashion, the poems were celebrations of the imagination in its secular sensual condition, "tootings at the wedding of the soul" pronouncing "the marriage/of flesh and air." The world of the imagination was presented as a carnival world drawing on florid Mexican landscapes and elaborate acts of invention.

Harmonium was a commercial failure that earned only $6.70 in royalties for its author in its first six months. Stevens himself saw the poems as early experiments and wished to subtitle the volume "Preliminary Minutiae." But for all its flamboyances, it was consistent with an enlarging and serious line of speculation. Coleridge, from whom much of that speculation in fact derived, would probably have called Stevens's primary poetic gestures acts of "fancy" rather than "imagination." Yet this was, in a sense, the point: after the pantheistic marriage of human imagination with transcendental force in the outward universe had lost all discernible divine guarantee, fancy, the imagination's ballyhoo, was what was left, as the poet, seeking to enrich the world by uttering its things into being, sought delight and awareness in fictive construct. The meditative impulse behind the poems was evident in the longer, more serious pieces of the collection, "Sunday Morning," "Le Monocle de Mon Oncle," "A High-Toned Old Christian Woman," "Peter Quince at the Clavier" and "Thirteen Ways of Looking at a Blackbird"—now seen as some of Stevens's finest work. "Poetry is the supreme fiction, madame," he declared, for the first but not the last time, in opening "A High-Toned Old Christian Woman." The line seems addressed to the personified Genteel Tradition itself which seeks to "Take the moral law and make a nave of it/And from the nave build haunted heaven." But the poet as sensual aesthete constructs his own heaven, whipping "a jovial hullabaloo among the spheres":

> This will make widows wince. But fictive things
> Wink as they will. Wink most when widows wince.

The task is secular, conducted within the limits of reality, seeking, as he said elsewhere, "Nothing beyond reality. Within it,/Everything. . . ." Art is "a compensation for what is lost"; "God and the imagination are one." The perennially baffling question of what links the self's image of the real to the actual world, how the creative imagination forms ideas of idea in a universe deprived of innate design, was to compel his work for the rest of his writing lifetime.

He had already posed these questions in "The Comedian as the Letter C," a characteristically witty journeying through the imagination's landscapes. Crispin, the central figure, has served his "Grotesque apprenticeship to the chance event" and crossed the overwhelming sea, where he is "washed away by magnitude," to the translinguistic worlds of Europe and the sensual, exotic Caribbean—much as, in inspiration, his author had. He returns, "the poetic hero without palms," to Carolina, hoping that "his soil is man's intelligence," and comes to the conclusion of Williams and Faulkner: "The man in Georgia waking among pines/Should be pine-spokesman." But the inexorable facets of the real multiply and Crispin ends among contradictory Muses, ironically defeated by "things as they are." Reality overwhelms the imagination, and the "plum" of life's goods remains elusive. Yet here was a quest that had to continue, through Stevens's complex volumes of the 1930s: *Ideas of Order* (1935), *Owl's Clover* (1936), *The Man with the Blue Guitar* (1937)—where "things are as I think they are/And say they are on the blue guitar." A growing seriousness and precision became evident; by *Parts of the World* (1942) and *Transport to Summer* (1947), his dogged exactitude was clear. This last contained "Notes Toward a Supreme Fiction," a title that summarized all his work as its subtitles summarized its principles: "It Must Be Abstract," "It Must Change," "It Must Give Pleasure." Stevens's poems were always based in an act of thought, always subject to the occasions that prompted them, always tuned as instruments of aesthetic delight. The world of his poetry was pared down by now, from summer elaborations to the harder light of autumn, through his desire to make the poem "the cry of its occasion,/Part of the res itself and not about it," as he wrote in "An Ordinary Evening in New Haven." Like reality itself, the task remained obdurate to the last, sustaining an unending inquiry into the relation of imagination and reason, subject and object, utterance and vision. His late, reflective *Auroras of Autumn* (1950) showed a deepened awareness of "poverty" and life's tragedies. When, at the age of seventy-five he published his stout *Collected Poems* (1954), he added a crucial section called "The Rock," his concluding encounter with life's resistant solidity.

Wallace Stevens carried the native Emersonian grain through French symbolism and American pragmatism into the epistemological revolution of the mid-twentieth century. As the commentary on his work and thought accumulates, it becomes more and more likely that he will assume a central position in the literature of his time for the seminal influence he has had on the generation of writers who succeeded him.

·III·

The war the United States entered in 1917 to make the world safe for democracy, as President Woodrow Wilson put it, was the nation's first major foreign conflict. Although its impact on American thought and development proved to be deep and wide-ranging, the United States, its soil untouched, seemed less directly affected than Europe; indeed it emerged from the war more convinced of its "basic" values, suspicious of foreign entanglements, uneasy about the direction of world affairs, distrustful of the progressive politics of the prewar years. Looking to itself, the nation concentrated on business, economic expansion, the advancing of technology, the spread of consumerism; new developments seemed simple extensions of traditional American principles of individualism and the pursuit of abundance for all. Yet change was everywhere visible as the economy boomed. Wealth spread, mores altered, the texture of life changed, new technologies appeared in every home and street. For Americans as well as Europeans, the war was felt as a point of crucial translation that marked the beginning of an era, the 1920s, as clearly as the Great Crash marked its end.

One did not need to have gone to the European trenches to feel the sense of change and generational separation, but many American writers *did* go, as if seeking necessary life experience. John Dos Passos, Ernest Hemingway, e. e. cummings and Edmund Wilson were in the ambulance corps; Hemingway was wounded on the Italian front and turned that wound into a primal metaphor for the pain of life in a troubled age. Scott Fitzgerald had just finished officer school and was about to embark for Europe when the armistice was signed; William Faulkner trained with the Royal Canadian Air Force and encouraged the myth that he had served as a pilot in France. For many of these writers the war was the subject of their first literary utterances, an image of fundamental transition, a challenge to the small-town values among which many of them had grown up, to old heroic ideas of battle, to the notion of "culture" as a body of established beliefs, modes, languages. "Culture" had also meant Europe, but now Europe, tearing itself to pieces on the battlefields, meant experience not as art and tradition but as horror, extremity, historical exposure.

The war produced the war novel: John Dos Passos's two works of growing disillusion, *One Man's Initiation—1917* (1920) and *Three Soldiers* (1921); cummings's *The Enormous Room* (1922), about his confinement in a French prison camp after expressing pacifist views; realistic battlefield works like Thomas Boyd's *Through the Wheat* (1925); novels about the "separate peace" of the disenchanted modern hero like Hemingway's *A Farewell to Arms* (1930). But what dominated the 1920s was the *post*war novel—the novel permeated by war as an apocalyptic metaphor, the sign of a world severed from its past, changed, darkened, modernized. "I was certain that all the young people were going to be killed in the war," Fitzgerald recalled in describing the genesis of *This Side of Paradise* (1920), "and I wanted to put on paper a record of the strange life they had lived in their time." Hemingway's *The Sun Also Rises* (1926) turns upon its castrating war wound, afflicting not just his hero but the surrounding "herd" of modern young people as they search for new values and life-styles in a suddenly vacant world. The writing of the 1920s abounds in images of fragmentation, waste, castration and sterility—not just in Pound's "Hugh Selwyn Mauberley" or Eliot's *The Waste Land,* but in the Valley of Ashes that darkens Fitzgerald's *The Great Gatsby* (1925), the genital wound that dominates Hemingway's *The Sun Also Rises* (1926), the wounded soldier who casts his shadow over Faulkner's *Soldier's Pay* (1926).

If a sense of purposelessness, decadence, cultural emptiness and political failure pervades the new American fiction of the 1920s, post-war developments made their contribution. The compromises of Wilson's Versailles Treaty, the refusal of the U.S. Senate to ratify his support of the League of Nations, the Red Scare, the extending of Prohibition, the fading of progressivism, the rise of isolationism—all made critical contemporaries and later observers see the 1920s as a decade of political ignorance, flaunted capitalism and material wealth, intolerance and Puritanism. But this conservative decade also set in motion some of the most profound changes of American history, though they were less directly political than behavioral, cultural, psychological and structural. America modernized and in so doing swept away many of the values ordinary Americans thought central to the meanings of their national life. As the economy shifted its center from production to consumption, as the focus moved from country to city, as credit ran free and personal spending boomed, as new technologies brought autos, telephones, radios and refrigerators to the growing numbers of middle-class homes, change moved at an ever-faster pace. The 1920s was an age of Puritanism and Prohibition, but also of psychoanalysis and flappers, jazz and film. The age that challenged innovation and looked back nostalgically to the rural past also saw massive new technological advances, the airplane, the interstate highway, sound in movies, the high-rise sophisticated excitement of the cities. The tension between nostalgia and novelty was exemplified in some of the key conflicts of the age—immigration restriction, the Scopes "monkey trial" in Tennessee about the teaching of Darwinian evolution in schools, the trial and later the execution of the anarchists Sacco and Vanzetti, a *cause célèbre* which split conservatives and radicals and repoliticized what had seemed a largely apolitical decade.

The American novel of the 1920s explored to the full this mixture of experimental excitement about the new and anxious awareness of historical loss. None showed it more than F. Scott Fitzgerald, a novelist who seemed to exemplify the decade and indeed virtually *became* the 1920s in literature. Born in 1896 in St. Paul, Minnesota, his age ran roughly parallel to the century's decades, his career matched the rising excitements of American life. Going to Princeton in 1913, he encountered and was allured by its world of wealth and privileged promise. He trained as an army officer but did not reach France until the expatriate season of the 1920s. That year his first book, *This Side of Paradise,* came out, to rival on the best-seller lists a work by another Minnesotan, Sinclair Lewis, but where Lewis's *Main Street* summed up the 1920s through a half-savage and half-loving portrait of Puritanic Middle America, Fitzgerald dealt with East Coast wealth and charm, college days, youthful excitement and above all with the new generation. Like James Branch Cabell's *Jurgen* (1919), his was a self-consciously decadent book. Its "golden boy," Amory Blaine, is a "romantic egoist," "hallowed by his own youth." He chases wealth, beauty and religion, and senses the dilemmas of the age. Style is all, history is personalized as fashion. Daring conduct, flamboyant self-presentation, sensitivity and desperate self-expenditure mark the modern spirit. Everything is evanescent, all the while promising transcendental possibility. A youthful and often ill-written book, it aimed to be, and became, the text for the postwar generation, launching its author as a style setter, writing, he said, for "my own personal public—that is, the countless flappers and college kids who think I am a sort of oracle."

To many of his critics, Fitzgerald still appears little more than a stylish chronicler—a man so immersed in the social life, the amusements, the illusory promises of his time, with its fashions, its wealth, its changing sexual habits—and its charm—that he could never stand back far enough to consider and test it. And certainly Fitzgerald is a novelist of immersion, deeply invested in the dreams, illusions and romantic vulgarities of his generation. Yet, as his later novels and his famous essay "The Crack-Up" make very clear, Fitzgerald not only knew he paid a very high price for his literary tactics, but he was able to measure and explore that price with the greatest critical intensity. "The Crack-Up" draws a close analogy between the historical development of the 1920s, from early euphoria to increasing strain, and his own psychic curve from early buoyancy to trauma. The Depression of 1929 becomes the crisis of his generation as they face their own economic, spiritual and psychic overexpenditure, and it parallels his own personal "crack-up." As the titles of the story collections that followed the first novel show—*Flappers and Philosophers* (1921), *Tales of the Jazz Age* (1922)—Fitzgerald dedicated himself not just to the task of capturing but of promoting the moods, fashions, styles and self-images of the age of flappers, jazz and flaming youth. But as the title of his second novel, *The Beautiful and Damned* (1922), also suggests, there was a darker side; he emphasized that all his stories now had "a touch of disaster in them." Gloria and Anthony Patch—just like that other exotic couple, Scott and his wife, Zelda—want to make their marriage a "live, lovely, glamorous performance," trusting that "something is going to happen." But the pressures of time and moral carelessness take their toll, and the book is dominated by an increasingly familiar postwar tone of fragility and self-induced destruction: "I don't want to live without my pretty face," Gloria cries.

Like his character Dick Diver in the most analytical of all his novels, *Tender Is the Night* (1934)—a summing-up of the 1920s from the 1930s, a look back over the Boom from after the Crash—Fitzgerald believed in involvement and saw the task of the writer and intellectual as that of risking himself in the chaos of the times, despite the danger that one will not remain fully "intact." The writer's role is to become a "performing self," an agent in the places where history, society and change are most conspicuously enacted. Fitzgerald's public style and his fictional style were both modes of involvement; in his later work, however, he began increasingly to understand the driving forces behind the social display and his own psychic and economic overextension and began to seek the literary forms for exploring them. Ironically enough, it was *The Great Gatsby* (1925), the book with which his early public success began to fade, that brought the elements into fully effective balance. Its indirect, often ironic first-person technique was learned from Joseph Conrad, and it is his masterwork, the book T. S. Eliot acknowledged as a modern classic. The mixture of involvement in and critical understanding of its story is held in perfect control; the author, rather like his hero Jay Gatsby himself, seeks a parvenu's entrance into the social world while standing romantically and critically outside it. As we have seen in comparing it to Dreiser's *American Tragedy*, it is a novel of modern dream life, its vision demanding a style well beyond naturalism, its approach requiring not conventional moral interpretation but an imaginative instinct. The narrator, Nick Carraway, becomes a voice of what Fitzgerald called "selective delicacy"—filtering sensations and impressions in an order appropriate to his growing understanding of Gatsby's nature, presenting a landscape of complex images so that Gatsby, initially just another corrupt product of his material world, is gradually distinguished from it and finally made the victim of its massive carelessness. The novel suffuses the material with the ideal and turns raw stuff into enchanted object. That partly reflects Gatsby's own romantic and obsessive qualities, but it is also the product of a symbolist mode of writing that informs everything—Gatsby's dreams, parties, even his shirts—with an enchanted glow.

Gatsby is searching for a transfiguring vision, a world beyond the clock of historical time, life seeming meaningless unless *invested* with meaning. Fitzgerald too projects meaning onto the book's troubled landscape, its surreal world of the metropolis and contemporary social life, its strange detail thrown up in startling instants and images of shifting fashions, sudden music, the decor of hotel rooms, the glamour of possessions, the crowded motion of the streets, the suburban ash heaps, the passing faces and the passing hearses that catch the narrator's eye. Fitzgerald plays off the two alternatives: the world romantically arrested, suspended in wonder and love, and the world in motion, filled with rootless, grotesque images of dislocation, fragments without order, a waste land. That tension still haunts the final pages where the dream of a pristine America commensurate with man's capacity for wonder is also a nostalgic desire for what time, change, selfishness and contingency defeat. Gatsby is an elusive, deceptive, almost counterfeited figure, but he is also a portrait of the artist—chasing, with his "creative passion," a symbol, Daisy and the green light, which is both transcendent and corrupt. The book becomes a symbolist tragedy about the symbolic imagination's struggle to persist in a lowered historical time. In its final backward look at the American Dream, it explores the inherent ambiguity of the native sense of wonder in a meretricious, deceptive world. Fitzgerald succeeds not just in internalizing his own times—the era of a "whole race going hedonistic, deciding on pleasure"—but in realizing them as the source of a serious literary form.

As 1920s unease grew, Fitzgerald internalized that too, sensing the economic cost yet to be paid, the moral interest that was coming due. He himself was now overextended, financially and emotionally. The relative economic failure of *The Great Gatsby* drove him to producing countless inferior magazine stories, some showing the touch of vision and genius he so evidently possessed but others disappointing to today's reader as they were to their own author. The stock market crash of 1929, Zelda's growing mental illness, the unpaid bills and his own alcoholism were weakening the inner self behind the public façade. He read Spengler and Henry Adams, Marx and Freud and sensed the need for a "Great Change." In the Depression of the 1930s, he saw the irrelevance of the rich he had so admired and grew more conscious of the roots of his own wealth and his psychic situation, more aware of the historical processes that underlay the displays and disorders of his age. All this went into his next novel, *Tender Is the Night,* a troubled and troublesome book, never quite completed, so we can still read it in two versions. It is a tale of psychic disorientation, carefully made typical. Of his central couple, Dick and Nicole Diver, Fitzgerald can say: "At that moment, the Divers represented externally the exact furthermost evolution of a class." Diver himself, trained as a Freudian psychologist, can also represent the endeavor to plumb the unconscious forces that lie beneath the postwar world of chance, violence, breakdown and unexplained death. Behind the glitter of wealth, the sunlit glow of luxurious expatriate life on the French Riviera and in Paris, there sound constant echoes of the war lately ended. The book's method is panoramic and expository, its historical reach framed by an awareness of endless inner violence, fragility and despair. The world appears one of surfaces, but the expressive action is propelled by underlying processes—a compositional challenge that explains why the book was twice written and set in two different orders, as Fitzgerald sought to balance the relation of inner and outer life, personal stories and larger themes.

Fitzgerald was never satisfied with his novel and continued to amend it even after publication. Imperfect as it is, lacking the completeness of *Gatsby,* it remains a major work; even its incompleteness seems appropriate, for incompleteness and psychic overextension were now Fitzgerald's preoccupation in the serious writing he continued to produce despite growing personal collapse. The essays of 1936 and 1937, "The Crack-Up" and "Early Success," display how frankly he tested art against disintegration, playing his own thirties against his twenties, interweaving historical and personal awareness of crisis. His alcoholism by now serious, his wife, Zelda, permanently hospitalized, his youthful reputation fading fast, his finances in chaos, he turned to Hollywood for work as a screenwriter. His final novel, *The Last Tycoon* (1941, posthumous), is one of the best Hollywood novels. But it too was left incomplete, interrupted by Fitzgerald's sudden, early death in 1940. Monroe Stahr is the last of the great producers, another master stylist who is gradually destroyed by the disintegrative forces of the world outside him but also by the fragmentation of his inner life. This is another testing of the American Dream, set in the great dream-factory, Hollywood itself, with its tinsel images and its hidden conflicts. Stahr's tragedy resembles Fitzgerald's own, for he too had struggled to reconcile form and time, art and history, creation and commerce, seeking to invest his actions with romantic and moral value while seeing many of his dreams turn to tinsel or dust. After Fitzgerald's death his reputation fell further but has since revived, as the major artist he could be when his powers were working has become more apparent and his formal achievement grown more clear.

The Last Tycoon, as we have it, unfinished, concludes with a working note Fitzgerald had written to himself: "ACTION IS CHARACTER." It was an appropriate epitaph, fitting his effort to find through living a literary form suitable to his times. It applied in another way to the life and work of his great friend and rival through the 1920s and 1930s, Ernest Hemingway. Here was another writer committed to his own times and bonded to his own generation, stricken by the "unreasonable wound" of war; he called his first real book *In Our Time* (1925). For Hemingway too the writer was a performing self who discovered, through action, areas of personal being and crisis he could use to challenge the truth of language and form. But where Fitzgerald tested himself in the social world, Hemingway tested himself on its fringes, in those places of existential encounter that bring selfhood and courage physically to trial. Another expatriate in Paris, he wrote of bullfighting in Spain, war on the Italian front, the Spanish Civil War, game hunting in Africa, rarely setting his key novels in the continental United States. The short stories that bring him to home materials deal largely with the Michigan woods in which he had spent much time in his youth and with the testing initiations of young manhood that he repeated and reproduced throughout his life. Life-style and art-style again merged in quest of the existential and moral economy that would express itself in the "one true sentence" he always sought to construct. The new artistic economy meant, exactly, economy—a bodily and stylistic toughness, a refusal of romantic illusions, a controlled use of words, a precise and tensile self-expenditure. Technique in life and writing was precision—a precision that in time Hemingway came to feel that Fitzgerald lacked. Fitzgerald seemed to emphasize weakness; Hemingway emphasized inner strength, the things one cannot lose. Fitzgerald amassed material but wasted it and to some degree himself; Hemingway's was a life where romantic feelings and pains were kept half-hidden, contained by an exact language. Fitzgerald's was an open world, Hemingway's a tight and exclusive one, specified, appropriated, with its own distinctive terrain, its sanctified places, its own drinks and guns and rods, its own types of speech. Over that terrain moves the Hemingway hero, crossing the dangerous estate with an air of ease that cloaks but does not entirely conceal what lies behind—tension, insomnia, pain, wounds, the nightmare of the age.

Hemingway's fictional world is always a clean, well-lighted place, a world of the carefully selected minimum; this led him to a style of pure limitation that at its best made him into an experimenter with the experience and form of his time. His "hard" technique was analogous to modernist poetic doctrines of "impersonality" and the "objective correlative" and to the work of the postimpressionist painters he admired. It was also shaped by personal experience. Born in 1899 in Oak Park, Illinois, he grew up in a family dominated by a genteel, evangelical and repressive mother. Male roles and functions were driven from the house into a nature both initiatory and often meaninglessly cruel—the Michigan woods, where his Nick Adams discovers life in several short stories. After journalistic training Hemingway extended his encounter with "reality" by serving on the Italian front in the First World War as an ambulance driver with the American Field Service. Here he sustained, while rescuing an Italian soldier, serious shrapnel wounds in both legs, his initiation into modern exposure. Some of his best writing—the stories of *Men Without Women* (1927) and the novel *A Farewell to Arms* (1929)—deals with this experience, his fundamental loss and his conviction that modern war and violence emptied the great heroic abstractions, the high notions of pure heroism and sacrifice. He found return to the United States hard and so chose an expatriate life in Paris, which provided the material of his first novel *The Sun Also Rises* (1926) and his late memoir *A Moveable Feast* (1964, posthumous). He had letters from Sherwood Anderson introducing him to several expatriate gurus, including Gertrude Stein, from whom he learned more than he was later prepared to admit. "Begin over again—and concentrate," Stein told him after reading some early stories, and concentration became his fictional aim. He worked for a formalized, antiadjectival prose style that seemed less like aesthetic mannerism than a plain elimination of all loose or evocative reference: "All you have to do is to write one true sentence," he says he told himself. "Write the truest sentence that you know."

Hemingway's tight linguistic economy, setting limits on false experience and rhetorical afflatus, was initially displayed in the short story. *Three Stories and Ten Poems* (1923) and *In Our Time* (1924), first printed in Paris, established his style and introduced, in seven of the fifteen stories of the latter volume, Nick Adams, whom we see both in the Michigan woods and in wartime violence where nature consumes its own creations and the corpses of the dead seem no more important than the slaughtered cattle in the Chicago stockyards. The tight style complements a tragic stoicism; Hemingway's purity is shrill, suffused with the personal experience, the historical loss and the suffering out of which it has been wrought. Edmund Wilson once remarked that Hemingway's surfaces seem always to suggest "the undruggable consciousness of something wrong." This manner of writing is a kind of existential realism that seems to derive directly from encounter with experience, but it also implies acquaintance with a new historical condition and so leads onward into a world of trauma, sleeplessness, an awareness of *nada,* of all meaning lost except that which can be arduously reconstructed. So the writing both focuses attention on the cleanness of its own line and on the stoic pain and integrity of the experience and its human witness.

Hemingway is usually at his most exact and brilliant in his short stories, which remain among his best work, but during the 1920s he extended his terrain into the novel, first parodying his mentor Sherwood Anderson in the amusing but slight *Torrents of Spring* (1916), and then in the far more substantial *The Sun Also Rises* (1926) (called in England *Fiesta*). With its memorable epigraphs, one from *Ecclesiastes* and the other from Gertrude Stein—"You are all a lost generation"—the book, set among the Parisian expatriates, indeed seemed a text for the times. Stein later denied calling the postwar writers, drinkers and wounded young people "the lost generation," but the phrase stuck, and so did the vision of a world of lost spirits like Lady Brett Ashley, the dangerously overromantic Robert Cohn and the war-wounded narrator, Jake Barnes. Jake and Lady Brett, the sexually wounded stoic and the nymphomaniac, share a modern initiation and know their task. "I did not care what it was all about," Jake notes. "All I wanted to know was how to live in it. Maybe if you found out how to live in it you learned from that what it was all about." "Learning to live in it" is the main concern of the book, Hemingway's most social novel, a Baedeker of social and moral knowledge—an existential education in the right drinks, the right places to go, the right level of feeling and sensibility. The characters seek a "damned good time" but also a purity of action and being at the point of maximum exposure. Jake's wound is the central symbol of the intolerable intrusion of pain and history into the self which is the ultimate reality, the fundamental modern initiation. It also keeps him in a tight world of male comradeship, of men without women, of the things one cannot lose. It would be "pretty to think" that things could be otherwise, but romantic prettiness is not to be had—only a contained survival in the primitive and pastoral life glimpsed in Spain at the bullfight and on the fishing trip. Here the abiding earth can be encountered and managed, if one has genuine finesse and craft—*afición*.

Much of Hemingway's later fiction would concentrate on that sense of a direct encounter between struggling man and the seemingly implacable universe. *A Farewell to Arms* (1929) returned to the Italian front of the war, with its mud, disease, slaughter and retreat. Its hero, Lieutenant Frederic Henry, is another stoic and modern stylist:

> I was always embarrassed by the words sacred, glorious, and sacrifice and the expression in vain. . . . Abstract words such as glory, honor, courage, or hallow were obscene beside the concrete names of villages, the numbers of roads, the names of rivers, the numbers of regiments and the dates.

Henry's love affair with the British nurse Catherine Barkley is his attempt to find a path of escape through love. But the harsh, rain-drenched landscape provides the gloomy images that lead toward the tragic outcome, as Catherine dies in childbirth: "That was what you did. You died." By the end of the novel Lieutenant Henry, conscious of the cruel indifference of nature, the danger of abstract illusions, the brutal mortality of all human life, is driven into a stoic isolation and a "separate peace" with nothing more to say, making his farewell to the dead Catherine: "It was like saying good-bye to a statue. After a while I went out and left the hospital and walked back to the hotel in the rain." The method is clarity itself; its stylistic rules are expressed in the book about Spanish bullfighting, *Death in the Afternoon* (1932). Writing must express "the real thing, the sequence of motion and fact which made the emotion and which would be as valid in a year or in ten years or, with luck and if you stated it purely enough, always."

During the 1930s, along with his generation, Hemingway moved away from the stoic isolation of his early novels toward more social and communal themes. He left Paris and in time moved to Key West, then Cuba, and recognized the changing mood of the times. *To Have and Have Not* (1937) tells of Harry Morgan, who tries to make a living by smuggling; as he dies he expresses the new Hemingway lesson: "No matter how a man alone ain't got no bloody fucking chance." With its heavy social satire the book is one of Hemingway's weakest, but it helped prepare him for his most directly political novel, *For Whom the Bell Tolls* (1940), set during the Spanish Civil War, which Hemingway visited as a correspondent and about which he also wrote a play, *The Fifth Column* (1938). The novel departs from *A Farewell to Arms* in its insistence that "No man is an Ilande," as the title, taken from John Donne, emphasizes from the start. Robert Jordan, its American hero, finds a growing sense of commitment and responsibility as he joins the Republican forces in a sabotage operation against the Fascist troops of Franco. The Hemingway prose grows lusher and more rhapsodic as Jordan falls in love with the Spanish girl Maria, who has been raped by the Falangists, murderers of her father. Hemingway mutes much of the sentimentality by using a pidgin-Spanish manner, but the suppressed romanticism of his earlier work now becomes far more open. Jordan is a Frederic Henry who has rediscovered the value of feeling, the romantic potential of nature itself and ultimately the worth of the great abstractions Henry had rejected. He suffers disillusionment but finally surrenders his life in a willed sacrifice, affirming that "the world is a fine place and worth the fighting for and I hate very much to leave it." It was an affirmation that seemed called for as the threat of Fascism rose in the world, but it represented a change in the spirit of Hemingway's work. One of the finest novels we have of the Spanish Civil War, *For Whom the Bell Tolls* also prefigures some of the weaknesses of Hemingway's later writing: a tendency toward too ready transcendental affirmation, a growing sentimentality, a ripe romanticism that gradually undermined some of the darker, deeper aspects of his earlier vision and drew Hemingway, always a novelist of male heroes, further toward becoming his own best hero.

Where Fitzgerald's career ended bleakly in 1940, Hemingway both as popular writer and flamboyant war correspondent found himself catapulted into ever-greater fame. He was a courageous and often foolhardy reporter of the Anglo-American invasion of Europe in the Second World War and single-handedly liberated the Paris Ritz. War was his natural subject, and in reportage and the later fiction he strove to express his view of it. He had become a soldier-writer, a heroic stylist. The legendary Colonel Richard Cantwell of *Across the River and into the Trees* (1950) is a thinly disguised self-portrait. Cantwell has an instinctive comradeship for "those who had fought or been mutilated," an insider's deep knowledge of war, sport, food and love-making. He reaches "accurately and well for the champagne bucket," "stands straight and kisses true": the Hemingway hero as embittered success. In the antiradical postwar climate, Hemingway's prewar sense of political commitment faded; what he was left with was his own legend and a sense of life's fundamental struggle. That was expressed in the plain, powerful myth of *The Old Man and the Sea* (1952), which won him the Nobel Prize for Literature. A tale of ritual encounter between an old Cuban fisherman and the destructive natural forces that surround him as he battles first with a giant marlin and then with the sharks who strip his prize to a skeleton, it is an affirmative work: "But man is not made for defeat. . . . A man can be destroyed but not defeated." That message was to take on a darker look as the legendary author-hero reached his last years. A man of action battered by action, his body was bruised, his brain damaged. He worked now on five more book-length manuscripts but found it hard to complete them. One, *A Moveable Feast,* was a memoir going back to the "wonderful" years of the 1920s. Two were novels: *The Garden of Eden*

(1986, posthumous), which also returned to France and ends on a note of literary confidence, and another, yet more moving, which appeared in 1970 as *Islands in the Stream*.

Islands was first intended as a trilogy about the Second World War, but it became three stories about Thomas Hudson, a painter and sailor living in Cuba, a broken stoic who keeps passing beyond the limits of his control as wear and tear break his grip on art, sport, strength, sexuality, comradeship, marriage and fatherhood. The book is a dark self-portrait, the more moving because it, too, was never quite completed. By the time of its publication, Hemingway was dead; on July 2, 1961, he killed himself, as his father had, with a shotgun, the victim of depression, paranoia and increasing physical debility. The dark shadows evident everywhere through his finest books had overwhelmed him, and the writer of physical action came to the end of his great strength. Today it is the early books that look the best—the most profound and self-discovering, the most finished in form and exact in style. In the contemporary climate, some critics have challenged Hemingway's masculine carapace, his insistence on the male hero preserving grace under pressure, his stress on bravery and solitude. A cliché about the Hemingway hero persists, and in his later years Hemingway did a good deal to encourage it. None of this should distract from the tragic strength and the exact prose of the early work. To return in particular to the early stories is to see how complex his fictional world is, how much lies under his plain prose surfaces. For readers throughout the world, Hemingway's prose expressed the hard clarity and underlying existential pain that for many characterized the modern age.

One more major novelist emerged from the fresh, confident atmosphere of the American novel in the 1920s, in some ways the greatest of all. This was William Faulkner, who grasped hold of the almost moribund tradition of American Southern fiction and brought to it the energy and resources of experimental Modernism, to the point where some of his finest fictional explorations of form and consciousness fully compare with those of Joyce, Proust or Virginia Woolf. What made Faulkner's historical and social vision so different from that of his contemporaries was the distinctive, defeated nature of Southern history, its great chivalric and rural traditions broken apart by the

American Civil War that already lay sixty years in the past but was everywhere present in Southern consciousness when Faulkner began to write of it. Faulkner always remained essentially a Southern writer; born in 1897, he grew up in Oxford, Mississippi, and spent nearly all his life there, apart from frequent visits to Hollywood to earn money by screenwriting. It was what he made of that engrained history and the angles he took upon it that made him a great writer. The impact of that terrible defeat that had wasted the South and fulfilled the curse that lay upon it, leaving it to the disorders of Reconstruction and the growing predations of industrialization and mercantilism, was one main source of his writing. But another was the impact of Romantic, Decadent and modern literature. During a brief bohemian spell in New Orleans he came under the experimental influence of Sherwood Anderson, as his own work was developing from *Winesburg, Ohio* (1919) to the more mannered experimentalism of *Dark Laughter* (1925). Faulkner also tried himself out as a poet in verse influenced by Keats and the French Decadents. The writing of his own time, above all Joyce's *Ulysses,* was to have a profound effect on him, yet at the same time he always insisted that his work was bred "by Oratory out of Solitude." In fact it was by linking the classic Southern romance, so influenced by Scott, with the modern sense of experimental form, by merging a deep-seated sense of regional history with an awareness of the fracture of historical time, that he became a major novelist.

Faulkner's first novel, *Soldier's Pay* (1926), which Sherwood Anderson got published on condition he did not have to read it, was a decadent text about the malaise of postwar society, its central figure a scarred and blinded World War veteran. *Mosquitoes* (1927) is about decadent life in bohemian New Orleans and reveals Faulkner's desire for a timeless poetic beauty as well as his sense of the sterility and narcissism of contemporary existence. But this was all beginning work, and it was with his next book, *Sartoris* (1929), that Faulkner found what he needed as a writer—of the "native soil" through which he could interpret the fundamental drama of a Southern society emblematic of human fate in an age of war, lost hopes, stress and profound transition. Yoknapatawpha County, like Hardy's Wessex, became a populous, rich, almost real literary landscape in which universal themes could work themselves out. Around its county seat, Jefferson, lies a distinctive world of dispossessed aristocrats, of carpetbaggers and entrepreneurs, sharecroppers and former slave owners, of woods, bear hunts and pine-winey afternoons, of a long history of settlement back to Indian days when the white man's curse was first brought to the virgin land, of past chivalry, lasting guilts and the defeat of 1865. Into this rooted universe Bayard Sartoris returns from world war, uneasy about his manhood and place, seeking a reckless death among modern machines in a latter-day version of the fate of his ancestors. The present, in debased form, releases, reenacts and contradicts the past. The Sartorises are contrasted with the Benbows, delicate, intellectual and narcissistic. And Sartorises, De Spains and Compsons are contrasted with the Snopeses, modern entrepreneurs and opportunists who act without historical sense and only from self-interest. And so, said Faulkner,

> I discovered that writing was a mighty fine thing. You could make people stand on their hind legs and cast a shadow. I felt that I had all these people, and as soon as I discovered it I wanted to bring them all back.

Sartoris is a loose, baggy monster of a book, originally to have been called *Flags in the Dust* and shaped out of a yet vaster manuscript, a wild outpouring of social and historical material that was to serve Faulkner as groundwork for most of his writing thereafter. The great change came with the next novel, *The Sound and the Fury,* astonishingly published in the same year yet totally different in its style and concept of form. It is best read in an edition that contains the appendix Faulkner added to it in 1946 giving the history of the Compson family back to 1699, though it should be remembered that much of this history was devised later when the many lives of Yoknapatawpha County had become more real for their author and more tightly interlocked. It has rightly been acclaimed as the great American equivalent of Joyce's *Ulysses,* which strongly influenced it, and its complex time scheme— the four narratives are set on four different days, three in 1928, one in 1910, not in consecutive order—and its stream-of-consciousness methods make it plainly Modernist. The first fractured story is set in the present of 1928 and belongs to the mind and perceptions of Benjy, an idiot with a mental age of five; then we move to the monologue of

Quentin Compson on the day of his suicide back in 1910. We next hear the voice of the surviving, opportunistic Jason Compson and finally the enduring voice of the black servant Dilsey. In this and the books that followed, Faulkner displayed a remarkable compendium of Modernist strategies, though the tactics are finally very different from Joyce's or Proust's and always at the service of a larger history, that of Yoknapatawpha itself. Faulkner's preoccupation with time has to do with the endless interlocking of personal and public histories and with the relation of the past to the lost, chaotic present. A central theme of *The Sound and the Fury* is Quentin's attempt to arrest both subjective and historical time by defending his sister Caddy's virginity from psychic corruption and time's flow; the book started, Faulkner tells us, from the single image of young Caddy's dirty drawers. Benjy himself is locked in a single continuous moment of time that removes all causality or consequence from his perceptions. Jason sees matters empirically, Dilsey from a patient sense of human continuity. Strange associative links—like the coincidence of Caddy's name and the caddie at the adjacent golf course—allow themes and images to multiply and give the novel its intense, dense symbolist qualities.

In the group of novels that followed—*As I Lay Dying* (1930), the deliberately sensational and commercial *Sanctuary* (1931), *Light in August* (1932) and *Absalom, Absalom!* (1936)—Faulkner's complex methods were extended.

> I think there's a period in a writer's life when he, well, simply for lack of any word, is fertile and he just produces. Later on, his blood slows, his bones get a little more brittle . . . but I think there's one time in his life when he writes at the top of his talent plus his speed, too,

Faulkner later commented. These are the books written at the top of his talent, and in them we can feel his experimental powers at full force. Each reaches, in small selective units, into the Yoknapatawpha experience, revealing it not so much in expository historical narrative as in distinct units of perception. So we feel the long underlying history—from the seventeenth-century moment of settlement in the not quite virgin, Indian South to the immediate present—as a process in which there are occasions of concentration, moments of temporal arrest, millennial instants where history intersects with deep points of psychic crisis or personal perception. Rape and corruption, miscegenation and human taint enact their historical cycles, making Faulkner frequently a novelist of gothic extremity and violence. The various fates of Southern aristocrats and poor whites, blacks and Indians, work themselves out in an apocalyptic landscape. It is a world where in 1835 the "stars fell" with the appearance of a comet, where in 1865 a whole nation and tradition went down to defeat, and where land as spirit has yielded to land as pure property, woods to axes, gardens to machines, South to North, timeless wonder to "progress." But in this fallen Eden of the South, there are still moments of promise as life is renewed in the cycle of eternal time, as human endurance reveals itself, as romantic wonder yields up a lyric and transcendental vision and a sense of symbolic significance.

As I Lay Dying tells the story of the six-day funeral journey of the Bundren family through fifty-nine interior monologues, reflections on movement and stasis, living and dying, as they travel beside the moving wagon "with an outward semblance of form and purpose, but with no inference of motion, progress or retrograde." *Sanctuary,* a more gothic novel, creates a remarkable figure of contemporary evil in Popeye, the emptied, sterile man who has "the vicious depthless quality of stamped tin" and who revenges his impotence by raping with a corncob the whore-woman Temple Drake. The much finer and more exact *Light in August* deals with miscegenation and a lynching through pursuing three cunningly interlocked narratives—that of the victim, the wandering orphan Joe Christmas, who commits murder in a confusion of racial identity, that of the Reverend Gail Hightower, who secludes himself from life in an attempt to relive one single moment of historical time, and that of the encompassing figure of Lena Grove, fecund and pregnant, weaving round the story her natural abundance and future promise. In *Absalom, Absalom!* Faulkner brings many of his previous characters together and tells again the story of the downfall of a family, the gothic tragedy of the house of Thomas Sutpen and his grand "design." Quentin Compson returns as the central figure, trying to understand and place the historical process that has led the Sutpen family to its fate. The complex chronology of the book is so dense that the new reader really needs the key to its time scheme constructed by Cleanth Brooks—who called the book the greatest of Faulkner's novels and proof that Faulkner always regarded history not as a set of facts but as a great imaginative reconstruction.

Certainly by now that imaginative history was becoming dense, and Yoknapatawpha County—"William Faulkner, sole owner and proprietor," 2,400 square miles of crossed histories, a web of dynasties and genealogies, heroisms and crimes, stories and storytellers—richly populous. A good part of Faulkner's later work went into filling in its spaces. In the stories of *The Unvanquished* (1938) and *Go Down, Moses* (1942), he gave his characters wider room and a richer history, exploring the transformation of the land and the growth and decay of its dynasties as they move toward a present of greed and expropriation. In the latter volume we find one of the finest of all modern long short stories, "The Bear," the tale of Ike McCaslin's initiation into nature and the demands of time. In the late trilogy about the sharecropping, predatory Snopes family, *The Hamlet* (1940), *The Town* (1957) and *The Mansion* (1959), Faulkner, ever extending his materials and the number of his storytellers, turned to comedy, and in his last novel *The Reivers* (1962) to farce. In his late *A Fable* (1954) he attempted a summative work, using the First World War to tell what is in effect an allegory of Christ's suffering and crucifixion for mankind. It lacks his earlier complexity and is not a success, but it affirms what Faulkner celebrated in accepting the Nobel Prize for Literature in 1950, his belief in "courage and honor and hope and pride and compassion and pity and sacrifice." Faulkner had always been interested not simply in the onerous pains of Southern history and its relation to the crises of the modern psyche, but in the plenitude of human nature, the lyrical and transcendental aspects of the natural world and the feeling that creativity and hope can be relived and passed from generation to generation, so becoming timeless. The endurance of Southern blacks as victims of the history he explored confirmed his belief. All this sometimes sentimentalized his work, but it also helped make it mythical. The work had, like many of the best modern American novels, originated amid the decadent despairs and the experimental artistry of the 1920s, and like Fitzgerald's and Hemingway's, it persistently reflects the tragic exposure, the abrasion, the sense of radical discovery through which modern American fiction found itself.

The achievement of the American novel in the 1920s spread much wider—to e. e. cummings's *The Enormous Room,* Gertrude Stein's *The Making of Americans,* Sherwood Anderson's *Dark Laughter,* John Dos Passos's *Manhattan Transfer,* Willa Cather's *Death Comes for the Archbishop* and much more. It represents one of the most remarkable periods of American literary history, and its hunger for new styles, new forms, new attitudes to human nature and human history, new modes of artistic self-discovery, generated an atmosphere of innovation perhaps even more powerful than what had been happening in the new poetry. It often began in expatriate withdrawal to Europe or in bohemian separation from a culture that was seen as Puritanic, materialistic and fundamentally hostile to art, but it took up European experiments and assimilated some of the cultural despair and the sense of psychic and historical crisis we recognize as part of what was coming to be called the Modern temper. Many of these writers found that what had been created at the radical fringes, in the hothouse aesthetic atmosphere of the 1920s, was quickly drawn toward the center. Hemingway won national and international success, Fitzgerald finally earned his belated recognition and Faulkner became internationally acknowledged as one of the most significant Modern experimentalists. Perhaps this was because they possessed both a distinctively Modern vision and the sense of cultural contradiction that existed in an American society looking both backward and forward, to a receding, half-mythic American past and a shock-laden present rushing onward into a yet more alienating future. Thus they expressed the novelty of the new and often European forms and their relation to their own culture, as it experienced the rape of an older American innocence. They revealed the existential crisis of the age, but also some of that half-ironic sense of wonder it still possessed, what Fitzgerald expressed in the final phrases of *The Great Gatsby* in speaking of the "transitory enchanted moment" of wonder that creates an aesthetic contemplation man neither seeks nor understands: "So we beat on, boats against the current, borne back ceaselessly into the past." The result was that they were able to construct an enduring tradition for their successors: Fitzgerald's bright yet also embittered and terrible social vision, Hemingway's existential sense of tragedy, Faulkner's gothic perspective—without which the work of successors like Eudora Welty, Carson McCullers and Flannery O'Connor, or Bellow, Updike and Pynchon, seems scarcely possible. Their impact continues, their expression of a modern America persists, right into the novel of the later twentieth century. If American poetry had found a new way to utter the meaning of the nation, so too had the American novel.

CHAPTER

· 10 ·

RADICAL REASSESSMENTS

· I ·

H. L. Mencken, the most entertaining and widely read of America's commentators during the first third of the century, once imagined himself standing on the French Line pier—"wrapped in the American flag"—waving farewell to yet another boatload of young artists and writers pursuing the aesthetic promise of Europe's greener fields. But while Stein, Eliot and Pound did settle permanently abroad, countless others paid their ritual visit and returned to share Mencken's United States at first hand—among them Frost, Hemingway, Anderson and Fitzgerald, Katherine Anne Porter, Sinclair Lewis, Eugene O'Neill and numberless lesser talents. Archibald MacLeish planned to live abroad for five years and did just that, writing poems and verse drama strongly colored by the work of Eliot and Pound. But on his return to the United States at the end of the 1920s, MacLeish repudiated the poetry he had admired and imitated, arguing that wasteland pessimism and alienation had isolated the expatriate poet from the needs of his countrymen. He called for "public speech" to address the economic, social and moral issues of the age. A few years earlier, Van Wyck Brooks in *The Pilgrimage of Henry James* (1925) had complained of severed roots and distanced audiences, and one of the major figures of the new Modernism, William Carlos Williams, had accused Eliot and the expatriates of betraying the liberating impulse of American Modernism by working to revive the conservative values and verse conventions of European tradition. For Williams, fruitful experimentation was possible only with American materials, with the settings and speech patterns that characterized a native culture abandoned or poorly understood by the cosmopolitan expatriates.

The note was a familiar one. The plea for cultural nationalism made by MacLeish, Williams and Hart Crane asserted yet once again the value, the necessity, of an art nourished in native soil. And yet by 1930 the argument was inescapably more strident and insistent. If literature exists to write an ever-changing world into comprehensible existence, then the world faced by MacLeish in 1930 posed a unique challenge. Thinkers as different as Henry Adams, William James, Santayana and the younger Holmes had warned of the fissures in American bedrock assumptions, of the strain an ever-increasing velocity of change would inescapably create. With the crash of the New York stock market in 1929, the decade of no tomorrows came to a frightening end, and Americans were stunned by the rapidity of their slide. "The country can regard the present with satisfaction and anticipate the future with optimism," President Coolidge announced in December 1928, and it is easy to understand his good spirits. The volume of activity on the New York stock exchange had topped a billion shares. During the previous three years, General Motors shares rose from $99 to $212; in the summer of 1929, industrial stocks climbed nearly 25 percent. That autumn the rising arc cracked and sent values tumbling. By 1932, the bottom of the Great Depression, industrials had fallen from 452 to 58. General Motors dropped from 212 to 8.

What had come to seem an irreversible ride on the celestial railroad became perhaps the most serious challenge the American Dream had faced since the Civil War. Life savings disappeared overnight. Suddenly there were fewer jobs and lower wages for those that remained. In 1932, the average monthly unemployment total reached 12 million with wages at 60 percent of the 1929 level and industry operating at half its 1929 volume. Some 5,000 banks had failed and everyone knew the song "Brother, Can You Spare a Dime?" In 1933, 2,000 rural schools did not open. There were 200,000 unemployed teachers and 2.3 million children without schools to attend.

President Roosevelt launched his New Deal reforms and social programs to get the nation back to work, but it was not until the industrial boom forced by the need for armaments after the Japanese attack on Pearl Harbor in 1941 that the nation's economic and social life regained a semblance of its earlier vitality. The intervening decade had raised questions for MacLeish and other American writers that no number of earlier warnings could have prepared them for. This time the traditional jeremiad seemed inadequate, for if it was painfully clear that little promise remained to American life, the sources of necessary renewal no longer spoke unequivocally from a simpler past. Capitalism and its trusted industrial and technological handmaidens seemed powerless to halt the slide and sustain an egalitarian society that could guarantee the welfare of all. The world the artist was asked to understand and interpret had become dominated by economic and social forces that questioned insistently the nature of the nation: What had America become? What future might it anticipate? Given the startling new circumstances, what in the nation's past now spoke meaningfully to its present and future?

The changes of the late nineteenth and early twentieth centuries that had made America an urban, industrial society were brought into sharpened relief when the entire edifice seemed to many on the brink of collapse. The challenges of poverty, of social justice and economic equity, of national identity and international power in a world feeling increasingly the presence of the Soviet Union—these were the issues that forced the American writer toward the subjects, languages and themes of the Depression and war years. As his nation threatened to disintegrate, the writer recognized the fragility of its coherence and undertook to number the diverse strands that had come to constitute it with the hope that the most vital could be made newly relevant.

When Van Wyck Brooks announced *America's Coming-of-Age* in 1915, he lamented the nation's inability to nourish itself on its rich past and insisted that the arts must function as a social force, that they had the power to cure the ills of a stagnant culture. Three years later Brooks anticipated some of the freshest thinking of the next decades in "On Creating a Usable Past." Initially a manifesto for the young rebels intent on challenging the critical authority of an older generation, the sacred quest it urges was eventually made by most of the era's serious writers. "The spiritual welfare of this country depends altogether upon the fate of its creative minds," Brooks wrote.

The present is a void, and the American writer floats in that void because the past that survives in the common mind of the present is a past without living value. But is this the only possible past? If we need another past so badly, is it inconceivable that we might discover one, that we might even invent one?

During the 1920s American writers expressed their dissent from a materialist America by expatriation, by engaging in experimental aesthetic adventure, by exploring new forms and joining in the excitements of surrealism and the revolution of the word. By the 1930s the attitude changed as writers both questioned and struggled to reinterpret the history of their own culture, which had changed so radically overnight. When the social machine seemed to have broken down completely and, as Leo Gurko put it, "there were whole schools of mechanics jockeying for the privilege of starting it up again," the earnest but ineffectual liberalism of Brooks and the others steadily gave way before the vitality of Marxism and the energetic conservative response it engendered. The serious dialectic of the 1930s demanded extensive reassessment of every aspect of the national life. From a literary perspective, the answers offered by the New Left and the Southern Fugitive-Agrarians emerged as most significant for the artistic future of the country. It is not difficult to understand the appeal Marxism held for critics like Edmund Wilson, Granville Hicks and V. F. Calverton and novelists like Dreiser, Wright and Dos Passos. With its faith in progress, science and a richer life through the humanitarian reform of industrialism, Depression Marxism was a clear development of *New Republic* liberalism and the foggy-headed socialism of writers like Floyd Dell. The Tennessee agrarians had their forebears as well in the ethical neohumanism of Irving Babbitt, Paul Elmer More and Stuart Sherman; their shared rejection of just this progress, science and industrialism, their emphasis on individualism and the need for a saving remnant, and their consequent conservative-reactionary political, social and religious platforms attest their debt to the earlier critics.

The 1930s changed and developed this map of intellectual and literary thinking. The expatriates of the 1920s came back, or stepped out of Greenwich Village into the real wastelands of the 1930s, and were both dismayed and invigorated by the changed America they found. As Malcolm Cowley has recalled,

> Thousands were convinced and hundreds of thousands were half-persuaded that no simple operation would save us. . . . There had to be the complete renovation of society that Marx had prophesied in 1848. Unemployment would be ended, war and fascism would vanish from the earth, but only after the revolution.

Marxist analysis of the social and economic wreckage, Edmund Wilson noted, "at least offered a discipline for the mind, gave a coherent picture of history and promised not only employment but the triumph of the constructive intellect." Since an appropriate past was an important component of their reform program, the American Marxists of the 1930s undertook a fresh reading of the nation's political and literary history. The *Partisan Review and Anvil* for April 1936 published a group of papers with the heading "What Is Americanism? A Symposium of Marxism and the American Tradition." The papers were replies to a questionnaire that asked, "What is your conception of Americanism?" "Do you think of it as separate and opposed to the cultural tradition of Western Europe?" The response from novelist Robert Herrick measured the sense many had of what was at stake:

> For all the years of my conscious life I have believed in what used to be called, fondly if rather vaguely, "the American tradition" . . . that is, a cultural base differing from that of all other peoples, due to the physical environment, racial inheritances, and historical development of the American people. . . . I do not feel today that this vigorous American tradition has survived the shock of the World War and its economic convulsions, and the still greater shock of bewildered disillusionment at the partial collapse of the economic structure. . . . If American civilization survives, without taking either extreme of left or right . . . the enduring and intrinsic value of "the American tradition" will have been demonstrated. That tradition is now in the crucible. The world awaits the outcome.

The tradition of the Left that emerged from Herrick's crucible included Edmund Wilson's *Travels in Two Democracies* (1936) and *To the Finland Station* (1940), Joseph Freeman's anthology *Proletarian Literature in the United States* (1935) and Bernard Smith's *Forces in American Criticism* (1939). Two Marxist readings of American literary history undertook a thorough revision of the nation's literary heritage: *The Liberation of American Literature* (1932) by V. F. Calverton and *The Great Tradition: An Interpretation of American Literature Since the Civil War* (1933) by Granville Hicks. Neither Calverton nor Hicks made a lasting impression on serious readers of literature, but the case was significantly different with a third ambitious literary survey, Vernon L. Parrington's three-volume *Main Currents in American Thought* (1927–30). Parrington's Jeffersonianism brought leftist economic determinism a sense of native continuity, and *Main Currents* swept the literary scene and dominated for more than a decade the nation's conception of its usable literary past.

Writers as different as John Dos Passos, Nathanael West and Richard Wright were drawn at one time or another to the stringent questioning of American values urged by the Marxist left, but by the end of the decade little of its intense energy and less of its newfound influence remained. Marxism would emerge again, in the decades following the Second World War, to challenge American consensus and easy assumptions about the social and political roles of artists and their art, but by 1939 the first wave of economic analysis had collapsed from its own mechanical reductionism and from its unhappy identification with the policies of the Soviet Union. For John Reed and countless others, Russia had become a viable alternative to an America that no longer seemed able to function, but Stalin's purge trials and the Nazi-Soviet Nonaggression Pact of 1939 destroyed the base in history for explanations that claimed to be above all others historical. As Edmund Wilson was to recall in 1943,

the young journalists and novelists and poets who had tried to base their dreams on bedrock, had the spectacle, not of the advent of "the first truly human culture," the ideal of Lenin and Trotsky, but of the rapid domination of Europe by the state socialism of Hitler and Stalin, with its strangling of political discussion and its

contemptuous extermination of art; and they no longer knew what
to think.

Franklin Roosevelt's liberal economic and social programs, the
industrial recovery stimulated by military rearmament and the slow,
painful realization of Soviet totalitarianism combined to destroy the
cohesion and efficacy of the American literary left just as its strongest
adversary recorded an important—what time would prove to be
decisive—triumph. In 1938 two young instructors at Louisiana State
University published a poetry textbook that signaled the literary frui-
tion of the Southern Fugitive-Agrarian movement and the eventual
revolution in literary taste and methodology that has become known
as the New Criticism. *Understanding Poetry,* by Cleanth Brooks and
Robert Penn Warren, taught a generation of Americans not only how
to read but also what was worth reading, and that generation in turn
transformed the study of literature in the nation's schools and colleges,
thereby authorizing and institutionalizing one version of Modernism
for countless aspiring young writers.

As students at Vanderbilt University in Tennessee, Brooks and
Warren had joined with Allen Tate, Donald Davidson and John Crowe
Ransom, a group of poets which had evolved from the early years of
The Fugitive magazine (1922–25) into the conservative—some feel
reactionary—sociopolitical analysis of *I'll Take My Stand: The South
and the Agrarian Tradition* (1930) by "Twelve Southerners." Of all the
sections of the nation, the South, or those who idealized the leisured,
stable aristocratic culture of the plantation South, felt the most threatened by the Northern urban-industrial civilization championed by her-
alds of the "New South" as remedy for the malaise of the Depression.
The Vanderbilt agrarians urged as an alternative a tradition rooted in
regionalism: life centered in the land and values of a less frenetic,
acquisitive time, and art nourished in the Western legacy of classic
and Christian humanism. Ransom, Tate and Warren wrote restrained,
elegant, learned verse much like Eliot's, whose work they revered and
whose "Tradition and the Individual Talent" (1920) helped shape their
thinking. Like the writers of the left they so passionately opposed, the
Southern regionalists drifted from their social commitments as the
1930s drew to a close, but they passed on a remarkably coherent and

influential literary program to the decades that followed. When Brooks and Warren selected their readings and prepared their representative analyses for *Understanding Poetry* in 1938, they drew upon what the Marxists and socialists had been unable to secure, a canon of allusively rich and challenging verse and a methodology of close attention to "the poem itself"—both legacies of Eliot's Modernism and his later cultural conservatism. When Ransom published his essay collection *The New Criticism* in 1941, he gave a title to a new era of literary discourse.

The South was not the only region to develop its literary potential in the years before the Second World War, but its success was the most remarkable, enduring into the 1940s and beyond as a celebrated "Southern Renaissance." Mencken had angered the entire region of the South with his coverage of the Scopes "monkey trial" and his gibes at "The Sahara of the Bozart." But the eventual influence of the Agrarian–New Critics in the nation's universities, the poetry of Warren, Tate and Ransom, the plays of Tennessee Williams and the fiction of Warren, Ellen Glasgow, Thomas Wolfe, Katherine Anne Porter, William Faulkner, Carson McCullers, Flannery O'Connor and Eudora Welty made the South for several years the center of the nation's literary achievement.

Jane Austen once remarked that all she needed for her novels was a single rural setting and a few country families. William Faulkner gradually came to understand his Modernist art in much the same way: "I discovered that my own little postage stamp of native soil was worth writing about and that I would never live long enough to exhaust it." This is what Tate and Davidson meant by *regionalism,* a cultural concept based in the aesthetic thinking of Modernism. Unlike the nostalgic sectionalism of the post–Civil War local-color movement, this regionalism saw in the local and the specific the only source of general, human value, either social or artistic; regionalism is thus one answer to the era's search for a usable past, a mode of radical literary discovery of materials and themes that speak through the particular to the needs of the entire nation. In this sense Willa Cather, Edgar Lee Masters, Carl Sandburg and Sherwood Anderson are Midwestern regionalist writers, with Cather moving on to exploit the correlatives of the Southwest; Edward Arlington Robinson and Robert Frost used New England

as Robinson Jeffers and John Steinbeck used California, not to celebrate the separate section but to question universal values through the
specific case.

Viewed as fecund source, cities like Chicago and New York were
also regions, as was not only Harlem but the life of black Americans
drawn upon in the writing of the Harlem Renaissance and its heirs—
Claude McKay, Jean Toomer, Wallace Thurman, Countee Cullen,
Langston Hughes, W. E. B. DuBois, Ralph Ellison, James Baldwin,
Gwendolyn Brooks. A similar quest for usable materials led to the
excited discovery of other overlooked regions: in the lives of women,
native Americans and the artists and literary bohemians who gathered
in Manhattan's Greenwich Village—"Inglorious Miltons by the score,
and Rodins, one to every floor," John Reed quipped. It would draw
as well on the worlds of European Modernism and Hitler's *émigrés*—
Thomas Mann, Hannah Arendt, Vladimir Nabokov, Albert Einstein
—who continued to arrive and undergo the assimilation that at varying
speeds would nourish the American grain. Perhaps the foremost case
in point is the psychoanalytic thought of Sigmund Freud, Alfred Adler
and Carl Jung, which touched writers as different as Edmund Wilson,
Conrad Aiken and Eugene O'Neill and has remained a staple resource
for any artist exploring the many-layered life of the mind. Like Marxism
and even Agrarianism, psychoanalysis can be seen as part of the
growing internationalization of the American literary intelligence. As
Laurence Holland notes, "By 1940 'the psychiatrist,' the 'archetypal
symbol' and 'the Oedipus Complex' had become part of modern
mythology"—yet another way in which the 1930s and 1940s saw
American and European thought developing together.

· II ·

The Europe that journeyed westward during these decades was less
the normative model of earlier provincial years, more one source among
many of constructs and vocabulary for grasping and expressing an
"American Century." The suggestions of cubism and James Joyce were
eagerly grasped as modes of manifesting a modern reality that could
no longer be seen whole from any single perspective but only surmised

from the intersection of varied perceptions. Whether one looked at the public world of Depression America or the inner life of the individual, what had once seemed single, coherent, whole, now lay in pieces. Ezra Pound had noted how the simple life of a village will nourish a sense of sequence, so that history and life itself can be thought of as continuous, coherent narrative. But "in a city, visual impressions succeed each other, overlap, overcross, they are 'cinematographic.' " With the success of the first full-length talking movie, Al Jolson's *The Jazz Singer* in 1927, the century found its truly representative art form; American writers were quick to adopt its shifting time-scales, its visual collage and montage, its sense of a whole composed of some 100,000 often obliquely related fragments. Dos Passos stitched together bits of films, newspaper stories and popular songs; Faulkner drew together "the rag-tag and bob-ends of old tales and talking."

In 1922, an entire year of moviegoing numbered some 40 million Americans; by 1930 the total was close to 100 million per week. Legitimate theater in the United States has never enjoyed such success, partly because of the nation's size and partly too because few significant talents or theatrical organizations endure long enough to register a lasting impact. O'Neill's association with the Provincetown Playhouse helped channel European currents into New York productions and launch a career that would bring him the Nobel Prize in 1936. But taken together the audiences of O'Neill, Maxwell Anderson, Clifford Odets, Robert Sherwood and Lillian Hellman never matched the growing numbers at the movie "palaces." And as Hollywood developed into the world's capital of filmed drama during the 1930s, it was not the playwright who journeyed to Southern California to participate and profit but novelists like Faulkner and Fitzgerald. After the war, however, the dramatist and the no-longer-new medium did establish a close working relationship to produce film versions of plays by Tennessee Williams, Arthur Miller, William Inge and Edward Albee. More recent writers in all forms know film and its techniques thoroughly—as do their readers; selling a work to a film maker for a percentage of the movie's receipts usually brings the highest financial reward a writer can hope for. The years since the first "talkie" have thus made the motion picture a dominant influence on American literature. A complex piecing together of myriad filmed fragments, the film has remained a fruitful model for writers trying to bring into formal unity a national life that has remained permanently fractured, for a diversity of audiences that resembles nothing so much—as Henry James once remarked—as a checkerboard of distinct and contrasting needs and interests.

If we distinguish between theatrical production and dramatic literature, we can say that America has a long history of theater but few playwrights and only a handful of plays that perennially hold the interest of both audiences and thoughtful readers. Visiting companies from Britain toured the colonies and led to the construction of playhouses from Boston to Charleston, but the persistent demand to fill the seats and show a profit often stocked them with minstrel, burlesque and vaudeville entertainments (some little more than the "Royal Nonesuch" of Huck's King and Duke), just as rising production costs have turned New York's Broadway toward lavish musical comedy and astronomical ticket prices. Such conditions have been unable to nourish and support an American Shakespeare, Molière, Ibsen or Chekhov and have limited many promising dramatists to a few notable plays before forcing them toward the more dependable, substantial returns of cinema and television writing. There have been poets and novelists who wrote plays, but very few writers remembered primarily as playwrights: Henry James tried his hand, as did e. e. cummings, W. C. Williams, Robinson Jeffers, Edna St. Vincent Millay, Frank O'Hara, Faulkner, Bellow and Richard Wilbur. Among the more successful efforts have been experiments with verse drama, such as Eliot's *Murder in the Cathedral* (1935) and *The Cocktail Party* (1950), MacLeish's *J. B.* (1958) and Robert Lowell's trilogy, *The Old Glory* (1964), based on tales by Hawthorne and Melville. And there have been a few plays that continue to receive attention from amateur and regional companies and their audiences: Maxwell Anderson's *What Price Glory?* (1924) and *Winterset* (1935), Thornton Wilder's *Our Town* (1938) and *The Skin of Our Teeth* (1942), Robert Sherwood's *Petrified Forest* (1935), *Idiot's Delight* (1936) and *Abe Lincoln in Illinois* (1938), William Saroyan's *The Time of Your Life* (1939) and Lillian Hellman's *The Children's Hour* (1934), *The Little Foxes* (1939) and *Toys in the Attic* (1960). Students of dramatic expressionism often date serious American drama from Elmer Rice's *The Adding Machine* (1923), but the play is rarely staged; similar historical interest surrounds the early political plays of Clifford Odets, *Waiting for Lefty* (1935) and *Awake and Sing* (1935). The only playwrights and playwriting to hold the boards for notable periods since the Second World War have been Arthur Miller (*Death of a Salesman,* 1949), Tennessee Williams (*The Glass Menagerie,* 1944; *A Streetcar Named Desire,* 1947; *Cat on a Hot Tin Roof,* 1955) and Edward Albee (*Who's Afraid of Virginia Woolf?,* 1962).

The notable exception, America's single playwright of world stature, has been Eugene O'Neill. In his posthumous autobiographical masterwork, *Long Day's Journey into Night,* O'Neill portrays the dilemma of the native theater in the career of the play's father, James Tyrone. Beginning his life as an actor with much promise and high aspirations, Tyrone has the fortune-misfortune to find himself starring year after year in the lucrative crowd-pleasing *Count of Monte Cristo.* Secure profit and easy applause draw him repeatedly from the goals of his youth until we meet him lamenting his life as bartered away and unfulfilled. James O'Neill earned a fortune playing the lead in *Monte Cristo* more than five thousand times; the constant travel drove his wife to morphine addiction and his two sons to alcoholism. "You might say I started as a trouper," Eugene O'Neill once remarked. "I knew only actors and the stage. My mother nursed me in the wings and in dressing rooms." Within ten years after committing himself to a career as playwright, O'Neill was acknowledged as a major force in the American theater; in another ten years he was known worldwide as winner of the Nobel Prize in 1936, the only American playwright to be so honored. And yet the young O'Neill had wanted nothing to do with the commercial theatrical world of his father. In 1906, after his rebellious life-style and drinking led to expulsion during his first year at Princeton, he spent several years "just drifting"—mining for gold in Honduras, working a cattle steamer to South Africa and ships sailing between New York and Southampton, combing beaches in Buenos Aires and briefly reporting for a Connecticut newspaper. He tried acting with his father's company but detested the mediocre vehicle that paid the bills.

The turning point in O'Neill's life was a six-month sanatorium stay for nervous exhaustion and tuberculosis in 1912. Forced to remain idle, he read Strindberg, Ibsen and the Greek tragic poets and decided that "I want to be an artist or nothing." With the submission of the one-act *Bound East for Cardiff,* he was accepted for one semester as a special student in George Baker's 47 Workshop at Harvard; the same year he published his first book, *Thirst, and Other One-Act Plays.* If American dramatists have been limited by the economic caution of popular theater, what growth there has been can be attributed to low-budget experimental companies like the Provincetown Players and the Washington Square Players, both founded in 1915, and the Group Theater, founded in 1931. O'Neill's long association with the Provincetown Players—with summer productions on Cape Cod and winter runs in New York—gave him the opportunity for extensive experiment in dramatic style and structure and earned for the Players a place in American literary history.

O'Neill was from the first an experimental—if independent—Modernist. As he looked at the relations of self and society, he was initially moved by the material forces that diminish human choice, and he came to share the perspective of the naturalistic determinists. But his wide reading, especially in Freud, Jung and Adler, gradually led him to attempt dramatizing the inner struggles and conflicts that govern the search for existential meaning. The theater he inherited valued realism above all else, often a realism achieved through the devices and artifice of the stage manager. Though occasionally naturalistic and often melodramatic, O'Neill struggled to free himself through his own experiments with psychological expressionism. Taping the nine-act stream-of-consciousness *Strange Interlude* (1928) for a television revival, actress Glenda Jackson remarked that O'Neill did not write dialogue, he wrote speeches. Many of the plays contain lengthy monologues; *The Iceman Cometh* (1946) ends with perhaps the longest such speech in recent dramatic history. *The Emperor Jones* (1920) uses powerful lighting and musical effects to portray its protagonist's disintegration through Darwinian stages to helplessness. Describing his use of sound in the play, O'Neill recalled:

> One day I was reading of the religious feasts in the Congo and the uses to which the drum is put there—how it starts at a normal pulse and is slowly accelerated until the heartbeat of everyone present corresponds to the frenzied beat of the drum. Here was

an idea for an experiment. How could this sort of thing work on an audience in a theater?

Some of O'Neill's dramaturgic experiments are more successful than others. He uses Greek choruses, single characters played by two actors, cinematic flashbacks and elaborate stage masks to portray the ways "the sickness of today" renders life hollow and intolerable—of his more than thirty plays, only *Ah, Wilderness!* (1933) is a comedy. In *Dynamo* (1929), an electric dynamo becomes symbolic of a new divinity, much as it had for Henry Adams. The play's theme, according to O'Neill, is "the death of an old God and the failure of science and materialism to give a satisfactory new one for the surviving primitive religious instinct to find a meaning for life." As the insistent symbolism of expressionist style has lost its innovative freshness, many of O'Neill's experiments have come to seem dated and forced, but his reputation as a dramaturgic pioneer seems secure. Like the European masters he admired, he worked to open the range and possibility of dramatic discourse. His language is often clumsy and his thinking the urgent profundities of the autodidact, but he took the opportunity of staged thought more seriously than any American ever had, almost single-handedly beginning a tradition of serious writing for a native theater that would continue to fight for place in an arena dominated by commercial entertainment.

Several of O'Neill's early dramas continue to play well and are occasionally produced: *Anna Christie* (1921), *The Hairy Ape* (1922), *Desire Under the Elms* (1924); a film version of *The Emperor Jones* with Paul Robeson has become a television staple. But it is the later writing, some of it produced posthumously, that sustains his reputation as a playwright who can hold audiences through long evenings of tragic discourse. *Long Day's Journey into Night* is precisely that, both for the haunted Tyrone family and for those who watch the painstaking anatomy of their cyclic self-punishment. Revivals of *The Iceman Cometh* (1946) continue to be well attended and well reviewed, an evening listening to the derelicts and has-beens waiting in Harry Hope's saloon for a kind of Godot, a traveling salesman named Hickey who attempts to bring the happiness of truth through the destruction of illusion. Pursuing the ghosts of his own personal memories, the later O'Neill used the illusion of theatrical performance to test the power, the disappointment of illusion itself. In *A Touch of the Poet* (1957), part of a cycle called "A Tale of Possessors Self-Dispossessed," happiness lasts only as long as a Pirandello-like mirror image sustains the illusions of the uniform-wearing tavern keeper, and illusion collapses into insanity as a way to sustain life in the play's sequel, *More Stately Mansions* (1964).

The three decades after the First World War loom large as the golden years of American drama. The work of O'Neill, Odets, Maxwell Anderson, Wilder, Saroyan—and later Arthur Miller and Tennessee Williams—represents for the most part the nation's only serious achievement in the world of dramatic literature. But even at the height of their power and influence, none of these writers, not even the best of them, Eugene O'Neill, could be thought of as an important cultural force in the nation's life. Modern America has watched its stories staged by film makers and, since the 1950s, by the ever-growing commercial industry of television. Neither of these forms owes much to serious theater, except as the currents of thought and aesthetic experiment passed from European precedent into the American film industry. Television has brought drama nightly into every home, but after the early years of live performances such as those presented by "Playhouse 90," the development of videotaping has replaced the art of the theater with the technology of film. Americans for the most part watch dramas constructed by editors working with segments of tape recorded by many cameras in a sequence dictated by production rather than dramatic or narrative priority. The writers of these dramas, like the authors of film scripts, work as part of a large team and follow the rigorous requirements of the genre—for the television writer this often means a thirty- or sixty-minute format with calculated interruptions for commercial announcements. Art has always been valued for the challenges it overcomes, and writing for film and television has been characterized by energy and impressive skill. But the genres involved bear only superficial resemblance to what has come to be known historically as the drama; their histories are only now being written and their relation to the world of letters remains as yet uncertain.

This is merely to repeat that American culture has been shaped by the size and diversity of the country. Serious playwrights require theatrical centers and sophisticated audiences to support the production of their plays and to absorb the implications of their thought. But American settlement soon outdistanced the influence of Boston, Philadelphia and Richmond; New York, with its highly commercialized theater and modest avant-garde off-Broadway and off-off-Broadway, has never been a London or Paris, accessible and central to the cultural life of the hinterland. Few Americans—there have always been a few—journey to New York to experience and support serious playwriting, and the companies that take to the road to bring New York's theater to the rest of the nation are usually composed of apprentice or moderately talented actors presenting material deemed readily accessible to provincial outlanders. Such road shows have become unprofitable and hence rare as their intended audiences choose to remain loyal to the family television set now supplied with made-for-cable films. Theater in America has become increasingly a matter for local resident companies. These are often thoughtful, experimental and committed to the highest values of theatrical craft; they have attracted in scores of communities across the land discriminating and supportive audiences. It is among these groups that the future of theater in America must be sought, and it is doubtless among these groups that its best playwrights are currently to be found.

· III ·

Yet American theater still draws upon both the Modernist drama of the 1920s (O'Neill and Rice) and the political or "agitprop" theater of the 1930s—agitation propaganda that sought instant appeal to popular audiences. John Bonn's *15 Minute Red Review* (1932) and Elia Kazan's and Art Smith's *Dimitroff* (1934) used Communist songs and slogans to stir their audiences to direct political action. The best of the group, Clifford Odets's *Waiting for Lefty* (1935), ends with the cast leading the audience on a purposeful march from the theater; 1960s happenings and performance theater owed much to this changed relation of play to spectator. The 1930s saw not only "proletarian theater," but also the "proletarian novel," for as the Great Crash of 1929 developed into a deep-seated national and world depression, it soon became apparent that the social and cultural mood that had dominated the 1920s was gone for good. In 1931 Fitzgerald announced the end of his "Jazz Age": "It ended two years ago, because the utter confidence that was its essential prop received an enormous jolt and it didn't take long for the flimsy structure to settle earthward." The same year Frederic Lewis Allen's "instant history," *Only Yesterday*, set the 1920s apart as "a distinct era in American history." What Malcolm Cowley called the "exile's return" began as the checks to Paris stopped and writers came home to articulate a changed America. They found that progressive and radical thought had not died in the 1920s. The left-wing Michael Gold had been arguing for a "proletarian literature" as early as 1921, and when he took over the Communist paper *New Masses,* he repeatedly assaulted the bourgeois "imbecility" of American writing. From 1927 to 1930 V. L. Parrington was publishing his liberal social history of American literature, *Main Currents in American Thought*. The radical voice sounded clearly, too, in the prose as well as the poetry of the Harlem Renaissance, with such works as Jean Toomer's *Cane* (1923), and in Jewish immigrant autobiography or fiction like Abraham Cahan's *The Rise of David Levinsky* (1917). In 1927 liberal intellectuals found clear political cause in protesting the executions of the anarchists Nicola Sacco and Bartolomeo Vanzetti, but it was not until the stock market frenzy of 1928 and the subsequent collapse of an overspending, overborrowed system that a new literary accounting seemed inevitable.

Naturalism, documentary, muckraking, political rage returned to the novel as writers like Sherwood Anderson, Upton Sinclair and Theodore Dreiser took up radical issues and explored the language of unemployment, bread lines, urban misery, rural decay. Radicalism was no longer disloyalty, for one could castigate the economic system yet identify with "real" America: "I am accepted by working people everywhere as one of themselves and I am proud of that fact," Anderson wrote. One could challenge the political order and yet praise the nation—"America" appeared in all the titles. Writers as different as John Dos Passos, Hart Crane and Thomas Wolfe showed the general desire to explore the disordered nation, celebrate its epic qualities and speak for its troubled populace. The year 1930 marked the turning point. That year, Michael Gold in *The New Republic* attacked the "genteel" experimentalism of the bourgeois, aesthetic fiction of Thornton Wilder and renewed the calls he had been making in the *New Masses* for author-fighters and worker-correspondents. Writers like the steelworker Jack Conroy or the black migrant to Chicago Richard Wright began to win attention. Gold's own *Jews Without Money* also appeared in 1930, along with works with disturbing social titles: Edward Dahlberg's *Bottom Dogs,* Mary Heaton Vorse's *Strike!* In November 1929, in the very wake of the Crash, the *New Masses* sponsored the "John Reed Club" for young writers, its slogan "Art Is a Class Weapon." By 1934 there were thirty such groups across the nation; the New York club founded what would become the major intellectual journal of the times, *Partisan Review.* Like the first American Writers' Congress of 1935, its position was Stalinist, and it set out to assault liberalism, repoliticize writers and engage them in the great class struggle. This was the peak; by 1937, in the wake of the dismaying Moscow show trials, the editors were already reacting against Marxism's "totalitarian trend" and showing increasing sympathy for the Modern movement and sophisticated critical theories. They announced that "the imagination could not be contained within any orthodoxy," but for a few fevered years the attempt had been made.

This development, the dissolving of committed radicalism into the postwar "new liberalism," was to emerge as a crucial fact of American intellectual life. Many events—the show trials, the Spanish Civil War, the signing of the Soviet-Nazi pact in 1939, the end of the Depression, the coming of war in 1941—all helped lead to the changed attitudes of post-1945, with whose consequences we still live. Little of the radicalizing spirit survived the 1930s in Marxist form. Writers associated with left-wing positions joined in the battle against Nazism and Fascism, often using documentary skills developed in Depression America to report from Europe or the Pacific. Hemingway and Steinbeck narrated the war from European battlefields, Dos Passos went to the Pacific, and by the 1940s they were writing for an America that had at last thrown off economic crisis. But we should remember that the move toward "proletarian literature" and its methods of realism, naturalism, reportage and documentary was not the only direction of 1930s writing. If Hemingway and Fitzgerald opened their fiction to new social concerns, they did not abandon their formal inventiveness of the 1920s. The 1930s saw Faulkner's most experimental and Modernist novels, and one of the decade's key works of fiction, John Dos Passos's three-volume *U.S.A.* (1930–36), uses complex formal experiment to reach from subjective consciousness to public event and create a powerful version of twentieth-century American history from 1900 to Sacco and Vanzetti. In the work of Djuna Barnes, Henry Miller and Nathanael West, the quest for a modern gothic surrealism and artistic extremism continued, while in novels like *Look Homeward, Angel* (1929) Thomas Wolfe made the social landscape the material for a prodigiously inclusive subjectivity.

Yet the turn toward a socially sensitive realism and naturalism did slacken the energy of Modernist experiment, especially among the writers who undertook to speak of poverty, ghetto alienation and social displacement and sought a language to express the immediacy of their engagement. According to Michael Gold, the Modern movement was over; in 1930 he described himself as "the first writer in America to herald the advent of a world proletarian literature as a concomitant to the rise of the world proletariat." Gold called for "Proletarian Realism," works that displayed not Modernist pessimism but revolutionary *élan* and expressed the poetry of the worker molding his own world. His own *Jews Without Money* (1930) attempted to express these convictions. A ghetto novel about Rumanian-Jewish immigrants on New York's Lower East Side at the turn of the century, today it reads less like "Proletarian Realism" than as a significant if sentimental contribution to the Jewish-American fiction that had begun to widen the social map of the American novel. Its ancestor is Abraham Cahan's *The Rise of David Levinsky,* published in the year of the Bolshevik Revolution, 1917, the story of a diaspora Jew looking to America as the promised land and leaving *shtetl* life in Lithuania to search for "marvellous transformations." Here the Columbus myth becomes a Jewish rite of passage as he shaves off beard and earlocks to follow the path from rags to riches, from the simple world of the *shtetl* to a new world of secularism, complex modern sexual relations, greed and alienation. It is the story of social success and moral dislocation that would find its echoes in many Jewish-American writers thereafter. Gold's book reproduces this myth in its most political form. His autobiographical hero makes a similar journey, but stays poor and finds identity with the proletariat, the true Jews, "Jews without money." At the end he undergoes conversion to Marxism: "O workers' Revolution, you brought hope to me, a lonely suicidal boy. You are the true Messiah."

If, as the Hungarian Marxist critic Georg Lukács has argued, a modern realism means recognition of the objective evolutionary conditions of history, Gold's book is hardly socialist realism. It feels far closer to another book that expressed the Jewish experience in America in yet deeper and more complex form, Henry Roth's *Call It Sleep* (1934), another story of a boy's growing up on the Lower East Side before the First World War with the paradoxical, collapsing myth of the Promised Land. Roth too shares the Marxist sympathies common at the time and uses naturalist description to present the bleak streets, the gross sexuality, the bitter father and life-giving mother that Gold had also drawn. But his book is concerned less with the search for a political solution than the necessity of a coherent and adequate language, a new gift of tongues. The child David Schearl lives in a world of endless pidgin street talk, a babel of politics, obscenity and illiteracy, the chaotic voices of the melting-pot world. Finally he plunges a metal ladle into the electrified streetcar track hoping for rescue through the intensity of a true inner language. *Call It Sleep* manages to combine both the fractured prose of chaotic modern life and the fierce intensity of its transcendental vision. It was among the best of a good many novels—by Daniel Fuchs, Meyer Levin and others—that attempted to capture the truth of urban Jewish experience and led the way to a rich efflorescence of Jewish American fiction. By the 1940s and 1950s Jewish-American novelists like Saul Bellow, Philip Roth and Bernard Malamud were attempting a similar reconciliation of realism and transcendentalism, European and American fiction. Drawing on the international heritage of Kafka, Isaac Babel and Isaac Bashevis Singer, they undertook a moral and artistic depiction of a new America of mass culture, affluent alienation, historical uncertainty and troubled patriotism. Their hunger to express their nation's life condition made them central to an age of general displacement, and the Jewish hero —Bellow's Herzog, Roth's Zuckerman—became for a time an emblem of the entire culture.

A similar widening of the American fictional tradition occurred in the black novel as it developed out of the Harlem Renaissance of the 1920s. In 1930, as the Depression began, Richard Wright, a rural black from Mississippi, moved north to the modern city, Chicago, where he joined the John Reed Club and in 1934 the Communist Party, an experience he explored in an essay ten years later, "I Tried to Be a Communist." After the vivid, troubling stories about black life in a brutal and racist South, *Uncle Tom's Children* (1938), he wrote his masterpiece, *Native Son* (1940), the story of Bigger Thomas, tried and executed for the "almost accidental" murder of a white woman. James Baldwin, a younger black writer who extended the same tradition, later called it "everybody's protest novel"; it is a painful story of social and racial oppression. Like Clyde Griffiths in Dreiser's *An American Tragedy,* Bigger Thomas is a victim of the violence of his culture and the shameful limitations of his environment. Yet he is more than this, for he is also modern identityless man, an exile who insistently feels that he lives on "the outside of the world peeping in through a hole in the fence." The book has such a powerful impact because of its intense immediacy but also because, under the close examination the literary imagination can bring to such matters, pure protest is transfigured into a deep sense of disordered human identity, an awareness of absurdity. In his later autobiographical *Black Boy* (1945), Wright gave a black American portrait of the troubled artist. After the war he moved to Paris and increasingly acknowledged the existentialist, absurdist aspect of his writing. His novel *The Outsider* (1953) not only has virtually the same title as Albert Camus's *L'Étranger* but a similar theme, as a rebellious black hero confronts with an act of murder a meaningless world. Later black writing has drawn repeatedly on Wright's double heritage. In Ralph Ellison and James Baldwin, Wright found successors who could extend his mixture of discovering vision and rage against injustice. In the civil rights battles of the 1960s that rage seemed to matter most, but later his broad sense of human exposure and artistic hunger proved even more powerfully influential. Black American fiction has flourished in recent decades and owes much to him; like the best fiction of the 1930s, Wright's work was reaching toward a visionary distillation of an oppressed human condition.

The social conditions of the 1930s led other American writers back toward naturalism and its concern with social determination, victimization and the radical expression of the values and circumstances of those who came from the underside of the culture. Books like Edward Dahlberg's poetic *Bottom Dogs* (1930), the story of the author's hobo wanderings in the prewar years, or Jack Conroy's *The Disinherited* (1933), about a young Missouri worker who moves to the auto factories of the Boom and then encounters the disinheritance of the Depression, exemplify both the radical anger and the documentary inclusiveness that nurtured much fiction over these years. James T. Farrell's Studs Lonigan trilogy—*Young Lonigan* (1932), *The Young Manhood of Studs Lonigan* (1934) and *Judgment Day* (1935)—is a carefully designed work of naturalism by an author of Marxist sympathies who nonetheless rejected the simplistic stereotypes of proletarian fiction. Farrell's subject is the world of Irish Catholicism on Chicago's South Side. Studs himself—"a normal young American of his time and his class," growing up "several steps removed from the slums and dire economic want"—was carefully selected, Farrell explains, "not only as a character for imaginative fiction, but also as a social manifestation." Yet what he manifests is not just economic but spiritual poverty, the collapse of a Catholic immigrant inheritance and community values that can no longer sustain him and his friends in a materialist age. Farrell's books indict the cultural emptiness of an Irish-American family, the barrenness of its social and religious life during the 1920s. In the absence of a nourishing culture, Studs exploits raw aggression, physical and sexual prowess, streetwise values, an embittered vitality. Around him Farrell constructs the world of his sensory and emotional experience, a brutalized ethnic Chicago. When Studs dies a drunkard at the age of 29, Farrell's indictment is complete, not simply of the city's political shortcomings but of the cumulative erosion of any meaningful culture.

Farrell's naturalism remains powerful exactly because he made his dense, dark Chicago a credible and well-documented system. John Steinbeck's naturalism grew from different sources—the desire he shared with previous naturalists like Frank Norris, Jack London and Theodore Dreiser to understand the basic springs of man's primitive nature. Steinbeck came to seem the prototype of the "physical" writer. Like Jack London, he had apparently done everything, been a carpenter, a surveyor, a ranch hand, a department store clerk. He also had a scientific curiosity like Theodore Dreiser and had been a marine biologist concerned with biological theories of life. He had, for good measure, a certain amount of formal education at Stanford University in his home state of California, about which he was largely to write. His fiction began with a historical romance, but during the 1930s his themes changed. He explored the crowd emotions of a strike in *In Dubious Battle* (1936), the brutality and grace of the simple Lennie in *Of Mice and Men* (1937), the spirit of nature in his Californian novel *Tortilla Flat* (1934) and his fine story "The Red Pony" (1937). *The Pastures of Heaven* (1932) and *To a God Unknown* (1933) showed his interest in social problems and in the allure of California, which he attributed to the "westering" movement of mankind.

> The fascinating thing to me is the way a group has a soul, a drive, an intent, an end, a method, a reaction and a set of tropisms which in no way resembles the same things possessed by the men who make up the group,

he noted, and this sense of a group biology shaped his subject matter.

Steinbeck will always be remembered however for *The Grapes of Wrath,* his Depression epic which appeared in 1939 to sum up the spirit of the 1930s. With its "Okies," the migrants driven from Oklahoma farmlands by the dust bowl and the foreclosing banks, it is a protest novel, a challenge to agronomic carelessness and the indifference of capitalism, but it is also another novel of corporate "westering," as the migrants make their slow way down Highway 66 toward California. It takes in the defeats of the Depression and the shame of the Hoovervilles, the temporary camps put up to house the migrant workers, but it also affirms the primal human spirit and its transcendental powers, a theme caught in the famous moment when Rose of Sharon suckles a starving man back to life. Steinbeck later denied the novel was ever intended as a social record or a work of protest and insisted its focus was "streams in man more profound and dark and strong than the libido of Freud." But as the book went around the world, it made known the impact of dust bowl and Depression on American farmers; it had much to do with the award of the Nobel Prize for Literature to Steinbeck in 1962. By this time his work was returning to the larger myths in which the Depression was but an incident. *East of Eden* (1952) is a neobiblical epic of tribal wandering and generational conflict; California becomes once again the virgin Western kingdom where the dreams and struggles of humanity are experienced. Steinbeck reminds us that an inclusive epic persisted behind the social dismay of 1930s writing and that transcendental American aspiration did not die in the Depression.

This attitude was equally clear in the work of another writer of epic intentions who undertook great wanderings in order to write of "night and darkness in America, and the faces of sleepers in ten thousand towns; and of the tides of sleep and how the rivers flowed forever in the darkness." This was Thomas Wolfe, a stonecutter's son from Asheville, North Carolina, the "Altamont" and "Libya Hill" of his vast novels, a writer prepared to engulf all of America and the troubled world of 1930s Europe in the great web of his words. After the University of North Carolina, Wolfe went to writing classes at Harvard before settling first in New York and then wandering around Europe, always larger than life, before he died at thirty-eight from a brain infection following pneumonia. In the period of his travels and writing, Wolfe produced millions of words, but organizing for publication his vast flow of confession, reportage, the imaginative re-creation of his own life and the great themes he celebrated—death and sleep, "the city of myself, the continent of my soul," the web (of tradition) and the rock (of the contemporary city)—was beyond him. Maxwell Perkins of Scribner's, who also edited Fitzgerald and Hemingway, came closest to being a novelist when he cut Wolfe's great outpouring into the book-length units of *Look Homeward, Angel* (1929) and *Of Time and the River* (1935). In the preface to the first of these Wolfe explained his intentions: "All serious work is autobiographical. . . . The book was written in simpleness and nakedness of soul. . . . It is a book made out of my life, and it represents my vision of life to my twentieth year." In a letter he said, "There are few heroic lives; about the only one I know a great deal about is my own." Like Whitman before him, his aim was to make both a great social record and a great symbolic myth, with the author's own romantic, ever-transcendental self at the center.

Wolfe's books were constructed from the deluge of his personal experience, his own role that of the experiencer and searcher. His novels are "enfabled" quests for, he said, a father, a meaning, a myth. They take us from the traditional local community where lives are well ordered into the world of self-exposure in the fast-moving city and on to the turmoils of changing history—works of extravagant rhetoric, particularly attractive to youthful readers. A later pair of novels, *The Web and the Rock* (1939) and *You Can't Go Home Again* (1940), both posthumously published, have certain different qualities, partly because they were ordered by a different editor, Edward C. Aswell. By now Wolfe had become more concerned with the terrible powers of historical change, especially as Europe moved toward disaster, and so he sought to give his confessional narrative greater distance, more symbolic weight, a more complex time scheme. These are better books, though the three great subjects that concerned him persist at the center—self, life and America. By now he is more ready to acknowledge the problems of political life, the disillusionments of experience, the darker side of transcendentalism. Nonetheless Wolfe was never capable of actual doubt: "I believe we are lost here in America," he asserted, "but I believe we shall be found."

There were, however, writers who believed that Americans were lost and that only rage and obscenity were appropriate articulations of a nation that had become an "air-conditioned nightmare," a "huge cesspool," the very opposite of an immigrant dream. Ignoring the prevailing current of expatriation, Henry Miller, born in Yorkville, New York City, in 1891, once employment manager for Western Union, moved to Paris in 1930 as most other expatriates were returning home; "America three thousand miles away," he exulted, "I never want to see it again." Paris brought him into contact with the surrealist revolution and made him a writer of books that would not reach publication in the United States until the 1960s because of their sexual explicitness and frank and open obscenity. "This then? This is not a book. This is libel, slander, defamation of character," begins the first of them, *Tropic of Cancer* (Paris, 1934; New York, 1961); "No, this is a prolonged insult, a gob of spit in the face of Art, a kick in the pants to God, Man, Destiny, Time, Love, Beauty . . . what you will." Miller refused not simply all established concepts of art, but those of morality, loyalty and social allegiance. In their way, his books were deliberate anti-novels, though as Leslie Fiedler has noted, his works of the 1930s were also Depression novels, novels of the economic underdog written out of economic fury and political dismay. In "Inside the Whale" (1939), an essay about the collapse of liberalism and humanism in an increasingly totalitarian age, George Orwell was to put it slightly differently. Miller was his example of the writer as quietist, a "Whitman among the corpses," enduring and recording the processes of a dead and corrupted world without offering any political solutions at all. He was, said Orwell, a "completely negative, unconstructive, amoral writer," expressing the defeat the modern writer has suffered in history while contenting himself with creating in the ruins a vivid, surreal rage.

Miller's novels do reject responsible action to claim the role of art as outrage, a challenge to liberal humanism, political faith, bourgeois guilt, Utopian optimism. At the same time there is, as in Thomas Wolfe, a strong transcendental intention, though Miller's is largely based on Taoism, surrealism and European anarchism. *Tropic of Cancer* records random couplings, poverty, a vision of extremity amid the general detritus of life; it was the first, perhaps the most outrageous, of a three-volume sequence that went on to include *Black Spring* (Paris, 1936; New York, 1963) and *Tropic of Capricorn* (Paris, 1939; New York, 1962). Its down-and-out self, more fictional than the confessional, open technique suggests, decides to be a writer and identifies himself as a dispossessed genius with the tradition of Rimbaud, Bosch, van Gogh, those who "lived like scarecrows, amid the abundant riches of our culture." The artist must eject himself right out of society: "All my life I have felt a great kinship with the madman and the criminal," he says in "Brooklyn Bridge," an essay in *The Cosmological Eye* (1945). "To me the city is crime personified. I feel at home." American society has made him an underdog, but the underdog, exploiting the system that has belittled him, becomes the accuser entitled to claim whatever redemption there is. "Today I am proud to say I am inhuman," he writes in *Tropic of Cancer,* "that I belong not to men and governments, that I have nothing to do with creeds and governments." As with Genet perhaps or Céline, violence could be "cosmological" and generate radical vision out of the cancer that surrounded it. *Tropic of Cancer* deals mostly with Paris as contrast to the American void, "a soil so saturated with the past that however far back the human mind roams one can never detach it from its human background." The other two volumes in the sequence increasingly turn to the underside of an urban America, a New York he describes as the city of dead souls where he acknowledges himself "perhaps the unique Dadaist in America, and I didn't know it."

Miller's actual return to America in 1940 marked an important transition. He traveled the continent to assault it in *The Air-Conditioned Nightmare* (1945), but after settling in Big Sur in 1942 he moved toward a kind of peace with his homeland. His fictional sequence *The Rosy Crucifixion—Sexus* (1945), *Plexus* (1949) and *Nexus* (1960)—continued the personal saga but made the mystical content of his work more apparent. He argued that what he sought was not a revolution in sexuality but a revolution in consciousness, an idea of significant appeal to the rising beat generation of the 1950s. He wrote extensively and, with his books no longer banned in the United States, became a guru of the new radicalism, a voice of American Romantic anarchism and a writer of visionary celebrations. He came to be seen as a type of post-Marcusean man, freely enjoying bodily and spiritual consciousness as witness to the power of the polymorphous perverse, his work an influence on many writers of the later 1950s and 1960s as model of a visionary surrealism. The dark nihilism of the earlier days no longer seemed the important feature of his work; rather it was his self-discovering vitalism, capturing out of the obscene, grotesque comedy of apocalyptic despair a new form of being. This second Miller was thus read largely as a transcendental optimist, a Whitman not among the corpses but among the flower people, an influential and much-celebrated American writer.

Miller was never alone in seeing a psychoanalytic, radical surrealism as one way forward for American writing. Anaïs Nin, his companion in Paris, produced a more poetic and sensuous surrealism all her own in works like *House of Incest* (1936) and *Winter of Artifice* (1939), as well as in her intensely mystical and sensuous *Diaries* (1966–76). Djuna Barnes, also an expatriate in Paris, showed similar preoccupations in her psychological fantasy-tale of a lesbian love affair, *Nightwood* (1936), for which T. S. Eliot wrote an admiring introduction. A more comic, grotesque vein of surrealism guided the work of

Nathanael West, born Nathan Weinstein, who took up his writerly pseudonym when he too moved to Paris in the late 1920s. It was here he began *The Dream Life of Balso Snell,* a parodic and nightmarish comedy about an American poet who enters the womb of the Trojan horse through the posterior door, finds it "inhabited solely by writers in search of an audience" and generates a world of massive literary pastiche and artistic self-mockery. But it was when West applied his surreal, parodic tone to American society in *Miss Lonelyhearts* (1933), a dark farce about a newspaperman who runs an agony column and comes to share the painful sufferings of his correspondents, that his work took on lasting importance. Behind the antics of his comic method a world of real pain emerges to give to his writing something of the despair of the later Mark Twain. West's American society is grotesque, a place of hopeful dreams that can never be fully satisfied. His next book, *A Cool Million* (1934), addresses the fragile American Dream in a terrible parody of the Horatio Alger myth of "rags-to-riches" success, a bitter satire exploring political and financial corruption, constant violation and exploitation of innocence, in an atmosphere of rising American Fascism. Lemuel Pitkin, the innocent hero, is deluded, cheated, mutilated and at last killed in the cause of the Dream, and like so many of West's heroes becomes the futile victim of a false faith which nonetheless fulfills human need.

By now West was a screenwriter working in the greatest American dream factory of all, Hollywood. His final novel, *The Day of the Locust* (1939), published shortly before his sudden death in an auto accident, takes Hollywood as its theme and fully exploits West's sharp, satirical, grotesque comic-strip method of construction. Unlike Scott Fitzgerald's *The Last Tycoon,* it is concerned less with the world of the studios, the film makers and the stars than with the frenzied atmosphere of dreaming aspiration which surrounds them. Hollywood becomes the center of American myth, desire, religious yearning that attracts fantasists filled with terrible boredom and deep hidden frustration, as the Californian illusion of renewal to which they were drawn fails to satisfy. "It is hard to laugh at the need for beauty and romance, no matter how tasteless, even horrible, the results of that are. But it is easy to sigh. Few things are sadder than the truly monstrous," reflects the book's protagonist, the painter Tod Hackett, as he goes about his task of trying to paint an apocalyptic canvas, "The Burning of Los Angeles."

The book itself paints an even larger apocalyptic canvas, for West's Hollywood dreamers are not the westering epic heroes of Steinbeck but a group of sensation seekers and freaks living on a daily media diet of "lynchings, murder, sex crimes, explosions, wrecks, love nests, fires, miracles, revolutions, wars." Tod's purpose is to understand these people and "paint their fury with respect, appreciating its awful, anarchic power and aware that they had it in them to destroy civilization." At the end of the book they do destroy, if not civilization, then Hollywood, rioting and looting after they have gathered hysterically for a picture premiere. The final scene enables Tod to finish his violently surreal painting, a portrait of the modern suffering mob, and West to complete his apocalyptic tragicomedy. More than most American writers of the 1930s, West actually creates a modern language, a hard, aesthetically sharp, satirical voice for expressing group rage, the psychopathology of the gathering masses, the narcissism of twentieth-century selfhood with its greedy lusts and overstimulated desires—the world of posthistorical tackiness. In some notes he made for *Miss Lonelyhearts,* West explained his methods: "Forget the epic, the master work. In America fortunes do not accumulate, the soil does not grow, families have no history. Leave slow growth to the book reviewers, you only have time to explode." He noted that what he was writing was "A novel in the form of a comic strip" that avoided inward psychology; what West creates are pasteboard characters, identityless identities who are nevertheless capable of suffering and tragedy. In many respects West is the most modern of the 1930s novelists; if George Orwell was right to say that Miller retreated "inside the whale" to avoid writing about totalitarianism and mass society, West did confront these matters and find an appropriate style. It is the style of "black humor" that nourished the gallows comedy of writers like Joseph Heller and Stanley Elkin as well as the later "cybernetic" Postmodern fiction of Thomas Pynchon and William Gaddis.

West, like Faulkner, was one of the true innovative stylists of the 1930s. So was John Dos Passos, who did not "forget the epic, the master work." His three-volume sequence of novels *The 42nd Parallel* (1930), *1919* (1932) and *The Big Money* (1936)—published together in 1937 as *U.S.A.*—is a vast experimental project that utters the 1930s in all its complexity. In some ways it was a 1920s novel—the story ends with the executions of Sacco and Vanzetti—and Dos Passos was a 1920s writer. Like a good many of his literary contemporaries, he had gone, after a Harvard education, to be an ambulanceman in France during the First World War. His first novels are reflections of that experience: *One Man's Initiation—1917* (1919) and *Three Soldiers* (1921). Their very titles suggest his gradual move from a subjective vision toward a wider and more collective view of history, the first book establishing his sensitive, aesthetic dismay at the war, the second the broader experience of mechanization and organization to which his soldiers are subjected. But it was with *Manhattan Transfer* (1925) that Dos Passos found his way to Modernist form. Like Joyce's *Ulysses,* Döblin's *Berlin Alexanderplatz* or Andrei Biely's *Saint Petersburg,* this is an attempt to convey the complex, simultaneous, cinematic consciousness of the massive contemporary city. With its expressionist techniques of startling juxtaposition, rapid cutting, fragmentation, it owes a good deal to the cinema of Eisenstein and Griffith. The high-rise city, the jostle of crowds, the transit of massed people through skyscrapers and subways dominate the book. As Jean-Paul Sartre said in an admiring essay, Dos Passos seems to invent for us the "authorless novel" with "characterless characters" guided by an overall sensation of urban experience. The book belongs with works like Hart Crane's long Manhattan poem *The Bridge* (1930) or the city paintings of Ben Shahn. It is a synchronic novel, a work of juxtaposition and simultaneity, pluralized narration and the intersection of documentary material with personal stories.

Many of these methods helped to shape *U.S.A.* but in the interest of tracing the growth of a modern history—the history of the United States from its optimistic and progressive hopes at the turn into the twentieth century, the "American century," through the crisis year of 1919, when Woodrow Wilson's hopes began to fail, and so to the crass materialism of the 1920s, the era of "the Big Money." It covers the dying of the progressive impulses that had animated early twentieth-century America, the move from simple to complex capitalism, from a production to consumption economy, from innocence to modern experience. Dos Passos sees all this corrupting the psychology of his characters as they break faith with any idea of community or even of a shared common language—he was early in expressing his sympathy for a left-wing interpretation of modern American culture. But *U.S.A.* avoids the methods of simple documentary or naive realism, drawing instead on the techniques of Modernist collage and fragmentation. The long sweep of the trilogy unfolds on four different narrative levels. There are the extended life stories of various fictional characters, like Margo Dowling, Dick Savage and J. Ward Moorhouse, not simply individuals but representative American types; some of these tales intersect, but most simply run parallel, collectively representing an ironic portrait of the American Dream. Then there are factual biographies of real public figures, some of them heroes of radicalism like La Follette, Thorstein Veblen, Randolph Bourne, Big Bill Haywood and Frank Lloyd Wright, others the major politicians of the era or representatives of corporate capitalism like J. P. Morgan and Samuel Insull, or the major politicians of the era. Then there are the "Newsreels," documentary collages of headlines, songs, speeches, newspaper reports, sometimes there to show the evolution of events, at other times to make ironic comment on the failure of rhetoric to encounter reality. Finally there are the "Camera Eye" sections, stream-of-consciousness perception essentially derived from the novelist's own viewpoint as he struggles through the painful world of broken images, able to do little more than register sense impressions and struggle toward meaningful speech.

U.S.A. is a work where Modernist experimental sensibility meets the radical and reformist spirit of the 1930s; it is both a vision and a critique. It both questions and records history as it traces the dissolution of epic while seeking an epic life somewhere behind the social order, in the hearts and minds of the people. What divides and limits this land of great prospects, popular energies and noble myths is the power of capital, the weight of war, the loss of community, the domination of indifference and greed. In the prologue the young Vag wanders the streets and highways and tries, like Whitman, to include all contradictions: "U.S.A. is the world's greatest river-valley fringed with mountains and hills, U.S.A. is a set of bigmouthed officials with too many bank-accounts." He places his hope where Dos Passos himself seeks to place it: "But mostly U.S.A. is the speech of the people." Yet if the book seeks, as the poet Carl Sandburg did during the 1930s, to recover the native speech of the people, it is also a complexly layered system of elaborate discourses. As with Pound's *Cantos,* its technical fragmentation seems to lead us to a vision of disconnection, a world where the gap steadily widens between rhetorical statement and actual meanings, between ideal and real. As history turns downward after 1919, the fragmentation increases and false rhetorics increasingly overwhelm the languages of humanity and personality. In the age of "history the billiondollar speedup," language must struggle to maintain contact with the world of actual experience: "America our nation has been beaten by strangers who have turned our language inside out."

Yet, Dos Passos writes, "We have only words against," and so he layers into his book an epic and celebratory intention, an attempt to document and recover the deeper America, the endurance of the land, the speech of the people—a major theme of much 1930s writing. Indeed *U.S.A.* now appears a key work of the times, expressing the conflict between populist history and a second history of wealth, power and politics and showing, for all its artistic ambition, the documentary outreach and political rage of the fundamental Americanism implied in its title. Dos Passos was for a while a Communist, though he soon decided that after all Henry Ford was preferable to Karl Marx or even Michael Gold. "I think there's more life in the debris of democracy than the comrades do." In due time he became an America Firster, and by the postwar years his novels—especially the later sequence *Mid-Century* (1961) meant to counterpoint *U.S.A.*—became patriotic and conservative assertions of American values.

Ironically, this shift to affirmation deprived his writing of much of its form, vitality and intellectual challenge. The liberal and left-wing attitudes of the 1930s were a reminder that a writer is a critical interpreter of his culture. Their enduring legacy was the challenging, often left-radical tradition later American writers could exploit as they confronted mass, anonymity, economic despair and urban disorder in their search for sustaining human value in contemporary American life.

· IV ·

The naturalistic, investigative literature of the 1930s brought American writing closer to public utterance than it had come in more than a century. Many of the best books were efforts at exploration and documentation, not the least of them the various guides to America commissioned by the Federal Writers' Project, which produced, for instance, Richard Wright's rich depiction of Harlem. The reporter was often accompanied by the photographer: James Agee's and Walker Evans's assignment for *Fortune* magazine to look at the poor white sharecroppers of the South eventually appeared in 1941 as *Let Us Now Praise Famous Men,* one of the most sensitive records of the American 1930s. It was not really a time to develop the more personal art of poetry. Archibald MacLeish, defiantly insisting that "a poem should not mean but be," was one of many who resisted the call to commitment: "How to conceive in the name of a column of marchers?" he asked. Yet although American poetry during the 1930s never managed to produce a group of politically radical *and* experimental poets comparable to the British Auden group, there were notable achievements by William Carlos Williams, Louise Bogan and many more. In the South the fugitive group of John Crowe Ransom, Allen Tate and others explored in poetry and criticism alike the problems of modern poetic identity and the relation of literary form to historical and social responsibility.

If the 1930s was not perhaps an important age of American verse, it was a significant period in the articulation of a native critical tradition. While Henry James had been enjoyed or reviled for his careful prose and complex structures and Poe was rejected for his bizarre themes and jingling verse or celebrated as the nation's first great master of the short story, neither had become established as a major critical voice. "What had criticism in America usually been if not predominantly social, even political in its thinking," Alfred Kazin noted in *On Native Grounds* (1942).

From Emerson and Thoreau to Mencken and [Van Wyck] Brooks, criticism had been the great American lay philosophy, the intellectual conscience and intellectual carryall. It had been a study of literature inherently concerned with ideals of citizenship, and often less a study of literary texts than a search for some new and imperative moral order within which American writing could live and grow. . . . It had always been more a form of moral propaganda

than a study in esthetic problems. . . . Just as the main tradition
of American letters for a century and more had been the effort to
create a truly national literature, a literature of broad democratic
reality, so criticism had usually sought . . . to unite American writers
in the service of one imperative ideal or another.

The tradition of wide public discourse described by Kazin was continued by critics as dissimilar as Irving Babbitt, Edmund Wilson, Lionel
Trilling, Irving Howe and Kazin himself. Though their social and
political philosophies might differ, though they might argue Marx with
V. F. Calverton and Granville Hicks or Freud with Ludwig Lewisohn,
most of them saw literature as a means to an end—a healthy citizen
in a just, comprehensible social world. They frequently attributed the
cultural ills of the day to the hegemony of scientific positivism, and
yet often they assumed a reality that could be known as they understood
science to know it, a reality that remained stable in the pages of history
and was reflected clearly and directly in the writings of the authors
they favored. In each of these areas, their assumptions about the nature
and purpose of literature now seem continuing echoes from the earlier
Genteel Tradition.

In such a climate, the suggestion that art offered an alternative
way of knowing could be found only in the fringe publications of the
avant-garde. For T. S. Eliot, the criteria of mainstream criticism ignored
what made art what it is and thus failed to see clearly how it participated
in and helped us know the world we live in. He agreed with his friend
Irving Babbitt that the greatness of literature could not be judged
solely in literary terms, but he had learned from Ezra Pound and the
French symbolists that whether or not a text was literature at all could
be determined *only* in literary terms. He also learned from the French
how to value Edgar Allan Poe, and with his admiration for Henry
James he not only introduced the literary world to the little-known
American formalist tradition but succeeded in making it prevail in the
bookshops and academies of his homeland. By the mid-1920s the
political and ethical concerns of neohumanism and Anglican Christianity were leading Eliot far from the aesthetic preoccupations recorded
in *The Sacred Wood* (1920), but for decades his insistence on "the
poem itself" was the rallying cry of the first near-total revolution in
the history of American literary criticism.

Eliot's quest for a viable literary and cultural tradition made him for many years a spiritual cousin of Irving Babbitt and Paul Elmer More. With enemies much like theirs—Romanticism, liberalism, the chaos of a self-indulgent society—he too constructed a carefully ordered literary, political and, ultimately, religious tradition. His literary pantheon had taken shape by the early 1920s: Dante, Dryden, the Elizabethan dramatists, the seventeenth-century Metaphysical poets. From the very beginning, his concerns were with European culture and European traditions. Living most of his adult life abroad, he seemed, in the words of Stanley Edgar Hyman, "almost entirely blind to the American tradition, if not in flight from it." Like most of the artistic exiles, Eliot left his country primarily because he could discern there no usable tradition. "It is inevitable," he remarked in a 1919 review of the *Cambridge History of American Literature,* "that any work on American literature should contain a good deal of stuffing. The fault is not in the lack of material so much as in its lack of cohesion." Eliot's inability to find "cohesion" led to a view of American writers much like Mencken's: "The great figures of American literature are peculiarly isolated, and their isolation is an element, if not of their greatness, certainly of their originality." In a later discussion of the subject, an address in 1953 on "American Literature and the American Language," Eliot's view remained the same. There is Poe, Whitman and Mark Twain, but no tradition. The New England writers—the best is Hawthorne—show some coherence, but then New England has never been characteristically American. As one might expect from his influence on the French Symbolists, it is Poe who most interested Eliot. He admired Poe's intellect, his originality, his unmistakable idiom. "He was the directest, the least pedantic, the least pedagogical of the critics writing in his time in either America or England."

Eliot's literary ideas owed a good deal to the theoretical training he received at Harvard University from 1906 to 1914. The eminent philosopher of pragmatism, William James, had retired in 1907, but his influence remained powerful on a faculty that included Josiah Royce and two of Eliot's mentors, Irving Babbitt and George Santayana. (A. N. Whitehead came to Harvard in 1924.) In addition to studying Elizabethan and Jacobean drama and the poetry of Donne and Dante, the young Eliot read deeply in social anthropology and philosophy.

During a brief period before moving to London he taught in the philosophy program, and by 1916 he had completed his doctoral dissertation on the Oxford idealist F. H. Bradley.

There are sufficient elements here to indicate the general direction of Eliot's life and career. His later choice of Christian conservatism would occur in a world he had been taught to see was his for the shaping: "The letter giveth life." And he had been taught as well, by Santayana, that

> beauty is a species of value. . . . If we approach a work of art scientifically, for the sake of its historical connexions or proper classification, we do not approach it aesthetically. The discovery of its date or of its author may be otherwise interesting; it only remotely affects our aesthetic appreciation.

Santayana's distinction anticipates the fundamental New Critical discrimination between an "extrinsic" approach to the literary text—the approach of traditional academic scholarship and other critical schools (biographical, psychological, socioeconomic, mythic)—and the "intrinsic" emphasis of formalist New Criticism.

In 1936, when John Crowe Ransom wished to distinguish his literary position from the ethical imperatives of the new humanists, he admitted that he too was a "dogmatical critic," but he insisted that

> there are categories of beauty to be discussed, and techniques of beauty, for beauty is comparatively rare, and probably it is achieved and maintained often with heroic pains. It has the same right to its connoisseurs that moral character has.

In *God Without Thunder* (1930) and *The World's Body* (1938), Ransom's cultural analysis parallels Poe's assault on science for robbing us of our necessary dream beneath the tamarind tree, the beliefs we need to give our life meaning, and he insists that poetry alone can supply the lack. We need, he argued in *The New Criticism* (1941), an ontological criticism. With its debts to Poe, James and Eliot, such a criticism was already building, and it took its name from Ransom's volume.

The side of Eliot and Pound which ultimately had such a profound influence on the creation and study of American literature was not political. It was in fact more closely related than either would admit to Croce and Spingarn. What Robert Spiller has called the "aesthetic existentialism" of the century's middle decades owed as much to these American expatriates, as writers and critics, as it did to the imagists and symbolists, to Gertrude Stein, T. E. Hulme and the freshly discovered aestheticism of Henry James. Additional support for the creative artist was provided by the psychological libertarians. Whatever their other differences, men like Ludwig Lewisohn and William Carlos Williams, for many years little more than a persistent undercurrent in American criticism, later provided valuable encouragement for the formalist *coup* of the 1940s and 1950s. And not far behind both Lewisohn and Williams was D. H. Lawrence.

Lawrence was interested in American literature, Edmund Wilson writes, for its "meaning in the life of the western world as a whole." But from almost every other angle *Studies in Classic American Literature* (1923) seems an American book, right down to its completion during Lawrence's stay in New Mexico and its impact on subsequent American literary thought. All the earmarks of the period's criticism are here: the opening, reminiscent of Brooks's *America's Coming of Age,* that recognizes the need for American artistic maturity; the insistence that this need can be supplied only through acceptance of the nation's true literary tradition; and, finally, the confidence that in this book that tradition has at last been formulated.

Lawrence's reading of the American literary past follows closely his theory of instinctual "blood consciousness." He begins by rejecting "snuff-coloured" Ben Franklin and Franklin's God, "the provider. The heavenly storekeeper. The everlasting Wanamaker." Crèvecoeur, Cooper, Poe, Hawthorne, Dana and Melville are only partially acceptable, because they only partially recognized the unconscious demands of the blood.

> Americans have never loved the soil of America as Europeans have loved the soil of Europe. America has never been a blood-home-land. Only an ideal home-land. The home-land of the idea, of the *spirit.* And of the pocket. Not of the blood.

Whitman was the first to escape this commitment to the superiority of the soul, the first to accept the soul as one with the senses and the flesh. He "was the first heroic seer to seize the soul by the scruff of her neck and plant her down among the potsherds."

Lawrence's psychological primitivism had its most direct American influence on William Carlos Williams. With *In the American Grain* (1925), Williams wanted to tap the spiritual resources of his country's past in order to nourish this same sense of "blood-home-land." Like Lawrence, Williams looked for myths that would encourage the sinking of roots, would provide a definite sense of place—such as his own feeling for Paterson or the need the later Agrarians felt to relate themselves to the mythic past of the South. He has looked, he tells us, under the surface of America's misunderstood past to determine its "true character," the "noteworthy stuff." "It has been my wish to draw from every source one thing, the strange phosphorus of life."

To see American history truly is, for Williams, to see from the beginning a tragic split that has sapped the nation's potential greatness. Men like Columbus and Champlain appreciated the fertile *newness* of the continent, while Cortés, Raleigh, Drake and their kind brought only the rapacity of the Old World. As a result, "almost nothing remains of the great American New World but a memory of the Indian." The vitality, the instinctive place-consciousness of this Indian was effectively destroyed by Puritanism. Williams's indictment of the Puritan is among the best-edged that appeared during the period, for he has read the men he attacks. He has read Cotton Mather and has decided that what is in his books still "lives and there hides, as in a lair from whence it sallies now and then to strike terror through the land." The Puritan remained a European, fearful of emotional contact with a new, "orchidean" land. Instead of embracing it, he exploited it, and Americans became the greatest moneymakers in the world. Williams's view of the Revolution echoes his friend Pound's: instead of freeing us from the tyranny of the Puritan the conflict plunged us into worse servitude, and "Hamilton was the agent." Williams's usable past includes those who protest: the Indian, the American woman with her healthy intuition, Thomas Morton, John Paul Jones, Aaron Burr. The sum of all these he finds in Daniel Boone and his literary counterpart, Edgar Allan Poe. Williams's Boone is a mythic figure of heroic proportions, while his Poe, suppressed by society like Brooks's James and Twain, becomes virtually the *only* truly American writer. America has followed the wrong leaders, taken the wrong turn. "However hopeless it may seem, we have no other choice: we must go back to the beginning; it must all be done over; everything that is must be destroyed."

Ludwig Lewisohn's *Expression in America* (1932), with its companion anthology, *Creative America* (1933), was a more systematic reinterpretation of the American past than either Lawrence or Williams had made, but it started from much the same premises. In his early *Nation* days Lewisohn concerned himself directly with the political and social implications of the theater he discussed so well. By the time he came to write his oft-postponed history of American letters, however, he had fallen under the spell of Freud. Where the work of Freud seemed to offer metaphoric systems highly useful for many of the period's creative writers, for Lewisohn Freud supplied a thesis. He accepted the idea of sex as the all-important motive force in human behavior, and his book became a study of repression and its effect on American letters.

Lewisohn's new aim involved him in something of a contradiction with his still lively social concerns. He persistently berated Spingarn for his Crocean blindness to the social function of art, but when he himself spoke of art as autobiography, as release and liberation, he unwittingly strengthened the case of the aesthetes. His books seemed to illustrate the sterility which followed conformity to society's moral code, and as a result he was welcomed by those artists and critics who found art and society incompatible concerns.

When Lewisohn laid aside his socialism for the methods of Freud he was merely trading one weapon for another. The enemy remained the same: the established Philistine values that Brooks and countless others had blamed for the aridity of American cultural life. Like Lawrence and Williams before him, Lewisohn traced these values back to the moral rigidity of the Puritan.

From the Colonial laws which punished incontinence by brands and lashings . . . to the latest experiments in Prohibition enforcement, American society, true to its origin, has compensated itself for its fierce sinning against the Indian, the slave, the business competitor, by bearing down with unparalleled harshness upon all the more amiable and expansive forces of human nature.

The only artist such a culture can tolerate is the mere artificer—like Longfellow—who observes "the rules of the social and moral game" and represents life "as emptied of both reflection and desire." The result is a tradition of "polite letters unintegrated with life until almost the other day." Such a tradition has no value for Lewisohn's historical moment. What is needed, he writes in *Creative America,* is "a revaluation of the past in the terms of the present." To supply this need he produced his two books, "embodying the ultimate effort and highest exercise of the American spirit . . . a usable past."

Lawrence, Williams and Lewisohn agreed in making the American past contemporary and thereby replacing a literature of historical continuity with an art of symbolism and timeless myth. Theories of veiled ambiguities, of racial unconscious, of Jungean prototypes and Freudian repressions have since inspired a host of able critics—Edmund Wilson, Richard Chase and Leslie Fiedler among them. None of these writers believed art should be separated from its social context, and yet their views found a sympathetic audience in those who hymned the integrity of the artist and the autonomy of his art. "Where the ego had once been a figure of speech," Alfred Kazin notes, "it was now a banner."

The first widely influential reordering of America's literary tradition was Vernon L. Parrington's three-volume *Main Currents in American Thought* (1927–30). It was in effect a capstone to one whole movement of literary criticism, for Parrington succeeded in doing what Van Wyck Brooks never could: he provided a coherent usable past for the liberals. From another point of view *Main Currents* was only the beginning, the tentative introduction to a decade of leftist literary interpretation. Looking back in 1943, the editors of *The New Masses* were forced to admit that leftist criticism during the middle 1930s had "not come directly from Marxist sources, but from bourgeois critics like Taine, Brandes, and Parrington."

Parrington's debt to Brooks and the diagnosis of contemporary ills Brooks popularized is apparent throughout *Main Currents.* It was as clear to Parrington as it had been to Brooks that industrialism was transforming the agrarian world of an earlier America, that "the passion for liberty is lessening and the individual, in the presence of creature comforts, is being dwarfed," while "the drift of centralization is shaping its inevitable tyrannies to bind us with." There was reason to doubt that the idealism and concern for human rights of the early Fathers could "unhorse the machine that now rides men." But Parrington took comfort from the very resistance Brooks had called for: "it is not without hope that intelligent America is in revolt. The artist is in revolt, the intellectual is in revolt, the conscience of America is in revolt."

To help direct this revolt, Parrington produced his comprehensive survey of the American past: he wanted to reassert those "germinal ideas that have come to be reckoned traditionally American." The ideas Parrington saw as germinal to the American tradition he explicitly affirmed as "liberal rather than conservative, Jeffersonian rather than Federalistic"—democracy as "a humane social order, serving the common well-being." He was looking for writers who still had something—the right thing—to say to his own generation and, as he put it himself, "very likely in my search I have found what I went forth to find." For Parrington, "the promise of the future has lain always in the keeping of liberal minds that were never discouraged from their dreams."

As Lionel Trilling saw some years ago, Parrington's was not a great intelligence. It appeared obvious to him that the true American vein was the liberal one; once he had accepted this premise it seemed the simplest matter to line up those writers and thinkers who had furthered what he saw as the Jeffersonian-liberal cause and to oppose them with those who fought this "main current": "The line of liberalism in colonial America runs through Roger Williams, Benjamin Franklin, and Thomas Jefferson. . . . Over against these . . . must be set the complementary figures of John Cotton, Jonathan Edwards, and Alexander Hamilton." The three volumes move neatly from Calvinistic gloom through Romantic optimism to a modern mechanistic pessimism. Cooper, Thoreau, Twain and Whitman—writers who came to grips directly with the true American experience—form the nucleus of a usable past. Poe and James, Lowell and Longfellow—those writers, in short, who dealt only with abstractions and idealizations—bear little relevance to the needs of the present and rarely detain Parrington long. Howard Mumford Jones, a historian on the scene, later recalled the excitement *Main Currents* aroused. "Who can forget," he writes,

> the tingling sense of discovery with which we first read these lucid pages, following this confident marshaling of masses of stubborn material into position, until book, chapter, and section became as orderly as a regiment on parade! . . . All other histories of literature were compelled to pale their intellectual fires. We were free of Anglophilism, of colonialism, of apology at last. . . . Here was a usable past, adult, reasonable, coherent.

There was excitement in other circles as well. America had possessed a small but gifted and dedicated literary left since before the First World War. With the deaths of Sacco and Vanzetti and the collapse of the early Depression years apparently verifying their reading of history and the weaknesses of American civilization, the early Marxists found their numbers growing daily as more and more writers and intellectuals either joined the party or traveled sympathetically alongside. The 1930s were substantially Marxist years. As these writers and critics cast about for an American past they could square with Marxist dogma, they came naturally enough to the work of Vernon Parrington.

It is easy to understand what the Marxists would find appealing in Parrington's work. He had taken his first impulse toward cultural criticism from Taine but had soon fallen under the influence of his close friend J. Allen Smith and his economic interpretation of history. He came to feel, in the words of his editor E. H. Eby, that "economic forces imprint their mark upon political, social, and religious institutions; literature expresses the result in its thought content." He was "up to [his] ears in the economic interpretation of American history and literature," Parrington wrote to his Harvard class secretary in 1918,

> I become more radical with every year, and more impatient with the smug Tory culture which we were fed on as undergraduates. . . . I have set the school down as a liability . . . to the cause of democracy. It seems to me the apologist and advocate of capitalist exploitation.

From the early years after graduation he had been an active populist, and it is said that before the war his salary was twice reduced because he would not limit his lectures exclusively to *belles-lettres*. By 1928 he could remark, "I was a good deal of a Marxian."

There are passages aplenty in *Main Currents* which must have given aid and comfort to the left. "Bad social machinery makes bad men," Parrington writes in his discussion of Sinclair Lewis:

> Put the banker in the scullery instead of the drawing-room; exalt the test-tube and deflate the cash register; rid society of the dictatorship of the middle class; and the artist and the scientist will erect in America a civilization that may become . . . a thing to be respected.

But in spite of words like these, Parrington was no Marxist, as Granville Hicks saw very clearly. Parrington obviously went to school to Marx and the Marxist method, as Hicks pointed out, but after all is said and done, Parrington accepted the American system while Hicks and other Marxists did not. He was able to envision an America saved without revolution because he was not truly scientific in his determinism. He saw clearly enough for any Marxist that the conservatives in American history had been motivated by economic considerations, but he never applied the same standard to his beloved liberals. These are always "free souls," "idealists" or "men of vision." As a consequence the tragedy of American history had been merely the inability of the right side to retain ascendancy. He always slips back, Hicks complained, "into the conviction that things might somehow have been different, if only men had been true to the ideals he believes in." When Parrington spoke of the "different path" America must take, he described a future far from the inevitable classless Utopia expected by the Marxists. He had understood "something of the interplay of economic forces and the significance of class ideologies, but his concept was not comprehensive," and so his ultimate position could not be satisfactory. Nor would his American tradition fit comfortably the masters of the new decade.

"Any Marxist knows what the 'different path' must be," Hicks asserted with a confidence he later retracted. But the role the writer and his critics should play in leading society along this path was not always equally certain. Floyd Dell and Max Eastman, for instance, thought the revolution could best be served by the absolute autonomy of the artist, that the poet must necessarily fail when his art is too directly subservient to party dogma. This attitude dominated the left in the early years of the *New Masses'* rebellion against what Eastman called "middle class monotonies," and it flared up again in the mid-1930s when the *Partisan Review* finally split from the *New Masses*. The *Partisan* group protested, they wrote, "against the official idea of art as an instrument of political propaganda" and the practice of Michael Gold and others of condoning bad art for reasons of political expediency. For them Marxism was merely "a method of analysis."

For left writers whose national identity outweighed their interest in things Russian, the creation of a usable past was a pressing issue. "It seems to me," Dos Passos wrote,

> that Marxians who attempt to junk the American tradition, that I admit is full of dry rot as well as sap, like any tradition, are just cutting themselves off from the continent. Somebody's got to have the size to Marxianize the American tradition.

"We do need tradition," V. F. Calverton agreed, "but it must be a new tradition in consonance with the new age. The task that confronts us is to establish that tradition."

The two most frequently discussed—and abused—attempts to formulate a Marxist literary heritage for America were Calverton's *The Liberation of American Literature* (1932) and Granville Hicks's *The Great Tradition* (1933). Calverton explicitly sets out

> to interpret American literature in terms of American culture. . . . It is only by an appreciation of the class psychologies dominant at the time, as Marx has shown, that we can understand the nature of a culture or the direction and trend of a literature.

Calverton's resemblance to Parrington manifests itself on nearly every page, and he follows Parrington in calling his book social history rather than literary criticism. There is a fundamental difference, however, between *The Liberation* and *Main Currents*. Calverton, Hicks and Parrington agreed that taste has a social basis and, in Calverton's words, "can only be significant when derived from a sound social philosophy." But where Parrington put his faith in the liberal motivation of the individual, the Marxists saw a healthy future solely in class terms, in the freedom from economic restraint that only man in the mass could win. Thus Calverton finds his literary heroes in the writers of the frontier, Artemus Ward, Whitman, Twain and Joaquin Miller, who helped the national literature escape the "colonial complex" of New England's aristocratic individualism by establishing the larger class independence of the bourgeoisie.

> The faith in the common man which Emerson and Whitman entertained was faith in him as an individual and not as a mass. . . . In that sense, their faith was founded upon a false premise; fitting and persuasive enough in their generation it led only to disaster in the next. . . . Their belief in the common man was a belief in him as a petty bourgeois individualist; our belief must be in him as proletarian collectivist. In that belief lies the ultimate liberation of American literature—and American life.

The same year *The Great Tradition* appeared, Hicks outlined his critical principles in the *New Masses*. "An adequate portrayal of life as it is would lead the proletarian reader to recognize his role in the class struggle," he writes:

> Therefore a book should be judged by its ability to have that kind of effect. . . . The critic . . . will insist on intensity: the author must be able to make the reader feel that he is participating in the lives described whether they are the lives of bourgeois or of proletarians. . . . And, inasmuch as literature grows out of the author's entire personality, his identification with the proletariat should be as complete as possible. He should not merely believe in the cause of the proletariat; he should be, or should try to make himself, a member of the proletariat.

Hicks's allegiance to this recipe in *The Great Tradition* is uneven; he judges principally on "centrality of subject matter." His tradition is confined to those we might call industrial realists, and a writer rises —but generally falls—by how much cognizance his work takes of the major historical development of the nineteenth and twentieth centuries, the growth of machine civilization.

Hicks's book is a good deal more penetrating and readable than Calverton's, but it is ultimately not much more than a sensitive rewriting. If we have made his approach seem simple and automatic, it is because we agree with Stanley Edgar Hyman in regarding Hicks and Calverton as mechanical Marxists. Hicks was, to use a phrase he once applied to another, a young man in search of certainty. Many of the left writers shared with Calverton and Hicks the sense of standing at the crossroads of history, since the momentum of earlier American art and life seemed clearly played out. The future could belong only to the left, for only the left showed any signs of vitality. "Revolutionary literature marks a new beginning," Hicks concluded:

> It is, in part and however imperfectly, something unprecedented in human culture, and what is new in it will grow into what is still newer and far greater. But it is also the only possible fulfillment of the spirit that moves in the noblest creations of all American writers.

Hicks's certainty, like Calverton's, lay in the confidence that he could identify these noblest creations by testing them against a fully comprehensible reality. The sterility of their approach comes not from the theories they sought to apply but from their limited conception of what is real. The Marxist world of the 1930s was a world preoccupied solely with the play of economic forces; the only place for literature in such a world was as a weapon in class warfare. "Things are what they are and nothing else," Lionel Trilling writes in description of another Marxist, Bernard Smith. "That things are what they mean, that things are what they make us do or what we do with them, Mr. Smith does not want to believe."

A central literary irony of the decade is that the left and the nearly-left failed to recognize their most threatening opposition. The real enemy was just consolidating its social views as the 1930s opened. Hicks followed Calverton in casting a brief glance at the Fugitive-

Agrarians of Tennessee: they "may deserve whatever admiration one can accord to a quixotic gesture," but "they . . . demonstrate that regionalism is meaningless as a literary program unless it can be founded on economic and political realities." The left critics did not see the threat because the threat was not political, but before the decade was out the Fugitive-Agrarian–New Critics would sweep all before them and be well on the way to absolute control of the American literary scene.

If the Marxists mistook their enemy, there was no such confusion on the part of the twelve Southerners who issued *I'll Take My Stand* (1930). Until the final editorial meeting, the title for the collection of essays was to be "Tracts against Communism" or something similar. For Allen Tate, John Crowe Ransom, Donald Davidson, Robert Penn Warren and the others, there were few values more central than social stability. Like the Humanists they saw science, industrialism and optimistic liberalism as prime threats to this stability, and they did not need to be reminded by Babbitt or More that the leading champions of machine civilization were working from the political and literary left.

Ransom, Davidson, Tate and Warren came by their political commitment gradually; their association was originally solely literary. As members of the Fugitive group at Vanderbilt, they met regularly with poets and those interested in poetry and poetic form. Between 1922 and 1925 these sixteen poets managed to publish nineteen issues of *The Fugitive,* a triumph in endurance for the decade's exclusively literary little magazines. Reminiscing some years later, Allen Tate said, "I think that I may disregard the claims of propriety and say quite plainly that, so far as I know, there was never so much talent, knowledge, and character accidentally brought together at one American place in our time."

During the Fugitive years industrialism was making rapid inroads in the South. With industrialism, Davidson recalled later, came

advocacy of a collectivist type of government, thoroughly materialist and antireligious in philosophy, controlling education and the arts no less than the means of production, and founded upon a dialectic that would insist on a complete break with the historic continuity of Western civilization.

Collectivism was making its bid under the guise of nineteenth century liberalism, and there were very few in the South able to recognize the danger and move to the defense. "At the time," Davidson continues,

> it was thoroughly surprising to some of us in the fugitive group of poets. We had been devoting ourselves almost entirely to poetry and criticism without giving much attention to public affairs. We rubbed our eyes and looked around in astonishment and apprehension. Was it possible that nobody in the South knew how to reply?

Fugitive poetry itself—poems like Tate's "Ode to the Confederate Dead" (1926) and Ransom's "Antique Harvesters" (1927)—contained the beginning of a response. The then-imagist John Gould Fletcher saw as much when he enlarged upon the group's obvious debt to Eliot:

> Where he was an uprooted expatriate, seeking for eternal and absolute values in a world that had gone back to chaos, they still kept a local point of reference for their art, in the shape of their feeling for the Old South and its Tradition.

But the major impulse moving Fugitive poet toward Agrarian social theorist came from outside the group. With the Scopes "monkey trial" of 1925 and the abuse it brought the South from, among others, H. L. Mencken, the leading spirits of the now defunct *Fugitive* began more and more to turn their attention to the modern world around them. It seemed clear to all of them that the South must be defended in historical terms, that, as Davidson had it, "some true and commanding image of its past must be restored." "I've attacked the South for the last time," Tate wrote to Davidson in March 1927, "except in so far as it may be necessary to point out that the chief defect the Old South had was that in it which produced, through whatever cause, the New South." Davidson replied, "You know that I'm with you on the anti–New South stuff. . . . I feel so strongly on these points that I can hardly trust myself to write." At almost precisely the same moment, Ransom was writing to Tate,

> Our cause is . . . the Old South. . . . Our fight is for survival; and it's got to be waged not so much against the Yankees as against the exponents of the New South. . . . We must think about this business and take some very long calculations ahead.

While the calculations were going forward, Tate examined the South's heritage in *Stonewall Jackson: The Good Soldier* (1928) and *Jefferson Davis: His Rise and Fall* (1929). At the same time he was reviewing a host of Civil War books, books of political and social speculation and books on the history of the South. In 1929 Robert Penn Warren contributed *John Brown: The Making of a Martyr*, in which he pointed out the danger of an idealism that is divorced from a sense of human community.

The "stand" that emerged in 1930 was, as the symposium's subtitle has it, for "The South and the Agrarian Tradition." That the "agrarian" label was a poor choice hardly needs to be repeated. It invited the charge of reaction, an attack which took too simple a view of the values asserted. It was not the drudgery or hardship of the farm that the twelve Southerners meant to defend, but the simplicity and cultural integrity of the husbandman's world view. The way to express the issue, runs the book's statement of purpose, is agrarian *versus* industrial. In a later debate with Stringfellow Barr, Ransom made clear the direction Southern industrialization—the "New South"—was taking. "Big business . . . which every day becomes bigger business, will call for regulation, which every day will become more regulation. And the grand finale of regulation, the millennium itself of regulated industrialism, is Russian communism."

After the late years of the 1930s—perhaps it was the collapse of Seward Collins's conservative *American Review,* perhaps it was the steadily diminishing threat from the left—these critics wrote less and less about political and social issues. But when the Fugitives became Agrarians, they did not lose their passionate concern for literature, and when the Agrarians became "New Critics," or "Aesthetic Formalist Critics," they did not give up their interest in the health of American society—they remained the conservative regionalists they had been from the beginning. In 1945 Ransom might repudiate his agrarianism as a "phantasy," but only because it had no chance of success. "The agrarian nostalgia," he felt, was still "very valuable," for it focused attention on the role the arts can play in expiation of the crimes of science. "The modes of art and politics have always, as now, been mixed," Tate wrote as early as 1933; "but no other age seems to have lost as completely as we have lost it, the distinction between the two modes." The Fugitive-Agrarian–New Critics never lost the distinction between the two modes. Their persistent attention to the aesthetic dimensions of literature distinguished them from the other major critical movements of the century. And their taste came eventually to dominate the 1940s and 1950s and shape the thinking of later decades.

There had been critics before in America who had defended the aesthetic autonomy of literature. Poe, for instance, had felt that as a special form of knowledge, a poem does not need an "ulterior motive";

> the simple fact is, that, would we but permit ourselves to look into our own souls, we should immediately there discover that . . . there neither exists nor *can* exist any work more thoroughly dignified . . . than . . . this poem *per se* . . . which is a poem and nothing more . . . written solely for the poem's sake.

A similar view can be found in the work of Henry James, in many ways the central hero of the twentieth-century aesthetic tradition. And it can be found in Spingarn, Stein, Eliot, Pound and the other writers, at home or abroad, who filled many of the little magazines before the Depression. But it was not until about 1938, with the publication of *Understanding Poetry,* the immensely successful poetry text of Cleanth Brooks and Robert Penn Warren, that this strain of American criticism reached full strength. As this text came more and more to dominate the teaching of literature in the college classroom, the aesthetic position acquired a methodology and was well on its way to clearing the field of all other approaches to the appreciation and understanding of literature.

The New Critics did not lose interest in politics and theology, but rather, following the early Eliot, they tried to compartmentalize their concerns and separate their literary criticism from their analysis of American life. "I have assigned the critic a modest, though I think an important, role," Cleanth Brooks explained. As a man, the critic is of course interested in and pursues other interests. But as a professional critic he must tell us "what the work is and how the parts of it are related." This is essentially the argument by which Brooks and the other early New Critics sought to confine themselves to what can be done with some objectivity and assurance, the argument which kept their attention focused on the private difficulties of Modernist poetry rather than the distracting cultural density of prose. In the hands of their less gifted disciples, this new critical credo ultimately led back to much the same genteel separation of literature from American life with which the century began. But as we shall see, developments of the past two decades that clearly rest upon the work of Eliot, Ransom and their fellows are often distinguished from it in what has come to seem a ritual killing of the fathers. Despite the views of recent ahistorical commentators, "autonomy" for the first New Critics did not mean placing poetry "in a vacuum." It meant only that they sought, as Malcolm Cowley observed about the entire formalist tradition, "to establish literature as an independent country, with a history and geography of its own." Allen Tate made the case every formalist from Poe to the present would urge against those whose readings of literary works center on the implications of their paraphrasable contents. Paul Elmer More "is primarily a moralist, which is a worthy and serious thing to be," Tate observed. But "his failure to understand the significance of style is a failure to understand most of the literature he has read."

The New Critics' insistence that the literary work represents an autonomous entity, linked to the workaday world in its genesis and materials but separable for purposes of examination, led to the method of critical explication presented in *Understanding Poetry* and its innumerable successors. Following the lead of Eliot and traditional rhetorical analysis—drawing, that is, on some of the same legacy employed by Kenneth Burke and Chicago neo-Aristotelians like R. S. Crane, Richard McKeon, Elder Olson, Norman Maclean and Wayne Booth —Brooks and Warren demonstrated a fine-toothed verbal analysis of individual poems. The works treated are usually short, often by Eliot's favorites, the English Metaphysicals. In the rhetorical ironies of Donne's densely packed lines, the rich resources of verbal play create mutually limiting tensions that the critic examines and describes as a universe unto itself. For the second-generation New Critics in the 1950s, the method would often become tediously mechanical and bloodless, but when used by what came to be called "good readers," the poetry being scrutinized yielded wonders of implication; the whole emerged as richly superior to the sum of its parts, with easy separation of content and form disappearing as varied elements fused into meaning.

In 1941—the year in which the United States entered the Second World War, when the Depression and the spirit of the 1930s already had begun to fade—two books appeared that put the critical contention and dialogue of the interwar years into perspective. One was John Crowe Ransom's *The New Criticism*, which not only settled the name of what had come to be called the "formalists," but gave them a history and a usable past going back to the "aesthetic existentialism" of the leading figures of the modern movement—Eliot, Pound, Stein, Hulme, Henry James. Two years before, Cleanth Brooks had demonstrated that the art of Modernism demanded a "radical revision of the existing conception of poetry." Now Ransom made it clear that a literary text was a way of knowing all its own, that reading it fully meant more than locating it socially, politically or philosophically. He also made it clear that criticism itself, in the growing university system, had become an institution, that there was now something that could be called "Criticism, Inc." By the 1950s the New Criticism had become an academic convention, continuing the reinterpretation of the Modern movement and concentrating attention on both the complexity and the dissent that literature could embody. In magazines like *The Kenyon Review* it represented the antithesis but also the complement to the arguments of the more historicist critics of the *Partisan Review* who continued to debate the role of the critic as public intellectual in an age when Marxism had become "the God that failed."

The other book of 1941 which seemed to sum up the position American literary interpretation had come to was F. O. Matthiessen's *American Renaissance,* a large study of "art and expression in the Age of Emerson and Whitman." Matthiessen mediated between the two contending traditions, the social currents of Parrington, the formalist readings of the New Critics. In the work of Emerson, Thoreau, Hawthorne, Melville and Whitman he identified a single concentrated moment of American expression, complex and elusive in its artistry, cultural in its force. Matthiessen was a liberal well aware of the threat of war, and he believed that the question of a creative national tradition was of crucial importance. He insisted that an artist's use of form and language was the most sensitive index of cultural history, and he argued that his central group of authors, in complexity and even dissent, had created a literature for democracy. Writing with critical judgment and deep cultural insight, he constructed a vision of American literature's usable past that with Parrington's was to shape the compendious *Literary History of the United States* (1948) and nourish the American Studies movement of the 1950s. Bringing these writers, some of them still on the fringes of discussion, to a central position in their own forming culture and in American national history, Matthiessen provided American writing with a definitive, unmistakable and powerful heritage, a formed literary tradition—no longer uncertain, tentative or too disordered to guide the present. The contemporary American writer had gained an artistic and a cultural basis, fashioned not only from the past but from the vital tensions of two contentious decades.

·11·

STRANGE REALITIES,
ADEQUATE FICTIONS

·I·

When the twentieth century opened, the United States was still a provincial country, though that provinciality was fading fast. Despite its 200,000 miles of railroad track, more than all of Europe, two-thirds of its 76 million people still lived in rural farm communities or small towns. Though there were 8,000 horseless carriages and 154,000 miles of surfaced road, the big city was often far distant, Europe remote, the Pacific unimagined, and most lives were lived in a single place. Now, as the twentieth century comes to its end and the prospects for the new millennium show over the horizon, the picture is profoundly different. Most of America's 250 million inhabitants live very mobile lives, in cities or suburban extensions of large metropolitan areas. They own more than 100 million automobiles and drive on some three million miles of highway; more land is now paved than remains in virgin wilderness. At the beginning of the century, they lived in a terrestrial world; now they live in the age of global space, of moonshots and the lunar module. They live at the center of a network of world communications linked by plane and satellite technology, microchip messaging, interactive video or fax, an age of polyglot noise and hypercommunication. At the beginning of the century it was thought American technologies would transform the twentieth century; they did. Biotechnology, cloning, cryonics and *in vitro* fertilization have changed the physiological rules of existence. For the fifty years following the Second World War, America has been a world-shaping superpower. Its citizens are thought by many in the world to lead typically Postmodern lives and to represent the essential principles and life-styles of late Modern capitalism. American culture, aided by possession both of the English language, the main world language, and the newer languages of communications technology, reaches everywhere, whether it is popular, serious, seriopopular or any mixture of both. American writing has reflected this position of power, growing more open to history, to the global proliferation of styles and forms, to the sometimes exhilarating and sometimes depressing new span of human curiosity.

Far away now from the experimental excitements of the 1920s and the dismayed, radical self-analysis of the 1930s, late-1940s America entered an era of postwar, postatomic and Postmodern culture. War restored the economic base, and since 1945 the American economy, with whatever jitters, has boomed. To be sure, the world's warlike atmosphere did not disperse in 1945, and a prolonged period of cold war fixed ideological opinion in a mind-set that is only now beginning to dissolve. But for a time, American society and American experience seemed placed well in advance of the experience of most others in the world; Europe had been left in ruins, once-colonial empires had to reshape and rediscover myriad cultural identities, and the rebuilding of the world's geopolitical map left confusion and chaos. In more recent years, as material wealth and modern technologies have reached worldwide, American historical leadership has changed. American lives now no longer seem quite so exceptional, and many feel that American power has been overextended and so has strained the nation's economic base. At various times in this postwar world, it has seemed that an old history was over. Daniel Bell at the end of the 1950s wrote of "the End of Ideology," and more lately we have heard of "the End of History" and even "the End of Philosophy," the coming of a phase where some of the extreme ideological oppositions forged in the history of the twentieth century have begun to dissolve along with the comfortable certitude that sustained them. What does seem certain is that the long-lived "Postwar world" is now over, and that a new era is in the process of formation.

The remarkable upheavals of war undoubtedly changed the spirit and direction of all American writing. As William Faulkner said, wars are not good for the novel, and the great shift from the Depression of the 1930s to wartime economy changed the basis of all the literary arts. Many writers served as war correspondents, and many others went abroad on active service. The aftermath of war, and above all the sudden awareness of the two great horrors it had left behind, the genocide of the Holocaust and the threat of nuclear annihilation, brought a terrible sobriety to all artistic and intellectual life. The war had stimulated many new technologies and vastly expanded American influence and world awareness. What followed the war was an age of materialism, military expansion, ideological anxiety and a sense of the rapid transformation of consciousness. This was an age of the media, the instant record, the new message system, the multiplication of styles, the accelerating confusion of levels of reality. As writers increasingly began to observe, it was an era in which reality came increasingly to resemble unreality, when actuality frequently outpaced the writer's ability to image it and fiction needed to become superfiction to cope with an ever more fictional age of history.

In intellectual life, the sense that all realities were constituting fictions was a notion not confined to artists alone—nor journalists (we had the "new journalism"), nor historians (we had the "new history"). Thomas Kuhn's *The Structure of Scientific Revolutions* (1962) had enormous influence by making it clear that science was not, and never had been, the possessor of certain truths, but rather fictive "paradigms." Mathematics examined the fiction of numbers, linguists described the slippage of words, architects learned the vast simultaneity of all styles and the certainty of none, as codes gave way to decodes. Quotation and parody, redundancy or dreck seemed the stuff of which the fable of life was made. The human self became an organic-cell, style-based object; the loss of the subject seemed a universal condition. "To see the gods dispelling in mid-air and dissolve like clouds," Wallace Stevens wrote, "is one of the great human experiences. . . . It was their annihilation, not ours, and yet it left us feeling that in a measure, we, too, had been annihilated." The gods that dissolved like clouds were not simply the gods of faith and theology. The limits of earth-based experience, of body-based consciousness, of the Eurocentric world, the Judaeo-Christian heritage, the humanist hierarchy, also shifted, much as Ptolemy's Earth found itself only one of many planets in the universe. In areas like anthropology, linguistics and comparative religion, from Franz Boas's *The Mind of Primitive Man* (1911) to Claude Lévi-Strauss's *Structural Anthropology* (1958), there was an insistent sense of relativity about cultural truth—much as Mandelbrot brought relativity to mathematical truth and Heisenberg to the law of physics. The whole new discourse of ideas brought writers face-to-face with Henry Adams's "multiverse," William James's "pluriverse."

"One geometry cannot be more true than another," Henri Poincaré had concluded in 1902. "It can only be more convenient." By mid-century, many came to see truth as James had described it, as a workable relationship in time with no knowable a priori or absolute status. The only reality that can be known is a contingent synthesis rescued by sheer force of human will from a Heraclitean ocean of flux. We are all, it seems, artists constructing homemade worlds of human design—much as Whitman and earlier Romantics had insisted we are, but now with chilling literalness that only courage like James's can embrace with enthusiasm. After Wallace Stevens, the word frequently used to describe the fabrications we inhabit is *fictions,* a synonym for belief whose ontological basis rests on the willed and timebound conviction of individual human minds. Onto an actual world we can never know, we project meanings which constitute all there is for us of reality; we formulate and reformulate from the flux of impressions the fiction that for us proves adequate, sufficient, if never quite supremely perfect.

By mid-century, the word *fiction* pointed everywhere to an epistemological sea change of truly revolutionary proportions. The postwar world, the cultural drive toward what has become known as the Postmodern, can be viewed as opposed responses to the challenge of heterodoxy, a root disagreement reducible to the distinction between the adjectives *the* and *a:* Is reality single and ultimately knowable? Is truth therefore verifiable and constant; or is it multiple and timebound? And finally, the question as central to interpretation in life as in art, can we hope for *the* meaning of a historical event or poem, or must we make do as best we can with *a* meaning? The implications of this simple distinction seem likely to alter irreversibly the future America her writers will endeavor to write into knowable existence. If the age before 1941 had been an age of the Modern, this was, the critics began to tell us, an age of the Postmodern.

· II ·

With the Japanese attack on American bases at Pearl Harbor in 1941 American life became irrevocably implicated in the disorders, the historical redirections, the confusions of the later-twentieth-century globe. With whatever misgivings about risking its special Western destiny, America now committed herself to the Allied cause in what quickly became a Second World War, and it became evident that a last stage in national innocence was over forever. The dying of an era, the fading of an earlier modern notion of American writing, was signaled by the deaths of several of the leading figures of previous decades: Scott Fitzgerald and Nathanael West died within a few days of each other in 1940, Sherwood Anderson in 1941 and then Gertrude Stein in 1946. Modernism itself seemed almost over, even though some important figures, from Faulkner to Eliot to William Carlos Williams, wrote on. And not just the experimentalism of the 1920s but the radical liberalism of the 1930s now found itself out of touch with the climate of cold war and new affluence. There was now a new liberalism, bloodied and anxious, shaken by the vision of human nature the war had left and by the expansion of Soviet power through Eastern Europe in the 1940s. Intellectuals themselves were humiliated by the new anti-intellectualism manifested by Senator Joseph McCarthy and the witch hunts of the 1950s, demanding confessions for "un-American activities" from the intellectual survivors of the 1930s. In this new climate, many wondered if writing could find its authority again or the avant-garde recover its voice. In his *After the Lost Generation* (1951) John Aldridge argued that the era of avant-gardism was now over and America no longer had sufficient moral or mythic power to create a serious art, while Malcolm Cowley in *The Literary Situation* (1954) saw with remarkable prescience that the fading of the experimental climate, the narrowing of ideological discussion and the co-opting of intellectuals away from the magazines and into the universities meant that the new age would not be less one of creation than of academic literary criticism.

The postwar mood was already being signaled in the literature of wartime. In Saul Bellow's first novel, *Dangling Man* (1944), the Kafka-esque hero, Joseph, finds his old political faiths and friends useless in time of war and retreats into a disorganized and lonely despair, until he is called for military service—which he welcomes in relief, crying "Long live regimentation!" Norman Mailer's powerful novel about the Pacific battlefront, *The Naked and the Dead* (1948), shows feeble liberalism giving way to new militarism, while in *Barbary Shore* (1951) his hero discovers he is lost in "the air of our time, authority and nihilism stalking one another in the orgiastic hollow of this century." As America rose in power, writers and their fictional heroes frequently declined into anxiety, hoarding, as Saul Bellow would put it, their spiritual valuables. As Malcolm Cowley pointed out, the new novel of war lacked the experimental vigor and the sense of personal crisis that had marked the war fiction of the 1920s. Instead, in many of these works—Irwin Shaw's *The Young Lions* (1948), Herman Wouk's *The Caine Mutiny* (1951), James Jones's *From Here to Eternity* (1951) and so on to Joseph Heller's *Catch-22* (1961)—the enemy seemed less the Germans, Italians or the Japanese than the American military machine itself and its continuance into the cold-war world to follow. Few of these works had any claim to experimentalism, though the surreal energy of John Hawkes's fine novel of postwar disorder *The Cannibal* (1949) and the moral squalor of some of J. D. Salinger's *Nine Stories* (1953) began to hint at some of the vigor to come. Theater looked at the hidden corruptions of war in Arthur Miller's *All My Sons* in 1949 and at the disquieting implications of the material American Dream in *Death of a Salesman* (1950). War poetry also betrayed the crisis of personal meaning felt by many. Randall Jarrell's poem in *Little Friend, Little Friend* (1945), "The Death of the Ball Turret Gunner," summed up the mood: "From my mother's sleep I fell into the State . . ./When I died they washed me out of the turret with a hose."

There was thus little buoyancy in the literary recording of the circumstances and atmosphere of America's rise to world influence. For much of this new writing, the naturalism of the 1930s, shorn now of some of its ideological conviction, seemed appropriate to capture a world of new historical horror, moral pain and rising alienation. Urban writing concentrated on the darkness and disconnection of the

American city, for instance in Nelson Algren's Chicago novel *The Man with the Golden Arm* (1949) or Saul Bellow's *The Victim* (1947). In the South, agrarianism offered no comfort. Carson McCullers's *The Heart Is a Lonely Hunter* (1949) and *The Member of the Wedding* (1946), Eudora Welty's *The Robber Bridegroom* (1942) and *Delta Wedding* (1946), Flannery O'Connor's *Wise Blood* (1952) and "A Good Man Is Hard to Find" (1955), showed that the flowering of Southern talent and the Southern sense of form were not over, but these books offered a dismayed, disturbing moral vision that passed on to Truman Capote, Walker Percy and James Dickey. A sense of spiritual emptiness and haunting evil, of failed love and broken connections, dominates *The Heart Is a Lonely Hunter* and several other of these books. A similar mood shapes the work of J. D. Salinger, one of the most striking talents of the time, whose *The Catcher in the Rye* (1951) became the student classic of an anxious age in which the very business of growing out of childhood innocence seemed to be a pathway not to experience but corruption. Salinger wrote, he indicated, of "love and squalor," and love and squalor dominate a good deal of this fiction—a fiction of troubled realism that fitted a time of continuing nuclear threat, lost historical optimism and a pervasive sense of human evil. A strong philosophical influence came from French existentialism, with its vision of the absurd, and the French novels of Jean-Paul Sartre and Albert Camus and the writing of Samuel Beckett, who carried the Modernist spirit forward into these darker days, encouraged this feeling. As W. H. Auden said in a poem born out of his expatriation to America, this was "the Age of Anxiety."

American fiction was attempting to express a world which brought home the urgency of history but offered few confident hopes of its prospects. Some of the best writing came from those who felt their kinship to the victims of the recent past—above all the Jewish-American writers, whose postwar work can often be read as an indirect version of the war novel, a fiction of shaken survivors hunting for the recovery of moral truths, speaking indirectly for the six million victims of a totalitarian age which had not fully disappeared. From the 1890s Jewish-American writing had been an important part of American expression, but it reached a remarkable flowering after 1945. There was the poetry of Delmore Schwartz, Theodore Roethke and many more and the forceful drama of Arthur Miller, but above all it found its expression in the novel. No longer predominantly a literature of immigration, the new Jewish-American writing concentrated on the nature of the American Dream, the rise of materialism, the experience of the modern city, the bonds that linked person to person in the moral chain. It documented alienation and disaffiliation but spoke, too, of new American opportunities and possibilities. It drew not only on the intellectual heritage of American writing and the line of naturalism, but on the Modernism of Europe, the heritage of Marx, Freud and Einstein. Many writers of lasting importance emerged: Saul Bellow, Arthur Miller, Bernard Malamud, Norman Mailer, Delmore Schwartz, Allen Ginsberg, Meyer Levin, Herbert Gold, Edward Louis Wallant, Chaim Potok, Stanley Elkin, Joseph Heller, E. L. Doctorow, Grace Paley, Tillie Olsen, Cynthia Ozick, along with critics like Lionel Trilling, Irving Howe, Alfred Kazin and Philip Rahv. Not a few of these had belonged to the left in the 1930s and been associated with magazines like *Partisan Review*. During the 1940s their emphasis shifted from Marxism to Modernism in general and to a concern with what Rahv called "the sixth sense," the awareness of history itself. Their Europeanism was reinforced by the influence of writers like Isaac Bashevis Singer, whose fiction built the bridge between prewar Poland and modern New York, and of other Jewish writers who had lived and died in the turmoils of Europe: Isaac Babel, Bruno Schultz, Franz Kafka—writers whose sense of history had been wedded to guilt and pain, suffering and black humor.

Postwar Jewish writing is generally marked by its concern with the historical, the moral and the human anxieties of the modern self and therefore has sometimes been described as displaying a return to realism in the contemporary American novel. If this is so, it is generally a realism that contains a metaphysical vigor and a surreal inner agony of the kind that Kafka brought to the modern novel. It is a fiction that still remembers the old myth of the American New World, the place of freedom from persecution and bondage, though in modern material America the dream now takes quirkier forms. In Philip Roth's *Goodbye, Columbus* the old dream has become a story of affluent Jewry awash in the "swamp of prosperity." In Malamud's *A New Life* the urban Jew comically tries to re-create the frontier myth of the West—and betrays and is betrayed by the now much more labyrinthine dream. Re-creating the idealism of a migrant's America, many of these books portray a world of arbitrary wealth or poverty which is now historically confident but spiritually incomplete. Often using the pained wit of Jewish humor, they express moral aspiration and vivid humanism but also a fear of victimization and sterility. The existential rage of Norman Mailer's novels, the nameless unease of Joseph Heller's *Something Happened* (1974), the cemetery wit of Stanley Elkin's fiction, the constant allusion in Philip Roth's novels to the ghosts of a cruel history, all form part of their report on contemporary American life. One clear feature of much of this writing is that it is moral rather than political in its spirit both of criticism and affirmation. (Lionel Trilling in his influential work of criticism, *The Liberal Imagination* [1950], had summoned novelists back from naive ideology to what he called "moral realism.") In time political realities were to return; E. L. Doctorow's work of fiction-and history *The Book of Daniel* (1971), for instance, is concerned both with the Jewish tradition and the ritual execution of the Rosenbergs as Russian spies in the 1950s. Typically, though—Bernard Malamud's fiction is notable in this respect—the enduring question of the relationship between social and artistic responsibility is kept alive. What, collectively, Jewish-American fiction brought to the American novel was a nexus of art and politics, history and moral and psychic self-knowledge which encouraged and helped establish a more complex, less ideological vision of reality.

In this evolution, a central figure was undoubtedly Isaac Bashevis Singer. Born in Poland, he was one of many mid-1930s exiles from Europe to the United States who changed its mental and artistic life. After his arrival in 1935, he continued to write—many novels and a wide range of short stories—in Yiddish. A significant part of his fiction—*The Family Moskat* (in English, 1950), the stories of *Gimpel the Fool* (1957)—deals with the often bizarre and superstitious world of peasant and ghetto Poland; another part, including many of his best short stories, explores modern urban America with a similarly impish sense of estrangement. Singer's highly imaginative influence reaches far, into the poetic prose of Delmore Schwartz (*The World Is a Wedding*, 1948) and the zany dark comedy of Stanley Elkin (*A Bad Man*, 1967; *The Rabbi of Lud*, 1988; *The MacGuffin*, 1991), the soul-searching hunger to understand history and the modern self in Saul Bellow (*Henderson the Rain King*, 1954; *Humboldt's Gift*, 1975; *More Die of Heartbreak*, 1987) and the searching novels and stories of Bernard Malamud (*The Assistant*, 1957; *A New Life*, 1961; *Dubin's Lives*, 1979). Dealing very directly with Jewish mores and types, these works draw magical or mythic elements from the European Yiddish tradition that give them a cosmopolitan breadth. They contain as well a persistent ethical strain: "He asked himself a question I still would like answered, namely, 'How should a good man live, what ought he to do?' " reflects the hero of Bellow's first novel *Dangling Man* (1944). Bellow, perhaps the most important single novelist of the American postwar period, and like Singer himself a Nobel prizewinner, was an early translator of one of Singer's most enduring stories, "Gimpel the Fool," a portrait of the Jewish schlemiel or wise fool who appears in much of this fiction.

Bellow was born in Canada, moved in childhood to Chicago, about which he frequently writes, and published his first story in *Partisan Review* before he established himself as a novelist with *Dangling Man*. That wartime book shows several influences: something of Singer, something of Dreiser in its urban naturalism, something of Kafka in its sense of estrangement from reality and its steady retreat from life into solitude. Ever since that book, Bellow's work, which now covers six decades, has traced postwar American life from the urban deprivation of ordinary Jews in the late 1940s to the wealth-laden supercities of contemporary America, where, he has said, there is more of the it than the we. The books also moved from the moral discovery of common humanity in the postwar stories to tales of spiritual discovery and transcendental adventure in the more exotic intellectual climate of the later, post-space-shot world. Roughly his work can be divided into two groups: the darker novels of soul-searching, like *Dangling Man, The Victim* (1947) and *Mr. Sammler's Planet* (1970), and the more epically inclined novels either of picaresque or mental adventure, like *The Adventures of Augie March* (1953) or his reflection on American Modernism and what succeeds it, *Humboldt's Gift* (1975). Both meet in what is probably his best work, *Herzog* (1964), the story of the "suffering joker" Moses Herzog, who, caught in "a shameless and impotent privacy" that leads him nearly to madness, is still capable of analyzing the intellectual heritage of popular and egotistical modern romanticism which has led him to despair. Herzog's attempt to resist exotic modern apocalypticism and too-easy alienation draws him into a transcendental silence, as, in this ambitious book, Bellow seeks a way toward inner understanding past all the "five-cent syntheses" so readily available in the modern world. With this novel Bellow showed himself a serious analyst of Byzantine modern confusions in the world of cultural pluralism and stylish prescriptions for selfhood. Later books like *The Dean's December* (1982), contrasting Eastern European political impotence with Western moral impotence, and *More Die of Heartbreak* (1987), a study of the torments of the mind in a world of confused modern sexuality, show his persistent vision of private wealth and spiritual sterility and his continuing quest for transcendental recuperation, even if it takes him (as it does in this last novel) to the margins of polar isolation.

The tradition of postwar Jewish-American fiction has endured through the various stylistic surges of the recent American novel, perhaps because it has assumed that the function of the novel is eternally serious, even though it can be intellectually playful. Bernard Malamud also wrote in a variety of modes, from the neonaturalism of his early work *The Assistant* (1957), to the skeptical meditation on biography and art of *Dubin's Lives* (1979). Art and the world of dross from which it comes has been a recurrent theme of Malamud's work, most playfully addressed in the stories of *Pictures of Fidelman* (1969). Similar half-guilty concerns with the relation of art to life also run through the work of Philip Roth, who established himself in the stories of *Goodbye, Columbus* (1959). Roth, too, showed himself to have a great repertory of techniques; a Jamesian moral vision informs *Letting Go* (1962) and *When She Was Good* (1967), while surreal and Kafkaesque experiment dominates *The Breast* (1972). Roth once remarked that America's actuality constantly outdid any literary realism: "The American writer in the middle of the twentieth century has his hands full in trying to understand, describe and then make *credible* much of the American reality." With the erotic *Portnoy's Complaint* (1968) he broke the mold of his earlier fiction, releasing it from ideas of "ethical Jewhood" to adventure among wild psychic urges. His various Zuckerman novels explored a fundamental Oedipal guilt about the critical offense of being a writer, and *My Life As a Man* (1974) and *The Counterlife* (1986) teased the entire notion that the life of the artist is one of formal and moral maturity, rather than of surreal self-confession. Though critical opinion has frequently tried to distinguish such writing from experimental Postmodernist fiction and define it as late-twentieth-century realism, it has very evidently been more than that. Artistic self-examination has been a strong element of most postwar Jewish fiction, from the writers mentioned previously to the work of Grace Paley (*The Little Disturbances of Man,* 1959; *Later the Same Day,* 1985), Tillie Olsen and Cynthia Ozick.

If one implication of the development of Jewish-American writing after 1945 is that a once marginal ethnic tradition has become central, much the same could be said of black American writing. Richard Wright had been the leading figure of the 1930s, but he bred many successors in the 1950s. Ralph Ellison's *Invisible Man* (1952) added to Wright's increasingly existential vision a Kafka-like absurdity by telling the story of a black whose color has rendered him invisible as a moral agent. A novel of existential namelessness, it recognized the universality of its central image: "Who knows but that . . . I speak for you?" For James Baldwin, the problem of the new black writer was to escape from the "cage" of humiliating conventions laid over black writing by white representation. Baldwin was the son of a bitter Harlem preacher, and his extraordinary and in many respects most successful novel *Go Tell It on the Mountain* (1953) re-creates the world of religion and urban poverty he knew in childhood. His subsequent novels— *Giovanni's Room* (1956), *Another Country* (1961), *Tell Me How Long the Train's Been Gone* (1968)—reveal his fictional form expanding and growing more polemical as his writing acquires a greater social and political rage. Baldwin possessed both a fine critical intelligence and a vigorous pulpit oratory, which he put to notable use in his deeply felt polemics on the issues of black identity and civil rights, *Nobody Knows My Name* (1961) and the apocalyptic *The Fire Next Time* (1963). Writing these at a time when civil rights protests and sit-ins were raising American consciousness of the plight of blacks, Baldwin not only called white consciences to account but played an important if sometimes contentious part in the rising movement of the black arts.

There were those, like Imamu Baraka (LeRoi Jones), who came to believe that a black separatism, a black writing for black audiences only, was the only way forward, but the most striking feature of the powerful black writing that has developed in the United States since the 1950s has been its breadth and variety. Chester Himes wrote his novels of protest—*If He Hollers Let Him Go* (1945)—but also became an important and successful detective story novelist (*The Real Cool Killers*, 1959). Ishmael Reed became a surreal experimentalist (*The Free-Lance Pallbearers*, 1967; *Mumbo Jumbo*, 1972) and Clarence Major (*All-Night Visitors*, 1969) a writer of self-reflective Postmodernism. In the 1960s, with the appearance of writers like Ernest Gaines and John A. Williams, a new black American writing began to flourish, much of it raising central questions of the historical identity of blacks in America and their chaotic urban life in the ghetto cities. In 1976 Alex Haley (*The Autobiography of Malcolm X*, 1965) published *Roots: The Saga of an American Family*, an enormously popular novel and television series that stimulated geneological interest among a wide range of American ethnic groups. Perhaps the most remarkable achievements of the 1970s and 1980s came with the emergence of several black women writers, including Toni Morrison (*Song of Solomon*, 1977; *Beloved*, 1987) and Alice Walker (*The Color Purple*, 1982).

There can be little doubt that the tensions of the Kennedy era did much to unsettle the postwar American novel and direct it toward new forms and methods. During the 1950s it was already apparent that American fiction expressed an edgy dissent and a world divided between personal experience and public events so vast and disturbing that, as Saul Bellow put it, "private life cannot maintain a pretence of its importance." It was perhaps not surprising that many American writers came to think of history as an absurd fiction, a massive plot that commanded the self while dissolving its sense of stable reality. Fiction undertook to reappraise the forces loose in the world and the individual's power to face them. William S. Burroughs's venomous satire *The Naked Lunch* (1959) and its various sequels traced the connections between anarchic inner space and overwhelming modern political systems. It was the beginning of a new mood, and in the following years works that mixed grotesque form with historical vision developed the theme. In 1961 Joseph Heller's cult classic *Catch-22* described contemporary America in a fantastic and wildly comic parable set on the Italian front in the Second World War. Kurt Vonnegut's *Mother*

Night (1961) and *Slaughterhouse Five* (1969) used the methods of what their author liked to call "gallows-humor" to explore the defeat of the self and of innocence by a historical world that could be counteracted only by the play of the imagination. Ken Kesey's *One Flew Over the Cuckoo's Nest* (1962) saw government as the totalitarian version of a madhouse, and the most remarkable new writer of the postwar years, Thomas Pynchon, attempted in *V.* (1963), *The Crying of Lot 49* (1966), *Gravity's Rainbow* (1973) and *Vineland* (1990) to give a parodic shape to the powers of world history, despite the entropic and disintegrating processes he discerned at work in it. In many such books, history is no longer a graspable progression but a stage set of lunacy and pain that turns the writer away from the immediacy of realism toward a mocking of the world's substance, a cartooning of character, a fantasizing of the "facts." This had implications as well for all forms of historical journalism. A period that had begun with John Hersey's documentary *Hiroshima* (1946) saw accurate reportage blur into the "non-fiction novel," as Truman Capote dubbed his *In Cold Blood* (1966), and the "real life novel," as Norman Mailer called his *The Executioner's Song* (1979). The elements that John Dos Passos in *U.S.A.* had categorically distinguished flowed together in a free interchange of historical data and imaginative fictionalizing, leading to the docudramas of cinema and television and the docufiction of William Styron's *The Confessions of Nat Turner* (1967), Robert Coover's *The Public Burning* (1977) and E. L. Doctorow's *The Book of Daniel* (1971), *Ragtime* (1975), and *Billy Bathgate* (1989).

In *The Armies of the Night* (1968), about a protest march on the Pentagon against the Vietnam War, Norman Mailer confronted the way "realities" are constructed by questioning the basic relation of historical actuality and fiction. Questions of reportorial subjectivity became overt in journalism itself, emerging in what Pete Hamill dubbed "the new journalism." For Tom Wolfe, its leading exponent, this displaced the "boring" novel by appropriating its methods of scene-by-scene construction, dramatic rendering of dialogue and detailed exploration of mores, style and status in order to record what he described, with characteristic *élan*, as "the crazed obscene uproarious Mammon-faced drug-soaked mau mau lust-oozing Sixties." Wolfe, along with other "new journalists" like Hunter S. Thompson,

Jimmy Breslin and Joan Didion (also a fine novelist), have tended to emphasize their stylistic innovations, but their chief contribution has been to define a journalism as willing to confess to its authorial subjectivity as were many of the "new histories" which were revising the nature of historiography. Thus it was possible to pursue the legacy of naturalism derived from Dreiser and Dos Passos while simultaneously drawing reportage toward the craft of fiction. This coincided with a turn away from conventional realism toward an emphasis on the "fictionality" of fiction, a move toward "fabulation" or "metafiction" generating a "self-reflexiveness" in the novel that recalled nothing so much as Laurence Sterne's *Tristram Shandy* (1759–67) and opened new freedoms of fantasy. Many have argued that fantasy is not so much an escape from reality as a way of interrogating the real, as Vonnegut does in *Slaughterhouse Five*. Much of this fiction thus becomes fantastic through its assault upon the historical and the real, while at the same time it makes clear that it derives from historical situations and processes. The gallows humor in writers like Vonnegut, Heller, Elkin, Thomas Berger and Bruce Jay Friedman was gradually replaced by a broad inquiry into fiction itself. Fiction began to celebrate its own loss of signification, sought to create independent worlds of textuality and consciousness and, in authors like Pynchon, John Barth, Robert Coover, William Gaddis, William H. Gass and Donald Barthelme, produced fables skeptical about genre, parodic or ironic in form that resist stable readings of the signified world.

This broad shift in fiction can be seen in the careers of many authors who started work in the immediate postwar climate, but whose writing then changed markedly. J. D. Salinger's *The Catcher in the Rye* (1951) was a bible of the postwar young, the story of Holden Caulfield, a middle-class adolescent schoolboy in New York just on the edge of losing his presocial and presexual innocence—which he is able to express, like Huckleberry Finn, in his own vivid vernacular and through his own intuitive independence before his revolt collapses. This vivid book was often read as a novel of generational protest, but essentially it is an attempt to discover a lyric religion and language of innocence that can offset social pressures so great that Salinger can only see the world as real, unphony, through the eyes of a child. In the linked narratives of *Franny and Zooey* (1961), *Raise High the Roof*

Beam, Carpenters and Seymour: An Introduction (1963), Salinger returns to this theme, bringing back the sensitive Glass family from an earlier narrative. But these are works that persistently experiment with their own form to become a corporate quest for transcendental vision through and beyond the world of psychic tension. In the stories and the world beyond them, the quest leads toward silence; Salinger himself, one of the most successful of *New Yorker* writers, also moved through broken form to literary silence. Happily other authors associated with the same magazine remained productive, above all John Updike and John Cheever (*The Wapshot Chronicle*, 1957; *Falconer*, 1977). Both became vivid recorders of American changes from the affluent 1950s into the liberated 1960s and the narcissistic 1970s. Updike in particular caught the new American world of expanding suburbs, postatomic young couples and the rhythm of their marriages, children, divorces, material hungers and spiritual and sexual desires —desires that in his work very often seem to be one and the same.

Born in rural Pennsylvania, Updike took that world for the landscape of several of his early novels and stories, but his geography soon widened into the attics and lofts of professional New York and out to the eastern commuter seacoast, its Puritan past strangely transformed but nonetheless haunting a number of his works, including the experimental *Roger's Version* (1986). Through his books we can read the fate and fortunes of the couples—*Couples* (1968) is the title of his sexually frankest book—who are radically changed and shaken by history, but whose lives largely circulate around domestic needs and aesthetic-religious desires for transcendent revelation in the age of what Updike, in *Marry Me* (1976), calls "the twilight of the old morality." The pressures of time and modern affluence dog Updike's most famous hero, Harold "Rabbit" Angstrom, whose story evolves through *Rabbit, Run* (1960), *Rabbit Redux* (1972), *Rabbit Is Rich* (1982) and *Rabbit at Rest* (1990). Updike is an experimental realist, an excellent parodist, as in his "Bech" books, a poet and serious literary critic. His work has attempted to test what remains of the realistic and the romance traditions of American fiction, and he writes with a vivid sense both of moral hunger and aesthetic purpose. From his first book, *The Poorhouse Fair* (1959), to the age of word processing and computer language that gives underlying metaphors to *Roger's Version,* he has provided the most fluent, continuous, aesthetically considered record of the postwar era of any contemporary American writer.

That key question of how one expresses both surface and soul of modern America is also central to the work of Norman Mailer, once called by Robert Lowell "the finest journalist in America." *The Naked and the Dead* (1948), which brought him public fame, is essentially a naturalist novel in which record of Pacific War violence intersects with Dos Passos–like "Time Machine" passages relating the war story to contemporary social realities. Mailer puts conventional naturalistic types—the petty criminal, the Brooklyn Jew, the Southern cracker, the Montana wanderer—to the tests of Pacific combat and military discipline in a world where "the individual personality is just a hindrance." But, Mailer stressed, his story was "a parable about the movement of men through history," which he saw in a distinctive way, as a process of massing power with oppressive psychic consequences. In the books that followed, therefore, he began fracturing his naturalism. He described *Barbary Shore* (1951), about America's political wasteland, as an attempt to build a contemporary political ideology by uniting Marx and Freud, the sexual body with the social. *The Deer Park* (1955) went on to pursue existential discovery won through untrammeled sexuality and apocalyptic violence. Mailer's aim was to construct the romantic-revolutionary savage who is at once sexually autonomous and historically evolutionary, and, as the essays of *Advertisements for Myself* make clear, that figure is inescapably Mailer himself. Trying to link Hemingway's existentialism with Faulkner's experimental complexity, he endeavors to assume responsibility for the consciousness of an entire generation.

This attempt is the basis of Mailer's famous essay of 1957, "The White Negro," where he described the new "Hipster" hero the age needed if the totalitarian cancer was to be resisted ("One is Hip or one is Square . . . one is a rebel or one conforms") and so defined the Manichaean struggle in which, Mailer thought, the American writer was engaged. His 1965 novel *An American Dream* showed the kind of fiction he envisaged. An unself-consciously obscene, semiautobiographical sex-and-power fantasy interweaving the psychic, sexual and political worlds of American life, it also reveals the kind of intervention in the times he thought the writer could make politically—as when, for instance, he himself ran for public office as a candidate for Mayor of New York. Mailer has also written several works of fictionalized journalism, including *Armies of the Night* (1968), subtitled "History as a Novel/The Novel as History"—though Frederick Karl has observed that "History as Autobiography/Autobiography as History" might be more appropriate. Although he has remained one of the period's most engaged and versatile writers, with a novel set in the Egypt of the Pharaohs, *Ancient Evenings* (1983), and a murder mystery, *Tough Guys Don't Dance* (1984), more of his energy has gone to journalism than fiction. *Why Are We in Vietnam?* (1967) is an interesting combination of both modes, a Reichian fantasy that relates an Alaskan bear hunt to the violence of the war in Vietnam. Throughout his career, Mailer has undertaken to portray an alliance of consciousness with that disorder and anarchy of event we call history, meanwhile putting less and less faith in the autonomy of the individual self, in controlling form, or a directly rational or humanistic response to that complex dreamworld of sex and violence he has identified as the true politics of the age.

Experimental as this may be, it nonetheless has refused to explore another major direction chosen by many postwar American writers—the turn toward the novel as a haven of epistemological questioning and pure aesthetic discovery. Various writers like Saul Bellow and Joyce Carol Oates have resisted this tendency with its inclination to reject the humanistic function of the novel and hence its capacity to represent the reality of action in a knowable world. Thus Oates, herself a powerful and prolific writer of fiction and criticism, has questioned "art forms in which language is arranged and rearranged in such a manner as to give pleasure to the artist and his readers, excluding any referent to an available exterior world." She is referring to that group of writers with various roots in Modernism and surrealism who have come to be known as "Postmodern" and who came to prominence over the later 1960s and the 1970s. Like Modernism itself, "Postmodernism" is an elusive term. It has been used to describe a diversity of strands, from the drug-culture writings of William Burroughs, Jack Kerouac and the "provisional" and "spontaneous" authors of the Beat Generation, to a body of writers influenced by the late-Modernist ideas of Vladimir Nabokov, Jorge Luis Borges and Samuel Beckett. This latter group, including Thomas Pynchon, John Barth, William Gass, Donald Barthelme and Walter Abish, has shown a thoughtful consonance with many of the philosophical ideas of current literary criticism and literary theory, the tendencies of Structuralism and Deconstruction.

Burroughs—a leading figure in the emergence of the Beat Generation—is associated with this approach because of his experimental method of "cut-up" and "fold-in" and his use of hallucinatory images and indeed of drugs themselves to write his books—the novel of homosexuality and drug addiction *Junkie* (1953), the sequence *The Naked Lunch* (1959), *The Soft Machine* (1961), *The Ticket That Exploded* (1962) and *Nova Express* (1964). Burroughs exploits "junk" in two senses—junk as drugs and junk as cultural rubbish, the floating detritus and loose images of contemporary life. Though he calls his works satires, that term implies a literary control his methods belie, as through loose and surreal associations the dreck of the world and the images of science fiction merge with the author's mind-blowing trips and homoerotic dreams to create violent fantasies of endlessly warring powers. Calling himself a "cosmonaut of inner space," Burroughs, like Mailer, sees a world of oppressive and authoritarian forces struggling with the free play of consciousness. His books are unstable, violent and often obscene texts which attempt to penetrate a public world far gone in barbarity, technological systemization and a violence which accurately reflects his inner life. His transgressive experimentalism emphasizes the provisional, improvisatory side of modern experiment and its pursuit of more open forms—much like abstract expressionism in painting or some of the improvised "total theater" or "performance theater" of the 1960s.

At around the same time, another more profound experimentalist was also challenging the referential basis of the novel. Vladimir Nabokov wrote his first books in Russian in the various European cities to which the Revolution of 1917 exiled him and his family. In 1940 he moved to the States, having already started in English *The Real Life of Sebastian Knight* (1941), an ostensible "true biography" which disintegrates in paradox and riddles of identity. So began his "love affair with the English language" which brought to American fiction an intricate tradition derived in part from Gogol, Pushkin and the

Russian symbolist movement. His English-language books include *Bend Sinister* (1947), by "an anthropomorphic deity impersonated by me," *Lolita* (1955), a chase across America for an elusive nymphet, *Pnin* (1957), about a Russian academic émigré in a position not unlike his own, and *Ada* (1969), in which the fictional landscape of American gothic is overlaid with the traditions of the Russian novel. These books, later ones like *Transparent Things* (1972) and *Look at the Harlequins!* (1974), earlier works later translated into English and his critical writings amount to a major inquiry into fiction and fictionality. "Reality," says Nabokov, is a word that means nothing without quotation marks; fiction is a place where words do not simply attach themselves referentially to things; any literary type or structure can be open to mockery, parody or "intertextuality," a distorting intersection with some prior text. So Nabokov's narrators often emerge as liars or madmen, characters' names may be puns, anagrams or emblems, and art becomes a form of game-playing where an artist chases transcendent butterflies with a verbal net, seeking some fleeting imprint of the real. Humbert Humbert in *Lolita,* who owes something to Nabokov's own past but quite a lot to Edgar Allan Poe, is himself an artist in pursuit of his fleeting, erotic symbol, Dolores Haze. The essence of Nabokov's art is that it displays both the epistemological justification and the means for seeing story as a model for the way we constitute the meaning of the world through the fictional constructs of the imagination.

"What the hell," John Barth once remarked, "reality is a nice place to visit but you wouldn't want to live there, and literature never did, very long." Barth actually parodies his own methods in "Life-Story" from *Lost in the Funhouse* (1968), a collection of fictions based on the Möbius strip that mixes items written for print, tape and live voice: "Who doesn't prefer art that at least overtly imitates something other than its own processes? That doesn't continually proclaim 'Don't forget I'm an artifice!' "—so runs his mockingly inverted account of himself:

> Though his critics . . . described his own work as avant-garde, in his heart of hearts he disliked literature of an experimental, self-despising, or overtly metaphysical character, like Samuel Beckett's, Marian Cutler's, Jorge Borges's. . . . His favorite contemporary

authors were John Updike, Georges Simenon, Nicole Riboud. He had no use for the theater of absurdity, for "black humor," for allegory in any form, for apocalyptic preachments tricked out in dramatic garb.

All this is a typical Barthean joke, down to the names of two invented authors (Cutler, Riboud): even the narrative self is a parody. For Barth does indeed represent the extension of Nabokov and Borges into recent American fiction. He is, in the better sense of the term (though now and again in the worse), an "academic" author, learned, burdened with the great history of storytelling and conscious of lying near the end of it in a state of exhaustion that he must turn to replenishment. His early books (*The Floating Opera,* 1956; *The End of the Road,* 1958) were comedies of existentialist absurdity, but *The Sot-Weed Factor* (1962) expansively mocked the manner of eighteenth-century adventure narrative to recount the story of Ebenezer Cooke, first laureate of Maryland. Since then his fictions have repeatedly spiraled around themselves, as in *Chimera* (1972), which goes back to the origins of storytelling in Greek myth and *A Thousand and One Nights* to seek the key to literary renewal. Later, larger-scale books have frequently replayed the materials and characters of earlier ones in new combinatorial systems. Barth is, essentially, a storyteller in an anxious time, ever questioning the nature of narrative and the meaning of fictionality in order to resuscitate its power and signification.

In this he has been close to the center of an experimental era of writing that has touched all of the approaches he mentions—absurdism, black humor, apocalyptic fiction—and more, where many other writers have been associated with the speculative rediscovery of fictional forms. Some have been self-consciously philosophical. "Reality is not a matter of fact, it is an achievement," says the philosopher-critic-novelist William H. Gass in *Fiction and the Figures of Life* (1970); a true storyteller must keep his reader "kindly imprisoned in his language, there is literally nothing beyond." These nominalist assumptions inform his works of fiction, *Omensetter's Luck* (1966), *Willie Master's Lonesome Wife* (1968) and the story collection *In the Heart of the Heart of the Country* (1968), as well as some superb criticism. Robert Coover has followed Barth's inquiry into the nature of story in *Prick-*

songs and Descants (1969), "seven exemplary fictions," but has addressed political realities as well in *The Public Burning* (1977), which is, like E. L. Doctorow's *The Book of Daniel,* a fictionalist's exploration of the Rosenberg case. Recent work has shown Coover a bitter social satirist as well as a teaser of narrative in works like *Gerald's Party* (1986), an extraordinary piece of sustained chatter which mixes-and-matches a multiplicity of narrative forms, and *A Night at the Movies* (1987), which retextualizes the visual narratives with which we have become familiar. This Postmodern mixing of forms and genres—Postmodernism sometimes seems essentially an art of stylized and mannered quotation from a splayed and glutted tradition—is also found in the work of Richard Brautigan, with its playful Californian contrasts of pastoral and tacky America. *Trout Fishing in America* (1967) teases the fisherman's manual, *The Hawkline Monster* (1974) is a "Gothic Western," a mix of two discrepant genres. Donald Barthelme brought Postmodernism to the *New Yorker* in mixed-media tales, collected in *Sixty Stories* (1981), which use pictorial illustration and printed text to capture modern sadness in a complex mixture of deletion, distortion and recombination.

Among the writers expressing this Postmodern impulse has been William Gaddis, author of *The Recognitions* (1955), which has been called the most experimental novel of the 1950s, the encyclopedic *JR* (1976), about American money as a system, and the briefer, tighter *Carpenter's Gothic* (1985), which yet manages to evoke a world of wide and wild event and intimate interconnection. John Hawkes is another writer who made his surreal mark in the 1950s with novels "committed to nightmare, violence, meaningful distortion, to the whole panorama of dislocation and desolation in human relationships." The tendency was always international and had close links with the French *nouveau roman,* as is manifest in the work of the French-American Raymond Federman—who called his *Take It or Leave It* (1976) "an exaggerated second hand tale to be read aloud either standing or sitting"—and with German speculative fiction like Peter Handke's and the work of the Austrian-Jewish-American writer Walter Abish, author of *How German Is It* (1980), about a Germany he had never visited. These experiments are far from being a negation of fictional meaning, any more than they deny Modernism. Indeed they have opened American fiction to a recovery of its own multiple national and international traditions: in gothic, in speculative romance, in Modernist experiment (especially the experiments of Dada and surrealism), in existentialist absurdism, in the contemporary kinship of American writing with the experimental postwar forms of French writers like Alain Robbe-Grillet, Germans like Grass and Handke, and of Italians like Calvino and Eco. Nor was their emphasis on irrealism and on fictionality a refusal of historical awareness, as is clear in the work of Thomas Pynchon.

Pynchon is a restless and unrelentingly difficult writer, but his novels *V.* (1963), *The Crying of Lot 49* (1966) and *Gravity's Rainbow* (1973) are major fictions of their time. *V.* tells the story of a quest for history in a chaotic, synchronic, cybernetic universe. Its two central figures are Benny Profane, an inanimate modern man, and Herbert Stencil, born in 1901 into Henry Adams's modern multiverse, the "century's child." While the profane Profane yoyos his way through modern urban entropy, Stencil searches the past for V., an elusive female figure who has been associated with major historical crises but whose name and identity constantly shift, like the lost significance of modern history. *The Crying of Lot 49* moves us to modern California in the age of bricolage, to San Narciso and the Galactronics Division of Yoyodyne, Inc., where, in a laid-back world of strange delights, high technology and obscure plots and conspiracies, Mrs. Oedipa Maas seeks the meaning of life. Pynchon is a bitter satirist but also the novelist of indeterminacy; it seems impossible for Oedipa to know whether there is "another mode of meaning behind the obvious, or none." Ambiguity still prevails at the end as, at an auction, she awaits the crying of the possibly revelatory Lot 49, perhaps the Pentecostal word itself. *Gravity's Rainbow,* set, as one critic puts it, in "the crucial, explosive, fecund nightmare of all our psychoses and all our plots," the Second World War, is Pynchon's largest endeavor to date; some have considered it the late-twentieth-century *Ulysses,* the exemplary Postmodern text. As German V2 rockets fall on London, the many characterless characters of the book engage in clue-rich searches for a "Real Text" to explain the seemingly random patterns of destruction. The book conveys both the author's quest for meaning and his massive historical research. But, perhaps like the world itself, it too ends in anxious indeterminacy, refusing that sense of completion and acceptance we get from *Ulysses* or most great works of Modernism—one reason why to describe this writing by a term like "Postmodernism" helps.

It may well be that as the century ends Postmodernism is on the wane. If so it will undoubtedly remain an influential and revealing phase not just in the history of American literature but of twentieth-century writing generally—a deep-rooted search for a late Modern form and style in an age of cultural glut that has been called an age of no style. Some of its works do have serious philosophical import, and some—like the novels of Gilbert Sorrentino—are closer to the joyous spirit of pure literary play. What it most sharply represents is the feeling that, still under the complex shadow of Modernism, the aesthetic and intellectual importance of which we have more and more grown to understand, we have both a stylistic situation all our own and a peculiar vacancy of meaning. History has upset the coherence of any single vision—we are after the Modern; we are no longer content with an innocent and confident realism. Nor do we still share the Modernist crisis which was related to the historical and political anxieties of the first half of a century whose fundamental direction has changed. Capitalism and radicalism have both had to reconstruct themselves, thereby changing our progressive expectations. The avant-garde is no longer *avant,* but our political, technological, social and artistic philosophies remain as perplexed as ever by the ironies, paradoxes and indeterminacies of a universe science has opened to much vaster exploration. We are abundant in commodities, clever in the creation of systems; we multiply the technologies of information, the powers of artificial intelligence, the channels of global interaction. All our stories have changed, but the fundamental task of stories—to help us discover for us the meanings we need and the tracks of the imagination down which we might reach them—remains, but anxiously, the same. Now we are no longer in the postwar world but near the close of a century that will give way to a new one with a yet more extensive conception of our modernity. By then it may well seem that our critical philosophies of structuralism and deconstruction were not just explorations but revelations of our awareness both of philosophical and historical indeterminacy—ambiguous, half-destructing products of an age that needed to replenish itself by turning toward the future while re-creating what was salvageable from the past.

Postmodernism now looks like a stylistic phase that ran from the 1960s to the 1980s and left the intellectual landscape looking very different—partly reshaped by the anxious, self-doubting liberalism of the 1950s, partly by the indeterminate, radical spirit of the 1960s which encouraged expressionist art, aleatory music, performance theater, the happening, the random street event. Today more conservative styles return to fashion, intellectually and artistically. Cunning experiment continues, as in the novels of Paul Auster, whose *New York Trilogy* (1987) is a detective story quest through both chaotic urban culture and its own literary tradition. A new realism, sometimes called "dirty realism," appears in the novels and stories of Raymond Carver (*Cathedral,* 1983) and Richard Ford (*The Sportswriter,* 1986), which offer a critical way of looking with stylistic exactitude at a sad, commonplace world. We have a return to regionalism in the Texas fictions of Larry McMurtry and the tales of Garrison Keillor, whose Wobegon world (*Lake Wobegon Days,* 1985) is a comic return to Winesburg. In *The Bonfire of the Vanities* (1988), Tom Wolfe uses traditional journalistic observation to capture the closed world of Wall Street insider trading in the age of high-tech capitalism and the chaotic outsider world of the wasted inner city beyond, while glitzy novelists like Jay McInerney (*Bright Lights, Big City,* 1984) and Bret Easton Ellis (*Less Than Zero,* 1985) record the sharp flavor of the Reagan years. Radicalism returns but from different centers—from Hispanic fiction, from gay fiction like that of Edmund White, and from feminist fiction by authors as various as Marge Piercy (*Woman on the Edge of Time,* 1976) and Kathy Acker (*Don Quixote,* 1986). Some of the striking writing comes from black women—Alice Walker, Toni Morrison, Maya Angelou—and shows the novel's complex involvement in the most serious issues of the time. The next generation of American storytelling is on the scene and at present in a state of its own becoming, as it too tries to deal with the present and rewrite the meanings of the recent past.

· III ·

If the spectacle of postwar narrative in the age of anxiety, the age of the new American empire, displays a flamboyant and varied stylistic abundance, very much the same can be said of the postwar scene in poetry. While the 1930s were not in general a period of remarkable poetic activity, this changed during the war. After it, the times nourished more poetry—or certainly more aspiring poets and more variety of poetic expression—than any other period in the nation's history. Perhaps the major war poet was Randall Jarrell, whose pained "The Death of the Ball Turret Gunner" captured the crisis of personal meaning many of his contemporaries felt. Typically, like James Dickey, Richard Wilbur and Howard Nemerov, Jarrell moved from the war to the university campus ("I'd pay to teach," he said) and became part of the new alliance between the writer and the academy; as Jarrell put it, "the gods who had taken away the poet's audience had given him students." The Modernist ethos of bohemia was displayed by a new landscape that Jarrell was himself to capture with affectionate irony in his novel *Pictures from an Institution* (1954). As poets and novelists supported their writing by teaching, often part-time, a fresh economy of literary production began to develop, a new relation of poetry to criticism and an efflorescence of little magazines with campus associations; many a campus became, as John N. Morris said of his own, "a nest of singing birds." Poetry was at last becoming a public institution, and twenty-five years after John F. Kennedy asked Robert Frost to read a poem at his presidential inauguration, Congress created, in 1985, the "Poet Laureate Consultant in Poetry" to the Library of Congress, so far granting the annual honor to Robert Penn Warren, Richard Wilbur, Howard Nemerov, and Mark Strand.

While opportunistic Senator Joseph McCarthy was persecuting prewar leftist idealists as un-American, the critique of American society they had launched during the Depression years continued into the 1960s in an unlikely guise. Dos Passos had complained that there were two Americas and he framed his *U.S.A.* trilogy with a destitute vagabond trudging a desolate road, "No job, no woman, no house, no city. . . . Wants crawl over his skin like ants." The "old words the immigrants haters of oppression brought to Plymouth" have become "ruined words worn slimy in the mouths of lawyers districtattorneys collegepresidents judges," while soaring overhead in the technological miracle of an airliner is an overfed businessman, sovereign of the modern state, the America of exclusion. The affluence of what Lowell called "the tranquilized fifties" only accentuated the commercial and acquisitive values the 1930s Leftists had condemned, and soon there was a fresh movement of social and political protest. Reading Thoreau and Whitman while pursuing the spiritual illuminations of Eastern mysticism, the Beat Generation of Allen Ginsberg and Lawrence Ferlinghetti followed novelist Jack Kerouac *On the Road* (1957), the road of Dos Passos's Vag that led not only to campus demonstrations against "the military-industrial complex" but to affirmations of personal liberation as well—through widespread experimentation with hallucinogenic drugs and rejection of traditional sexual taboos. In a sense, the wide availability of illegal chemical substances brought earlier resistance to psychological repression even closer to the arena of political protest than had been the case during the early Greenwich Village days. The wisdom of Freud seemed captured in a pocket of pills, and the newly freed self joined with the more politically motivated in condemning the war in Vietnam and marching on the Pentagon.

For many European readers, the Beat Generation wrote the most representative American poetry of the postwar years. The label had been coined half in jest by Kerouac and his friends to suggest not only the beaten alienation of the socially disaffected and the rhythmic celebrations of the marginal music of jazz—whose hip jargon colored the speech of the cognoscenti—but also the beatitude awaiting the rootless wandering pilgrim who sought it at the fringes of conventional society. The most visible pilgrim of the age has been Allen Ginsberg, whose "Howl" of 1956 attracted as much attention as Eliot's *The Waste Land* some thirty years before. "Howl" is a wasteland poem, but its roots reach not to Eliot's tradition of European culture but back through Dos Passos's camera eye and William Carlos Williams to the native leaves of Walt Whitman. Ginsberg's writing has been in many ways a return and response to Whitman's vision; he has measured the nation's fall from grace and sounded his own barbaric yawp of pain and disappointment. "Hold back the edges of your gowns, Ladies, we are going through hell," Williams wrote to introduce the poem. But Ginsberg's vision is very much his own, and he often tints it with a humor not common in Whitman's writing. His "Supermarket in California" imagines Whitman amid a modern microcosm of American plenty: "Shopping for images, I went into the neon Fruit supermarket, dreaming of your enumerations. . . . Whole families shopping at night! Aisles full of husbands! Wives in the avocados, babies in the tomatoes!"

> I saw you, Walt Whitman, childless, lonely old grubber, poking among the meats in the refrigerator and eyeing the grocery boys. . . .
> We strode down the open corridors together in our solitary fancy tasting artichokes, possessing every frozen delicacy, and never passing the cashier.
> Where are we going, Walt Whitman?
> . . . Will we walk all night through solitary streets?
> . . . Will we stroll dreaming of the lost America of love past blue automobiles in driveways, home to our silent cottage?
> Ah, dear father, graybeard, lonely old courage-teacher. . . .

Ginsberg's extended "song of myself" writes of an urban America, and as "Kaddish" (1959), his majestic celebration of his mother's life as a Jewish immigrant, suggests, it is an America of twentieth-century tension and suffering. From his earliest associations with Kerouac and San Francisco poets Kenneth Rexroth, Gregory Corso, Robert Duncan and Gary Snyder, Ginsberg set himself to give literary presence to the Jews, beatniks, homosexuals and Vietnam protesters his unorthodox life-style brought his way. He has worked steadily for reform of the nation's strict laws against homosexual relationships and drug use— even though he has himself rejected chemically induced visions as incompatible with a fully free human life. Ginsberg is best understood as a public figure, a gentle guru moving from cause to cause, from campus to campus, speaking always for antinomian freedom from state and corporate invasion of the self, whether through draft laws or violation of the natural environment.

"My feeling is for a big long clanky statement," he notes with regard to his Whitmanian lines—

> not the way you would *say* it, a thought, but the way you would think it . . . we think rapidly, in visual images as well as words, and if each successive thought were transcribed in its confusion . . . you get a slightly different prosody than if you were talking slowly.

Ginsberg admired Kerouac's "oceanic prose," and he learned, too, from William Burroughs, author of *Junkie* (1953) and *Naked Lunch* (1959) and elder counselor of the Beats. Ginsberg lived for a time with Burroughs and acquired from him an appreciation for the European Modernism of Kafka, Yeats, Rimbaud and Céline. But Ginsberg's literary roots run steadfastly in Williams's American grain, so much so that his high visibility and widespread popularity among the young seem to measure the decline of Eliot's authority and the waning of Europe's influence on postwar American writing.

This is only partially true, but the Beat writers did define themselves through their opposition to the reigning literary orthodoxies of the 1940s and 1950s, the overseas Modernism of Eliot and Pound institutionalized in the nation's universities by Ransom, Tate, Brooks and Warren and the other New Critics. In the late 1940s, Eliot was firmly established as the controlling voice in American poetry, partly through the forceful impact of *Four Quartets* in 1943 and partly through his overwhelming dominance as a critic: his influential definitions of the terms for poetic criticism, his authoritative reshaping of poetic tradition. In the *Quartets* Eliot moved beyond his earlier classicism and impersonality, but the meditating self of these poems remains far indeed from the open explorations of individual consciousness the age would soon embrace. Eliot's effort to capture the rhythm of the thinking mind would nourish other poets of philosophic meditation like Ashbery and Ammons, but his personal integration of the finite and infinite, the temporal and eternal, seemed to many to limit rather than encourage either metaphysical speculation or poetic experiment.

The poets of the postwar years were almost without exception highly educated, and the literature classes of their college years brought them into close contact with Eliot's authority through the New Criticism which had become the controlling orthodoxy of the nation's English departments. John Crowe Ransom, Allen Tate and especially Robert Penn Warren and Cleanth Brooks turned Eliot's readings in the witty and highly complex verse of Donne and Herbert into the country's dominant literary tradition. The poetry and critical methodology of the Fugitive-Agrarian–New Critics created a separate place in art for the reader repelled by what seemed the empty experience and general meaninglessness of current American life. Many of the younger poets of the 1940s and 1950s learned to write Eliot's kind of poetry, rich in metaphysical conceit, irony and mythic echoes, a poetry contained, impersonal, carefully crafted. "Frozen poems," Karl Shapiro remarked, "with an ice-pick at the core,/And lots of allusions from other people's books."

As Eliot's influence gradually waned, other prewar Modernists found readers and imitators. Pound, Stevens, Williams and Frost continued to publish, although Frost rarely matched his earlier work and became instead a widely known public figure, the nation's unofficial poet laureate. Unlike Eliot, the other three opened new avenues for younger poets. Despite his closeness to Eliot in other ways, Pound's vision of the Romantic ordering self, apparent in "Hugh Selwyn Mauberley" (1920) but dominant in *The Pisan Cantos* (1948), pointed away from the conservative impersonality of Eliot and his Southern disciples. Fully conversant with the European roots of Eliot's Modernism, Wallace Stevens nevertheless displaced his classicism with Romantic theories of imaginative creation—and Emersonian Romanticism at that. For Williams, too, it was the American grain that contained the future of the nation's art; he had condemned *The Waste Land* as an atom bomb destroying what was vital in contemporary poetry. With his persistent Whitmanian celebration of America, his rejection of the European iamb for the "American foot"—so much closer to American speech—Williams lived into the postwar decades as perhaps the most fecund legacy of prewar Modernism. With the sections of *Paterson* that appeared at intervals between 1946 and 1958, Williams seemed to many to assert continuing vitality and effectively displace Eliot's principles and practice.

Williams's growing influence can be attributed partly to the increased social and political activism that made Eliot and his followers appear disconnected from the passional world of everyday life. Younger poets sought a voice that spoke out of, that was adequate to, backgrounds and experiences that differed vastly from Eliot's. At one extreme were the anarchic Beats, who rejected all received structures as betrayal of individual response, but few of the newer poets were willing to follow Ginsberg's "Howl"—though some, like Lowell, did learn from the freshly asserted selves of Ginsberg and Kerouac. But the agitation of the times prompted exploration in other directions as well. With the loosening of Eliot's hold, diverse areas of concern began to displace the hegemony of European literary tradition; activism was fed by and in turn nourished fresh awareness of longstanding, if usually silent, cultural assumptions. The term was "consciousness raising," and its beam touched first the de facto racism of American life, then the larger issue of women's rights in a reputedly egalitarian society, then—almost by necessary association—the second-class citizenship of Native Americans, Chicanos and other minority groups. For many the literary tradition of Whitman and Williams, of Sandburg, Dos Passos and Steinbeck identified newly discovered regions crying for expression, the other America, neglected, denied, virtually unseen by the white, male, Anglo-Saxon establishment.

During the 1960s and 1970s the nation became increasingly alert to, actually seemed to acknowledge for the first time, over half its population. No one living or writing during these decades could escape having his consciousness raised, could escape a new awareness of the preconceptions that colored commonly shared perceptions of reality. But not all writers undertook exploration and articulation of the newfound American lands. Some, like Ginsberg, Berryman and Lowell, continued in the century's Freudian fascination with the self as a parallel and infinitely engrossing geography; theirs is the most explicit autobiographical revelation to be found in American poetry, songs of selves far more personal and searching than anything ventured by Whitman. Other poets have remained absorbed in the problems of knowledge highlighted by the new concern with perceptual relativity. They look, not to Williams or psychoanalysis, but to Emerson, William James and Wallace Stevens and a poetry of ideas. Writers like John Ashbery and A. R. Ammons share the concerns of Barth and

Pynchon and the literary theorists who dominate the writing of the 1970s and 1980s in raising fundamental questions about the relations between the world, the artist and his art.

While college students chanted "Hell no, we won't go" at antiwar rallies, the armed forces drew their strength from the poor and under-educated. Black men who risked their lives in Europe and the Pacific, in Korea, Vietnam and Cambodia, expected their service to make a difference in the life that awaited their return. But they found that almost nothing had changed. Once out of uniform they were expected to disappear into the urban ghettos of Harlem and Watts, the rural anonymity of Southern small towns. The school desegregation agitation following *Brown* v. *Board of Education* of Topeka (1954), the race riots of the 1960s, the assassinations of Medgar Evers, Malcolm X and Martin Luther King, Jr., heightened awareness of black disaffection, not only among whites but among blacks as well. As W. E. B. DuBois had recognized, the parallel prosperity of the two races—that Booker T. Washington had predicted—would never evolve easily from the generosity of white, the tractability of black. The Civil War had never ended and slavery was still the issue.

The new militancy of the black consciousness movement reopened debates of the 1920s. Should the black writer perfect his craft on the standard of mainstream American culture, white and Eurocentric as it was? Would he thereby demonstrate that he was in fact the equal of white artists? Or was the very aspiration demeaning in its acceptance of implied inequality? Pressure mounted in the 1960s, from black rights organizations and radical whites, for black authors to write first as blacks, to fashion a black sensibility, a black aesthetics. The search for a black literary tradition led to renewed interest in the writers of the Harlem Renaissance and in the roots of the 1920s movement—in Phillis Wheatley, Frederick Douglass and slave narrative, in Paul Laurence Dunbar, Claude McKay, Arna Bontemps, Countee Cullen, Langston Hughes and the other poets collected by James Weldon Johnson in *The Book of American Negro Poetry* (1922, 1931), in the fiction of Charles W. Chesnutt, Jean Toomer and Zora Neale Hurston. Among the most aggressive converts to black activism in the arts—and beyond—has been Imamu Amiri Baraka. Born LeRoi Jones in Newark, New Jersey, in 1934, he attended Howard University, a predominantly black institution, and then earned an M.A. in German literature at Columbia in New York. He knew Ginsberg and Frank O'Hara and read Lorca, Williams, Pound and Charles Olson. Adopting as well the currents of earlier black writing, including blues music, Jones began as a poet of black self-torment seeking a personal voice for personal suffering, but the upheavals of the 1960s converted him to a larger social vision. His adoption of a Muslim name signaled his distance from his early writing, from its "preoccupation with death, with suicide. . . . Always my own, caught up in the deathurge of the twisted society. The work a cloud of abstraction and disjointedness . . . that was just whiteness." His college experience, he came to feel, "let me understand the Negro sickness. They teach you how to pretend to be white." In "The Myth of a Negro Literature" he rejected most black writing as mediocre because "most of the Negroes who've found themselves in a position to become writers were middle-class Negroes who thought of literature as a way of proving they were not 'inferior.' " Baraka has transformed his own writing into an instrument of his political activism. He founded the Black Repertory Theater of Harlem and has written several plays, among them *Dutchman* (1964), a vividly realized encounter between a black man and a white woman in a deserted subway car that leads to the death of the man and the suggestion that the woman will continue her journey of black entrapment and destruction. With such a vision of relations between the races, it is perhaps not surprising that Baraka participated in the Newark riots of 1967, narrowly escaping conviction for carrying a concealed weapon, or that his book of poems, *Black Magic* (1969), has sections titled "Sabotage," "Target Study" and "Black Art."

Baraka's career recalls the committed Leftists of the 1930s whose dream of revolution came to absorb the purpose and direction of their writing. The less well known work of Robert Hayden stands as an implicit rejoinder to Baraka and a powerful argument for a larger, more fully formed—and informed—vision. Hayden was a university teacher, at Fisk and the University of Michigan. With *Heart-Shaped in the Dust* (1940) and a succession of volumes in the 1960s and 1970s, he illustrated a protest poetry free of agitprop simplifications. Formally sophisticated, it draws on the entire history of the black people to bring resonance to a voice that must speak outside of time for all who cannot speak for themselves. In his two lengthy sequence poems, Hayden portrays racism with a richness of historical understanding notably missing from other black poets. "Runagate Runagate" recounts Harriet Tubman's 1849 escape from slavery; "Middle Passage" describes the agonies of the black journey to slaveholding America with Melvillean depth and power. Hayden has shown younger writers such as Michael Harper and Rita Dove an alternative to the traditional black course of imitating English verse forms or sacrificing craft to the passions of protest.

The best-known and most successful black poet of the postwar years has experienced the same pressures but stopped short of the violent public gestures Baraka and his admirers feel are necessary. With *Annie Allen* (1949) Gwendolyn Brooks became the first black writer to win the Pulitzer Prize. She has long been identified with the black community of Chicago; during the early decades of her career, with the encouragement of Langston Hughes and James Weldon Johnson, she worked to express the lives of the urban poor she knew well, creating, as one critic wrote, black portraits more than black protest. "Although I called my first book *A Street in Bronzeville*," she remarked, "I hoped that people would recognize instantly that Negroes are just like other people; they have the same hates and loves and fears, the same tragedies and triumphs and deaths, as people of any race or religion or nationality." These are the themes of her early books, and although she drew on the biblical speech of black preachers and the vivid talk of the ghetto streets, she remained, like Phillis Wheatley and Countee Cullen before her, a poet in the orthodox literary tradition, writing sonnets and short lyrics and using strongly accented and rhymed lines. Like Baraka and so many others, however, Brooks has been forced to accommodate the upheavals in postwar race relations. In 1967 she attended the second Black Writers' Conference at Fisk University and undertook a radical change of direction. No longer content with what Hughes had called "the ordinary aspects of black life," she has acquired a black publisher and writes primarily for black audiences. Gone are the traditional forms of her early poetry. The new verse juxtaposes fragments of anger, bafflement and protest. "Poets who happen also to be Negroes," she notes, "are twice-tried"; they must both "write poetry and . . . remember they are Negroes."

This has remained the challenge of black poets in America, writers as diverse as Etheredge Knight, June Jordan, Michael Harper, Don Lee, Sonia Sanchez, Nikki Giovanni and Audre Lorde. Several of these are women, and like Brooks they often link their racial protest to the current agitation over culturally determined gender roles. The civil rights demonstrations of the 1960s attacked de facto racial segregation in housing and education and led to concerted denunciation of white-only lunch counters, drinking fountains and bus seating. Before long the libertarian energies aroused on behalf of some 20 percent of the population turned to a much larger group that was learning to see that it too had been forced to accept minority status by an authority struc-ture that was not only white but also predominantly male. Through large-scale meetings, organizations like the National Organization for Women (NOW) and journals like *Ms.* magazine, this newly conscious "minority" remains the strongest legacy of 1960s activism; it continues to work with great energy and imagination to elect women can-didates—Geraldine Ferraro's history-making vice-presidential bid is a case in point—combat sexual discrimination in the marketplace and its male-biased salary scales, and secure an amendment to the nation's Constitution to guarantee women equality by act of law.

So Gwendolyn Brooks might have described the black woman writer as thrice-tried. Poet Adrienne Rich recalls "the split . . . between the girl . . . who defined herself in writing poems, and the girl who was to define herself by her relationships with men." In her essay on women writers, "When We Dead Awaken" (1972), Rich recalls that women poets usually looked to established male writers for guidance—in her case Frost, Stevens, Yeats, Auden and Dylan Thomas. Even when she read women writers, she was "looking . . . for the same things I found in the poetry of the men, because I wanted women poets to be the equals of men, and to be equal was still confused with sounding the same." Not only has the literary establishment his-torically been predominantly male, but the most revered writers of the American literary tradition have been, not only white, as the blacks complain, but male as well. With the establishment of journals and presses dedicated to the work of women writers, efforts have been made to define a feminist usable past, a legacy of writing by women offering a viable alternative to the male-dominated canon. Interest grew in Anne Bradstreet and Mary Rowlandson, in the domestic "scribblers" Hawthorne had lamented, in Fuller, Stowe, Jewett and Freeman, in Charlotte Perkins Gilman and ostensibly undervalued authors like Wharton, Cather and Stein, Elinor Wylie, H. D., Katherine Anne Porter and Edna St. Vincent Millay. Emily Dickinson and Kate Chopin, who had slowly been making their way into the standard anthologies without apparent attention to their gender, suddenly became central exhibits in the defense of an art by and for women. As more and more young women begin research careers at the nation's universities, the volume of published commentary on this newly defined literary tradition continues to grow. Poets like Elizabeth Bishop, Anne Sexton and Sylvia Plath may not pursue the overt lesbian concerns of Adrienne Rich or Audre Lorde, but they do show increased awareness of early conventions and they resist "ladylike" writing; they reflect the political concerns of their time by insisting on, and fashioning, a distinctive feminine voice in American poetry, enriching it with all that is available to an other-than-male vision. In *On Lies, Secrets, and Silence* (1978), Rich notes that

> Women's work and thinking has been made to seem sporadic, errant, orphaned of any tradition of its own.
>
> In fact, we do have a long feminist tradition, both oral and written, a tradition which has built on itself over and over, recovering essential elements even when those have been strangled or wiped out. . . .
>
> Today women are talking to each other, recovering an oral culture, telling our life-stories, reading aloud to one another the books that have moved and healed us, analyzing the language that has lied about us, reading our own words aloud to each other . . . to name and found a culture of our own.

Interest in the distinctive vision of women, the quest for a "woman's voice" has paralleled similar quests for the voice of the black poet, of the Native American poet. Further, each of these has shared in the turn from Eliot's impersonal poet and the political energies of the 1960s toward the uniquely personal utterance of what might be called the lyric of a new romanticism. That is, in each of these newly examined regions of concern, the same debate has occurred between those committed to the interests which define the group and those exploring the private needs colored and shaped by gender, race, religious or sexual preference and so on. In the poetry of women from Bradstreet to Dickinson, a self can be heard beneath the woman's voice, molded by the experience of being a woman and yet reaching for comprehension and expression beyond the orientation of gender. The work of Marianne Moore has helped shape this tradition, and it can be examined as well in the poetry of Elizabeth Bishop, who met Moore while still a student at Vassar. Bishop learned too from Dickinson and George Herbert and devised a poetry well tuned to the orphaned estrangement of her life. She traveled widely throughout the world and—like Wallace Stevens—absorbed the lush imagery of Key West and then Brazil, where she lived for sixteen years. She early saw the analogy between the traveler's map and a poem; as Helen Vendler has remarked, "Each represents—but in an arbitrary, schematic, and conventionalized way—a reality independent of its charting." Bishop's maps are drawn with an exquisite eye for detail, but her quiet description turns always toward questioning the journey itself, the meaning that she and her reader of either sex cannot escape seeking: "Continent, city, country, society:/the choice is never wide and never free./And here, or there . . . No. Should we have stayed at home,/wherever that may be?"

Most poetry written during the past three decades has explored this landscape of personal experience, but the terrain has differed as widely as the purposes prompting the explorations. What might be called the disguised confessional self of Eliot's Prufrock or Pound's Mauberley reappears openly as Whitmanian voice for the laments of the nation, its inarticulate minorities or the psychological and philosophical questionings that life in modern America presses on the poet's sensibility. It can be heard in Ginsberg, Jarrell, Bishop and Baraka, in Olson, Snyder, O'Hara and Ammons. But nowhere is it so painfully naked as in the poetry of Berryman, Roethke, and Lowell, and two of Lowell's writing students, Anne Sexton and Sylvia Plath. Rarely has plumbing of the self as a metaphor for life in the world reached so deeply or pictured such painful misery. "Don't you feel," John Berryman once asked Irving Howe, "that Rimbaud's chaos is central to your life?" Some of the most creative writing of the period begins in the nightmare shadows of Poe, Rimbaud and Céline and leads finally, graphically, to acute alcoholism, mental breakdown or suicide. If the life in the poetry is taken to mirror the life of the poet, then several of these writers have declared it, by their word and deed, unlivable.

> It is not seemly a man should rend open by day
> The huge roots of his blood trees.
> A man ought to hide sometimes. . . .
> And some human beings
> Have need of lingering back in the fastidious half-light
> Even at dawn.

These lines were written by James Wright, a student of Theodore Roethke at the University of Washington, a few years after Roethke's death in 1963. Roethke had been a remarkably popular teacher whose alcoholism and mental breakdowns disturbed and shortened his life. Like Berryman, Lowell, Sexton and Plath, Roethke made his pain his principal subject; he learned from Blake how to use the voice of his childhood to comment on his adult world, and he learned from Freud how to locate in the bewilderment and fears of the child the moments that haunt the later poet. The method was developed further by John Berryman in some four hundred "Dream Songs" (1964, 1968), a sequence of remarkable short lyrics modeled, Berryman said, on *Leaves of Grass,* "the greatest American Poem." After early work as a traditional academic poet, Berryman began what he thought would be a short poem on Anne Bradstreet. Led into extensive research in the American past, he eventually produced the first of his two major works, the fifty stanzas of *Homage to Mistress Bradstreet* (1956). His other significant achievement is the dark wit and verbal virtuosity of the "Dream Songs."

As a child, Berryman had watched while his father committed suicide. The experience haunted him during his career as scholar, poet and teacher, through his episodes with drink, drugs and mental disorder until he took his own life in 1972. The father and his act of violence appear frequently in the "Dream Songs," along with Berryman's sorrow, anger and unsuccessful effort to understand and accept the violence he finds echoed around him and ultimately in himself:

> All the world like a woolen lover
> once did seem on Henry's side.
> Then came a departure.
> Thereafter nothing fell out as it might or ought.
> I don't see how Henry, pried
> open for all the world to see, survived.

Berryman suggests a demonic e. e. cummings in the skewed inventiveness of a language that is all his own, part street slang, baby talk and exaggerated minstrel-show black dialect. He splits his poetic voice into a Freudian drama of three, the commenting "I" of the lines above, the questioning superego Mr. Bones from the vaudeville stage and finally Huffy Henry, the pleasure-seeking id without inhibitions or patience for the restraints he feels forced upon him. After the "departure," as Henry—and Berryman—fought to survive,

> What he has now to say is a long
> wonder the world can bear & be.

The poetry of Roethke and Berryman, of Lowell, Sexton and Plath has become known as "confessional," a term often decried as at best of little use, at worst implying whining self-pity. But there can be no doubt that these decades saw widespread exploitation of the poet's psychological life, a driven willingness to reveal innermost experience for the sake of art—and for the sake too, no doubt, of mental balance and survival. Many of these writers looked back to Delmore Schwartz, whose poetry and personal life provided an instance of the modern poet as near-mad sufferer. As poetry editor of *Partisan Review,* Schwartz was known by many as a writers' writer; his best work is perhaps the story "In Dreams Begin Responsibilities" (1938), but his witty, personal poems of the 1930s and early 1940s won him the admiration of Berryman and the respect of Lowell. As a tragic presence in Bellow's *Humboldt's Gift* (1975), Schwartz evokes the anguished misunderstood artist in the modern world, a fate that Schwartz and similar writers both welcomed and endured as the price of their gift.

In his poem to Schwartz, Robert Lowell has him misquote Wordsworth: "We poets in our youth begin in sadness;/thereof in the end come despondency and madness." Lowell himself did not begin as a "confessional" poet, however. His series of books from *Land of Unlikeness* (1944) and *Lord Weary's Castle* (Pulitzer Prize in 1946) trace rather a Wordsworthian growth of the poet's mind from his deep roots in the American past to assimilation of Eliot's legacy and eventually the autobiographical revelations of *Life Studies* (1959). Lowell gradually came to accept, as he wrote in "For John Berryman" (1977), that " . . . really we had the same life,/the generic one/our generation offered/. . . first students, then with our own,/. . . our fifties' fellowships/to Paris, Rome and Florence,/veterans of the Cold War not the War. . . ." Lowell's version of this life took him from patrician Boston to imprisonment for refusing to serve in the Second World War and later antiwar fellowship with writers as unlike himself as Ginsberg, Levertov and Mailer. The career and the poetry provide a paradigm of one kind of artistic life in the United States of the postwar decades.

In "Reading Myself" (1973), Lowell calls "this open book . . . my open coffin." While it may be true to date his confessional period from his appreciation for the spontaneity and candor of Ginsberg and the Beats and the publication of *Life Studies,* Lowell drew from the first, as all writers do, on the experience that was his alone. Like Henry Adams before him, he was blessed and cursed by a hallowed New England name; he was related to a former president of Harvard, to James Russell Lowell and Amy Lowell, "big and a scandal, as if Mae West were a cousin." The first poems treat the tensions of such a legacy and look with a New England conscience on the conscience of New England, the intensity and constriction so large a part of the Puritan bequest.

Lowell found ways to break away and begin refashioning himself, an ordeal which joined personal upheaval to serious mental strain. In 1937, after two years at Harvard, he transferred to the Kenyon College of John Crowe Ransom, where he learned to admire Eliot and Allen Tate and the tight formal poetry of John Donne. In search of stability outside his inherited tradition, he followed Eliot's path into the Church, becoming a Roman Catholic in 1940. He later came to feel that his conversion was as much a search for form as a matter of spiritual conviction—a rejection of Protestantism and mercantile Boston as well as a need for structures to help him "begin a poem and bring it to a climax." Catholicism provided him with ritual symbols and a detached position from which to judge the "sublunary secular sprawl" of his America, but he left the Church after ten years. His involvement in public affairs became increasingly immediate, and after listening to readings by Beat writers and seeing the deeply personal poetry of his own student, W. D. Snodgrass, Lowell undertook yet another departure. His own poetic style, he decided, was "distant, symbol-ridden, and willfully difficult. . . . I felt my old poems hid what they were really about, and many times offered a stiff, humorless and even impenetrable surface."

Lowell occupies a special place in American cultural history. He was an unusually gifted poet whose verse experiments transformed the face of American poetry. As a Lowell, he touched principal moments in the earlier life of the nation, and he was directly involved with the political and social changes of his own time. He succeeded better than any of his contemporaries in turning his personal experience, especially his suffering, into an expression of general public-historic concern. Like Yeats and Whitman he bridged the gap between private sensibility and public utterance. From the harsh New England portraits of "The Quaker Graveyard in Nantucket," "After the Surprising Conversions" and "Mr. Edwards and the Spider," he moved to his well-known "For the Union Dead," a passionate linking of the nation's Civil War past to his own boyhood dreams and eventual disenchantment with his native Boston. Just as the South Boston Aquarium of his youth stands with boarded windows while "giant finned cars nose forward like fish," so, too, Saint Gaudens's memorial to the first all-Negro regiment shakes during the construction of a parking garage under Boston Common; "when I crouch to my television set,/the drained faces of Negro school-children rise like balloons" in films of contemporary civil rights confrontations. Another popular poem, "Skunk Hour," responds to "The Armadillo" by his friend Elizabeth Bishop with an apparent relaxation of personal pain into the calm of ordinary natural life. After crying "I hear/my ill-spirit sob in each blood cell, as if my hand were at its throat. . . ./I myself am hell . . . ," he can yet stand

> . . . on top
> of our back steps and breathe the rich air—

a mother skunk with her column of kittens swills the garbage pail.
She jabs her wedge-head in a cup
of sour cream, drops her ostrich tail,
and will not scare.

Lowell joined the protesters in the march on the Pentagon in 1967, where Norman Mailer observed that he "gave off at times the unwilling haunted saintliness of a man who was repaying the moral debts of ten generations of ancestors." When he died a decade later, he was widely appreciated as the most accomplished poet of his generation, not only for his ten volumes of varied and intense verse but for his exemplary, if tortured, life as a public man of letters. Unlike so many of the self-examining writers who took him for a model, Lowell insisted on facing simultaneously both his own and his nation's pain.

Two of Lowell's heirs, Anne Sexton and Sylvia Plath, were his students at Boston University. They became friends and shared each other's interest in the particular problems of women and in the agony of life that led each to attempted and then successful suicide. Poetry, Sexton said, "should be a shock to the senses. It should also hurt." Her own verse owes as much to Snodgrass's *Heart's Needle* (1959) as to Lowell, but the candor and intensity of her subjects are all her own. She brought sex, illegitimacy, guilt, madness and suicide into her poems as if these topics, and her woman's sense of them, were necessary components of the mental disintegration suggested in book titles like *To Bedlam and Part Way Back* (1960), *All My Pretty Ones* (1962), *Live or Die* (1967), *The Death Notebooks* (1974) and *The Awful Rowing Toward God* (1975). Lowell remembered Sylvia Plath with an "air of maddening docility. . . . I sensed her abashment and distinction, and never guessed her later appalling and triumphant fulfillment." The Plath of the autobiographical novel *The Bell Jar* (1963) does indeed seem docile in the face of the limited roles available to the women of her generation, but with the poems of *Ariel* (1965) she found a strong voice, often fierce and joyous at the same time, to test the "private and taboo subjects" of her family tensions and mental breakdowns. Like marriage and motherhood, writing helped Plath cope with the chaos of her inner world:

> I cannot sympathize with those cries from the heart that are in-
> formed by nothing except a needle or a knife. . . . I believe that
> one should be able to control and manipulate experiences, even
> the most terrifying . . . with an informed and intelligent mind.

A poem like "Black Rook in Rainy Weather" reflects the tight restraint
and clarity she sought, while the deceptive whimsicality of "The Ap-
plicant," "Lady Lazarus" and the often reprinted "Daddy" only emphasizes the angry energy that eventually overcame her power and will
to control.

The so-called "confessional" poets of these years brought American poetry closer to European traditions of anguish and madness than
it had ever been. Many readers were surprised at what seemed a violent
turn from Eliotic classicism toward an intensely expressive romanticism, but the sources of the new work were evident in a Protestant
legacy of intense self-scrutiny, the modern secular language of psychoanalysis and widespread conviction that the self and its expression
were the only artistic resource in an otherwise incomprehensible world
The questions raised seem likely to remain part of the nation's literary
culture: To what extent can a poetry of private and often obscure
suffering express a public, a universal, agony? To what extent can
madness in an individual be taken for the derangement, the meaninglessness of society as a whole?

Not all the recent autobiographical poetry portrays emotions on
the edge, desperation, madness, outrage. The very different needs of
very different writers have been served by a widening of expressive
range and an ever-deepening self-scrutiny. Autobiography of one kind
or another has again become legitimate in poetry, has in fact become
as dominant as it was in the nineteenth century. Writers as dissimilar
as James Merrill, Adrienne Rich, Frank O'Hara and A. R. Ammons
have, like Levertov and Olson, found uses for personal experience that
touches, comments upon and shapes the world around them. As Daniel
Hoffman has noted, one may deal with chaos by inviting it in or by
holding it off. A number of accomplished poets have chosen to hold
it at bay; the result may be a loss of intensity but a gain in clarity, wit
and formal achievement. Picking and choosing among the styles and
verse patterns available, these writers fall into no particular school.

Many saw no need to reject the formal devices employed by Eliot—the masks, allusions and regular formal patterns—but neither did they feel the need to use them, unless the poem in hand would be well served by them. The list here is lengthy: John Ciardi, Richard Wilbur, Stanley Kunitz, Richard Eberhart, Howard Nemerov, W. S. Merwin and James Wright come most readily to mind. There continue to be poets who associate themselves with specific geographical places, like Frank O'Hara in New York or Robert Penn Warren and James Dickey in the South or Gary Snyder and Richard Hugo in the Northwest. The self has both an outer and an inner landscape; as has always been the case with the best of the regionalists, the locale is chosen to express the geography of the artist's inner life. As Hugo put it, "the place triggers the mind to create the place."

The poets of uninhibited and passionate self-revelation cannot properly be called a "school," but to give some shape to the abundance of poetic output during the postwar years we can speak of three more or less coherent groups. In addition to the Beat poets with their roots in San Francisco, there have been the adherents of Charles Olson, one-time rector of Black Mountain, an avant-garde college in North Carolina, and the so-called "New York School" of Ashbery, Frank O'Hara and Kenneth Koch. In 1950 Olson published *Projective Verse,* a radical manifesto describing a poetry of immediate notation, a typography stretching words and spaces unevenly across a page to indicate the individual poet's "breath" and to score as in music the pauses and emphases the reader should observe. Olson saw a poem as the mark of a self at a specific moment, not the summary or description of a completed experience. His own poetry, notably the sequential *Maximus Poems* (1953–68), adapts the approach of Pound's *Cantos* to Olson's vision of America's pre-European past: "The substances of history now useful lie outside, under, right here, anywhere but in the direct continuum of society as we have had it." Like D. H. Lawrence and Williams before him, Olson sought to escape the false turns of civilization by digging for the instinctive vitality he associated with primitive North American cultures like the Mayas of the Yucatán. His combined aesthetic and cultural departures made him something of a guru for enthusiastic followers like Robert Creeley, Robert Duncan and Denise Levertov. Olson's interest in the redemptive energies of the unconscious can be found as well in "deep image" poets like Robert Bly, W. S. Merwin and James Wright and in the Native American and Asian researches of Gary Snyder.

Snyder introduced a forester's term into poetics with the title of his first book, *Riprap* (1959). A riprap, he explained, is "a cobble of stone laid on steep slick rock to make a trail for horses in the mountains." A student of ritual and myth, Snyder seeks spiritual insight through the painstaking accumulation of observed detail: poetry is "a riprap on the slick rock of metaphysics." Poetry as a point of purchase, as the process "of the mind in the act of finding/What will suffice," as Stevens wrote in "Of Modern Poetry" (1940)—these poems of the postwar years comprise a new genre of meditative art. Wallace Stevens was, as Berryman quips, a "funny money man./Mutter we all must as well as we can./He mutter spiffy." Stevens muttered of "metaphysics" more directly and more creatively than any other American poet; he was, it has been said, a man made of words. He sang into being a world made of words and celebrated his fictions for the human acts that were their creation. His legacy reaches deeply into the fiction of Barth, Pynchon and Barthelme and the poetry of A. R. Ammons and John Ashbery. Ammons, with his command of science, the worlds of both microscope and telescope, resembles Pynchon as a man of the time pressing the present into comprehensible shapes. Like Emerson and Thoreau, Ammons looks at the natural world of his upstate New York home for representation of transcendent implication, but in his case it is the human dimension he seeks, not the divine. His reader is likely to hear Frost and Emily Dickinson in his lines and to think of Williams and Moore—but principally Stevens. The underlying aspiration is most often epistemological, a desire to capture in words, to create with words, not so much the meaning of experience as the act of seeking that meaning. "I found a/weed/that had a/mirror in it/and that/mirror/looked in at/a mirror/in/me that/had a/weed in it," he writes in "Reflective" (1966). In one of his colloquies with a mountain, the poet remarks that "I don't know your/massive symmetry and rest"; in another the mountain says, "I see you're scribbling again." The poet replies with a central image in the thought of late-twentieth-century America, the river of Heraclitus and the paradox of its ever-changing sameness: "I said/well, yes, but in a fashion very/like the water here/

uncapturable and vanishing. . . ." "Next," the mountain says, "you'll be/arriving at ways/water survives its motions." Ammons is a poet of flux who rejects "narrow orders" and embraces random change, entropy and "temporary meaning." He limits punctuation, drawing heavily on the colon to suggest uninterrupted flow: he composed one book-length poem, *Tape for the Turn of the Year* (1965), on a roll of adding-machine tape, letting its width dictate the length of his lines and its length the duration of the poem. In "Corson's Inlet" (1965), he declares himself "caught always in the event of change." "Manifold events of sand/change the dune's shape that will not be the same shape/ tomorrow." "The Overall," he admits, "is beyond me," but he will accept no explanations that he cannot see clearly for himself: "no forcing of image, plan, or thought:/no propaganda, no humbling of reality to precept." Ammons's reality is the knower's stream of consciousness described by William James; it receives its fullest expression to date in *Sphere: the Form of Motion* (1974), a single full-length poem of 155 four-tercet sections with no full stops whatsoever.

The bearing of William James on American writing of the last decades will concern us again in a moment. It has proven remarkably fruitful in the meditative poetry of ideas produced by Stevens, Ammons and John Ashbery. Ashbery seems to some the century's ultimate symbolist-solipsist, the poet of intense phenomenological awareness recording the consciousness focusing and unfocusing, thinking and feeling, forming and dissolving amid the rush of random thoughts and moments. Outer events seem merely the occasion for registering response, or rather response to response. As with Stevens, poetry becomes very serious play, the process of meditation being meditated upon. Again like Stevens, Ashbery and other members of the "New York School"—Kenneth Koch, James Schuyler and Frank O'Hara— drew important inspiration from contemporary painting, in their case cubism and abstract expressionism. To the iconoclastic playfulness of Klee, Matisse and the dadaists, cubism added the age's preoccupation with the conditions of seeing, experiments with perspective suggesting that various ways of looking at an object—or, by extension, an experience or idea—may be equally "true."

Like Stevens and Ammons, Ashbery thinks of a poem as a picture of the act which creates it, much like the "action paintings" of Jackson

Pollock. In the lengthy *Self-Portrait in a Convex Mirror,* he attends as much to the painter's sense of his undertaking as he does to the final painting which prompts the poem—and even more to his own reaction to both. Such a poem must always be partial, a falsification of the layered life that must be reduced to the limited dimensions of the formal object. "I think that any one of my poems might be considered to be a snapshot of whatever is going on in my mind at the time," he has suggested, "—first of all the desire to write a poem, after that wondering if I've left the oven on or thinking about where I must be in the next hour." Ashbery's collected snapshots have appeared in a series of volumes that display remarkable inventiveness and equally remarkable shifts and departures, from the unsettling and baffling *The Tennis Court Oath* (1962), a wholly unexpected successor to his first book of lyrics, *Some Trees* (1956), to the prose poems of *Three Poems* (1972), the lyrics of *Houseboat Days* (1977) and the unrhymed sonnets of *Shadow Train* (1981). In 1975 *Self-Portrait in a Convex Mirror* won all three of the year's major poetry prizes.

Ashbery's work displays an original intellect indebted to the writing of Keats, Eliot, Auden and Stevens. He returns persistently to primary questions about the relations of art and knowing in a cyclic life that seems without verifiable meaning or purpose. "Why be hanging on here?" he asks, "Like kites, circling,/Slipping on a ramp of air, but always circling?" We turn on a "waterwheel of days" or we spin on a "damaged carousel," with "Dozens of as yet/Unrealized projects, and a strict sense/Of time running out, of evening presenting/The tactfully folded-over bill. . . ." "I know," he admits, "that I braid too much my own/Snapped-off perceptions of things as they come to me./They are private and always will be." But these fictions, the "occasional dream, a vision," are the only way to hold on "to the hard earth so as not to get thrown off." Life is "a metaphor made to include us," and so Ashbery turns to the "Fables that time invents/To explain its passing"—

The being of our sentences, in the climate that fostered them,
Not ours to own, like a book but to be with, and sometimes
To be without, alone and desperate.

But the fantasy makes it ours, a kind of fence-sitting
Raised to the level of an esthetic ideal. . . .

Ashbery imagines each of us "strapped" to our "mindset," each with "one big theory to explain the universe/But it doesn't tell the whole story. . . ." Nor can it, as the river of Heraclitus suspends meaning in what Ashbery calls the emulsion of time. Tomorrow will "alter the sense of what had already been learned. . . . The learning process is extended in this way, so that from this standpoint/None of us ever graduates from college."

Faced with the multiplicity of early modern life, Henry Adams had turned to writing for the coherence he could not find in the world around him. In "Negative Capability and Its Children" (1984), Charles Simic defines a similar role for the poetry of the century's last years. He finds contemporary relevance in Keats's term, negative capability —"that is, when a man is capable of being in uncertainties, mysteries, doubts, without any irritable reaching after fact and reason." Anyone might make, Simic reminds us, "a long list of intellectual and aesthetic events which question, revise and contradict one another on all fundamental issues." If we add all the political upheavals of our time, we might ask, "how, in this context, are we capable of being in anything *but* uncertainties? Or, since we are thinking about poetry, ask how do we render this now overwhelming consciousness of uncertainty, mystery and doubt in our poems?" Today's poet encounters uncertainties on every side, and the poem, too, is "in the midst" of them, an adequate fiction, "a kind of magnet for complex historical, literary and psychological forces, as well as a way of maintaining oneself in the face of that multiplicity."

· IV ·

A main concern of this book has been with the way writers from the sixteenth century to the present have participated in one of the more important tasks of the post-Renaissance mind: the task the Mexican historian Edmundo O'Gorman once called "the invention of America." The "Newfounde land" that challenged existing images of the world forced a unique creative enterprise, and those who undertook it faced a problem of expression—the very American problem, as Horace Bushnell put it in 1849, "of how to get a language, and where." What literature is, what America is, has been and will become, are large questions. For Americans the nature of art has often been defined very broadly, from painted canvas to painted barn, from statuary to the technology of manufacturing, from poem to doggerel, from experimental fiction to movie script. Americans very much wanted to have a literature of their own—as Noah Webster said, "Honor demands . . ."—and they discussed the question with remarkable frequency. They were certain that a new land, a new history, a new theory of government and society, a new "nation of nations" could not express and define itself simply by imitating the arts of Britain or Europe. But what this literature should look and sound like, from what materials and what attitudes of mind and spirit it should be composed, were questions that often did not lead far beyond patriotic simplicities. American literature has its many triumphs, but they have most often arisen from disparate and largely unexamined theories of writing.

The history of literary ideas in America has not been predominantly philosophical but rather social, political, "a search for some new and imperative moral order," as Alfred Kazin wrote, "to unite American culture in the service of one imperative ideal or another." Over the generations, different assumptions have guided these activities. Puritans insisted on "the plaine style" as a religious duty in the daily drama of spiritual life and death. The eighteenth century supported a neoclassicism influenced by Pope, Addison and Goldsmith. Emerson declared that the literary work should be judged by its power to point toward transcendental truth. Poe offered his distinctive version of the doctrine of art for art's sake, discriminating between truth and beauty and asserting the value of the "poem which is a poem and nothing more." Writers who did examine their work theoretically, like Poe or Henry James, were generally not seen as typically American in their concerns, and they certainly had little impact on criticism as it was generally practiced in America in the nineteenth century.

In the earlier part of the twentieth century these debates revived with vigor as critics returned to large questions about the nature and history of American literature—a usable past, a viable canon. They did this once again largely in the setting of a broad social dialogue which explored the nature of national life as much as it did literary values, and critics attracted large audiences for their speculation. Political, ethical and literary discussion reached a high level of public relevance; as H. L. Mencken put it in the 1920s,

> Ears are bitten off. Noses are bloodied. There are wallops both above and below the belt . . . [that] melodramatize the business of the critic, and so convince thousands of bystanders, otherwise quite inert, that criticism is an amusing and instructive art.

Criticism was made public, and it was made interesting. But by the 1950s observers were already noting that debate was shifting into the universities and away from creative practice, leaving bystanders not only inert but thoroughly bewildered.

Today we unquestionably live in an age of critical theory, and as a consequence there is no agreement or anything like one on standards of judgment or a canonical tradition. Critical debate has grown highly philosophical, crossing frontiers that even Eliot, Pound, Stevens and their Modernist contemporaries approached with reluctance. The same indeterminacy that prevails in accounts of the physical world is equally present in the philosophy of serious literary criticism as it struggles without any certainties to construct an adequate usable account of itself. The pluralism of the age has multiplied theories of art, reading and culture; these in turn have led to disputes that for the moment seem unresolvable. Indeed the position of criticism resembles that of the arts themselves, a situation of plurality without resolution. We have learned—from thinkers like William James, Eliseo Vivas, Ernst Cassirer—that we live in a world of symbol systems, that we are largely the artists of our own realities, that we all build fictions, provisionally "adequate," never "supreme." We have learned to see a pluralistic, perceiver-shaped reality, and, as Elder Olson put it, "The number of possible critical positions is relative to the number of possible philosophical positions."

In the years after the war, formalist theories largely derived from Modernism passed into the New Criticism and into the general teaching of literature. These have contended with a rebirth of sociological and political theories, often developed from 1930s Marxism and the Frankfurt School with its emphasis on the "false consciousness" of bourgeois society. Champions of other groups—women, blacks, Chicanos, Native Americans—began to look past "false consciousness" to "consciousness raising," seeking less an ideologically created world than one of greater justice and equity. Also important has been mythological criticism that sees literature leading less to matters of social organization than to shared, structural forms of common experience, to the larger narrative systems constitutive of human culture. Myth criticism found its most complete expression in Northrop Frye's ambitious *Anatomy of Criticism* (1957), which sees myth not so much as eternal human narrative as art's power of discovery through its own metacommentary. Art is, he says, an "autonomous verbal structure," which yet contains "life and reality in a system of verbal relationships." For Frye its enormous symbolic discourse is scriptural and study of intertextual and intergeneric relationships and underlying archetypal motifs can reveal meanings analogous to those hitherto available only through divine revelation.

If for Frye literature becomes scriptural, for French structuralist critics working in the 1950s it becomes *scriptible*. Structuralism was a large project which drew from anthropology, in Claude Lévi-Strauss, to psychoanalysis, in Jacques Lacan; but essentially it was a science of signs, or a semiology. Influenced by Gottlob Frege, Ferdinand de Saussure and Roman Jakobson, it challenged theories of language which linked words directly to the material world. Language for the structuralist is a system of signs arbitrarily employed in signification. Any declarative statement draws on the relations of its terms to others in the system and to the auditor's conversance with the total language, the *langue* that is being employed. As with Frye's archetypes, meaning is purely a matter of convention, as we grasp the part in what might be called the ecology of the whole. The argument became powerful in the United States as a development beyond the New Criticism; in 1966 Geoffrey Hartman welcomed it as "a new kind of criticism which could view literature as an institution with its own laws or structural principles, yet relate these to both local traditions and the societal as such." Like Frye, Hartman sees an escape from what appears to be the narrow, closed, aesthetic world of New Criticism and formalism into time and the sweep of history.

From the point of view of the practicing writer, the price has often seemed high. Structuralist and myth critics are primarily concerned with the *network* of relationships that exist among the parts composing the whole, whether that is the *langue* of the structuralists or the collective myth of Frye's anatomy of criticism. Arguments about "the Death of the Author" (Roland Barthes) and the "Disappearance of the Subject" (Michel Foucault) appear to make the work of the individual writer a single star in a vast galaxy, his written text no more than the result of his inescapable programming, the flowing through him of prefabricated perceptions. As an actor in the drama of literary creation, the author was indeed dead. At the less cosmic level, the semiological approach sees each literary text as a linguistic complex drawing its meaning from the relationship between the writer's shaping discourse and the larger *langue*. It was through semiology that the linguistic and philosophical currents of Europe came, over the 1960s and 1970s, to have their greatest impact on theoretical criticism in the United States. Two existing native traditions enhanced its impact. One was the tradition of formalism that had evolved out of Poe, Henry James, Eliot, Pound and the New Critics. The other was the heritage of pragmatism, the lineage of William James, Charles Sanders Peirce, John Dewey and Clarence Irving Lewis, which reached back to Emerson and forward to Richard Rorty to regard the universe as a system of signs drawing its meaning from the relation of its parts as grasped through the intentions of its human perceiver. For William James, as for his brother Henry, the "truth" is the successful connection of perceiver and world, "successful" when the perceiver can thereby function for his ultimate well-being. James's way of "reading" the material world anticipated the contemporary semiologist's approach to a poem as a formal verbal system. From this approach, a successful reading is one in which the complex relations of the poem's details are apprehended to render the fullest possible awareness of the total work as a paradigmatic instance of coherent meaning rather than *the* univocal reflection of its author's intention.

Semiology can thus be viewed as New Criticism moved from a

symbolist to a pragmatic epistemological base, a shift that has proven wholly unacceptable to a large segment of the literary community. If the new critical methods for finding meaning captured in the intricacies of literary symbol systems have been wed to belief in absolute truth, a truth closely linked, as it was for many New Critics, with the premises of their personal religious traditions, then the modern epistemological revolution which American pragmatism has nourished can come to seem—to recall Andrews Norton on Emerson's transcendentalism— "the latest form of infidelity." At issue, as it was in the biblical criticism of the previous century, has been the "ontological status" of a textual work's meaning. Is it single and fixed, placed in the language of the text by its author and available to the humble and careful seeker like treasure in a chest? Or does a poem's meaning reside elsewhere, perhaps in the relationship of an individual reader or community of readers to the systematic arrangements that are the text? Is there only one system present *to* be read, or is any linguistic discourse a Byzantine overlay and virtually an indecipherable scramble of coherent but competing systems? In America at present there is a wide gulf between many new critical formalists and younger critics attracted to Postmodern conceptions of meaning. M. H. Abrams, to cite an eminent example, labors through scholarship and carefully refined taste to read literary works as he believes they were devised by their authors to be read, while readers like J. Hillis Miller object on basic philosophical ground to Abrams's quest for single and correct interpretations, *the* reading rather than simply *a* responsible reader's response.

Critics as dissimilar as Hillis Miller, Paul de Man, Harold Bloom and Stanley Fish have demonstrated repeatedly how formalist methods of literary analysis can be continued and enhanced by awareness of semiological theory. But they insist as well that the revolution in thought that has moved this century from a world of determinable truth to one of multiple, often conflicting interpretation has totally and irrevocably altered how we think of—and teach—works of literature and the reading appropriate to them. Their views have separated them from their academic forebears and from the wide public arena as well in controversy that is gradually being recognized for what it is, a philosophical debate, but since the epistemological certainties of earlier centuries seem at present to have a shrinking number of serious defenders, we can assume that the newer viewpoints will gradually transform many of the literary and educational practices of the nation.

One of the earliest discussions of these antipathetic views and their far-reaching implications was E. D. Hirsch's *Validity in Interpretation* (1967). Hirsch's title suggests two foci of critical discussion during the past twenty years. As Jane P. Tompkins argues in her excellent survey, *Reader-Response Criticism: From Formalism to Post-Structuralism* (1980), the common ground of twentieth-century criticism distinguishes it from that of earlier centuries: a great deal of it focuses on the interpretation of literary texts. Hence the recent flurry of theoretical activity, by frequently pursuing the same ends, allies itself more than its often ahistorical proponents are willing to admit with the interpretive goals of mid-century formalism. Hirsch uses the word "hermeneutics" to describe this concern, drawing on the long tradition of biblical and legal exegesis to explore what a text might be taken to be and what we might mean by interpreting it. The notion of "validity," however, marks the chasm where New Critics and their successors part company. As we have seen, if the critic's presumption is that a single textual interpretation can be isolated as somehow the "right" one, he is implicitly affirming an epistemological authority—or, as is now commonly said, he is "privileging" one reading over another. Hirsch's imaginative resolution of the dilemma is to have it both ways, using the term "meaning" for the recoverable intent of the original creative act and "significance" for the varied interpretations subsequent generations of readers have found "valid." But few critics have accepted his distinction to describe alternative responses to a literary work.

The discussions of tradition prompted by Eliot's *The Waste Land* (1922) and "Tradition and the Individual Talent" (1919) signaled a crisis in the theory of history—an inability to establish whether the past has absolute value in itself or whether, like any other text, the past concerns us only as we variously read and interpret it from the multiple perspectives of today. Our loss of confident faith in our inherited scriptures and traditions has deprived us not only of the wellsprings of explanation and value but also of the very means of establishing the "validity" of our individual readings of reality. In this historical context, the arc of current critical discourse takes discernible shape. A world without absolute, unchallengeable norms, without epistemological certainty, is a world of ultimate Protestantism: every man becomes his own philosopher, his own arbiter of the true and the real. "He always has been," we are told. But he has never accepted the responsibility so universally nor has he turned his ingenuity so diligently to exploring the implications of his newly acknowledged autonomy.

In literary criticism, analogous concerns have led to intense debate over the role of the reader in discovering—or determining—the meaning or meanings any text may be said to have. Earlier critical discourse had addressed the relation of the author to his work (biographical and psychological criticism), the interdependence of work and world (sociopolitical criticism and the determining conventions of literary history and myth) and the shaping internal tensions operative in the work itself (formalism, structuralism, semiotics). Recent inquiry has turned to the neglected participants in the entire process; if a text may be said to speak, its discourse has come to be seen as less a monologue than a dialogue. For many recent theorists, a text exists only through the participating perception of its reader; some go so far as to affirm that any individual work has as many meanings as it has readers, for meanings are created or at least completed by readers or "interpretive communities." As in the larger philosophic universe, so in the more modest realm of literary criticism: the challenge to interpretive certainty has made each individual consciousness—each reader or group of readers—an active partner in creating the meaning of the object perceived.

Varying degrees of centrality have been granted to the reader-perceiver in creating the meaning of a literary work. The phenomenology of Georges Poulet and the early Hillis Miller concerns itself with a passive, almost erotic subjection of reader to the author's presence in the text, while for Michael Riffaterre and Jacques Derrida the role of the human agent in establishing meaning is limited by the shaping power of structural and semiological codes—those "systems of intelligibility," as Jane P. Tompkins puts it, "that operate through individuals" and determine their observations. Following in the footsteps of William James and I. A. Richards, the psychoanalytic critic Norman Holland has argued that "interpretation is a function of identity," that all our experience is "creative and relational" and that we treat a work of literature just as we do anything we encounter: we identify what we can use and then interpret and assimilate it to maintain our stability and sense of identity. Like Emerson before him, Holland affirms the separateness of the self and the otherness of the object, but all knowing is reciprocal and—in the tradition of I. A. Richards—healing. The early work of Stanley Fish posits something like a structuralist reader, asking—the words are Jonathan Culler's—"what must an ideal reader know implicitly in order to read and interpret works in ways which we consider acceptable?" A poem is thus not simply a formal object in space but an experience in time; its meaning is what happens as the reader negotiates its lines. But more recently Fish has concluded that conventions are important only in the use we make of them and that readers actually create the works they read—meaning is not on the printed page but in the "interpretive strategies" by which readers "produce" texts.

Walter Benn Michaels has seen most clearly how much this Postmodernist thinking in America owes to the pragmatists, especially C. S. Peirce. To an extent new to history, the individual human self has been made constitutive of reality and so, for Michaels, Descartes's separation of subject and object or the New Critics' separation of reader and text can be ignored because both the self and the world it knows are cultural, historical constructions. In this view, *any* meaning—of text or world—is relative, timebound and inescapably self-interested.

The last decade has seen increasing interest in the New Historicism, less a school or movement than an academic tendency to revive historical scholarship in a Postmodern world. Originating in the Renaissance studies of Stephen Greenblatt and Louis Montrose and centered in the journal *Representations,* New Historicism has baffled efforts at univocal definition. To some observers it seems reactionary, a return to old-fashioned philological fact-finding and absorption in the pastness of the past—in short a flight from Postmodern relativism. To others it seems the expansion of that relativism into cultural analysis, the displacement of conventional literary history by broad and deep "thick description" of carefully selected cultural moments which seem rich in significance. In this view, New Historicism joins the epistemological skepticism of Poststructuralism with the methodology of anthropologist Clifford Geertz. Or, as Hayden White puts it, at one moment or another the New Historicists import "models, methods, and strategies borrowed from Geertzian cultural anthropology, Foucaultian discourse theory, Derridean or de Manian deconstructionism, Saussurian semiotics, Lacanian psychoanalytic theory, or Jakobsonian poetics into historical studies." H. Aram Veeser has recently tried to formulate "key assumptions" that define New Historicism, "for all its heterogeneity":

> that every expressive act is embedded in a network of material practices; that every act of unmasking, critique, and opposition uses the tools it condemns and risks falling prey to the practice it exposes; that literary and non-literary "texts" circulate inseparably; that no discourse, imaginative or archival, gives access to unchanging truths nor expresses inalterable human nature; finally . . . that a critical method and a language adequate to describe culture under capitalism participate in the economy they describe.

In practice, the New Historicist's energizing sensibility may be declaredly political or not. His goal may be enriched understanding of a literary work through awareness of its complex cultural immersion. Or he may resist foregrounding or privileging the artwork by regarding the historical moment as itself a text—to be interpreted and used with full awareness of the reader's inescapable subjectivity and the consequent fictionality of his narrative account.

It is perhaps not a large step from this individual creation of meaning to denial that anything at all is meaningful—or has value that is related to meaning. The most extreme version of these views has become known as Deconstructionism, an aggressive impressionism that places reader-response at the center of any quest for meaning in the literary experience. Vincent B. Leitch suggests that the Deconstructive approach begins when "Nietzsche, Freud and Heidegger call into question and destroy the metaphysical concepts of being, truth, consciousness, self, identity, and presence." Since the Poststructural Deconstructionist recognizes no referential connection between linguistic signs and any world outside them, a literary text becomes in effect a cognitive playground. As Jonathan Culler notes,

Although Derrida's writings all involve close engagement with various texts, they seldom involve interpretations as traditionally conceived. There is no deference to the integrity of the text, no search for a unifying purpose that would assign each part its appropriate role. Derrida characteristically concentrates on elements which others find marginal, seeking not to elucidate what a text says but to reveal an uncanny logic that operates in and across texts, whatever they say.

The logic "revealed" is controlled only by the Deconstructive critic's ingenuity and the linguistic determinations he finds encoded in the text, and so the improvisational opportunities of the approach resemble, as many have noticed, the creative independence assumed by the jazz musician in his elaborations on a composer's melodic score.

American interest in Deconstruction largely began when Jacques Derrida delivered his paper "Structure, Sign, and Play in the Discourse of the Human Sciences" at Johns Hopkins University in 1966, and it prospered especially at Yale—ironically enough, the center of New Criticism two decades before. The work there of Paul de Man, J. Hillis Miller and Geoffrey Hartman imprinted a powerful neo-Romantic impulse on contemporary American thought, arguing that criticism is a performative art and the critic in a fundamental respect a creative artist. Just as Leslie Fiedler called his study of the American novel yet *another* American novel, so Harold Bloom called his intricate meditation on modern literary intertextuality *The Anxiety of Influence* (1973) a poem. Bloom would therefore doubtless accept Yale colleague Geoffrey Hartman's view of his fellow interpretive improvisers as "the unknowledged poets of our time," though he does stop short of what he has called the "serene, linguistic nihilism of Deconstructionism." Some of the most notable works of Structuralism and Deconstruction, French and American, do fairly take their place as part of the experimental discourse they decode, the literature they challenge, the Postmodern climate they perceive. Others, however, fall too readily into the category of obscure pedantry. Structuralism and Deconstruction have also encouraged feminist and new Marxist approaches to writing and led to a large-scale examination both of the power and the practice of discourse. While some of this writing has been couched in a language of hermetic abstraction and while some of its argument has appeared anticreative, these movements at best *have* contributed to contemporary writing. For writing itself has always deconstructed its constructions, decoded its codes, decanonized its canons, especially in periods when a large-scale transition of forms is taking place. There is good reason to suppose that the ending not just of a century but of a millennium, when dominant twentieth-century ideologies are either collapsing or transforming, will prove a time when criticism has the potential to stir the creative imagination into new vision.

Two different views could be taken of the present state of writing in the United States, and indeed elsewhere in the West. One view is that we live in a moment of creative exhaustion, of labyrinthine aesthetic pluralism, of critical mystification, an age of decadence. But another notes that ages of decadence in the past have usually generated the impetus toward new artistic enterprise and new stylistic discovery. At such times the role of criticism often becomes crucial. Back in 1928, Edmund Wilson wrote in "The Critic Who Does Not Exist" of his regret "that some of our most important writers . . . should work, as they apparently do, in almost complete isolation, receiving from the outside but little intelligent criticism and developing, in their solitary labors, little capacity for supplying it themselves." He saw the absence of a sufficient critical debate in America as "a sign of the rudimentary condition of our literature in general." American criticism lacked, he said, "the interest of the intelligence fully wakened to the implications of what the artist is doing. . . . There is one language which all French writers, no matter how divergent their aims, always possess in common: the language of criticism." It was a breach that Wilson himself attempted to heal in his role as public critic, the kind of person-of-letters that America largely lacked. There have been other seminal times when the creative and critical traditions in the United States have profitably intermingled: in the philosophic inquiries of Poe, in the metaphysical and aesthetic speculation that was an essential part of transcendentalism, in the explorations of the pragmatists and in the theories of the early Modernist era. As the century draws to a close, there is no reigning theory of literature in America, and consequently there is no dominant theory of criticism or agreement on a canonical literary tradition. The epistemological pluralism of our age multiplies theories of art; these in turn generate revisions of the literary canon, anthologies which embody them and continuing—often acrimonious—debate over who the significant American writers are and how they should be read and taught.

"The traditional canon is elitist" is the blunt conclusion of Professor Sue Howard, and she speaks for many who fear that accepted traditions based on unexamined ideological bias may force low estimation of unfamiliar works simply because readers lack sufficient background knowledge to appreciate them. The established canon, she says, is "concerned with the writing primarily of privileged white men. Women's writing, writing of people of color, people of the working class—those voices need to be brought into the study of literature." Ferment of this kind, a grudging agreement to disagree, characterizes contemporary critical discourse in America. It has fueled warm interest in the history of criticism, in its issues, dialogues, persistent questions and timebound answers and may well betoken a new literary era where these restructured traditions nourish new creative possibilities. For a time, this critical writing that so resembles and asks to be read as poetry has been the freshest, most imaginative literary work produced in the United States. As long as historians continue to debate the meaning of history and historical study and literary students quarrel over the nature of literature and literary history, we will have contending canons, and no one can say which or whether one will become standard for a season. As we noted at the start, amid the present din of disputed reassessment our effort has been to describe a central thread in the nation's literary conversation with itself. Whatever is ultimately added to this basic formulation, the writers and works touched upon here will continue to hold a place in America's understanding of what it is, and what it has been, and will provide language to express its hopes for the future.

Near the end of *The Golden Bough,* Sir James Frazer concludes that "magic, religion, and science are nothing but theories of thought . . . that ever-shifting phantasmagoria of thought which we dignify with the high-sounding names of the world and the universe." Literature too is yet another theory of thought in which writers try, as William Carlos Williams has it, "Through metaphor to reconcile/the people and the stones." It is the story of that enterprise in America over three centuries we have sought to tell. During the twentieth century, the promises ushered in by the early discoverers, the glories of westward creation awarded by Bishop Berkeley, the expectations of "the American Century," were largely fulfilled and the United States was leading the way into postmodern experience for many more people than the Americans themselves. In consequence, the writing of the American story has taken on a new kind of meaning as American writers have found themselves interpreting a modern history and experience for a larger world. At the same time the concerns of that larger world impinged upon them, as never before, and so did the imaginative experience of other peoples. The émigrés of the 1930s, the Eastern European dissidents of the cold war era, the writers of South America, the Caribbean, Africa and the Pacific have joined the increasingly multiethnic and multicultural expression of the contemporary United States itself in the quest. As the world map changes again and old ideological frontiers crumble the issues of what Elizabeth Bishop called "the worst century yet" give way to the coming issues of the twenty-first, and already there is a new story to tell. When centuries and millennia end, the imaginative arts are apt to take on a special significance. Time as well as space is a new frontier, another "Newfounde land." And it too demands its discovering fictions, fictions adequate to explore the strange, ever more plural world to come.

INDEX

442 · Index

FOR THE BEST IN PAPERBACKS, LOOK FOR THE 🐧

In every corner of the world, on every subject under the sun, Penguin represents quality and variety—the very best in publishing today.

For complete information about books available from Penguin—including Pelicans, Puffins, Peregrines, and Penguin Classics—and how to order them, write to us at the appropriate address below. Please note that for copyright reasons the selection of books varies from country to country.

In the United Kingdom: For a complete list of books available from Penguin in the U.K., please write to *Dept E.P., Penguin Books Ltd, Harmondsworth, Middlesex, UB7 0DA.*

In the United States: For a complete list of books available from Penguin in the U.S., please write to *Dept BA, Penguin*, Box 120, Bergenfield, New Jersey 07621-0120.

In Canada: For a complete list of books available from Penguin in Canada, please write to *Penguin Books Canada Ltd, 10 Alcorn Avenue, Suite 300, Toronto, Ontario, Canada M4V 3B2.*

In Australia: For a complete list of books available from Penguin in Australia, please write to the *Marketing Department, Penguin Books Ltd, P.O. Box 257, Ringwood, Victoria 3134.*

In New Zealand: For a complete list of books available from Penguin in New Zealand, please write to the *Marketing Department, Penguin Books (NZ) Ltd, Private Bag, Takapuna, Auckland 9.*

In India: For a complete list of books available from Penguin, please write to *Penguin Overseas Ltd, 706 Eros Apartments, 56 Nehru Place, New Delhi, 110019.*

In Holland: For a complete list of books available from Penguin in Holland, please write to *Penguin Books Nederland B.V., Postbus 195, NL-1380AD Weesp, Netherlands.*

In Germany: For a complete list of books available from Penguin, please write to *Penguin Books Ltd, Friedrichstrasse 10-12, D-6000 Frankfurt Main 1, Federal Republic of Germany.*

In Spain: For a complete list of books available from Penguin in Spain, please write to *Longman, Penguin España, Calle San Nicolas 15, E-28013 Madrid, Spain.*

In Japan: For a complete list of books available from Penguin in Japan, please write to *Longman Penguin Japan Co Ltd, Yamaguchi Building, 2-12-9 Kanda Jimbocho, Chiyoda-Ku, Tokyo 101, Japan.*